T0299068

STUDIES IN ECONOMIC HISTORY AND POLICY
THE UNITED STATES IN THE TWENTIETH CENTURY

Regulation and the revolution in United States farm productivity

STUDIES IN ECONOMIC HISTORY AND POLICY
THE UNITED STATES IN THE TWENTIETH CENTURY

Edited by
Louis Galambos and Robert Gallman

Other books in the series:
Moses Abramovitz, *Thinking About Growth: And Other Essays on Economic Growth and Welfare*
Michael A. Bernstein, *The Great Depression: Delayed Recovery and Economic Change in America, 1929–1939*
W. Bernard Carlson, *Innovation as a Social Process: Elihu Thomson and the Rise of General Electric*
Richard Gillespie, *Manufacturing Knowledge: A History of the Hawthorne Experiments*
Michael J. Hogan, *The Marshall Plan: America, Britain, and the Reconstruction of Western Europe, 1947–1952*
David A. Hounshell and John Kenly Smith, Jr., *Science and Corporate Strategy: Du Pont R&D, 1902–1980*
Simon Kuznets, *Economic Development, the Family, and Income Distribution: Selected Essays*
Peter D. McClelland and Alan L. Magdovitz, *Crisis in the Making: The Political Economy of New York State since 1945*
William N. Parker, *Essays on the Economic History of Western Capitalism: Volume 1: Europe and the World Economy*
Volume 2: America and the Wider World
Leonard S. Reich, *The Making of American Industrial Research: Science and Business at GE and Bell, 1876–1926*
Hugh Rockoff, *Drastic Measure: A History of Wage and Price Controls in the United States*
Christopher L. Tomlins, *The State and the Unions: Labor Relations, Law and the Organized Labor Movement in America, 1890–1960*
Richard H. K. Vietor, *Energy Policy in America since 1945: A Study of Business–Government Relations*

Regulation and the revolution in United States farm productivity

SALLY H. CLARKE
University of Texas at Austin

CAMBRIDGE
UNIVERSITY PRESS

CAMBRIDGE
UNIVERSITY PRESS

32 Avenue of the Americas, New York NY 10013-2473, USA

Cambridge University Press is part of the University of Cambridge.

It furthers the University's mission by disseminating knowledge in the pursuit of
education, learning and research at the highest international levels of excellence.

www.cambridge.org
Information on this title: www.cambridge.org/9780521441179

© Cambridge University Press 1994

First published 1994
First paperback edition 2002

A catalogue record for this publication is available from the British Library

Library of Congress Cataloguing in Publication data
Clarke, Sally H .
Regulation revolution in the United States farm productivity /
Sally H. Clarke.
        p.   cm. – (Studies in economic history and policy)
Includes index.
ISBN 0 521 44117 X (hc)
1. Agriculture and states – United States – History – 20th century.
2. Agricultural productivity – United States - History – 20th century.
I. Title.   II. Series.
HD1761.653   1995
338.1'873–dc20   94-5959   CIP

ISBN 978-0-521-44117-9 Hardback
ISBN 978-0-521-52845-0 Paperback

For Louise Hammond Clarke and Albert Byrd Clarke

Contents

List of tables   *page* viii
List of figures   xi
Acknowledgments   xiii

Part I   Regulation and productivity
1 Introduction   3
2 Agriculture and the organization of knowledge in
   the early twentieth century   22
3 Accounting for the slow rate of productivity
   growth   50

Part II   "Power Farming" in the Corn Belt, 1920–1940
4 The tractor factor   83
5 Depressed markets and market regulation   136
6 "If You'll Need a Tractor in 1936 You Ought to
   Order It Now"   162

Part III   A legacy for New Deal regulation
7 Regulation, competition, and the revolution in farm
   productivity   203
8 Conclusion   246
   Epilogue: The credit crisis of the 1980s   255

   Appendix A   The tractor's threshold, 1929   271
   Appendix B   The tractor's threshold, 1939   287
   Appendix C   Sources of preharvest and harvest
   labor productivity, 1929–1939   297

   Index   305

Tables

3.1   Rates of interest and terms of farm mortgage loans   *page* 69
     by major lenders, 1911–71
3.2   Percentage of farm mortgage debt held by lenders,
     1910–70   74
4.1   Number of tractors purchased by farmers, 1910–39   86
4.2   Percent of farms that passed the tractor's acreage
     threshold and the percentage with tractors, 1929   93
4.3   Financial crisis among midwestern states, 1910–30   108
4.4   Descriptive statistics for Iowa and Illinois counties,
     1929   126
4.5   Estimated regression coefficients for counties in Iowa,
     1929   129
4.6   Estimated regression coefficients for counties in Illi-
     nois, 1929   130
4.7   Difference-of-means test for counties in Iowa and Illi-
     nois, 1929   132
5.1   Delinquency rates of farm mortgage loans reported by
     life insurance companies and federal lenders, 1929–37   138
5.2   Value of farm mortgages held by life insurance compa-
     nies, 1933   149
5.3   Proceeds of federal loans used to refinance farm mort-
     gages held by lenders, 1933–7   151
6.1   Land and labor productivity in corn production, the
     Corn Belt, 1920–40   164
6.2   Mechanical corn picker's acreage threshold, 1937   172
6.3   Mechanical corn picker's acreage threshold, 1929   174
6.4   Percentage of farms that passed the tractor's acreage
     threshold and the percentage with tractors, 1939   176
6.5   Cost of production of corn and CCC loan prices, the
     Corn Belt, 1932–40   184
6.6   Average rates of interest for new farm mortgages,
     1932–8   191

6.7   Capital expenditures, cash receipts, and the diffusion
      of the tractor in the Corn Belt, 1930–9   195
7.1   Corn, cotton, and wheat owned by the CCC, 1949–87   214
7.2   Government support prices and payments for acreage
      restrictions, 1963–72   218
7.3   Year-to-year changes in prices of farm commodities,
      1921–80   220
7.4   Indexes and rates of growth of farm productivity,
      1910–80   230
7.5   Investments in technology, 1910–80   231
7.6   Measures of financial leverage for U.S. agriculture,
      1946–89   234
7.7   Value of farm sales, off-farm income, and debt-to-asset
      ratios by farm size, 1975   237
E.1   Annual rates of farm failures as reported by lenders,
      1959–90   258
E.2   Percentage of farms by sales class with debt-to-asset ra-
      tios of 40–70, 71–100, and 100 + percent, 1985   259
A.1   Annual fixed cost of tractor, equipment, wagon, and
      horses, 1929   272
A.2   Corn equipment and farm size, 1929   273
A.3   Fixed costs for farms with and without a tractor, 1929   274
A.4   Hours per acre spent raising and harvesting different
      crops, 1929   275
A.5   Distribution of crops and weighted work hours per
      acre, 1929   276
A.6   Variable costs per acre, 1929   277
A.7   Adjustments to hours spent by five as compared to six
      horses in raising crops, 1929   278
A.8   Adjustments to hours spent by three horses and a trac-
      tor as compared to four horses and a tractor in raising
      crops, 1929   280
B.1   Changes in prices of farm resources, 1929–39   288
B.2   Fixed costs for farms with and without a tractor, 1939   290
B.3   ·Variable costs per acre, 1939   291
B.4   AAA acreage restrictions and variable costs, 1939   292
B.5   Adjustments to hours spent by five as compared to
      six horses in raising crops, given acreage restrictions,
      1939   293

B.6 Adjustments to hours spent by three horses and a trac-
     tor as compared to four horses and a tractor in raising
     crops, given acreage restrictions, 1939   294
C.1 Preharvest labor hours in 1929 and 1939   298
C.2 Harvest labor hours in 1929 and 1939   300
C.3 Total labor savings, 1929–39   301

Figures

2.1	Morrow Plot, University of Illinois, 1906	*page* 30
2.2	Farmall tractor, late 1920s	38
3.1	A farmer's cost of production	52
3.2	Threshold model and the adoption of a mechanical invention	55
3.3	Adoption of a mechanical invention when prices decline	56
4.1	"Be the Master of Mechanical Power"	84
4.2	"For Utility and Economy no Tractor can Match a McCormick-Deering"	85
4.3	"The Great Emancipators"	88
4.4	Distressed assets per $100 of farm investment in the Corn Belt by life insurance companies, 1929 and 1932	112
4.5	Tractor's rate of diffusion in Illinois and Iowa, 1929	118
4.6	Subregions within the Corn Belt	119
4.7	Lag in the tractor's adoption in Illinois and Iowa, 1929	122
5.1	W. W. Eral displaying cash obtained from CCC loan, 1933	147
5.2	Receipts and disposals of mortgage applications for federal loans, 1933–6	153
6.1	Soil conservation meeting, Illinois, 1937	167
6.2	Examining hybrid corn, Iowa, 1939	169
6.3	"Firestone Ground Grip Tires"	177
6.4	A Farmall tractor, 1939	178
6.5	"Ever-Normal Granary" seal, Iowa, 1939	183
7.1	Number of foreclosures per 1,000 farms, 1912–80	208
7.2	Number of voluntary transfers per 1,000 farms, 1912–80	210
7.3A	Government support prices and market prices: corn, 1942–87	213

7.3B   Government support prices and market prices: cotton, 1942–87   217

7.3C   Government support prices and market prices: wheat, 1942–87   219

7.4   Ratio of purchased to nonpurchased resources, 1913–82   233

E.1   Exchange value of the U.S. dollar and U.S. agricultural exports, 1967–84   264

Acknowledgments

Inasmuch as this book benefited from generous amounts of advice, scrutiny, and good humor, I want to convey my sincere thanks to Naomi R. Lamoreaux, Louis Galambos, and Peter Jelavich. I also would like to thank individuals who commented on earlier portions of this project or otherwise took part in this scholarly enterprise; they include Nini Almy, L. B. Boyce, Sherri Broder, Gregory Clark, Lewis Gould, K. Austin Kerr, William Lazonick, Robert Moffitt, James T. Patterson, Richard Pells, Thomas Weiss, Thomas L. Whatley, members of the Berkeley/Stanford Economic History Group, the UC-Davis Economic History Seminar, and a group of anonymous but very helpful referees.

As part of my research, I traveled to a number of archives and libraries. I would like to thank Gregory Lennes of Navistar International Transportation Corporation for the use of the International Harvester Company Archives; Arline Schneider, director of the archives of the Equitable Life Assurance Society; Maynard Brichford, director of the University of Illinois Archives of the University of Illinois at Urbana-Champaign; Richard Maier of the American Council of Life Insurance; Andrea Garber of Connecticut Mutual Life Insurance Company; Linda S. Jett and Thomas Wood of Sangamon State University; Paul C. Lasewicz of Aetna Life and Casualty Company; Robert A. McCown of the University of Iowa; Daniel B. May of Metropolitan Life Insurance Company; E. Cheryl Schnirring of the Illinois State Historical Library; Stanley Yates and Glenn C. McMullen of Iowa State University; the librarians at the University of Illinois at Urbana-Champaign; the staff of the National Archives; and the librarians at the National Agricultural Library. I thank the American Council of Learned Societies, the National Endowment for the Humanities, the University of Texas at Arlington, and the University of Texas at Austin for funding my research and travel.

In completing this project, I have acquired a greater appreciation of the work inherent in the various steps of publishing a book. To this end, I want to thank my copy editor, Brian R. MacDonald, and my production editor, Helen Wheeler. I want to express my gratitude, as well, to Frank Smith.

PART I. Regulation and productivity

1. Introduction

In the wake of the Great Depression, Franklin D. Roosevelt's administration launched several new regulatory programs as experiments intended to mitigate if not resolve the economic crisis. Although the New Deal failed to pull the economy out of the Depression, many of its programs became seemingly permanent elements in the nation's modern administrative state. Farm regulation fit this pattern. Three agricultural programs of the 1930s outlived the crisis and have persisted to the present: a voluntary system of acreage controls designed to cut production; a price-support loan system intended to raise prices; and a revised system of public lenders designed to provide special sources of long- and short-term credit.[1]

Viewed some sixty years later, farm regulation typically calls to mind its costs. Certainly, farm programs resulted in artificially high prices, sustained excess stocks of commodities, and saddled taxpayers with a large bill for annual subsidies and storage. If these problems were not enough, there was also the personal trauma and the special costs stemming from the farm crisis of the 1980s.

Yet, from a historical perspective, what is striking about the inherited system of regulation is its long-term relationship with farm productivity. Americans typically do not equate regulation with efficiency, but in the case of agriculture, the introduction of these farm policies coincided with the start of a "revolution" in U.S. farm productivity.[2] To be sure, the extraordinary gains in productivity would not have been possible without the availability of new sources of technology. Tractors, trucks, combines, mechanical corn and cotton

[1] The federal government first offered price supports for corn and cotton in 1933. In 1938 wheat and tobacco were added to the program, and in World War II a large number of commodities were put under the system of price supports.

[2] Wayne D. Rasmussen, "The Impact of Technological Change on American Agriculture, 1862–1962," *Journal of Economic History*, 22 (December 1962), pp. 578–91. Also see William N. Parker, "Agriculture," in Lance E. Davis, Richard Easterlin, William N. Parker, Dorothy S. Brady, Albert

3

pickers, and a series of larger and more complex implements gradually displaced farmers' older source of power, horses and the equipment used with them. So too, hybrid seeds, insecticides, herbicides, and chemical fertilizers downgraded, and then eliminated farmers' "rule of thumb" choices for seeds, fertilizers, and pest controls.

But technology alone provides an inadequate explanation of the revolution in productivity. For one thing, many of the technical innovations predate the 1930s, and yet the 1930s marked a long-term break in the pattern of productivity gains. In the three decades prior to 1930, labor productivity and total factor productivity in the farm sector increased at a rate of less than 0.5 percent per year. For the first two decades of the century these measures showed no gains. In the 1920s changes began to be felt as both indexes rose at a 1.2 percent annual rate. But after 1935, gains were striking. Total factor productivity increased at a 3 percent annual rate, or at twice the pace set in the 1920s, and at six times the rate recorded over the years from 1900 to 1930. Labor productivity showed similar results: from the middle of the 1930s through the 1970s, it rose at roughly a 4.5 percent annual rate, or almost four times the pace of the 1920s.[3]

These gains in productivity brought dramatic changes to the farm sector. From 1930 to 1965, as the number of labor hours needed to raise and harvest a field of corn or wheat (or many other crops) declined, more than thirty million individuals had no choice but to seek industrial or service sector jobs. In these thirty-five years, more

Fishlow, Robert E. Gallman, Stanley Lebergott, Robert E. Lipsey, Douglass C. North, Nathan Rosenberg, Eugene Smolensky, and Peter Temin, *American Economic Growth: An Economist's History of the United States* (New York: Harper and Row, 1972), pp. 369–417.

[3] Choosing the mid-1930s as a starting point, rather than 1940, does not significantly alter the growth rate because total factor productivity in the farm sector increased at a rate of 2.8 percent per year between 1933–5 and 1938–9. Labor productivity reflects increases in output per unit of labor. See John W. Kendrick, "Productivity," in Glenn L. Porter, ed., *Encyclopedia of American Economic History* (New York: Charles Scribner's Sons, 1980), vol. 1, p. 161; John W. Kendrick, *Productivity Trends in the United States*, National Bureau of Economic Research (Princeton: Princeton University Press, 1961), pp. 136, 152, 362–4; John W. Kendrick and Elliot S. Grossman, *Productivity in the United States: Trends and Cycles* (Baltimore: Johns Hopkins University Press, 1980), pp. 34–5; and John W. Kendrick, *Improving Company Productivity: Handbook with Case Studies* (Baltimore: Johns Hopkins University Press, 1984), pp. 87, 93.

Americans deserted the rural parts of the country than had come to this nation in the great immigration waves between 1820 and 1960.[4]

By the late 1980s only 2.7 percent of the civilian work force earned an income from raising livestock or growing crops. This did not mean that family farms vanished. As recently as 1990, the majority of farms were still operated by families. But by that date a "family farm" had become an extremely large, capital-intensive enterprise.[5] With highly mechanized operations and farms that were nearly three times larger than their counterparts of the 1930s, each farmer supplied food for ninety-seven individuals (farmers included) in 1989, up from eleven in 1940, and seven in 1900.[6]

This exceptional pace for gains in farm productivity remains striking when compared with other parts of the economy. The manufacturing sector recorded a 2.1 percent annual rate of increase in total factor productivity both from 1900 to 1930, and again from 1948 to 1976. Whereas in the first period, agriculture's rate of productivity growth was not even a third as fast as the manufacturing sector's, in the second period farmers achieved a rate nearly 50 percent higher. In the thirty years since World War II, out of twenty individual

---

[4] Rasmussen, "The Impact of Technological Change on American Agriculture, 1862–1962," pp. 578–91; for changes in farm population, see John L. Shover, *First Majority Last Minority: The Transforming of Rural Life in America* (DeKalb, Ill.: Northern Illinois University Press, 1976), p. 4.

[5] Based on the 1987 Census of Agriculture, families accounted for 86.7 percent of all farms and 65 percent of all farmland. Within the class of partnerships and corporations, "family-held corporations" accounted for 2.9 percent of farms and 11 percent of land in farms. This left 9.9 percent of farms as partnerships or nonfamily corporations; together they held 17.3 percent of all farmland. Put another way, as of 1978, 95 percent of all corporate farms were held by ten or fewer shareholders, indicating that they were most likely family-run operations. See U.S. Department of Agriculture, "Agricultural Outlook," AO-161 (March 1990), p. 28. Also see U.S. Department of Commerce, *Statistical Abstract of the United States: 1982–1983* (Washington, D.C.: U.S. Government Printing Office, 1983), p. 653.

[6] For the size of the agricultural labor force, see *The Economic Report of the President, 1988* (Washington, D.C.: U.S. Government Printing Office, 1988), p. 284; for the number of persons fed per farm worker, see U.S. Department of Agriculture, "Economic Indicators of the Farm Sector: Production and Efficiency Statistics, 1980," Statistical Bulletin No. 679 (January 1982), p. 63; and U.S. Department of Agriculture, "Economic Indicators of the Farm Sector: Production and Efficiency Statistics, 1990," ECIFS 10-3 (May 1992), p. 36.

manufacturing industries, only two (chemicals and electrical machinery) surpassed the farm sector.[7] For labor productivity, agriculture ranked first against mining, construction, durable and nondurable manufacturing, transportation, communications, electrical and gas utilities, trade and finance, and services – that is, all other major sectors.[8] Thus, by the standard of productivity growth, the farm sector represented one of the most dynamic parts of the U.S. economy in the years after it began to be actively regulated.

My purpose in this book is to assess the consequences of government regulation for the long-term changes in farm productivity, particularly in the years from World War I to the farm crisis of the 1980s. It is not intuitively evident how regulation affected farm productivity. It may have been that the productivity increases took place in spite of regulation. Alternatively, regulation may have been neutral, which is to say insignificant. But a third possibility is that the regulation was related positively to the productivity gains. This last choice, however, runs sharply counter to our prevailing concepts of government regulation. Indeed, in recent years, to pair "innovation" or "productivity" with regulation would seem paradoxical to the popular mind as well as to academic scholars.

This has not always been the case. It was not true more than a century ago, when Americans first began to advocate extensive government regulation of private markets. Fearing that large-scale corporations – because of their size and power – would undermine democratic principles of individualism and fair competition, many

[7] The communications sector also set a higher rate than the farm sector. See Kendrick, *Productivity Trends in the United States*, pp. 65–71, 136–7, 464. For the comparison of agriculture with the twenty individual manufacturing industries, see Kendrick, "Productivity," p. 162. Angus Maddison reports similar figures. In the years 1909 to 1948, agriculture and industry reported annual rates of labor productivity of 1.6 and 1.5 percent, respectively; by contrast, from 1950 to 1973 the rate of growth for agriculture was 5.4 percent as compared with 2.2 for industry. From 1973 to 1984, both sectors reported slower rates: 2.5 percent per year for agriculture and 0.8 percent for industry. See Angus Maddison, "Growth and Slowdown in Advanced Capitalist Economies: Techniques of Quantitative Assessment," *Journal of Economic Literature*, 25 (June 1987), p. 684; and Angus Maddison, *Dynamic Forces in Capitalist Development: A Long-run Comparative View* (Oxford: Oxford University Press, 1991).
[8] Edwin Mansfield, "Technology and Productivity in the United States," in Martin Feldstein, ed., *The American Economy in Transition* (Chicago: University of Chicago Press, 1980), p. 565.

Americans asked the government to control prices so as to curb monopoly power. Fear of monopoly figured in the regulation of railroads and, later, the regulation of various utilities, such as the electrical, gas, and telephone industries. A second, and different, wave of regulation occurred in the 1930s, this time in response to depressed markets. New Deal policies were introduced in an effort to shore up prices and restrict production not only for agriculture, but for other industries, including oil and gas, airlines, and trucking.[9] Policy makers hoped regulation would give a measure of stability to these troubled industries, and in turn help promote economic growth.

Many of these regulatory initiatives lasted long after the Great Depression ended. For nearly two decades after World War II, the economy performed quite well and calls for deregulation were rare. But beginning in the 1960s and gathering storm in the 1970s, elite and then public sentiment swung clearly against regulation. Markedly slow gains in productivity caused Americans to ask whether the policies they put into place to restore competition or to promote stability and economic growth were now to blame for the nation's economic malaise.[10] The historian Naomi R. Lamoreaux summarized Americans' skepticism by stating in 1984 that

[9] The literature on regulation is voluminous. For a sophisticated model relating changes in markets to the demand for and shape of regulation, see Richard H. K. Vietor, *Energy Policy in America since 1945* (Cambridge: Cambridge University Press, 1984); a model relating individual behavior to institutional change is developed in Peter Temin, *Taking Your Medicine* (Cambridge, Mass.: Harvard University Press, 1980); and a cultural analysis of regulation is found in Ellis Hawley, *The New Deal and the Problem of Monopoly* (Princeton: Princeton University Press, 1966), and Thomas K. McCraw, *Prophets of Regulation* (Cambridge, Mass.: Harvard University Press, 1984). Two overviews are Naomi R. Lamoreaux, "Regulatory Agencies," in Jack P. Greene, ed., *Encyclopedia of American Political History* (New York: Charles Scribner's Sons, 1984), pp. 1107–11; and Thomas K. McCraw, "Regulation in America: A Review Article," *Business History Review*, 49 (Summer 1975), pp. 159–83.

[10] Numerous scholars have studied the slowdown in productivity; an introduction to the varied perspectives is found in an issue of the *Journal of Economic Perspectives*. See, for instance, Zvi Griliches, "Productivity Puzzles and R&D: Another Nonexplanation," *Journal of Economic Perspectives*, 2 (Fall 1988), pp. 9–21; and Dale W. Jorgenson, "Productivity and Postwar U.S. Economic Growth," *Journal of Economic Perspectives*, 2 (Fall 1988), pp. 23–41. Also see Martin N. Baily, "What Has Happened to Productivity Growth?" *Science*, 234 (October 24, 1986), pp. 443–51. For a comparison of sources of productivity from 1913 to 1984 as well as a comparison of the performance of the U.S. economy with that of five

mounting costs – both actual and threatened – caused by the late 1970's a tremendous backlash against regulation and the beginnings of what may prove to be the first great wave of deregulatory legislation. It became fashionable for both scholars and politicians to belabor the inefficiencies of regulation, to denigrate the abilities and ambitions of federal officials, and to denounce the menace posed by big government to the prosperity and growth of the economy.

Thomas K. McCraw delivered a similar message, saying that "the fact remains that in popular perceptions over the last three decades regulation has been regarded as a synonym for failure."[11]

This notion of failure is perhaps clearest in studies of the economic consequences of price regulation. Consider, for instance, the well-known experience of airlines.[12] In 1938 Congress created the Civil Aeronautics Authority, later renamed Civil Aeronautics Board (CAB), to protect firms in a new industry and a depressed market. In the years after World War II, regulators set airline fares, restricted competition between destinations, and predetermined the number of competitors. This caused airline companies to replace price competition with many unproductive strategies. They offered frills, like movies and fine meals, and added more flights between cities. As the number of flights increased, the load factor (passengers per flight) sank to just 56 percent by the 1970s. In an effort to prevent ruinous competition, regulators had created a cartel and reduced the efficiency of the entire industry.

In 1975 Congress began to respond. Senator Edward M. Kennedy directed hearings in which witnesses highlighted the ineffectiveness of airline regulation. Then in 1977 President Jimmy Carter appointed

other industrialized nations, see Maddison, "Growth and Slowdown in Advanced Capitalist Economies," pp. 649–98. Among business scholars the concern about recent economic growth finds a historical model in Paul Lawrence and Davis Dyer, *Renewing American Industry* (New York: Free Press, 1983).

[11] McCraw went on to note, "Even in some of the best scholarship on regulation, failure has often been applied not merely as a conclusion but also as a premise, a tacit assumption hidden behind apparently scholarly explanations presented in theoretical forms: the theories of capture, of public choice, of taxation by regulation, and several others." Lamoreaux, "Regulatory Agencies," p. 1108; and McCraw, *Prophets of Regulation*, p. 308.

[12] McCraw, *Prophets of Regulation*, pp. 261–2, and Richard H. K. Vietor, *Contrived Competition: Regulation and Deregulation In America* (Cambridge, Mass.: Harvard University Press, 1994), pp. 23–90.

the economist Alfred Kahn as chairman of the CAB. Kahn championed competition as a remedy for the airlines' problems, and in 1978, Congress took this advice when it passed the Airline Deregulation Act. The days of frills and price controls are gone, and many economists contend that the industry is more efficient as a result. Fares for most consumers are cheaper and flights are more diverse. If there are any less fortunate aspects of the competitive airline industry, they receive little emphasis from the supporters of deregulation.[13]

This economic critique of regulation is appealing, particularly in academic circles, because it fits closely with modern principles of competitive equilibrium. Economic theory teaches that in the short run, efficiency is achieved when market forces of supply and demand determine prices freely. Regulation of market prices, by its very nature, misallocates resources: any price fixed above the market equilibrium generates excess supply, and any price set below the equilibrium creates excess demand. In the long run such tampering with the market stymies economic growth because it distorts or eliminates entirely the price signals that tell producers when to increase or decrease output, and when to furnish new products or eliminate old ones. To sustain gains in productivity, economic theory suggests, one should increase competition.

Although this prescription is intuitively appealing, it long ago encountered a formidable challenge from the economist, Joseph Schumpeter. Writing in the interwar years, Schumpeter was among the first economists to theorize how entrepreneurs were vital to the dynamic growth of an economy. He began with the assumption that in the absence of entrepreneurial activity, the economy rested at a steady-state equilibrium in which there was neither productivity growth nor growth in producers' earnings. In order to achieve higher levels of productivity, entrepreneurs were needed. Although they typically did not invent new products or production processes, entrepreneurs had the ability to see beyond daily competitive routines, visualize how an

---

[13] Since the 1978 act, the airline industry has encountered various financial and operational problems that have caused different constituents – passengers, labor unions, and management – to rethink the consequences of a freely competitive market. My point here, however, is to recall that regulation of prices and entry contributed, as conventional economics would expect, to efficiency problems in the 1970s. For an analysis of both the regulated and deregulated eras, see for instance Vietor, *Contrived Competition*, pp. 23–90.

idea might change the economy, and fight entrenched interests to introduce a new product or process. When they succeeded, other competitors either had to copy the idea quickly or be forced out of business. Once the cycle of innovation and imitation played itself out, the economy would arrive at another stationary equilibrium, but this time at a higher level of productivity. Schumpeter called this process the "creative destructive" cycle. In the creative phase entrepreneurs introduced new ideas. In the destructive phase they cleared out unproductive firms, thus enabling the economy to attain a more efficient equilibrium.[14]

This dynamic view of the economy prompted Schumpeter to question the dominant concept of the relationship between market structure and economic growth – that is, he questioned the extent to which competition promotes growth. In the short run, Schumpeter acknowledged, perfect competition insures the most efficient allocation of resources. But, he argued, entrepreneurs need the promise of extraordinary profits to offset the risks they must assume. In a perfectly competitive market the entrepreneur's idea will be imitated as soon as it is introduced. All competitors will benefit from reduced costs of production, and as they pass on their benefits to consumers in the form of lower prices, the entrepreneur will go unrewarded. In a perfectly competitive economy, then, the entrepreneur has no incentive to introduce new productivity-enhancing ideas. By contrast, with monopoly power, an entrepreneur can limit imitation and reap large profits. In this way, the entrepreneur is rewarded for and willing to undertake the costs of developing and introducing a new product or process. Schumpeter concluded that monopoly power can benefit society in the long run through its stimulus to innovation and productivity growth.[15]

[14] Joseph Schumpeter, *Capitalism, Socialism and Democracy*, 3rd ed. (New York: Harper and Row, 1950; originally published, 1942), especially pp. 61–163.

[15] See Robert L. Allen, *Opening Doors: The Life and Work of Joseph Schumpeter* (New Brunswick, N.J.: Transaction, 1991); Morton Kamien and Nancy Schwartz, *Market Structure and Innovation* (Cambridge: Cambridge University Press, 1982), pp. 7–10; F. M. Scherer, "Schumpeter and Plausible Capitalism," *Journal of Economic Literature*, 30 (September 1992), pp. 1416–33; and F. M. Scherer and David Ross, *Industrial Market Structure and Economic Performance*, 3rd ed. (Boston: Houghton Mifflin, 1990), pp. 613–60. A recent revision of Schumpeterian competition is found in William Lazonick, *Business Organization and the Myth of the*

In the years since Schumpeter challenged existing theory, many economists have attempted to assess the ties among market structure, innovation, and economic growth. They sought to determine whether monopoly power stimulates innovation and productivity, as Schumpeter argued, or whether it restricts economic growth because, without competition, the monopolist feels no pressure to be creative. Results have been mixed. Some scholars have found market concentration to be closely tied to large research expenditures. Others have come to just the opposite conclusion. Still others have found that market concentration can stimulate innovation if some further condition is met. One scholar, for example, discovered that concentration could stimulate innovation if – despite the large size of firms – barriers to imitation were low (as was true in the consumer nondurable industries). Others have emphasized the importance of rivals, arguing that the threat of rivals can force dominant firms to pursue their own innovative efforts with greater vigor. Still, other scholars have tried to distinguish between different types of innovation, finding that large-scale enterprises may be better able to pursue certain projects that require process development. In combination, these economic studies suggest that some reduction in perfect competition may stimulate higher rates of innovation, but they warn that pure monopoly is not the optimal industrial structure.[16]

Other scholars have approached this problem from an institutional perspective. Business historians, in particular, have replaced Schumpeter's focus on the entrepreneur with studies of the structure of the firm and institutions inside the firm (such as research laboratories) or

Market Economy (Cambridge: Cambridge University Press, 1991), chap. 3.

[16] Wesley M. Cohen and Steven Klepper, "The Anatomy of Industry R&D Intensity Distributions," *American Economic Review,* 82 (September 1992), pp. 773–99; W. S. Comanor, "Market Structure, Product Differentiation, and Industrial Research," *Quarterly Journal of Economics,* 81 (1967), pp. 639–57; F. M. Scherer, "Market Structure and the Employment of Scientists and Engineers," *American Economic Review,* 57 (1967), pp. 524–31. Surveys of the field are found in William L. Baldwin and John T. Scott, *Market Structure and Technological Change* (Chur, Switzerland: Harwood Press, 1987); Kamien and Schwartz, *Market Structure and Innovation,* pp. 7–11, 22–33, 70–104; Jennifer F. Reinganum, "The Timing of Innovation: Research, Development, and Diffusion," in Richard Schumalensee and Robert Willig, eds., *Handbook of Industrial Organization* (Amsterdam: North-Holland Press, 1989), vol. 1, pp. 849–908; and Scherer, "Schumpeter and Plausible Capitalism."

outside the firm (such as regulatory agencies). How institutions operate, they argue, is an important element of our explanations of why some firms are more successful than others and, in turn, why some industries or economies are more dynamic than others.[17]

Consider, for example, the industrial research laboratory. David Mowery and Nathan Rosenberg contend that the standard neoclassical interpretation of research and development (R&D) "focuses largely on the incentives of firms to invest in R&D and views internal structure and process as unimportant."[18] By contrast, Mowery and Rosenberg reason that how research is organized may have very important consequences for innovation. They illustrate this point in their comparison of institutions for industrial research in U.S. and British firms. "The effectiveness of R&D within British firms was often limited by the incomplete rationalization of internal firm structure. In short, the structural development of American industrial enterprises allowed for a more effective exploitation of the complementarities between research activity and production activity."[19] In other words, British firms relied on independent subsidiaries and research organizations outside the firm. But because U.S. companies fully integrated research with other activities within the firm, they were better able to translate research into new products or pro-

[17] A large body of literature exists about the role of institutions inside the firm. An important study with theoretical insights about technological innovation is W. Bernard Carlson, *Innovation as a Social Process: Elihu Thomson and the Rise of General Electric, 1870–1900* (Cambridge: Cambridge University Press, 1991). An economist's revision of the role of the firm and the question of innovation is found in Lazonick, *Business Organization and the Myth of the Market Economy.* Other business historians have emphasized the importance of internal firm structure. See Alfred D. Chandler, Jr., *Scale and Scope* (Cambridge, Mass.: Harvard University Press, 1990); and Alfred D. Chandler, Jr., *The Visible Hand* (Cambridge, Mass.: Harvard University Press, 1977). Other important examples include Louis Galambos and Joseph Pratt, *The Rise of the Corporate Commonwealth* (New York: Basic Books, 1988); David Hounshell and John Kenly Smith, Jr., *Science and Corporate Strategy: Du Pont R&D, 1902–1980* (Cambridge: Cambridge University Press, 1988); and Leonard S. Reich, *The Making of American Industrial Research: Science and Business at GE and Bell, 1876–1926* (Cambridge: Cambridge University Press, 1985).

[18] David C. Mowery and Nathan Rosenberg, *Technology and the Pursuit of Economic Growth* (Cambridge: Cambridge University Press, 1989), pp. 7–8, 3–16.

[19] Ibid., p. 99.

cesses.[20] Although U.S. and British corporations faced similar market conditions, U.S. firms better utilized research and proved more innovative.

Taken together, these two bodies of scholarship – the first about market structure, the second about business institutions – qualify the conventional notion that competition will promote economic growth. The studies of market structure indicate that there is no clear and unambiguous relationship between a given market structure and an industry's economic performance. One reason for this is suggested by the studies of institutions. This scholarship indicates that although markets send signals to producers, much still depends on how firms respond internally to those messages. Put another way, within a given market structure, what needs to be understood is the nature of the institutions and the processes by which they promote or hinder innovation.

I find these two fields of research useful even though their focus is slightly different from mine. First, most research about business institutions or market structure has addressed highly concentrated industries in the manufacturing sector. My study, by contrast, concerns itself with agriculture – a sector characterized by highly competitive markets. Second, whereas most studies of business examine innovation as a source of productivity (by asking how firms create and introduce new products or processes), I study productivity in terms of the diffusion of technology (i.e., by asking how farmers invested in such things as tractors or hybrid seed).

Despite these differences, I have turned to these two bodies of scholarship because their conceptual insights about innovation complement my analysis of the diffusion of farm technology and the role of regulation. Studies about economic concentration indicate that market structure in itself does not allow us to predict the nature of innovation in a given industry or sector of the economy. In the case of agriculture, farmers' competitive markets may not alone explain changes in the pace or pattern of farm productivity. Why this would be the case is suggested in the work about institutions. These studies tell us that particular types of institutions are important for encouraging technological innovation, but even though they may have similar

[20] Mowery and Rosenberg note two other problems. One was the government's weak antitrust policy, the other the small number of engineers and scientists trained in British universities. Ibid., pp. 98–119.

forms they are not all equally adept at promoting change. Thus these two bodies of literature convinced me that regulation, while interfering with markets, could have acted to encourage gains in productivity. It did so, following this literature, by altering the institutional character of farms and related firms so as to spur investment. This investment in turn yielded gains in productivity.

My purpose in this study is to assess the plausibility of this proposition – that is, to examine how regulation could have stimulated productivity growth even though it interfered with farmers' markets. I break down this proposition into a set of systematic questions. First, I ask whether, despite their competitive markets, farmers delayed purchases of productivity-enhancing technology. Prior to 1930, did farmers achieve few gains in productivity simply because scientists and engineers had not developed new products? Or did farming lag because farmers delayed purchases? If farmers delayed purchases of productivity-enhancing inventions, why did they do so? What problems did they face, and did regulation address these problems? That is, did New Deal farm policies alter farmers' assessment of the profitability of investing in new machinery or scientific resources? Once established in the 1930s, did the farm policies continue to shape the diffusion of technology and stimulate gains in productivity in the years after 1940?

To answer these questions, we must investigate farmers' investment calculus, looking at when and why farmers adopted technology. Neoclassical theory would hold that competition was the most important factor shaping individuals' decisions. Simply stated, given that farmers had no control over prices, their one strategy to remain competitive was to reduce costs. If farmers followed this formula, then the diffusion of technology would proceed according to an invention's profitability; farm regulation, by implication, would distort this process.

This hypothesis is intuitively appealing, and I test its explanatory value by employing the so-called threshold model. Developed by the economist Paul David and used by many other economic historians, the model is designed to compare two different production techniques. It operates from the premise that given competitive markets, individual producers will select the technique that offers comparatively greater cost savings. The model goes one step further. Because the cost of an invention will vary with the size of the farm applying it, we can ascertain the acreage or threshold at which one technique will offer farmers greater cost savings than another technique. Economic historians have used the threshold model – as I do – to predict when farmers should switch from an old to a new technique and how many farmers should do so.[21]

This model offers a useful conceptual framework for analyzing the cost determinants of technological diffusion. If farmers responded to their highly competitive markets and adopted an invention on the basis of its cost savings, then their actual level of adoption should have matched the rate predicted by the threshold model. If their actual rate fell short of the predicted rate (as was the case), then something hampered their investment calculus. The model does not enable me to identify what caused the pace of technological diffusion to deviate from its predicted rate, but it will provide evidence of the extent to which farmers were hesitating to purchase new technology.

This leaves me with the task of explaining why they hesitated and what might have caused them to change their investment patterns. To investigate these questions, I go beyond competition and the threshold model, and create a broader conceptual framework of what I call farmers' "investment climate." This refers to the dynamic interplay among farmers, their various markets, regulation, and the different actors vital to farm investment – creditors, implement manufacturers, agricultural researchers. All of these actors shaped the diffusion of technology and hence the rate of productivity growth. In looking at these disparate elements, I begin with the premise that while they all influenced investment patterns, they did not necessarily interact in ways that would prompt high rates of investment or productivity growth. Manufacturers and agricultural researchers certainly encouraged the use of technology. But the products' rates of diffusion depended on farmers being able and willing to use their earnings or credit to finance investments.

Farmers' willingness to invest in technology was in turn clouded by the nature of their markets. Here the problem did not relate to the high level of competition, but to the unstable nature of crop prices. Scholars have long recognized that large and unpredictable swings in

[21] Paul David, "The Mechanization of Reaping in the Ante-Bellum Midwest," in Henry Rosovsky, ed., *Industrialization in Two Systems: Essays in Honor of Alexander Gerschenkron* (New York: John Wiley and Sons, 1966), pp. 3–39.

the supply of and demand for particular commodities created special risks for producers.[22] Because farmers could estimate only with a wide range of error what would be next year's prices for corn, wheat, or many other crops, they could not determine with any certainty what their income would be or how they should use their earnings for capital expenditures.

To understand how this type of risk hampered investments in technology, we must look closely at a series of important agricultural institutions. Farmers responded to unstable prices in terms of the institutions they used to organize production, which is to say the family farm. I examine how farm families could select among different inputs to try to limit their exposure to losses resulting from low prices, and argue that this selection process led farmers to assess new techniques with criteria other than an invention's relative cost savings. Given these conflicting criteria, farmers could choose to delay investments, thereby slowing the overall rate of diffusion of technology.

As an alternative, farmers could turn to credit markets. Here too we must look at the basic institutions that helped to shape the consequences of farmers' actions. Various creditors – commercial banks, life insurance companies, and individuals in the private sector, as well as federal land banks and production credit associations in the public sector – made farm loans. But lenders made funds available and set the terms of loans in response to market conditions along with their own institutional constraints. As a result, they might offer loans that did not fully suit farmers' investment needs. Again, this process was capable of slowing the diffusion of technology.

By analyzing farmers' investment climate in this context, regulation takes on a new perspective. New Deal farm policies, primarily

---

[22] The literature is very large. For two early studies, see D. Gale Johnson, *Forward Prices for Agriculture* (Chicago: University of Chicago Press, 1947); and Theodore W. Schultz, *Agriculture in an Unstable Economy* (New York: McGraw-Hill, 1945), pp. 258–72. Also see Lawrence A. Jones and David Durand, *Mortgage Lending Experience in Agriculture,* National Bureau of Economic Research (Princeton: Princeton University Press, 1954); and William G. Murray, "An Economic Analysis of Farm Mortgages in Story County, Iowa, 1854–1931," Iowa State University Agricultural Experiment Station Research Bulletin No. 156 (January 1933).

through price supports, altered the pattern of prices as well as their volatility. Regulatory policies – including price supports, acreage controls, and special sources of credit – also affected the outlook of those actors who were vital to farmers' investment calculus. Public policies caused manufacturers to rethink how they promoted or sold their machinery and prompted banks and life insurance companies to rethink how they made loans to farmers. Although regulation clearly interfered with farmers' markets, these policies seem to have shifted the dynamic among farmers, their markets, creditors, and manufacturers so as to stimulate investment and promote productivity growth.

My study therefore follows Schumpeter's concern with the dynamic process of economic growth, but my approach differs. I study the diffusion of technology, not innovation, and rather than focus on the role of the entrepreneur, I ask how farmers interacted with their investment climate to shape the diffusion of technology. Still, I find that by opting for a dynamic perspective in place of a static neoclassical model, I can better explain why farm productivity increased in the late 1930s, and what role New Deal regulation played.

My point of departure is the reorganization of sources of knowledge in the early twentieth century. By the 1920s and 1930s, both public and private institutions for formal research in scientific and mechanical knowledge made possible the introduction of complex farm technology. In this sense, agriculture was no different from manufacturing. But the process by which knowledge was organized and technology introduced indicated two important distinctions. First, the organization of knowledge in manufacturing was associated with the creation of the industrial research laboratory and the firm's vertical integration. In agriculture, by contrast, the introduction of technology based on the formal use of knowledge was associated with a reverse process. Farmers began to replace activities once performed on the farm with technology developed off the farm. Second, unlike the manufacturing sector, agricultural markets remained highly competitive. Farmers presumably would want to adopt technology so as to reduce production costs. But the potential existed for farmers to hesitate to do so insofar as technology altered a farmer's finances.

To assess the effects of competition and finances, in Part II, I trace the diffusion of specific technology in the Corn Belt during the years immediately before and after regulation took effect (roughly 1920 to

1940).[23] Judged by its size alone, the Corn Belt is an important part of the agricultural sector: it accounted for roughly a quarter of production in the years spanning the two great wars. Conveniently, two developments in this region permit an analysis of the effects of regulation. First, the Corn Belt was one of two regions – the other being the cotton South – that took part in all three types of New Deal regulation in 1933. In the case of the South, the role of sharecropping and race relations complicated the diffusion of technology.[24] Because I want to single out the effects of regulation on farm investment patterns, I chose to study the Midwest. The second development in the Corn Belt that favored my analysis was the introduction during the interwar years of three major inventions: the tractor, the mechanical corn picker, and hybrid corn.

The most important invention was the tractor. Its use enables me to compare farmers' investment calculus in the years before and after regulation took effect. If farmers responded to competition and adopted tractors on the basis of their cost savings, then the machine's relative cost advantage should have determined its rate of diffusion in both the 1920s and the 1930s. Alternatively, if conditions hampered investments, then the tractor's rate of diffusion should have taken a course at odds with the threshold model's predicted rate. Further, with this calculation, we can ask what caused the delay and how regulation altered this equation in the 1930s. Hybrid corn and the mechanical corn picker offer two additional tests of these hypotheses. Because the mechanical corn picker did not become widely available until the middle of the 1930s, I use its introduction to determine

[23] The Corn Belt includes parts of the following states: Ohio, Indiana, Illinois, Michigan, Wisconsin, Minnesota, Iowa, Missouri, North Dakota, South Dakota, Nebraska, and Kansas. In several states, however, farmers devoted more time and resources to other crops, notably wheat, than they did to corn. In my analysis I concentrate on the five main Corn Belt states: Ohio, Indiana, Illinois, Iowa, and Missouri.

[24] Although I study labor in terms of family operations, I do not pursue questions dealing with wage labor or sharecroppers – problems that assumed particularly important and pernicious consequences in the South. There exists a broad literature dealing with this topic. Different perspectives are found in Pete Daniel, *Breaking the Land: The Transformation of Cotton, Tobacco, and Rice Cultures since 1880* (Urbana: University of Illinois Press, 1985); Robert A. Margo, *Race and Schooling in the South, 1880–1950: An Economic History* (Chicago: University of Chicago Press, 1990); and Gavin Wright, *Old South, New South: Revolutions in the Southern Economy since the Civil War* (New York: Basic Books, 1986).

whether farmers continued to delay investments despite the coming of regulation. Hybrid corn enables me to compare variable- versus fixed-cost resources. Taken together, the three inventions help me separate the relative influence of competition and regulation. This leaves one further task: to estimate the consequences of farmers' investment calculus for changes in productivity.

Going beyond this case study of the Corn Belt, in Part III I trace the consequences of regulation in the years after 1940. As before, I examine farmers' investment climate by looking in particular at the relationships among market prices, regulation, and farmers' finances. But I do not concentrate on specific inventions, nor do I focus only on the Corn Belt. Instead, I examine the relationship between farmers' investment climate and the dynamic process by which smaller, less efficient, less affluent, or financially conservative farmers left agriculture, and their more aggressive counterparts survived. Among those who survived, the most obvious change was the increase in the size of farms, but farms also underwent a transformation that the economist William N. Parker called "vertical disintegration." Whereas operators had once integrated many activities on the farm itself, after 1940 they shed several functions. Farms became, in Parker's words, "small factories pouring industrial inputs into the land over the year and extracting a raw product for immediate sale."[25]

These changes in the competitive character of the farm sector grew out of the kind of climate that families faced in those years, a climate that was shaped by regulation. This role was not constant, however, but varied in relation to trends in market prices. From the end of World War II to the early 1970s, prices tended to fall; in the 1970s, by contrast, a boom in exports ushered in an era of rising and more volatile prices. Using these two different market conditions, I describe how regulation, in shaping farmers' investment climate, first promoted both the rapid decline in farms and the emergence of a small number of capital-intensive enterprises. I then examine why regulation left these large operators vulnerable to the credit crisis that emerged after the boom years of the 1970s.

Throughout the book, I use a number of different sources. I never could have conducted this study without the quantitative information collected by the U.S. Department of Agriculture (USDA); these data

[25] Parker, "Agriculture," p. 402.

series include information on farmers' cost of production, prices, land values, debt, rates of foreclosure, and other subjects. I also use data from state agencies and, for my analysis of the Corn Belt, county-level census data. To study the relationships among farmers, creditors, and manufacturers, I use many qualitative sources, including trade journals, government hearings and investigations, records of state politicians, bulletins of state experiment stations, manufacturers' advertisements, and, where possible, company archives.

There are certain limitations as to what I could accomplish with these latter materials. In some cases, they suggest questions that could have been answered had I obtained other forms of quantitative information. In particular, I would have liked to have had county-level data about the effect of New Deal credit agencies and price supports for the 1930s (to compare better farmers' investment patterns in the 1920s and the 1930s). The narrative sources provided more plentiful information for some individuals or organizations than for others. For instance, in looking at lenders, information was more detailed for life insurance companies than for commercial banks or private individuals. The archives of individual insurance companies, the most important of which was the Equitable Life Assurance Society, proved to be an especially valuable source of information. Similarly useful were the records of implement manufacturers, but here too the results were uneven: I received more information about the International Harvester Company (especially from its archives) than I was able to obtain about Deere & Company. Finally, although I found relatively few sources (such as diaries) for individual farmers, I was able to secure useful proxies. I examined agricultural researchers' own bulletins to determine whether farmers followed researchers' advice; I also examined the records of politicians on the premise that they addressed the concerns of their constituents and discussed farmers' problems.

In using these varied sources, I combine the techniques of economic and business history to write my account. As is common in economic history, I use theoretical ideas and quantitative evidence to offer a degree of clarity about the effects of competition and the timing of the diffusion of technology. Although this quantitative evidence is important, it cannot by itself enable me to explain the emergence of an investment climate conducive to a sustained era of high rates of productivity growth. For this reason, I turn to qualitative materials more commonly associated with business history, especially those concerning relevant institutions. This blend of economic and business history, I sense, holds the most promise in ascertaining how competition, farmers' investment climate, and regulation conditioned the revolution in U.S. farm productivity.

One final note. This study is not designed to promote economic regulation. Government regulation takes so many forms that it would be difficult to define, let alone defend, any "typical" or "representative" policy.[26] Nor, in my specific focus on farm regulation, do I offer any overall assessment. As I noted at this chapter's outset, in many ways regulatory policies subsidized farmers at taxpayers' expense. These costs are well known because they have been quite large. My intent, instead, is to study a problem that is more complex and is not intuitively evident – that is, to assess regulation's long-term consequences for investment patterns and productivity growth. I want to emphasize that these effects were often unintended and unexpected. I do not, therefore, equate consequences with "performance." That regulation had certain effects, intended or not, does not mean that it was a "success"; in this regard, I seek to avoid lumping the consequences of regulation into an overall assessment of either good or bad, successful or unsuccessful. Instead, my focus remains historical. I study regulation's long-term consequences because they suggest how institutions interacted with farmers' markets to shape the pace and pattern of investment and productivity growth in this important sector of the economy.

[26] McCraw, *Prophets of Regulation*.

2. Agriculture and the organization of knowledge in the early twentieth century

In the 1920s the United States attracted international attention for its technological "leadership" – leadership that reflected two strands of knowledge.[1] One, mechanical knowledge, had a long history dating back to the early nineteenth century. Numerous individuals acquired mechanical skills by working in textile, railroad, and other machinery-using industries. These mechanics created new machine tools, increased the speed of existing machinery, and refined the precision with which machines cut and shaped metal. Such knowledge was central to Americans' system of interchangeable parts and was reflected in several products, including firearms, clocks, hardware, and reapers.[2] At the close of the nineteenth century a second source of knowledge emerged in American universities. There researchers acquired highly specialized training in abstract laws governing biological, chemical, and physical processes; similarly, engineers acquired specialized training in different fields – mechanical, civil, chemical, and agricultural engineering. They systematically applied their abstract knowledge to concrete problems, and as they expanded their theory, they broadened the realm of projects they could tackle successfully.[3]

By the 1920s American business was effectively exploiting sources of scientific and mechanical knowledge to create and mass-produce complex goods. Although it is easy to relate mechanical knowledge to

[1] Richard R. Nelson and Gavin Wright, "The Rise and Fall of American Technological Leadership: The Postwar Era in Historical Perspective," *Journal of Economic Literature*, 30 (December 1992), pp. 1931–64.

[2] David Hounshell, *From the American System to Mass Production* (Baltimore: Johns Hopkins University Press, 1984); Brook Hindle and Steven Lubar, *Engines of Change: The American Industrial Revolution, 1790– 1860* (Washington, D.C.: Smithsonian Institution Press, 1986).

[3] Thomas P. Hughes, *American Genesis* (New York: Viking, 1989); Nathan Rosenberg, *Technology and American Economic Growth* (Armonk, N.Y.: M. E. Sharpe, 1972).

mass production and sciences to the development of products, the two sources of knowledge often made joint contributions to new products and processes. For instance, in the most talked-about case for the 1920s, Henry Ford fashioned machinery to mass-produce automobiles. But General Motors supported formal research in chemistry, physics, and engineering and used this knowledge to redesign and refashion automobiles. Conversely, formal research in the sciences found its way into products like rayon and cellophane, but this knowledge also became important for refining liquids. The application of chemistry to petroleum refining, for example, led to more efficient methods of cracking crude oil. These two sources of knowledge mingled with one another as management created new products and improved methods of mass production.[4]

Although the exploitation of mechanical and scientific knowledge was most readily seen in technology found in manufacturing, examples abounded in agriculture: chemical fertilizers, fungicides, insecticides, pesticides, hybrid seed, along with complex machinery – tractors, combines, mechanical corn and cotton pickers – all exemplified the exploitation of scientific and mechanical knowledge. My purpose in this chapter is, first, to trace the emergence of institutions where scientific and mechanical knowledge was organized for the development of farm technology and, second, to examine the implications of technology based on the formal use of knowledge for the process by which farmers acquired gains in productivity.

Compared with manufacturing, agriculture clearly differed in terms of the organization of research: manufacturing establishments organized knowledge inside the firm in the so-called industrial research laboratory; farms were too small to do so. Instead, formal sources of knowledge were organized in institutions off the farm. Federal and state governments created a public system for research in agricultural sciences and engineering; private firms, especially implement manufacturers, applied mechanical knowledge to the development and mass production of machinery. To translate research into gains in

[4] John Enos, *Petroleum Progress and Profits* (Cambridge, Mass.: MIT Press, 1962); Hounshell, *From the American System to Mass Production*, pp. 217–98; David Hounshell and John Kenly Smith, Jr., *Science and Corporate Strategy: Du Pont R&D, 1902–1980* (Cambridge: Cambridge University Press, 1988), pp. 119–317; Stuart W. Leslie, *Boss Kettering* (New York: Columbia University Press, 1983); Nelson and Wright, "The Rise and Fall of American Technological Leadership," pp. 1944–6.

productivity, firms and farmers adopted different strategies: manufacturers concerned themselves with invention and innovation, farmers with the adoption of technology.

This distinction carried over to changes in the structure of the two enterprises. Prior to 1880 most manufacturers concentrated on single activities; one would not describe them as integrated enterprises. Later, when management established research laboratories, it did so as part of a larger process of integrating different functions within a single firm. For farmers, their relationship to the sources of relevant knowledge followed a reverse sequence. Prior to 1900, farmers – despite the small size of their operations – performed several functions needed to grow crops and raise livestock. The arrival of new technology, based on the formal use of sources of knowledge, called on families to change the structure of their enterprises – to shed resources obtained (or activities performed) on the farm and, instead, purchase technology off the farm.

"Anybody can cross corn": Farmers as entrepreneurs

Before 1900 agricultural sciences offered farmers little systematic knowledge. Sociologist Jack Kloppenburg observed: "Agricultural science is heavily grounded in biology, and that field was, in 1900, still immature. The truth is that agricultural science did not have much to offer the farmer that would greatly increase productivity."[5] The economic historian William N. Parker likewise wrote, "The state of scientific knowledge about biochemistry and genetics in the nineteenth century was one of profound ignorance on many points. Successful innovation was largely a process of trial and error. . . . Every farmer did things a little differently from his neighbor and was sure his own way was best."[6]

To be sure, this did not imply that farmers shunned the markets that

[5] Jack Ralph Kloppenburg, Jr., *First the Seed: The Political Economy of Plant Biotechnology, 1492–2000* (Cambridge: Cambridge University Press, 1988), p. 77.

[6] William N. Parker, "Agriculture," in Lance E. Davis, Richard Easterlin, William N. Parker, Dorothy S. Brady, Albert Fishlow, Robert E. Gallman, Stanley Lebergott, Robert E. Lipsey, Douglass C. North, Nathan Rosenberg, Eugene Smolensky, and Peter Temin, *American Economic Growth: An Economist's History of the United States* (New York: Harper and Row, 1972), p. 389.

could provide them with up-to-date products. Throughout the nineteenth century farmers purchased inputs they needed to raise and harvest their crops. Professional horse breeders bought, sold, and raised
desirable draft animals. Seed growers raised seed, but also traveled to
neighboring areas to obtain new strains. Farmers purchased lime and
fertilizers. These markets were widespread, and farmers made use of
them. Still, individuals were flexible. Although they purchased items,
they also relied on their own "rule of thumb" knowledge, meaning
their accumulated experience, to select seed, fertilize their land, or
solve problems involving insects or plant diseases.

Consider, for example, the seed most widely planted in the United
States: corn. Rather than buy seed corn, farmers typically selected
ears from the previous harvest and mixed the seed for the next
spring's planting. Henry A. Wallace, before serving as secretary of
agriculture during the 1930s, described corn improvement as an activity very much in the average farmer's control. Prior to the 1920s,
he included regular articles about corn selection and farmers' own
experiments in *Wallaces' Farmer;* he instructed readers that "anybody
can cross corn."[7] Apparently, farmers took this advice to heart.
Nearly all seed corn came from farms themselves; so too, nearly all
seed for wheat came from farms. Reflecting this fact, few seed companies earned their revenues from farmers; instead, most sold seed to
urban dwellers (often for vegetable gardens).[8]

For problems dealing with insects, diseases, and questions of soil
fertility, farmers turned to commercial products. In 1910, the USDA
estimated that farmers used 946,000 tons of lime and 856,000 tons
of other plant nutrients (nitrogen, potash, and phosphoric oxide).[9]
The USDA also reported sales of various insecticides and pesticides
(calcium arsenate, sulfate of copper, sodium arsenate, Bordeaux mix-

[7] Quoted in Deborah Fitzgerald, *The Business of Breeding: Hybrid Corn in Illinois, 1890–1940* (Ithaca, N.Y.: Cornell University Press, 1990), pp. 11, 50–4.
[8] Kloppenburg reports that, in 1915, 97 percent of the seed used for growing wheat came from the farm itself. See Kloppenburg, *First the Seed,* pp. 54–7, 61–2, 70–1.
[9] U.S. Department of Agriculture, "Changes in Farm Production and Effi-ciency: A Summary Report," Statistical Bulletin No. 233 (August 1958), pp. 14–16. Fertilizers are reviewed in K. D. Jacob, ed., *Fertilizer Technol-ogy and Resources in the United States* (New York: Academic Press, 1953).

ture, lime sulfur solution) by the 1930s.[10] Yet these quantities were relatively small. In Illinois the application of fertilizer was just 7 pounds, and in Iowa 6 pounds per acre of corn. In some older states in New England plus New York, New Jersey, and Pennsylvania (where farmers applied from 140 to 255 pounds of commercial fertilizers to an acre of corn) there was greater reliance on commercial fertilizers.[11]

Even so, there and elsewhere, farmers often depended on their own solutions. Manure, for instance, supplied nitrogen to the soil (one ton released roughly twenty pounds of nitrogen). Farmers also understood that corn yields rose sharply with regular rotations of oats and legumes. These two practices, in turn, helped to combat insects and plant diseases. Nutrients, particularly phosphorus, worked against one of the more common corn diseases, diplodia stalk rot. Crop rotations alleviated problems stemming from the insect corn rootworm. To combat many other problems, farmers altered the time for performing specific operations. To reduce noxious weeds, they cultivated with rotary hoes or spike-tooth harrows soon after the weeds sprouted. In these and many other cases, farmers based decisions on their accumulated experience, or advice they acquired and shared with their family and neighbors.[12]

Unlike these cases involving biology and chemistry, farmers purchased several earth-moving implements (plows, disks, harrows, cultivators), and important types of machinery, notably the reaper. But in other regards, they relied on their own resources. For power, farmers used draft animals, typically mules or horses. They purchased these animals from professional breeders, but they also reared them on the farm itself. This case should not be shrugged off. Draft animals were crucial for all field operations and many other activities as well. The replacement of horses by tractors was the single most significant innovation on U.S. farms in the twentieth century.

In the case of harvesting machinery, the reaper was in a sense exceptional. For corn and cotton, farmers picked the harvest by hand. Again, the experience of Henry Wallace offers an instructive example.

---

[10] U.S. Department of Agriculture, *Agricultural Statistics, 1940* (Washington, D.C.: U.S. Government Printing Office, 1940), p. 710.

[11] Ibid., p. 708.

[12] George F. Sprague, ed., *Corn and Corn Improvement* (New York: Academic Press, 1955), pp. 343–612.

In 1922 he called for cornhusking contests; the champion would be chosen not only for his or her speed in husking but also for his or her ability to strip the husks clean. In the next two decades, contests acquired enormous fame in midwestern states, and even in the nation at large. Although they were entertainment, recreating in county and state fairs the atmosphere of a big-time football game (Wallace likened them to a "Yale–Harvard" game), these fairs also promoted innovation since they brought farmers together to share information for saving time and money in this arduous task.[13]

Into the early twentieth century, then, farmers still relied on their accumulated experience to increase profits and raise productivity. They selected their own seed and conducted their own experiments; they raised their own draft animals; they assessed soil problems; and through crop rotations, they attempted to boost yields. Certainly, farmers turned to the market on many occasions. Yet what stands out in the years prior to 1920 is their flexibility, which is to say, their ability to be innovative through their own experience.

Given that theoretical research had yet to produce desirable technology on a large scale, most farmers were skeptical about the value of institutions intended to support agricultural research. Kloppenburg writes that farmers' "uneasiness about the hybridization of these two words [agriculture and college] centered on a fear that education would teach them nothing about farming that they did not already know and yet cost them much."[14] Although farmers were not eager to sponsor institutions designed to support research, those who profited from farmers were. Manufacturers who bought farm products, banks who loaned farmers money, and those actively engaged in research itself (experiment station scientists, deans of land grant colleges, officials at the USDA) took advantage of federal and state

[13] Betty Fussell, *The Story of Corn* (New York: Alfred A. Knopf, 1992), pp. 304–7. Even in the case of the reaper, farmers shared capital to purchase the machine, and labor and horses to effectively operate it. This case is discussed in more detail in the next chapter.

[14] Kloppenburg, *First the Seed*, p. 58. See also David B. Danbom, *The Resisted Revolution: Urban America and the Industrialization of Agriculture 1900–1930* (Ames: Iowa State University Press, 1979); Paul Gates, *The Farmer's Age: 1815–1960* (New York: Holt, Rinehart and Winston, 1960); Charles E. Rosenberg, *No Other Gods: On Science and American Social Thought* (Baltimore: Johns Hopkins University Press, 1976); and Roy V. Scott, *The Reluctant Farmer: The Rise of Agricultural Extension to 1914* (Urbana: University of Illinois Press, 1974).

governments to create a public system of institutions devoted to the agricultural sciences.[15]

Institutions for research in the agricultural sciences

Between 1862 and 1914 Congress passed three acts that created a federal and state system for agricultural research. In 1862, the same year that the Department of Agriculture was created, Congress provided the initial legislation: the Morrill Land Grant Act gave each state 30,000 acres of the public domain for each senator and representative in Congress, and stipulated that revenue derived from the land be used to establish and maintain agricultural and mechanical (A&M) colleges. In 1887, with a surplus in its budget, Congress passed a second important bill, the Hatch Act. It granted states annual appropriations of $15,000 to establish and support experiment stations, and created the Office of Experiment Stations to communicate findings among universities and experiment stations around the nation. The last important institution was added with the Smith–Lever Act of 1914, which appropriated funds to each state to create an extension service; within the states an agent was assigned to each county.[16]

The three acts initiated a sustained program for agricultural research. Universities sponsored the fundamental study of various sciences. Experiment station scientists tailored general ideas to the soil, climate, and crops of specific states or areas within a given state. Finally, county agents acted as a communication system carrying researchers' results to farmers, and farmers' complaints to researchers. The three institutions, although national in scope, proved enormously flexible for treating problems that varied by state or region.

Despite its flexibility, this complex system fell short of its potential

---

[15] Danbom, *The Resisted Revolution*, pp. 23–74; Rosenberg, *No Other Gods*, pp. 35–184; Scott, *The Reluctant Farmer*, pp. 138–205.

[16] See Gladys L. Baker, Wayne D. Rasmussen, Vivian Wiser, and J. M. Porter, *Century of Service: The First One Hundred Years of the Department of Agriculture* (Washington, D.C.: U.S. Government Printing Office, 1963); Margaret W. Rossiter, "The Organization of the Agricultural Sciences," in John Voss and Alexandra Oleson, eds., *The Organization of Knowledge in Modern America, 1860–1920* (Baltimore: Johns Hopkins University Press, 1979), pp. 215–16; Scott, *The Reluctant Farmer*, pp. 3–36. For an organizational perspective, see Louis Ferleger and William Lazonick, "The Managerial Revolution and the Developmental State: The Case of U.S. Agriculture," *Business and Economic History*, 22 (Winter 1993), pp. 67–98.

for many years. The USDA and many land grant universities lacked funding and personnel until the early 1900s. Not surprisingly, education suffered: as late as 1909, the Carnegie Foundation reported that land grant institutions were so weak that they were in effect offering a form of secondary education. But just as the foundation was producing its report, officials at these colleges were beginning to tap state and federal governments, as well as private interests, for the money they needed to improve their programs.[17]

The emergence of the agricultural program at the University of Illinois is instructive. When Eugene Davenport became dean of the College of Agriculture in 1895, he found no single agriculture building, a barn on the verge of collapse, and little if any equipment.[18] In the next fifteen years Davenport organized farmers throughout Illinois. Committees with specialized interests in distinct areas (crops, orchards, dairying, among others) lobbied state officials, and Davenport won additional funding.[19] His first victory came in the 1900–1 academic year when the state appropriated the agricultural college $8,000 and the experiment station $54,000; in 1902–3, funds jumped to $61,000 and $85,000, respectively; and by 1911–12, the budgets, which lumped funds together, totaled nearly $500,000. In that year the faculty numbered 100, a considerable increase from 3 in the early 1890s. Further, 1906 – the year that the Morrow Plot was photographed (Figure 2.1) – marked the start of the graduate program: whereas there had been no graduate students prior to the 1905–6 academic year, by 1920–1 63 had enrolled.[20] In succeeding years, the school enjoyed so much national prestige that officials often forgot the college's troubled start.

Illinois was not exceptional. At Cornell, H. H. Whetzel supported his new department of plant pathology in good part by soliciting

[17] Fitzgerald, *The Business of Breeding*, p. 100. See, as well, Carnegie Foundation for the Advancement of Teaching, *Fourth Annual Report* (Boston: Merrymount, 1909). A comparative perspective to land grant universities is found in Rosenberg, *No Other Gods*, pp. 160–72.

[18] Richard Gordon Moores, *Fields of Rich Toil: The Development of the University of Illinois College of Agriculture* (Urbana: University of Illinois Press, 1970), pp. 105–49. Also see Fitzgerald, *The Business of Breeding*, pp. 77–8.

[19] This strategy, while increasing funding, had its own costs. It allowed farm leaders to interfere with the hiring of experiment station staff. Moores, *Fields of Rich Toil*, pp. 111–49; and Rosenberg, *No Other Gods*, pp. 162–3.

[20] Data reported in Moores, *Fields of Rich Toil*, pp. 240–1.

Figure 2.1. Morrow Plot, University of Illinois, June 23, 1906. From Record Series 39/2/20, Box 27, University of Illinois Archives, University of Illinois at Urbana-Champaign.

funds from private firms. After reading an article in 1907 about "industrial fellowships" for agricultural research at the University of Kansas, Whetzel said he had found the "key to my quandary." He solicited his first industrial fellowship from the Niagara Sprayer Company. Luckily, this project resulted in the commercialization of a lime-sulfur solution to replace the Bordeaux mixture then used as a fungicide to spray apple trees. Whetzel parlayed this success into more industrial fellowships. From one in 1909, the number jumped to eight in 1911, thirty-three in 1922, and fifty-eight in 1944. Not only were these funds a large part of the department's budget, but they helped encourage the state legislature to appropriate additional funds. Despite an apparent conflict-of-interest, Whetzel was pleased with his ability to muster private funds for public research.[21]

[21] H. H. Whetzel, "The History of Industrial Fellowships in the Department of Plant Pathology at Cornell University," *Agricultural History*, 19 (April 1945), pp. 99–104.

In the early 1900s, the federal government also increased its support. Under the Adams Act of 1906 Congress doubled annual appropriations for experiment stations to $30,000; in that year it also provided generous increases in the USDA's budget. As a result, the number of employees increased sharply. From 1905 to 1914, personnel at experiment stations doubled from 845 to 1,852, and rose to 2,415 by 1925. Within the USDA, the gains were also large. At the Bureau of Plant Industry, the number of employees increased from 127 in 1897 to 2,128 in 1912. Other bureaus (for chemistry, soils, entomology, biological survey, and statistics) were smaller, but they nevertheless experienced growth of a similar magnitude.[22]

In addition to new funding, Congress provided important assistance to research with the Smith–Lever Act (1914). Before then, experiment station scientists had experienced tension with their presumed clients. Farmers submitted numerous requests for simple procedures, such as soil samples or fertilizer tests, which they expected experiment station scientists, as "public servants," to perform quickly. Scientists, however, saw this as time lost from valued research and, for this reason, the arrival of the extension service was a welcome relief. Farmers could turn to agents for their routine tests or demonstrations; researchers (even if they still complained) could devote far more time to their own projects.[23] By the early 1920s the extension service was nearly complete. In 1923 all but six states had at least one agent for every two counties; and in many states, like New York and Illinois, the ratio was almost one for one.[24]

As this public system for research emerged, it promoted the growth of several scientific professions specializing in agriculture. By 1920

---

[22] Rosenberg, No Other Gods, pp. 173–84. Alfred Charles True, "A History of Agricultural Extension Work in the United States, 1785–1923," U.S. Department of Agriculture Miscellaneous Publication No. 15 (October 1928), pp. 137, 190, 212, 273.

[23] Kloppenburg, First the Seed, pp. 75–7; Scott, The Reluctant Farmer, pp. 254–313; Rosenberg, No Other Gods, pp. 154–9.

[24] Some relief had already existed. Before the extension service was established, farmers in individual states had created so-called farm institutes to communicate research findings. The institutes sponsored lectures and demonstrations, and by 1914 close to 9,000 institutes were conducted in forty-four states, most in the North and the West. After the Smith–Lever Act was passed, federal and state agencies shifted their energies from institutes to the extension service. Scott, The Reluctant Farmer, pp. 170–287; True, "A History of Agricultural Extension Work," pp. 14–33, and table 7, p. 200.

disciplines included economic entomology (the study of the control of insects), agronomy, plant and animal pathology, plant breeding, animal nutrition, and soil science. Each one acquired the marks of an established field by claiming its own body of theory and touting its own collection of "breakthroughs"; each organized its own professional societies and published its own journals.[25]

The growth of public institutions plus professional fields also contributed to private research. With the development of public research institutions, small firms were able to tap this source of information. Take, for example, the commercialization of hybrid corn. In 1917 the USDA placed a plant breeder, J. R. Holbert, at a newly created federal field station, located next to the Funk Brothers Seed Company of Bloomington, Illinois. Holbert remained a USDA employee, but he worked closely with Funk Brothers, the DeKalb Agricultural Association, and Lester Pfister of El Paso, Illinois. Advice from Holbert, as well as from university and USDA researchers, helped the three develop commercial products by the early 1930s. Presumably, the companies would have developed hybrid corn without this cooperation, but it would have taken more – perhaps considerably more – time. Without building large research facilities of their own, the firms were able to draw on officials from the land grant colleges. Once the link had been made, it helped individual firms enlarge their own research programs.[26]

This public system of research also made the findings available to farmers, as the law required. One preferred method was to write bulletins and circulars. Even in cases where private firms sponsored research, the findings typically appeared in the form of a masters thesis or dissertation, which often became the basis of a bulletin or a circular. If farmers chose not to read technical papers, they could turn to farm journals. Popular presses like *Wallaces' Farmer* and *Prairie*

---

[25] Rossiter summarizes the professional development of the agricultural sciences in "The Organization of the Agricultural Sciences," pp. 211–48. For plant technology, see Kloppenburg, *First the Seed*, pp. 66–84.

[26] Allan G. Bogue, "Changes in Mechanical and Plant Technology: The Corn Belt, 1910–1940," *Journal of Economic History*, 43 (March 1983), pp. 1–25; A. Richard Crabb, *The Hybrid Corn Makers: Prophets of Plenty* (New Brunswick, N.J.: Rutgers University Press, 1947); Fitzgerald, *The Business of Breeding*, pp. 112–14, 148–61, 178–89; Kloppenburg, *First the Seed*, pp. 71, 94–116; Rosenberg, *No Other Gods*, pp. 190–5; Sprague, *Corn and Corn Improvement*.

Farmer discussed findings, and after the Civil War their readership rose sharply. According to a 1913 survey, almost all farmers in the Northeast and the eastern Midwest read at least one such paper; in the South figures were not so high, but nevertheless readership rose sharply in the early 1900s.[27]

By the 1920s U.S. farmers had become the beneficiaries of an extraordinary public system devoted to agricultural research. At the USDA and at land grant universities, studies in various agricultural sciences were supported, and their results were tailored to local conditions at experiment stations. When it came to the distribution of results, county agents demonstrated products, while official publications and the popular press helped circulate information. As of the 1920s no other industrialized nation (Britain, France, and Germany included) provided agriculture with similar institutions on this scale.[28]

Implement manufacturers and farm machinery

While the agricultural sciences were emerging, other changes of note were taking place. These included the development of the gasoline tractor, an innovation that provided, one historian of science noted, a "visible and dramatic demonstration of the new usefulness of 'science' on the farm."[29] Implement manufacturers dominated the production and sale of tractors, equipment, and machinery. Like manufacturers in many other industries, they went through a process of consolidation during the great merger movement (1895–1904) and, afterward, individual firms consumed several years resolving questions of internal organization. The development of the tractor and other complex machinery came as these firms developed research programs, acquired

[27] Whetzel, "The History of Industrial Fellowships," pp. 100–1. The USDA discovered in a survey in 1926 that more than 40 percent of farmers thought their best source of information came from farm papers; for this finding and for circulation rates of popular farm papers, see Scott, *The Reluctant Farmer*, pp. 20–1; also see Rossiter, "The Organization of the Agricultural Sciences," pp. 219, 241–2.

[28] Rossiter notes that Japan had established stations by the 1890s, and that while little is known about them they were well funded. See Rossiter, "The Organization of the Agricultural Sciences," p. 242. Also see A. C. True and D. J. Crosby, "Agricultural Experiment Stations in Foreign Countries," U.S. Department of Agriculture, Office of Experiment Stations, Bulletin No. 112 (1902; rev. ed., 1904).

[29] Rossiter, "The Organization of the Agricultural Sciences," p. 245, n. 18.

new sources of mechanical knowledge, and pushed aside the competitive threat posed by Henry Ford when he entered the tractor market in 1917.

The industry's consolidation had its origins in the "Great Harvester War" of the 1890s. Although McCormick Harvesting Machine Company was the largest firm, it could not discipline its smaller competitors. Cyrus McCormick, the inventor's grandson, wrote:

> The saturation point of natural absorption had been reached about 1890, and the production capacities of the sixteen larger companies fighting for the business was far in excess of the normal demand. The jobber had already disappeared in the face of the desire of the companies to own their own branches and thus get closer to the ultimate consumer. Such a system of distribution tied up much invested capital in property and stocks of machines and bore heavily on treasuries which were none too robust.

All firms, McCormick continued, "had to try to find ways of increasing their volume to help carry the load."[30] The two largest competitors had different capabilities to apply to that goal: McCormick maintained the better sales force; but its next largest competitor, the Deering Company, had a more fully integrated operation, which included rolling mills for manufacturing and sources of crucial raw materials. Neither firm had a decided edge, however, and they finally escaped the hardships of competition by merging. In 1902 J. P. Morgan arranged the deal at a fee of $3 million. After its formation, the International Harvester Company (IHC) controlled between 70 and 85 percent of the harvesting market.[31]

[30] Cyrus McCormick, *The Century of the Reaper* (Boston: Houghton Mifflin, 1931), pp. 96–7.

[31] Despite it being a "family history," Cyrus McCormick wrote a surprisingly useful history in *Century of the Reaper*, pp. 89–127. Federal investigations provide a great deal of information about Harvester, and the industry as a whole. See U.S. Department of Commerce, Bureau of Corporations, *The International Harvester Company* (Washington, D.C.: U.S. Government Printing Office, 1913); and Federal Trade Commission, *Report on the Agricultural Implement and Machinery Industry*, 75th Congress, 3rd sess., House Document 702 (June 6, 1938). For the "little plow trust," see Wayne G. Broehl, Jr., *John Deere's Company: A History of Deere & Company and Its Times* (New York: Doubleday, 1984), pp. 278–87, 298–305. Harvester's experience fits closely with that of many manufacturers during the late nineteenth century. For the sector as a whole, see Naomi R. Lamoreaux, *The Great Merger Movement in American Business, 1895–1904* (Cambridge: Cambridge University Press, 1985), pp. 14–117.

Despite its size, IHC faced several problems in the next two decades. Internal organization, especially the sales force, presented one difficulty. Management had to persuade dealers who had come to despise each other to work together. As a compromise, but hardly as an efficient solution, IHC established two dealerships (one Deering and the other McCormick) for each farming community and created two lines of farm implements and machinery. Another problem concerned capacity. After the merger as sales tapered off, IHC was left with a good number of idle plants. Management's response, McCormick recalled, was a new strategy of product diversification: "An immediate benefit resulting from the amalgamation was the plan, not originally formulated, but soon to be developed, of filling idle factories and curing the abuse of part-time operations with various new lines of product."[32] Some products were developed internally, but many others were acquired by buying independent companies. Then, in 1912, Harvester entered lengthy antitrust proceedings. All three tasks – consolidation, diversification, and the antitrust case – took time to resolve, and in the process Harvester's market share slipped.[33]

The rest of the industry went through a second consolidation in the teens and twenties. By 1929 just seven "long-line" companies (meaning firms that carried a full line of implements and machinery to meet all of a farmer's needs) remained: Allis-Chalmers, J. I. Case, International Harvester, Deere & Company, Massey-Harris, Minneapolis-Moline, and Oliver. The two largest manufacturers were International Harvester and Deere. Together, they controlled 70 percent or more of various implement markets.[34]

As the firms consolidated, they began to develop new products, notably the tractor. Unfortunately, there is no scholarly account of research and development within an implement company. Yet, if the tractor is an indicator, it suggests that prior to 1920 most implement producers relied heavily on knowledge acquired through machine tool

[32] McCormick, *Century of the Reaper*, p. 116.
[33] Ibid., pp. 111–27.
[34] Wayne Broehl details several organizational problems Deere faced in these years. See *John Deere's Company*, pp. 288, 312–49, 400, 488–91, 804–5; Federal Trade Commission, *Report on the Agricultural Implement and Machinery Industry*, pp. 150–3; McCormick, *Century of the Reaper*, p. 146; and Warren Wright Shearer, "Competition through Merger: An Economic Analysis of the Farm Machinery Industry" (Ph.D. dissertation, Harvard University, 1951), pp. 122–34, 236.

shops. These manufacturers could profit from techniques developed in the automotive industry – techniques embodied in Henry Ford's new tractor, affectionately titled the Fordson.

Prior to the Fordson's introduction in 1917, tractors had begun to diminish in size, but they still were built on the principles of implements, not autos. By applying mass production ideas from autos, Ford cut the cost of production for the tractor far below that of existing manufacturers.[35] He also altered the tractor's design. Before the Fordson, drive gears and clutches were left exposed to the open air, and as a result, dust and dirt damaged the parts and cut short a tractor's life. By enclosing drives, as was common for automobiles, Ford improved the tractor's design and increased its life expectancy. These changes plus the reduction in production costs made the Fordson better fit the needs and pocketbook of many medium-sized farmers. By 1920 Ford's tractor claimed more than half of a small but rapidly growing market.[36]

Ford's challenge was short-lived. Despite the tractor's advances in design, it was flawed in many ways. Ford also erred in his marketing strategy: rather than develop his own line of equipment to suit the tractor, Ford worked with other manufacturers to design implements. This error compounded another: rather than work through existing implement dealers, Ford instructed his auto dealers to sell tractors. The automobile dealers were not, however, prepared to handle this new market. This became evident in 1921 when farmers' demand for tractors collapsed. To cover his large investment in mass-production

[35] Randy Leffingwell writes, "the tractor was designed in three units: a transmission housing contained the gearbox, the differential, and the worm-wheel drive to the rear wheels; the engine included flywheel and clutch assemblies; the front end included mounts for the steering assembly and axle. Farkas planned tractor parts to support the entire machine without needing a separate frame. All these units were designed to be run on rails to a central point in the factory for final assembly." Randy Leffingwell, *The American Farm Tractor* (Osceola, Wis.: Motorbooks International, 1991), pp. 10–11, 109–12.

[36] Ibid.; McCormick, *Century of the Reaper*, p. 162; Marvin McKinley, *Wheels of Farm Progress* (St. Joseph, Mich.: American Society of Agricultural Engineers, 1980), p. 83; Charles E. Sorenson, *My Forty Years with Ford* (New York: Norton, 1956), pp. 233–6; Robert C. Williams, *Fordson, Farmall, and Poppin' Johnny: A History of the Farm Tractor and Its Impact on America* (Urbana: University of Illinois, 1987), pp. 29, 33–5, 47–9, 55; Reynold Wik, *Henry Ford and Grass-roots America* (Ann Arbor: University of Michigan Press, 1972), pp. 82–102.

technology – that is, to keep his plants running full – Ford slashed prices.

Initially, firms responded to Ford in a way that seemed to recall the 1890s. At International Harvester, Alexander Legge ordered large price cuts despite the fact that the firm then ran at a loss. In other respects, however, the crisis differed. In the 1890s various firms had escaped competition by merging, but this battle centered around two large firms, Harvester and Ford, and IHC ultimately forced Ford out of the domestic market. Aside from cutting prices, IHC took advantage of Ford's long-term marketing problems and the Fordson's design flaws. Harvester succeeded because in the years since the 1902 merger, its management had clarified the firm's internal organization and – with its new effort in research – developed a superior tractor.

One ingredient for IHC's organizational capabilities was marketing. In 1918 its antitrust suit produced a consent decree in which Harvester agreed to maintain only one dealer per farming community. The requirement was not really a hindrance, as it enabled Harvester to consolidate its sales force and product line. It also left Harvester with a national network of some 13,000 dealers; IHC backed them with extensive advertising, a credit system, and a distribution system of branch houses that coordinated the rapid delivery of equipment and replacement parts. Harvester was not alone in this regard. Deere & Company, the second largest firm, had filled out its own distribution system and supported roughly seven thousand dealers. In its investigation of the industry, the Federal Trade Commission concluded that aside from the market power the two firms might acquire through their size, they held a decided cost advantage through their comparatively more efficient distribution systems and dealership networks.[37]

[37] Warren Wright Shearer analyzed the Federal Trade Commission data and concluded that Deere and Harvester had much lower marketing costs than most other competitors, and this gave them a decided advantage. Shearer, "Competition through Merger: An Economic Analysis of the Farm Machinery Industry," pp. 122–34, 236; also see, Broehl, *John Deere's Company,* pp. 488–91, 804–5; Federal Trade Commission, *Report on the Agricultural Implement and Machinery Industry,* pp. 150–3. For Harvester's distribution system, see Paul B. Coffman, "International Harvester Company, Organization and Policies," in U.S. Federal Trade Commission, "Farm Machinery Investigations (1936)," Record Group 122, Box 1485, pp. 15–17, National Archives, Washington, D.C. McCormick, *Century of the Reaper,* pp. 185–8, 226–46.

Figure 2.2. Farmall tractor, late 1920s. Courtesy of the International Harvester Company Archives, Navistar International Transportation Company, Chicago, Illinois.

Harvester's dealers were an important part of its short- and long-term strategies because they served as a feedback system. Much like county agents who reported farmers' complaints to experiment station scientists, dealers referred farmers' ideas and problems back to the central office. Ford was less able than Harvester to sustain this type of feedback because the firm's dealers only sold tractors; many of the farmers' problems concerned the relation of tractors to implements. Harvester was better organized to address the relationship between the tractor and its implements, and this connection was at the heart of its innovative tractor, the Farmall (Figure 2.2).[38]

Harvester introduced the Farmall in 1924. Its superiority to the

[38] Broehl notes that branch houses served this function in the nineteenth century. See Broehl, *John Deere's Company*, pp. 184–7; McCormick, *Century of the Reaper*, pp. 195–200; Williams, *Fordson, Farmall, and Poppin' Johnny*, pp. 60–1.

Fordson was so clear that by 1928 Ford quit the domestic market. The historian of Deere, Wayne G. Broehl, Jr., wrote: "It is difficult to overemphasize the breakthrough in farming technology brought by this one new tractor. The response from the field was instantaneous – the Farmall became an abiding success. It was patently clear to the farmer that the Farmall could do things that the Fordson could not do, that the Deere Model D could not do."[39] What all existing tractors could not do was a set of complicated tasks, like planting seed or cultivating corn, in addition to plowing and disking land. The Farmall was innovative precisely because it could perform these sorts of operations. Even if Farmalls were not used for all tasks – even for a few extra tasks – they still proved more flexible and desirable than existing tractors.

To develop this tractor, IHC had undertaken a sustained research project. Its engineers raised the rear axle so as to give ample clearance for cultivating row crops like corn; they created driving wheels that slid on their axle "so that the width of the track could be adjusted according to the requirements of individual row crops."[40] The front tires were reorganized and closely paired so that they ran down a single crop row. With these changes, the tractor could rotate in a small, eight-foot radius so as to allow it to make tight turns at row ends, and thereby execute field tasks like planting seed and cultivating corn.[41]

The Farmall came equipped with another improvement, the "power take-off," which had been introduced two years earlier (in 1922). As the sales brochures explained, in tractors with a power take-off the "transmission is designed so that power can be transmitted from the engine directly to the driven machine by using a revolving shaft."[42] When horses were used, the farmer had to employ a far more cumbersome mechanism, a bullwheel, which rolled along,

---

[39] Broehl, *John Deere's Company*, p. 479.
[40] Hard Barger and Hans H. Landsberg, *American Agriculture, 1899–1939: A Study of Output, Employment, and Productivity* (New York: American Book-Stratford Press, 1942), p. 207.
[41] Leffingwell, *The American Farm Tractor*, pp. 102–3; McCormick, *Century of the Reaper*, p. 211; Williams, *Fordson, Farmall, and Poppin' Johnny*, pp. 86–8.
[42] "McCormick-Deering Farmall," n.d., n.p., John C. Blood Papers, Box 7, Illinois State Historical Library, Springfield, Illinois; McKinley, *Wheels of Farm Progress*, p. 83.

transmitting power to an implement. But with the power take-off, the rotating drive shaft directly "empowered" implements needed to perform field tasks.[43] When the Farmall was introduced in 1924 and fully marketed in 1925, it plowed, disked, planted, and cultivated crops. Even if farmers did not use the Farmall for every one of these operations, the new tractor was clearly more versatile than the Fordson thanks to its ability to rotate in small spaces.

Harvester's ability to develop the Farmall had not simply been a question of engineering; it reflected as well the corporation's financial and organizational capabilities. Edward A. Johnston, who had been named director of the Experimental Division in 1910, supervised the research effort. Between 1910 and 1921, his department worked through the design of a lighter, tricycle-framed tractor. While this project was in place, Ford's competition in 1922 caused management to decide, the firm's chronicler wrote, to "accelerate the Farmall program." In the next two years, the Experimental Division revised the tractor several times; they redesigned implements to attach to the tractor, including cultivators, mowers, and corn planters. In 1922 and 1923, IHC assembled and tested prototypes; a small number of Farmalls were introduced in 1924, and larger numbers in 1925.[44]

This was a fruitful and expensive venture into R&D in an industry not usually identified with modern research. Some estimates hint that millions of dollars were spent in the intervening years. While no exact figures exist, one proxy is the size of Harvester's research staff. In response to the National Research Council's 1927 survey of U.S. "industrial research laboratories," Harvester said that it maintained a staff of 27 chemists, 51 engineers and designers, and 539 other personnel. Research covered the "development of materials; development of devices and machines applied to agriculture, power, transportation; revamping machines to new conditions; development of specifications; development of standards." Although Harvester's staff

[43] McCormick, Century of the Reaper, p. 209; Williams, Fordson, Farmall, and Poppin' Johnny, pp. 62–3.

[44] C. W. Grey, "Farmall History," pp. 24–5, Document No. 13865, and Arthur C. Seyfarth, "Tractor History," manuscript, pp. 55–63, Document No. 13864, International Harvester Company Archives, Navistar International Transportation Corporation, Chicago, Illinois. Also see Leffingwell, The American Farm Tractor, pp. 101–3; Barbara Marsh, A Corporate Tragedy: The Agony of International Harvester Company (New York: Doubleday, 1985), pp. 54–5.

may seem small by present-day standards, for the 1920s it ranked among the forty-four largest manufacturing research laboratories in the United States.[45]

Aside from Harvester, the only other response to the National Research Council's 1927 survey came from Allis-Chalmers, a diversified manufacturer, which reported that its staff included six chemists and one engineer, along with some other (unspecified) laboratory workers. Other firms did not report data on laboratories, indicating that their methods of research did not, for the most part, conform to the idea of an "industrial research laboratory."[46]

Deere's experience supports this conclusion. While it established an experimental department by 1920, Deere left the design of products decentralized – that is, in the control of factory managers. As such, research activities were split between Theo Brown, the head of Deere's experimental department, and the heads of individual factories. Throughout the 1920s these factory engineers continued to hold the upper hand; new machines – the combine, corn picker, and tractor – came out of individual factories. Brown's experimental department was given the authority to investigate all product lines, and in the 1920s it received generous funding.[47] Yet when it came to product development, his department had to work closely with engineers in specific factories. As a result, Brown's organization concentrated on the development of new components, especially those that won patents. One innovation was the tractor's power lift, a device that used the tractor's own power to raise and lower implements, developed in 1926.[48]

By 1933, nearly all implement firms reported to the National Research Council that they maintained some form of industrial research, but most firms reported small staffs. My suspicion is that these reports understated the resources actually devoted to R&D. Yet, even

[45] Leffingwell, *The American Farm Tractor,* p. 102; National Research Council, "Industrial Research Laboratories of the United States," Bulletin No. 60 (Washington, D.C.: National Research Council, 1927), p. 60; George Perazich and Peter M. Field, *Industrial Research and Changing Technology,* National Research Project Report M-4 (Philadelphia: Works Progress Administration, 1940), p. 66.
[46] National Research Council, "Industrial Research Laboratories of the United States," Bulletin No. 60, p. 6.
[47] Broehl, *John Deere's Company,* pp. 400, 471–2, 477, 480–8.
[48] Ibid., pp. 480, 486–9.

at a later date, say 1940, Harvester maintained a significantly larger program of research than any of its competitors.[49] Size alone, then, may not have dictated all research activities. For instance, Allis-Chalmers, working with Firestone, introduced pneumatic (rubber) tires in the early 1930s. This example and others suggest that IHC's competitors addressed important topics and improved farm machinery.[50]

In addition to spurring investments in research and development, Ford's entry stimulated the industry's competitors to invest in new methods of mass production. Cyrus McCormick recalled that at the time of Ford's entry into the market, standards

> were hardly up to date in terms of manufacturing progress. The record annual production of four thousand Mogul 8–16's in 1915 had been non-progressively assembled; and at a period in its early existence the flywheel of the Titan 10–20 traveled exactly one mile around the factory (as compared with a subsequent three hundred feet) before it was mounted in the tractor.[51]

But the competition with Ford brought a rapid transfer of information about mass production to the implement business. McCormick recalled:

> The automobile men . . . adopted exactly the same theory that, for example, had underlain the development of mower-frame boring

---

[49] By the 1940 survey, reports seemed more accurate, and firms gave much larger figures for the size of their laboratories. Even so, IHC's lab was still considerably larger than other firms. For example, Caterpillar reported a lab with 5 chemists, 43 engineers, 51 other technical persons, and 45 other persons. IHC, by contrast, reported 93 chemists, 33 metallurgists, 70 physicists, 102 engineers, 302 layout men and draftsmen, 805 mechanics, 108 other technical and scientific personnel, 66 road engineers and field mechanics and testers, and 223 other persons. See National Research Council, "Industrial Research Laboratories of the United States," Bulletin No. 104 (Washington, D.C.: U.S. Government Printing Office, 1940), pp. 4, 55, 77, 152, 188, 207; and National Research Council, "Industrial Research Laboratories of the United States," Bulletin No. 91 (Washington, D.C.: U.S. Government Printing Office, 1933), p. 126.

[50] National Research Council, "Industrial Research Laboratories of the United States," Bulletin No. 91, pp. 9, 42, 55, 102, 126, 138. For the pneumatic tire, see R. B. Gray, The Agricultural Tractor: 1855–1950, part 2, rev. ed. (St. Joseph, Mich.: American Society of Agricultural Engineers, 1975), pp. 15–16; Leffingwell, The American Farm Tractor, pp. 71–2; tests of pneumatic tires are covered in the entire issue of Agricultural Engineering, 15 (February 1934).

[51] McCormick, Century of the Reaper, pp. 195–6.

machines, and arranged to machine the different faces of a crank-
case at one pass through a milling machine. They devised multiple
drills and prepared types of speed wrenches to enable a nut to be
screwed more quickly on a bolt.[52]

In the next five years, IHC's tractor and truck divisions converted
machinery and reorganized plant floors so as to mass-produce trucks,
tractors, and other complex machinery. By 1928, when IHC's Farmall
dominated the tractor market, its factory was able to produce 24,000
machines in a year.[53]

Although private firms, especially Harvester, designed and produced complex machinery, public universities trained most of the
engineers needed to achieve these goals. As with other agricultural
disciplines, agricultural engineering remained small until the early
1900s; then, along with the tractor, the profession flourished. In 1907
the American Society of Agricultural Engineers was organized, and in
1920 it established its official journal, *Agricultural Engineering*. By
the early 1920s, several land grant schools were running specialized
programs in agricultural engineering.[54]

Agricultural engineering differed from other types of engineering,
particularly automotive engineering, in the sense that many problems
associated with tractors and implements were unique to agriculture.
Tractors operated in fields not just on roads; they needed to match
weight to pulling power; and they had to be designed to coordinate
and power implements whose moving parts interacted with different
soils and crops.[55] Agricultural engineers at universities, experiment
stations, and the Bureau of Agricultural Engineering of the USDA
(established in 1931) all addressed these sorts of topics.

Public officials also began to check the validity of manufacturers'
claims. University professors and experiment station scientists fur-

[52] Ibid., p. 253.
[53] Ibid., pp. 255–7; Leffingwell, *The American Farm Tractor*, p. 101; Marsh,
A Corporate Tragedy, p. 55.
[54] J. Brownlee Davidson, "Launching a New Engineering Society," *Agricultural Engineering*, 12 (June 1931), pp. 182–3; Raymond Olney, "The
A.S.A.E.: 1906–1931," *Agricultural Engineering*, 12 (June 1931), pp.
185–6; B. B. Robb, "Agricultural Engineering Extension," *Agricultural
Engineering*, 12 (June 1931), p. 194; Philip S. Rose, "Engineering's Service
to Agriculture," *Agricultural Engineering*, 12 (June 1931), pp. 183–4;
H. B. Walker, "Agricultural Engineering Education," *Agricultural Engineering*, 12 (June 1931), p. 193.
[55] See, for example, McCormick, *Century of the Reaper*, p. 150.

nished lengthy evaluations in farm bulletins, circulars, and pamphlets. In the important case of tractors, farmers could turn to the Nebraska State Fair tractor contest. In 1919 the state legislature determined that any tractor sold in the state had to enter the annual contest. Tractors were judged for their speed, weight, maneuverability, and power.[56] The issue of power was especially important, and the contest evaluated both drawbar power (the ability to cover fields, and thus the speed in plowing or disking land) and "belt power" (the ability to operate stationary equipment such as a thresher). Well beyond Nebraska's borders, the annual event became a standard for judging one tractor against another. It allowed farmers to check manufacturers' sales claims and to ascertain how different tractors could best suit their specific needs.

By the start of the 1920s, there was in place a formidable dual system of promoting innovation in agriculture. Public institutions supported the biological and chemical sciences, and trained agricultural engineers. Private manufacturers used this specialized staff to develop and mass-produce complex machinery. For the dissemination of products, the two again overlapped. Manufacturers advertised their products, but officials followed up with their own evaluations. This institutional foundation encouraged the development of new professions which in turn initiated substantial changes in agricultural technology in the years following World War I.

Research, technology, and the farmer as investor

By the 1920s both public researchers and private manufacturers assumed greater authority in determining biological and chemical resources (seed, chemical fertilizers, pesticides), and for developing new machinery (tractors, combines, and mechanical corn pickers). As a result, from 1920 to 1940 farmers began to shift their focus: they dwelled less on questions of innovation and more on problems of adoption.

Although farmers had acted as their own entrepreneurs for many functions, this did not preclude scientists at public institutions from making important contributions. For the most part, however, their contributions were based on systematic investigations, not on theoret-

[56] Gray, *The Agricultural Tractor: 1855–1950.*

ical knowledge. For example, to fight the "cottony cushion scale" epidemic of 1888, California officials responded by finding its biological predator (the lady bug); though widely applauded, the solution did not require theoretical research. Rather, it required the systematic analysis of predators – a project that exceeded an individual farmer's capacity. This example fits with others, including the Babcock butter test, the collection of new seed, and the Bordeaux mixture for spraying insects. Referring to such cases, Kloppenburg notes that they were not "transformative; they tended to provide immediate solutions to discrete problems, but did not move productivity to qualitatively different levels. Experiment station research focused on the 'putting out of fires' rather than on more theoretical work that might have led to a radical reconstitution of the agricultural production process."[57]

As the new system for research evolved, however, the agricultural sciences gradually acquired the theoretical framework they needed to "move productivity to qualitatively different levels." In animal pathology, for instance, Theobald Smith discovered the role of insects in transmitting disease, and Marion Dorset found that certain viruses and bacteria caused diseases in animals. In plant pathology, in the 1870s scientists showed that fungi and bacteria were the source of plant diseases. In the case of plant breeding, the rediscovery of Gregor Mendel's laws for inheritance in 1900 launched another branch of research.[58]

As a result of the theoretically oriented research, farmers were encouraged to make purchases rather than depend on their own seed and fertilizer or on their own solutions to problems with insects and plant diseases. In the case of hybrid corn, by the early 1920s researchers and active observers like Henry Wallace understood that corn improvement no longer was an open sport. Experiment station researchers established that through specialized methods they could breed hybrid seed on a commercial basis.[59] Once hybrids were introduced in the 1930s, it no longer was in a farmer's interest to experiment (as they had with open pollinated corn).[60] Instead, farmers

[57] Kloppenburg, First the Seed, pp. 60, 75; Rossiter, "The Organization of the Agricultural Sciences," p. 222.

[58] Kloppenburg, First the Seed, pp. 67–71, 77–80, 94–116; Rossiter, "The Organization of the Agricultural Sciences," pp. 26–9.

[59] Fitzgerald, The Business of Breeding, pp. 54–6.

[60] Kloppenburg writes, "seed of these hybrid combinations could not be saved and replanted. . . . Mendelian segregation decrees that subsequent

concerned themselves with the selection of hybrids, judging seed for its yield, resistance to drought, cold weather, wet soil, or a variety of other features.[61]

As scientists acquired greater control over the creation and introduction of biological and chemical resources, mechanical engineers acquired greater control over the development of complex machinery. When in 1917 the Society of Tractor Engineers joined the larger Society of Automotive Engineers, Cyrus McCormick wrote that "immediately" automotive engineers passed on knowledge about several aspects of the mass production and design of complex machines: the use of machine tools; ways to improve the layout of factories; standardization of parts; selection of materials and metals; improvements in internal combustion engines; and techniques to improve fuel efficiency, among other topics.[62] Yet, to supplant the Fordson and similar tractors, IHC depended on the knowledge of agricultural (not just automobile) engineers. Their training included the study of the nature of crops, soils, and terrain – that is, information needed to design the "all-crop" or "general-purpose" tractor. "Such factors influenced height, clearance, tread, center of gravity, turning radius, attachment points ahead, behind and beneath."[63] The same kind of knowledge applied to the design of implements. Referring to the development of a cultivator for a general-purpose tractor, Theo Brown, head of Deere's experimental department, stated that several questions arose including those involving sufficient clearance, wheel tread, balance, the method used to hang the cultivator from the tractor, and the tractor's center of gravity.[64]

generations ... will be increasingly heterozygous and uneven in yield. Thus, although hybrid seed is not biologically sterile like the mule, it is in effect 'economically sterile.'" See First the Seed, p. 97.

[61] Ibid., especially pp. 112–14, 148–61, 178–89. Also see Deborah Fitzgerald, "Farmers Deskilled: Hybrid Corn and Farmers' Work," Technology and Culture, 34 (April 1993), pp. 324–43.

[62] Leffingwell, The American Farm Tractor, pp. 101–3; McCormick, Century of the Reaper, p. 163; Williams, Fordson, Farmall, and Poppin' Johnny, pp. 27–8, 69–70. Annual changes can be tracked in the trade journal, Agricultural Engineering.

[63] E. J. Baker, Jr., "A Quarter Century of Tractor Development," Agricultural Engineering, 12 (June 1931), p. 207.

[64] Theo Brown, "The Requirements and Design of Cultivating Equipment for the General-Purpose Tractor," Agricultural Engineering, 11 (February 1930), pp. 63–4.

As automotive and agricultural engineering knowledge coalesced in the twenties, manufacturers were able to develop machinery suited to medium-sized farms. The single most important innovation was the tractor, but manufacturers also developed combines and mechanical corn pickers. Instead of needing to know how best to raise, break, and care for their horses, farmers now wanted to ask how to invest in complex machinery – how to read the Nebraska reports on tractor contests, how to use university experiment station bulletins, and how to judge the technical advice they received from county agents.

By the 1920s, the products of public and private research – hybrid corn, chemical fertilizers, mechanical corn pickers, smaller combines, and, of course, tractors – made possible new gains in productivity. They also involved structural changes in the nature of family farms. Farmers now had the option of replacing their existing source of power, their horses, as well as changing their use of labor. When they invested in a tractor, farmers made not one but a series of decisions. Now they needed to buy fuel, lubricants, and repair parts rather than raise feed for horses. Horses no longer supplied manure. The farmers had to switch to commercial fertilizers. Moreover, they often needed to purchase additional land to better realize the machinery's cost savings.

As farmers took up the question of investing in modern technology, they did so in a market setting that was still extremely competitive. Here there was a decided contrast between agriculture and manufacturing. In manufacturing industries, the exploitation of sources of knowledge in the industrial research laboratory demanded large, long-term financial commitments. Small firms in very competitive industries did not undertake such costly efforts.[65] Thus, large research laboratories were found in the chemicals, electrical communication, petroleum, rubber, electrical machinery, and iron and steel indus-

[65] In the textile, apparel, lumber, furniture, printing, and leather industries, research intensity, as measured by the ratio of the number of industrial researchers to the number of wage earners in an industry, was less than 0.7 in the years prior to 1946 and, where data are available, prior to 1963. In most cases, the level of research intensity was less than 0.3. See David C. Mowery, "The Emergence and Growth of Industrial Research in American Manufacturing, 1899–1945" (Ph.D. dissertation, Stanford University, 1981), pp. 66–70, 150. Also see David C. Mowery and Nathan Rosenberg, *Technology and the Pursuit of Economic Growth* (Cambridge: Cambridge University Press, 1989).

tries.[66] Within these industries, a few of the very largest corporations
accounted for a sizable share of the researchers: overall, in 1927, 59
percent of all researchers still worked for only forty-four firms (or less
than 5 percent of all research-oriented corporations). Even as the
number of laboratories nearly doubled by 1938, forty-five firms still
accounted for more than half of all research personnel.[67] Managers,
thanks to their firms' size, could dictate the nature of research, and by
collecting patents, could exercise some influence over the flow of new
products and products' prices, thereby enhancing their market power
and restricting competition.[68]

In agriculture, by contrast, the new sources of scientific and mechanical knowledge were organized separately from the farm. Public
research institutions controlled and freely disseminated information.
Private manufacturers likewise advertised and distributed their machinery and equipment to all who could afford to purchase them.
From a farmer's perspective, no single individual could appropriate
the results of technical innovation. Competition created the incentive
for individuals to adopt technology so as to reduce costs, but that
same competition made it difficult for farmers to realize profits from
their innovation.

After 1920, then, the sources of productivity were changing, but
farmers' competitive markets were not. In the nineteenth century,
gains in productivity had been associated with the extensive growth
of agriculture. Migration to more fertile land, the use of new seeds,
the use of horses, and horse-drawn machinery all contributed to new
levels of productivity. By contrast, in the years after 1920, productivity growth was associated with thoroughgoing changes in the internal
operations of farms: families replaced traditional resources with com-

[66] Perazich and Field, *Industrial Research and Changing Technology.*
[67] In 1921, there were 462 industrial research laboratories, which employed
a total of 9,350 researchers. In 1927, the number of industrial research
laboratories had grown to 929 and employees to 18,982. Ibid., pp. 66, 68.
[68] Louis Galambos, "The American Economy and the Reorganization of the
Sources of Knowledge," in Alexandra Oleson and John Voss, eds., *The
Organization of Knowledge in Modern America, 1860–1920* (Baltimore:
Johns Hopkins University Press, 1979), pp. 270–1, 273; Leonard S. Reich,
"Industrial Research and the Pursuit of Corporate Security: The Early
Years of Bell Labs," *Business History Review,* 54 (Winter 1980), pp. 504–
29, and Leonard S. Reich, "Research, Patents, and the Struggle to Control
Radio: A Study of Big Business and the Uses of Industrial Research,"
Business History Review, 51 (Summer 1977), pp. 208–35.

plex machinery and biological and chemical products developed in public and private research facilities. As they did so, the timing and pace of the growth in productivity began to turn increasingly on how farmers dealt with the size and nature of their enterprises, on the one hand, and the effects of competition, on the other.

3. Accounting for the slow rate of productivity growth

In the spring of 1929 county agent S. Lysle Duncan announced to farmers in Johnson county, Iowa, that "Lime-Livestock and Legume Demonstrations" would be held soon. "Four specialists from Ames will be present to answer questions and to lead the discussion. Soil samples will be tested for you at the meetings." So "Tie up your team or shut off your tractor," Duncan urged, "and attend the nearest meeting." Duncan conducted many demonstrations. He gave lectures on multiple hitch (or eight-horse hitching), colt breaking, pruning trees and protecting young trees from pests, and identifying and destroying "noxious weeds" like "quack grass, buffalo burr, [and] horse nettle." To fill out his responsibilities, Duncan brought in specialists from Ames, home of Iowa State University, the state's agricultural and mechanical college. Like county agents, university specialists gave instructions to farmers as to how they could raise crop yields and save labor time and cost with new machinery.[1]

While public officials promoted technology, it is not altogether clear how quickly farmers adopted all techniques. To recall, it was not until after the mid-1930s that farmers achieved notable gains in productivity. From 1920 though 1935, gains were small, ranging from 0.5 to 1.5 percent per year for most types of farming. But after 1935, gains amounted to 3 percent or more each year.[2] How are we to explain this pattern? One hypothesis is that the technology failed to reduce costs until 1935. Another is that the size distribution of farms acted so as to slow the rate of technological diffusion until the mid-thirties. The threshold model, which ties the basic cost-savings analysis for machinery to the size of farms, should enable us to test this hypothesis. A third possibility is that farmers were concerned

---

[1] County Extension Agents, State of Iowa, *Annual Narrative Reports*, vol. 11, 1929, Johnson County, pp. 125–6, 129–30, Department of Special Collections, The Parks Library, Iowa State University, Ames, Iowa.

[2] U.S. Department of Agriculture, "Changes in Farm Production and Efficiency," Statistical Bulletin No. 561 (1978), pp. 44, 68.

about reducing risks as much as costs. It is possible that farm families tried to acquire safety against fickle markets by relying on the integrated structure of their farms. Their concern for security, then, suggests an alternative account: if technology reduced a farm's financial safety, it may have caused farmers to delay investments and miss potential gains in productivity.

Implications of competition: Assessing the cost savings of technology

In considering the various explanations, we should bear in mind that farm commodities closely fit the notion of competitive markets. By the early twentieth century, the United States had developed a series of specialized markets or "belts": the Corn Belt in midwestern states, primarily Ohio, Indiana, Illinois, Iowa, but also parts of Missouri, Nebraska, Minnesota, and Michigan; the Cotton Belt in several southern states; the Wheat Belt in the Plains states (Oklahoma, Kansas, Nebraska, South Dakota, and North Dakota). These three crops accounted for the largest share of agricultural production, but more specialized markets existed for fruits and vegetables in states like California and Florida; dairy farming likewise became more specialized to states like Wisconsin and New York.[3]

Within each market, producers sold a homogeneous product (corn, cotton, wheat). Few farms were exceptionally large, and they did not account for a significant share of farm production. In Iowa, for example, less than 1 percent of all producers worked farms of 500 or more acres in 1920, and they held just 4 percent of all acreage. In the next smaller size category (260–499 acres) 11 percent of Iowa farms (25,879 enterprises) held 23 percent of all acreage.[4] In other states, the average size of farms varied, but no farmer held any significant share of output and no sway over commodity prices. Instead, the one

[3] William N. Parker, "Agriculture," in Lance E. Davis, Richard Easterlin, William N. Parker, Dorothy S. Brady, Albert Fishlow, Robert E. Gallman, Stanley Lebergott, Robert E. Lipsey, Douglass C. North, Nathan Rosenberg, Eugene Smolensky, and Peter Temin, *American Economic Growth: An Economist's History of the United States* (New York: Harper and Row, 1972), pp. 378–82.
[4] Iowa figures are calculated from the U.S. Department of Commerce, *Fifteenth Census of the United States: 1930* (Washington, D.C.: U.S. Government Printing Office, 1932), Agriculture, vol. 2, part 1, p. 894.

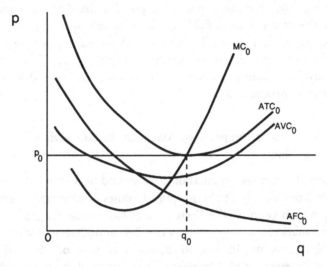

Figure 3.1. A farmer's cost of production. p_0 denotes the going market price; q_0 denotes the amount of land under production where the farmer's marginal cost curve equals p_0. ATC_0 denotes average total costs; AVC_0 denotes average variable costs; AFC_0 denotes average fixed costs; MC_0 denotes marginal costs.

way for a farmer to remain competitive presumably was to reduce costs.

This logic can be formalized with a few standard economic principles. Total supply and demand determine a crop's market price; farmers seek to maximize their earnings at this price. Figure 3.1 depicts a farmer's average fixed costs (AFC_0), average variable costs (AVC_0), average total costs (ATC_0), and an upward-sloping marginal cost curve (MC_0). A farmer produces at the point where marginal cost equals marginal revenue – that is, where the additional (marginal) cost of producing another unit of output is just offset by the additional revenue earned from that unit. Under perfect competition, marginal revenue equals the market price, p_0. The farmer produces $0q_0$ in output. Because the market is perfectly competitive the price equals marginal cost, and the farmer neither earns a profit nor incurs a loss.

When faced with a new method of production, the farmer will want to adopt the technology provided it is more efficient than the older substitute. The exact process varies somewhat for technology based on scientific as compared with mechanical knowledge. For chemical and biological inventions (fertilizers, pesticides, seeds), a farmer's strategy is relatively simple. All that needs to be determined is the item's net effect on variable costs (meaning costs that may vary during the production season, mostly labor, feed, fuel, fertilizers, seed). Inventions like hybrid seed or chemical fertilizers initially raise variable costs due to their higher purchase price, or in the case of a fertilizer to its application costs. But as they secure higher yields, they lower per-acre costs. If the reduction in per-acre costs due to higher yields more than offsets the initial increase in costs, then farmers will want the product.[5]

An experience recorded by county agent S. Lysle Duncan illustrates this logic. A farmer by the name of Adams declared that he had used a new commercial fertilizer in 1928 but with no satisfactory results. Duncan took this complaint as a challenge. He tested five different fertilizer mixtures on Adams's farm in 1929, and kept careful figures for the cost of the fertilizer, changes in the yield per acre of corn, and finally the profit or loss per acre. After testing the corn for moisture content and sending samples off to Ames for the state statistician, Duncan reported a profit in all five cases ranging from $1.21 to $8.32 per acre. The agent gave Adams and his neighbors clear evidence of the returns from various fertilizers.[6]

The process for establishing the relative cost savings of mechanical technology is more complicated. Mechanical inventions alter both variable and fixed costs (fixed costs being mostly interest and depreciation on machinery and horses, and a portion of feed for horses). Since average fixed costs fall as the size of the farm increases, the profitability of a tractor, combine, or mechanical corn or cotton picker depends not only on relative costs but also on the size of a farm. Paul David's "threshold" model incorporates the effect of farm

---

[5] The relationships can also be expressed in terms of per-acre profits, as Zvi Griliches did in his famous research on hybrid corn. Griliches defined per acre profitability as the "increase in yield due to the use of hybrid seed, times the price of corn, and minus the difference in the cost of seed." See Griliches, "Hybrid Corn: An Exploration in the Economics of Technical Change," *Econometrica*, 25 (October 1957), p. 516.

[6] County Extension Agents, State of Iowa, *Annual Narrative Reports*, vol. 11, 1929, Johnson County, pp. 121–2.

size along with variable and fixed costs to determine when a new technique becomes profitable.[7] More will be said about the model in the next chapter, but at this point what is important to recognize is that, depending on the size of farms, not all farmers will reduce costs by using the new method. Here the threshold model measures the existing and new techniques' fixed and variable costs so as to determine the acreage or "threshold" beyond which farmers will save costs by employing the new technique.

Figure 3.2 illustrates a farmer's cost calculus when faced with two choices for fixed-cost technology. The existing technique's costs are pictured, as well as the new technique's marginal, average fixed, and average total cost curves (MC_1, AFC_1, and ATC_1, respectively). The new method's average fixed cost curve (AFC_1) is set higher than that of the existing method (AFC_0). Given the higher fixed costs, the new method's average total cost curve initially generates greater expenses. But as a farmer works more land, the new method generates smaller variable costs, notably in labor time and expense, than does the old method. Thus, while both methods' average total costs fall, the decline is steeper for the new technique. At the acreage size, T^*, the new method's average total cost curve crosses below the existing method's average total cost curve.[8] Any farmer with more than T^* acres will

[7] David's original article, "The Mechanization of Reaping in the Ante-Bellum Midwest," is reprinted in *Technical Choice, Innovation and Economic Growth* (Cambridge: Cambridge University Press, 1975), pp. 195–232; also see introductory remarks on pp. 4–5. His logic is reviewed by Alan Olmstead, "The Mechanization of Reaping and Mowing in American Agriculture, 1833–1870," *Journal of Economic History*, 35 (June 1975), pp. 327–52. Olmstead is reviewed by Lewis Jones, " 'The Mechanization of Reaping and Mowing in American Agriculture, 1833–1870': Comment," *Journal of Economic History*, 37 (June 1977), pp. 451–5. David also used the threshold model in "The Landscape and the Machine," in Donald C. McCloskey, ed., *Essays on a Mature Economy: Britain after 1840* (London: Methuen, 1971), chap. 5.

[8] The assumption that the mechanical mode of production has greater fixed costs and smaller variable costs relative to its alternative, horses, is taken from empirical research by scholars who assessed the costs of various methods of production. Many other economic historians have used this model to assess the tractor, the mechanical corn picker, and the mechanical cotton picker. By and large, they have found mechanical technology saved variable costs. See for example Robert E. Ankli, "Horses Vs. Tractors in the Corn Belt," *Agricultural History*, 54 (January 1980), pp. 134–48; Robert E. Ankli, H. Dan Helsberg, and John H. Thompson, "The Adoption of the Gasoline Tractor in Western Canada," in Donald J. Akenson, ed., *Canadian Papers in Rural History* (Gananoque, Ontario: Langdale Press,

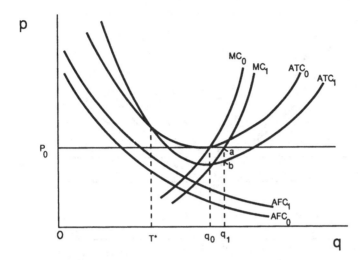

Figure 3.2. The threshold model and the adoption of a mechanical invention. For the new technique, ATC_1 denotes average total costs; AFC_1 denotes average fixed costs; MC_1 denotes marginal costs; q_1 denotes the amount under production where p_0 equals marginal costs. T^* denotes the acreage threshold where the invention's average total cost curve crosses under the existing method's average total cost curve.

reduce costs by using the new method of production. These farmers set marginal cost (MC_1) equal to marginal revenue, or the market price (p_0). Each one increases production from $0q_0$ to $0q_1$, and earns ab in per unit profits. Total profits amount to ab times $0q_1$. Eventually the increases in production drive prices down to point b where a farmer no longer earns a profit. But the point is that in order to reduce costs and remain competitive, farmers with more than T^* acres should invest in the mechanical invention.[9]

1980), vol. 2, pp. 9–39; Moses Musoke and Alan L. Olmstead, "The Rise of the Cotton Industry in California: A Comparative Perspective," *Journal of Economic History*, 32 (June 1982), pp. 385–412; and Warren C. What-ley, "Institutional Change and Mechanization in the Cotton South: The Tractorization of Cotton Farming" (Ph.D. dissertation, Stanford University, 1983). For an exception – that is, a case in which the tractor was found to save fixed costs and expend greater variable costs relative to a team of horses – see Robert E. Ankli and Alan Olmstead, "The Adoption of the Gasoline Tractor in California," *Agricultural History*, 55 (July 1981), pp. 213–30.

[9] David's threshold goes beyond Griliches's work in its ability to relate changes in production costs to the proportion of farmers who would want

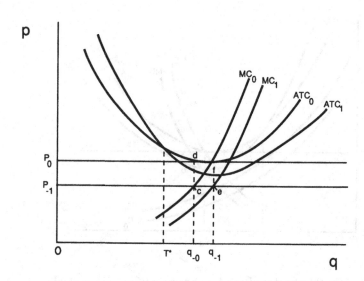

Figure 3.3. The adoption of a mechanical invention when a farmer faces a decline in prices. p_{-1} denotes a lower price at which the farmer loses money regardless of the method of production chosen; q_{-0} denotes the amount of production where p_{-1} equals marginal costs under the old method of production; and q_{-1} denotes the amount of production where p_{-1} equals the marginal cost curve with the new mechanical invention.

Implicit in this case, and that of science-based technology, is the notion that prices for farmers' crops — corn, wheat, cotton — matter insofar as they send signals to farmers telling them how much land they should devote to their crops, given marginal costs and revenues. For even if prices decline, and a farmer loses money, it may still make sense to adopt a new technique because the invention will lower costs and reduce the amount of the losses. Figure 3.3 illustrates this situation for a mechanical invention. The going market price declines from p_0 to p_{-1}. If the farmer sets the original marginal cost curve (MC_0) equal to the lower price, production will equal $0q_{-0}$, losses amount to

to invest in a new technique, and thus the timing of the diffusion of the particular invention. David's work also differs in his focus on a class of inventions that entailed fixed costs, whereas Griliches's study addressed hybrid corn, an invention that altered variable costs. The two works are compared in Nicholas Peter Sargen, *"Tractorization" in the United States and Its Relevance for the Developing Countries* (New York: Garland Publishing, 1979), pp. 54–63.

cd per unit, or to cd times $0q_{-0}$ for total losses. If, however, the farmer adopts the new technique, then the new marginal cost curve (MC_1) is set equal to the lower price. At this juncture, the farmer will produce $0q_{-1}$ and lose ef per unit. Total losses equal ef times $0q_{-1}$. The important point is that as a result of switching production methods, the size of the losses shrink. The exact reduction equals the difference between losses under the original method (cd times $0q_{-0}$) and losses under the new method (ef times $0q_{-1}$).

In the case of a scientific invention, the market price may curtail investments, depending on the magnitude of the drop in prices. Recall that a scientific invention's cost savings equal the increase in a crop's yield times the market price. As the crop's price drops, so will the invention's cost savings. If the crop's price declines to a point where the savings due to higher yields no longer offset the initial costs associated with the invention, then the farmer should forgo the investment.

The two cases thus share a common criterion for making an investment: a farmer invests in the invention if the technology reduces costs. Before purchasing a scientific input, a farmer ascertains the extent to which yields will increase and costs per acre will fall. The profitability of mechanical equipment, on the other hand, depends on its relative effect on variable and fixed costs. A farmer evaluates how much labor time and cost the machinery will save. If this decline in variable costs more than offsets the machinery's fixed expenses, the farmer should adopt the equipment.

Explaining slow rates of technological diffusion: Land settlement patterns and financial demands

Insofar as farmers reported small gains in productivity, the cost analysis offers one explanation: that a new technique offered cost savings only for the very largest farms. Economic historians, however, have gone beyond this obvious observation and have used the threshold model to investigate a second explanation. Here they have asked: what determined the size distribution of farms? Did certain factors cause a large proportion of farms to have been too small to utilize effectively a new technique? According to two case studies, the answer is yes, although the precise reasons for why farms were too small varied, as did their consequences for farm investments.

One study by Paul David assessed the diffusion of reapers in the Midwest during the mid-nineteenth century. Wheat farmers adopted reapers at a time when they were starting new farms and in the process of clearing their property. With a rise in the price of wheat during the 1850s, farmers cleared more land and increased their wheat acreage. Further, because the cost of harvest labor rose relative to the cost of the reaper, the machine's threshold fell. As farmers increased their wheat acreage and discovered the drop in the reaper's threshold, larger numbers profited from and invested in the machines.[10]

In a second study, Warren Whatley assessed the diffusion of tractors in the delta region of the South during the 1920s and 1930s. The tractor's record in this region differed in several ways from the reaper's experience in the Midwest. Rather than starting new farms, families in the Cotton South had well-established land patterns by the early twentieth century. More to the point, these families labored under the peculiar institution of sharecropping. Aside from its social and racial intentions, sharecropping had taken hold in the South in response to risks landowners faced in securing harvest labor. Picking cotton was an extremely labor-intensive process. One worker needed eighty hours to clear an acre, allowing the harvest of perhaps twelve to fifteen acres over the course of four months.[11] Landowners feared that workers would desert the farm once the harvest began. Sharecropping secured this labor because it tied a worker's annual earnings to the crop's final harvest. Once established, however, this system of labor fragmented land into small plots, and this fragmentation became an obstacle to mechanization. In the case of the tractor, it reduced costs for farmers who worked roughly 83 or more acres of cotton. But given the small size of most farms, few individuals profited from mechanization. Until the system of land tenure changed – that is, until landowners consolidated individual plots of

---

[10] David, "The Mechanization of Reaping in the Ante-Bellum Midwest."
[11] Whatley reports that it took eighty hours to harvest an acre of cotton. With four months allotted for harvesting, and a ten-hour day, then a worker could harvest up to fifteen acres. If time-off is allowed for Sundays, the work capacity would amount to 12 acres. Warren C. Whatley, "Southern Agrarian Labor Contracts as Impediments to Cotton Mechanization," *Journal of Economic History*, 47 (March 1987), especially pp. 48–9, 69–70. By contrast, a farmer in the Corn Belt spent five to seven hours harvesting an acre of corn. For more detail, see Appendix C.

land (or until the tractor's threshold fell further), the nature of farm settlement slowed the pace of "tractorization" and delayed gains in labor productivity.[12]

Using the threshold model, then, Whatley explained part of the pattern in the rate of growth of farm productivity. Prior to 1930 in certain areas of the South farmers "missed" gains in productivity insofar as sharecropping restricted the size of farms and limited the profitability of tractors. With the coming of the Great Depression, however, high rates of unemployment gave landowners more "security" in obtaining harvest labor. Further, landowners found that they could profit from one New Deal program – the Agricultural Adjustment Act – by consolidating their land and relying on wage labor. In the course of the late 1930s, a number of landowners in delta counties consolidated small farm plots and purchased tractors. This process accelerated during World War II and the postwar years.[13]

Although farmers' experience with the reaper in the mid-nineteenth century cannot answer any specific questions about the pattern of productivity growth between 1920 and 1940, that earlier experience with new technology nevertheless pointed to a different explanation for changes in productivity – one that dwelled not on questions of the distribution of land, but on the consequences of technology for farmers' finances. The reaper clearly harvested wheat faster than the traditional grain cradle, but its financial demands often exceeded a single farmer's resources: to operate it, most farmers needed extra horses and more land; and to purchase it, most needed extra capital. Manufacturers made loans, but once the loan was extended beyond its original term (typically six months), interest rates could be quite high. Farmers circumvented this financial conflict, however, by drawing on their community. They formed partnerships and divided the reaper's financial expense. Similarly, they spread the machine's fixed costs over two or more farms. Growing conditions might have hampered this tactic, but in this case, they did not do so. For even when split

---

[12] Whatley, "Southern Agrarian Labor Contracts." Also see Warren C. Whatley, "Labor for the Picking: The New Deal in the South," *Journal of Economic History*, 48 (December 1983), pp. 905–29.

[13] See Whatley, "Institutional Change and Mechanization in the Cotton South." The change in sharecropping is also described in Gavin Wright, *Old South, New South: Revolutions in the Southern Economy since the Civil War* (New York: Basic Books, 1986), pp. 226–38.

among farms, the reaper offered better insurance than the grain cradle of harvesting each farmer's wheat in a short period of time.[14]

Although these farmers found a simple financial strategy – sharing – their experience raises general questions about how farmers' investment climate influenced the diffusion of technology. The basic cost analysis described for scientific and mechanical technology assumes that once farmers found an invention profitable they readily adopted it. The threshold model offers more than a simple cost-oriented analysis; it can be used to investigate how land patterns affected the size distribution of farms and the diffusion of technology. Another factor that needs consideration, however, is risk. Farmers responded to perceived risks when deciding how to use their income or sources of credit to invest in technology. Risk might not be related to the size distribution of farms, but it could have a similar result, hampering families' investments. If perceived risks prompted farmers to delay purchases, farmers would slow the diffusion of technology, eliminating or reducing potential gains in productivity.

To understand how their finances could cause farmers to delay investments, we need to look again at the process by which farmers adopted technology. A cost-oriented analysis – as described earlier – simplifies how one looks at farms, technology, credit, and market prices. Farms are described as production units and technology is evaluated in terms of its cost savings. Producers are assumed to adopt technology readily once it demonstrates its value. Finally, prices matter insofar as farmers, given their competitive markets, seek to equate marginal costs with the going market price. All of these relationships, of course, are actually more complex than theory allows and all have a history, that is, a complicated past. By characterizing their history, we will be able to describe an investment situation within which farmers made financial choices about the desirability of purchasing technology.

In the model, farms are portrayed as production units, but in reality these enterprises differed from most other capitalist businesses in important regards. For many farms there was no division between ownership and labor: families who owned their land supplied most of the labor. Even the large number of farmers who rented or share-

---

[14] Olmstead, "The Mechanization of Reaping," especially pp. 333–44. Also see Jeremy Atack and Fred Bateman, *To Their Own Soil: Agriculture in the Antebellum North* (Ames: Iowa State University Press, 1987), pp. 194–200.

cropped land still supplied the vast majority of their own labor. Unlike many other family enterprises, farm families conducted many other activities on the farm. It is true, of course, that by the start of the twentieth century, many functions once performed on the farm had long since been eliminated. Families no longer provided their own clothing or preserved all their food. Yet even with these changes, families still raised a large part of the feed for their livestock and work animals; they saved seed from the previous harvest; manure was a fertilizer; and horses were raised on the farm. Farmers grew crops or raised livestock for part of their own food and relied on their own labor rather than hiring help.[15]

On these sorts of family farms, technological change frequently caused farmers to alter their finances. By replacing resources already available (horses, seed, manure), new techniques (tractors, hybrid seed, commercial fertilizers) often shifted the composition of expenses from noncash to cash outlays. Existing resources, like seed, entailed no direct cash outlay, and other resources, like horses, entailed relatively modest cash demands. With new technologies, however, farmers needed to expend cash or, alternatively, use credit. They turned to short-term credit markets to borrow in order to buy implements, machinery, livestock, and related inputs, such as fertilizer. They also borrowed in order to buy land.

These financial concerns did not cause farmers to ignore relative cost savings. Certainly farmers had no reason to adopt technology unless it saved costs. Yet because they made investment decisions whose consequences stretched over the course of several years, their choices were shaped by two other factors: one concerned market prices, the other credit. Long-term patterns of prices and sources of credit helped shape the investment climate within which families responded to competition and evaluated technology.

Unstable market prices

In the standard cost-oriented analysis, prices matter insofar as they send farmers signals about the relative profitability of different crops. Yet, along with the level of prices, the volatility with which markets

---

[15] Parker, "Agriculture," pp. 396–8, 400–1. Also see Harriet Friedmann, "World Market, State, and Family Farm: Social Bases of Household Production in an Era of Wage Labor," *Comparative Studies in Society and History*, 20 (October 1978), pp. 545–86.

set prices was also significant. This volatility brought unexpected changes to farmers' incomes; sudden and sharp changes in prices could also incite credit crises.

Economists and politicians alike have long recognized that farm prices fluctuated and that this instability created problems for individual farmers. Several factors – changes in foreign markets, wars, drought, and insect plights – made commodity prices unpredictable and volatile. Moreover, these events took place in markets in which the demand for crops was inelastic. From the turn of the century to the Great Depression, the price elasticity of demand for corn, cotton, wheat, potatoes, oats, barley, rye, and hay, among other crops, was less than unity.[16] Any change in a crop's output therefore prompted wider swings in its price. For instance, the prices of many cash crops, including wheat, corn, cotton, and hogs varied more than 15 percent from year to year between 1890 and 1924.[17]

Although farmers had no control over fickle markets, they could insulate themselves from the consequences of low prices. Farmers could do so because they obtained many of their resources – food, feed, fertilizer, seed, labor – from their families and farms. By avoiding cash payments, farmers acquired a degree of safety: prices could fall sharply, but actual cash losses might be small. Thus, although farmers could not predict when or how sharply prices might fall, they could limit their exposure to cash losses.[18]

[16] Price elasticity measures the sensitivity of the quantity demanded to changes in price. In technical terms, the price elasticity of demand equals the percentage change in quantity associated with a given percent change in the price of a good. If this ratio is less than one, then the price elasticity of demand is said to be inelastic. Henry Schultz estimated the price elasticity of these crops and others. Henry Schultz, *The Theory and Measurement of Demand* (Chicago: University of Chicago Press, 1938), especially pp. 548–9.

[17] D. Gale Johnson, *Forward Prices for Agriculture* (Chicago: University of Chicago Press, 1946), p. 79. Also see F. C. Miller, *The Behavior of Prices* (New York: National Bureau of Economic Research, 1927), pp. 489, 497.

[18] Economic historians have recognized farmers' concern about unstable prices and their desire for financial safety. In one study of the antebellum South, Gavin Wright and Howard Kunreuther accounted for farmers' behavior in terms of a strategy they called "safety first." They argued that small cotton farmers distinguished the cash crop (cotton) from food crops, devoting enough land to guarantee their food supply and planting what land remained in cotton. By not paying cash for food, these farmers did not expose themselves to losses in the event that the price of cotton declined. Although Wright and Kunreuther defined this safety-first strategy

We can see how this mechanism worked by comparing family enterprises and the great bonanza wheat farms of the late nineteenth century. The giant (nonfamily) farms relied completely on wage labor and heavy machinery. Once the land was cleared, the largest expense came from paying cash wages to migrant labor. For many years this did not matter. Because yields were plentiful and prices firm, the farms prospered. But in the late 1880s and 1890s, prices slipped and yields declined. Unable to cover cash costs, bonanza farms disappeared and family units took their place. Family operators in the Red River Valley survived because they relied on their own labor and restricted their standard of living during years of low prices. They also benefited by diversifying their crops.[19]

Although many families acquired some safety through these measures, they were not rigid about their strategy of conserving cash. Farmers frequently had reason to use credit to purchase land or technology, or to make cash outlays for hired labor. In one of the most well known studies of agricultural finance, William G. Murray argued that the initial cost of starting a farm gave families good reason to employ credit. It took several years to save the necessary cash for the farm's purchase, equipment, and livestock. A farmer starting out might have saved part of the investment, but rarely the total sum. Murray thought it reasonable for such farmers to borrow funds. He specifically cited young operators: "The competent young farmer between the ages of 20 and 35 with a family to support has everything needed for farming except the $7,000 of capital."[20] After land, the next largest outlay was for the purchase of machinery and

in terms of the mix of crops, farmers' actions may be described in general terms as an effort to conserve cash and protect their cash flow. See Gavin Wright and Howard Kunreuther, "Cotton, Corn and Risk in the Nineteenth Century," *Journal of Economic History*, 35 (September 1975), pp. 526–51; and Gavin Wright, *The Political Economy of the Cotton South: Households, Markets, and Wealth in the Nineteenth Century* (New York: Norton, 1978).

[19] Fred A. Shannon, *The Farmer's Last Frontier: Agriculture, 1860–1897* (New York: Rinehart, 1945), pp. 154–61. Also see Friedmann, "World Market, State, and Family Farm," pp. 545–86.

[20] Murray noted that for 1920 the value of a farm was $10,300 and in 1930, $7,600. In addition, the farmer needed $1,500 in working capital. William G. Murray, *Agricultural Finance* (Ames: Iowa State College Press, 1941), p. 3. For an overview of credit, see Allan G. Bogue, "Land Credit for Northern Farmers 1789–1940," *Agricultural History*, 50 (January 1976), pp. 68–100.

implements. Farmers often paid cash, but they also used short-term credit, especially for expensive items like the reaper. Similarly, farmers at times purchased livestock and supplies with credit. When they hired labor, especially at the time of the harvest, they would have to make cash outlays.

To be sure, the amount of money spent varied by region and even within a given region, according to the size of a farm, the effects of weather, the nature of different crops, and other variables. Still, across different regions and growing seasons, farmers who wanted to maintain or expand operations needed to make cash outlays. In doing so, they experienced a tension between safety and productivity: purchases of new land or machinery enabled them to expand production or to reduce costs, but the cash required for these purchases – either for interest or for the immediate cash expense – reduced the margin of safety farmers maintained between their expenses and their earnings.

Inasmuch as farmers needed credit to purchase land and technology, they exposed themselves to a second problem associated with market prices. Credit always entailed some degree of risk because a mortgage obligated the borrower to make regular payments despite variations in a farmer's cash earnings. These earnings were unlikely to be stable because of the variance of prices. In most cases, farmers could not expect a rise in prices to persist for more than one or two years. If, however, farmers sensed that prices would rise or remain high for several years, then a significant number were likely to alter their expectations and assume larger quantities of debt. As long as these higher prices remained stable, the borrowers did not suffer. But when prices dropped suddenly and swiftly, indebted farmers could not readily lower their nominal costs, particularly their debt obligations. Even though the new investment in land and equipment had increased total output, farmers would find themselves hard pressed to secure the cash to pay their mortgages. If enough farmers were involved, their failure to meet debt payments could result in a full-blown credit crisis.[21]

Looking at the 130 years prior to the Great Depression, five epi-

[21] Murray had been one of the first agricultural economists to study the relationship between long swings in market prices and the potential for a credit crisis. For his initial study, see William G. Murray, "An Economic Analysis of Farm Mortgages in Story County, Iowa, 1854–1931," Iowa State University Agricultural Experiment Station Research Bulletin No. 156 (January 1933).

sodes of "violent" movements in prices had interrupted the general pattern of variations in market conditions. The first case dated from the late 1810s; the second spanned the years before and after the panic of 1837; the third followed events in the Civil War; the fourth took place with events of the 1890s, at which time prices had reached a low point after the panic of 1893.[22] Unfortunately, the consequences of these earlier events for farm failures cannot be ascertained since in the years prior to 1912 the USDA did not systematically collect data. But in the last case involving the surge and fall in prices during and immediately following World War I, the outcome can be outlined.

After fighting began in World War I, prices of basic commodities like wheat, corn, cotton, and potatoes rose sharply; although farmers could not readily adjust production, they bid up land values. Higher land values translated into higher equity values, and farmers took out larger loans. All of these trends were exaggerated in states where farmers raised cash crops: land values rose further and debt levels were higher. Farmers were able to add to or improve their land, but ultimately this did not mean greater profits. In 1920 prices broke. The price of corn fell 78 percent, wheat 64 percent, and cotton 57 percent. Once prices settled in the early 1920s, they actually averaged, in nominal terms, 30 percent more than they had in the prewar years.[23] But because farmers had accumulated wartime debts at wartime prices, it was difficult for them to meet their payments. Rates of foreclosure (for all farms in the United States) rose from less than 4 farms in 1,000 just prior to the war to 11 between 1921 and 1925, and then to 17 in the late 1920s. As Murray anticipated, younger operators were more likely to be at risk. By 1929 farmers aged twenty-five to forty-four (who would have been ten years younger during World War I) held a quarter of all farms, but a third of all indebted farms. A significant number had gotten into debt at a time

[22] Lawrence A. Jones and David Durand, *Mortgage Lending Experience in Agriculture*, National Bureau of Economic Research (Princeton: Princeton University Press, 1954), pp. 3–5.

[23] Between 1910 and 1914, the index of prices received by farmers equaled 72 as compared to 94 for the period 1921 to 1925. From 1926 through 1929, prices equaled or surpassed 94. U.S. Department of Commerce, *Statistical Abstract of the United States: 1932* (Washington, D.C.: U.S. Government Printing Office, 1932), p. 604. For changes in prices after 1920, also see A. B. Genung, *The Agricultural Depression Following World War I and Its Political Consequences* (Ithaca, N.Y.: Northeast Farm Foundation, 1954), pp. 10–11.

when they would have been starting their farms and were likely to borrow money.[24]

This sort of credit crisis was ironic considering the general instability in the markets that farmers faced. The unpredictable ups and downs in prices normally prompted farmers to be cautious, to hesitate to invest in a new productivity-enhancing device. In the case of dramatic swings in prices, however, some farmers apparently acquired a false confidence; encouraged by the sharply rising prices, they acquired debts to expand operations. Alternatively, young operators had the bad fortune to need credit to start farms in years of rising prices. In either case, when prices ultimately collapsed, many faced a difficult financial future. Individuals who had avoided debts could look at these troubled neighbors to confirm that their original strategy of conserving cash was the right one.

Sources of credit

Credit – its availability and its terms – was another important factor in farmers' investment strategies. Implicit in the analysis of technology based on its cost savings is the assumption that farmers could readily finance investments. Certainly, manufacturers recognized the importance of credit for sales. John Vance, an official at International Harvester, put the issue in these words:

> The sale of farm operating equipment in the United States has always been a credit business. . . . the nature of the farmer's operations is such that, however sound his assets, they usually are not readily available in liquid form. The farmer invests money, time and

[24] For an analysis of the credit crisis that began after 1920, see Lee J. Alston, "Farm Foreclosures in the United States during the Interwar Period," *Journal of Economic History*, 43 (December 1983), pp. 885–903. Alston reports that in all but eight states land values rose by at least 140 percent between 1912 and 1920. He also charts the relationship between changes in land values and levels of debt by state. For changes in prices, see U.S. Department of Commerce, *Statistical Abstract of the United States, 1925* (Washington, D.C.: U.S. Government Printing Office, 1926), p. 636. On the size of mortgages, see Donald C. Horton, Harald C. Larsen, and Norman J. Wall, "Farm-Mortgage Credit Facilities in the United States," U.S. Department of Agriculture Miscellaneous Publication No. 478 (1942), p. 235. For the rate of indebtedness, see U.S. Department of Commerce, *Fifteenth Census of the United States: 1930*, Agriculture, vol. 4, p. 447; for the proportion of indebted farmers by age, see pp. 460–3.

labor in crops which require months to produce. His income is
received at irregular intervals and in irregular amounts as crops
mature.[25]

The same justification could be made for long-term debt used to
purchase land. In either case, farmers turned to various private creditors – individuals, commercial banks, implement companies, life insurance companies. When creditors set loan policies, they had in mind
how they raised funds, their alternative investment options, their
sense of market risks. As a result, farmers' ability to obtain credit and
to obtain "desirable" terms (meaning the rate of interest and the
length of loans) varied a good deal between local creditors (individuals and banks) and "centralized" lenders, notably life insurance companies.

Among the two important local lenders, the USDA surveyed banks'
policies in 1921. That study indicated that because they depended on
demand deposits for their loanable funds, and because customers
could readily withdraw their deposits, banks concentrated their funds
in short- rather than long-term credit; (in 1920 banks held $3.9
billion in short- versus $1.4 billion in long-term debt). Banks set loans
with rates that ranged from 6.5 to 7 percent, and kept the length of
loans short. Most terms ran for three to six months or nine to twelve
months, but rarely extended beyond a year.[26] Officials concluded:

> One of the greatest defects of bank loans to farmers under existing
> conditions is that credit is not available for such a length of time as
> is frequently needed by the farmer to mature his products and to
> market them in an orderly manner. For the production and market-
> ing of crops, loans for a term of from 8 to 12 months are frequently

[25] John W. Vance, "History of Credits and Collection Policies" (1941), p. 2,
Document No. 959, International Harvester Company Archives, Navistar
International Transportation Corporation, Chicago, Illinois.

[26] For a short-term personal or collateral loan, a survey conducted in March
1921 reported that commercial banks' prevailing short-term interest rates
ranged from 6.8 in Ohio and Illinois to more than 7 percent in Indiana,
Iowa, and Missouri. It is difficult to find studies of bank loans, but see
Roy J. Burroughs, "Experience of Michigan Rural Banks with Short Term
Loans to Farmers," Michigan State College Agricultural Experiment Sta-
tion Special Bulletin No. 311 (August 1941). For short-term bank credit,
see Norman J. Wall, "Agricultural Loans of Commercial Banks," U.S.
Department of Agriculture Technical Bulletin No. 521 (July 1936); V. N.
Valgren and Elmer E. Engelbert, "Bank Loans to Farmers on Personal and
Collateral Security," U.S. Department of Agriculture Bulletin No. 1048
(February 1922), pp. 6–9, 22–3.

needed, and the producer of livestock . . . often needs credit for a period of from 1 to 3 years. To obtain a loan under existing conditions, farmers not infrequently are obliged to agree to repay the same at a time prior to that at which they have any expectation of being able to meet it, and to rely on the hope of being able to renew the loan when it falls due.[27]

This problem was exacerbated by a second. Demand deposits were closely tied to farmers' own income. In flush years, deposits rose and banks looked for outlets to make loans, but in depressed years, customers would be more likely to withdraw funds, and banks would want to be prepared for this outflow. Thus the ability of banks to make loans varied with farmers' fortunes: in years of low prices – years when farmers needed loans – banks were least able to offer them.[28]

In the case of long-term credit, private individuals appear to have set terms similar to those of the banks. Farmers had always relied on private individuals for credit, and in the early nineteenth century many owners took back paper as a way of selling their farms. Alternatively, relatives used mortgages to transfer farms to the next generation. In these cases the mortgage acted as a kind of retirement annuity.[29] For whatever reason, individuals wrote short loans, ones that typically matured in less than four years, and carried rates of interest at 6.2 percent (Table 3.1). These figures were close to those of the banks; their loans matured on average in fewer than three years, and their rates averaged 6.6 percent (Table 3.1).[30]

Compared with these local lenders, businesses that operated in several states were more flexible about credit, and they tended to offer

[27] Valgren and Engelbert, "Bank Loans to Farmers on Personal and Collateral Security," p. 26.
[28] Wall, "Agricultural Loans of Commercial Banks," pp. 10–13.
[29] Bogue, "Land Credit for Northern Farmers 1789–1940," pp. 71–83. See as well Allan G. Bogue, *Money at Interest: The Farm Mortgage on the Middle Border* (Ithaca, N.Y.: Cornell University Press, 1955); Allan G. Bogue, *From Prairie to Corn Belt: Farming on the Illinois and Iowa Prairies in the Nineteenth Century* (Chicago: University of Chicago Press, 1963); Margaret Beattie Bogue, *Patterns from the Sod: Land Use and Tenure in the Grand Prairie, 1850–1900* (Springfield: Illinois State Historical Library, 1959).
[30] Valgren and Engelbert, "Bank Loans to Farmers on Personal and Collateral Security," pp. 4, 7–9; and V. N. Valgren and Elmer E. Engelbert, "Farm Mortgage Loans by Banks, Insurance Companies, and Other Agencies," U.S. Department of Agriculture Bulletin No. 1047 (December 1921), p. 21.

Table 3.1. *Average rates of interest and terms of farm mortgage loans by major lenders, selected years, 1911-71*

Year	Life insurance companies	Commercial banks	Federal land banks	Individuals & other lenders	All lenders
A. *Average rates of interest*					
1911-30	5.8%	6.6%	5.4%[a]	6.2%	6.2%
1931-5	5.6	6.5	5.1	6.2	5.9
1936-40	5.3	5.8	3.8	5.5	4.8
1941-5	4.7	5.4	3.6	5.0	4.4
1946-50	4.3	5.1	4.1	4.7	4.5
1951-5	4.4	5.2	4.1	n.a.	4.7
1960-4	5.2	5.9	4.9	5.1	5.2
1965-9	5.6	6.1	5.4	5.3	5.5
1971	6.0	6.7	6.4	5.6	6.0
B. *Average terms of farm mortgage loans (years)*					
1917-21	7.5	2.7	30.9	3.7	[c]
1922-6	8.7	2.5	29.6	3.3	[c]
1927-31	8.1	2.1	28.8	3.1	[c]
1932-5	7.2	1.9	20.7[b]	2.9	[c]
1945	15.0	4.5	22.9	4.9	[c]
1949-59	18.3	4.2	25.1	7.0[d]	9.4
1961-9	20.7	6.8	29.4	11.5[d]	17.2
1971	20.7	7.3	29.1	11.7[d]	15.9

[a]The interest rate is reported for years 1918 to 1930.
[b]Average terms were reported for federal land banks and Land Bank Commissioner loans.
[c]Information is not available.
[d]Includes miscellaneous lenders -- mortgage and investment companies, state and local government agencies, merchants and dealers, and unidentified lenders.
Sources: For rates of interest, see U.S. Department of Agriculture, "Agricultural Finance Statistics," AFS-3 (July 1976), p. 43; and U.S. Department of Agriculture, "Major Statistical Series of the U.S. Department of Agriculture," Agriculture Handbook No. 118 (October 1957), vol. 6, p. 22. For terms of loans, see "Size, Terms, and Conditions of Farm Mortgages Recorded," *Agricultural Finance Review*, 9 (November 1946), p. 56; U.S. Department of Agriculture, "Farm Mortgages Recorded in 1959, Interest Rates, Terms, and Sizes with Historical Data, 1949-1959," ERS-61 (April 1962), p. 33; and U.S. Department of Agriculture, "Farm Mortgage Characteristics: 1/1/71 and Historical Data, 1961-1969," ERS-527 (August 1973), pp. 23, 24, 26.

better terms. In the case of short-term credit, farmers obtained loans to purchase machinery from implement companies. Over the years, these implement firms began to extend the length of loans to assist the purchase of expensive machinery, notably the tractor. For the 1920s, IHC wrote loans that carried terms of two or three years (which for a bank would have been the length of a mortgage). A farmer paid 20 percent of the cash price in the first year and 40 percent of the tractor's price in the next two years.[31] Similar policies were offered by other firms. Although the length of their loans was longer than those set by banks, the rates of interest were similar, ranging from 6 to 7 percent. If a farmer extended the loan beyond its maturity date, then rates often were raised a point to 7 or 8 percent.[32]

Until the entry of federal creditors, the single largest group of centralized lenders offering long-term credit was composed of life insurance companies. Insurance firms accumulated funds from their collection of premiums, and they could be more flexible than banks because the funds were not subject to quick withdrawal. They also had greater flexibility given the scope of their markets. Whereas banks made loans in their immediate vicinity, insurance companies developed a network of financial correspondents who lived in several states. Correspondents submitted mortgage applications, and an inspector assessed the value of the property. The farm mortgage department then determined whether and when to approve the loan. In this way, insurance companies generated profits on volume, as an official at Connecticut Mutual explained in 1917:

> The cost of handling farm loans is relatively small and decreases in proportion as the volume of loans increases. . . . in fact our Company, whose outstanding volume of loans has trebled within the past fifteen years, handles the larger volume with practically the same number of clerks and with only slightly heavier other contingent expenses.[33]

As a result, insurance companies offered loans on better terms than did local lenders. Their rates of interest averaged 5.8 percent between

---

[31] Vance, "History of Credits and Collection Policies" (1941), p. 16.

[32] Federal Trade Commission, *Report on the Agricultural Implement and Machinery Industry*, 75th Congress, 3rd sess., House Document 702 (June 6, 1938), p. 656.

[33] "Farm Loan Investments" (1917), Docs 1. Exec. / Pres. 6 (Taylor) / Investments – Farm Loans, p. 10, Corporate Library, Connecticut Mutual Life Insurance Company, Hartford, Connecticut.

1910 and 1930, or nearly a point below rates charged by banks. They also set longer maturities, averaging seven to eight years, compared with bank averages of fewer than three years (Table 3.1). Across the different farm regions in the United States, insurance companies offered rates roughly half a point lower than those of other lenders.[34]

Although insurance companies set relatively low rates, they faced other concerns that caused them to limit the availability of funds and to restrict the terms of loans. They were dependent on loan correspondents who earned a commission when farmers renewed their loans. Renew they normally did. The agricultural economist, David Wickens, estimated that the average farmer remained in debt for twenty to thirty-five years. He concluded that "most farmers would save inconvenience and expense by taking out mortgages that have terms much longer than are now covered by most loans. . . . farmers who contract for mortgages with 5-year terms should realize that before the debt is paid they will probably have to make at least four or five renewals."[35] Bankers Life explained this outcome from the lender's side: "The bulk of farm loans are made for a term of five years. This office would rather make the term ten years. The man who secures the application however wants the shorter term." Aetna's treasurer concurred: "It is natural for the agent to desire a short loan, as he can then obtain an additional commission on its renewal."[36]

In periods of tight money, insurance companies could not always meet farmers' requests and responded – not surprisingly – by raising rates. E. H. Lougee, a loan correspondent for Connecticut Mutual, described how this process worked for the corn farmers in his community of Council Bluffs, Iowa, in 1910. An internal memo at Connecticut Mutual pointed out "that farmers did not realize a full return from last year's crops, and that there is still a large amount of corn being held for sale." Their actions carried over to banks: "local banks have been loaned up to the limit; the country banks borrowing of the banks of the Iowa cities, and they in turn borrowing of the New York

[34] Horton et al., "Farm-Mortgage Credit Facilities," pp. 229–31.

[35] David L. Wickens, "Farm-Mortgage Credit," U.S. Department of Agriculture Technical Bulletin No. 288 (February 1932), pp. 75–7.

[36] Bankers Life to Rural Organization Service, August 29, 1913, p. 2; M. B. Brainard, Aetna, to Rural Organization Service, October 31, 1913, p. 2; and Robert W. Huntington, Jr., Connecticut General, to C. W. Thompson, November 1, 1913, pp. 3–4, "Bank Survey," Record Group 83, Entry 114, Box 9, National Archives, Washington, D.C.

and Chicago banks."[37] In the winter of 1910, banks "unloaded such loans on hand as they could, and the full demand was turned back onto the insurance companies, who found that even their large funds for investment became exhausted." As demand increased Lougee reported that "The Northwestern has raised its rate to 6%, but that is practically prohibitive." The treasurer proposed the same tactic: "I think a 6 % rate will check to a very lar[ge] extent the buying of lands and . . . would very largely curtail the farm [illegible] business." He further noted that "The Company's supply of investment funds is far from inexhaustable [sic]. Not infrequently, in its present loan field, it is obliged to suspend for a time making new loans because of lack of available investment funds."[38]

In periods of tight money, lenders frequently found alternative investment opportunities more attractive than farm loans. In reply to the 1913 survey, Aetna wrote: "Quite frequently during periods of tight money we receive numerous applications to take up loans made by the local banks. These loans we presume are short time ones, and are called by the banks during the periods of financial stringency." Connecticut General stated: "At such times also the price of first-class railroad and other bonds is apt to be very attractive. The company has therefore practically removed [sic] from the farm loan market at a time when money is tightest."[39]

Given their scope and institutional concerns, life insurance firms normally limited their operations to selected regions of the United States. Because they based profits on the ratio of loans to correspondents, they concentrated their business in regions with good farmland where they could write many comparatively large mortgages. Overall, in 1920, 79 percent of all debt held by insurance companies was loaned to farmers in states in the East and West North Central –

[37] E. H. Lougee Memo (June 25, 1910), Docs. 2. Records / Correspondence – Incoming / Iowa Farm Loans – June, 1910, Corporate Library, Connecticut Mutual Life Insurance Company.
[38] Ibid.; Treasurer to M. J. Haire, Fort Dodge, Iowa, July 1, 1910, Docs. 2. Records / Correspondence / Iowa Farm Loans July – August, 1910; and "Farm Investment Loans" (1917), p. 14, Corporate Library, Connecticut Mutual Life Insurance Company.
[39] M. B. Brainard, Aetna, to Rural Organization Service, October 31, 1913, p. 1; Robert W. Huntington, Jr., Connecticut General, to C. W. Thompson, November 1, 1913, Record Group 83, Entry 114, Box 9, National Archives.

meaning the Corn and Wheat Belts – and 10 percent in the West
South Central, notably Texas. Insurance firms avoided regions with
small farms and areas where farming entailed greater risks; they only
held debt in selected areas of southern states and had very small
shares of the debt in the "Mountain" states.[40] The behavior of insurance companies was shaped in part by the risks and investment
opportunities in the several farm regions. In the Corn and Wheat
Belts, interest rates ranged from 5 to 6 percent for most years in the
early 1900s. In the South and the West, interest rates ranged from 6.5
to 8 percent, or from one to two points above the national average.[41]

Given the competitive and institutional concerns of these creditors,
farmers were unable to obtain loans on terms that suited their investments – at least as they defined them. While insurance companies set
the best terms, the availability of these loans varied by region and
fluctuated according to the companies' alternative opportunities.
Moreover, as late as 1920, most farmers depended on local lenders:
private individuals accounted for the vast majority – 70 percent – of
farm mortgage debt; banks held another 14 percent of the outstanding debt (Table 3.2). These borrowers faced the prospect of renewing
loans with comparatively shorter terms and higher rates of interest.
In years of rising prices, many banks were pleased to make loans or
renew old ones, but in depressed years as deposits were withdrawn,
banks cut back – sometimes sharply – on their loan activity. If
farmers during these years seemed preoccupied about prices and
credit, they had every reason to be concerned and to express those
concerns through the political system.

Politics, prices, and credit

In the early years of the twentieth century, the problems of farm
credit and farm prices frequently found their way into national politics. Members of Congress (both Democrats and Republicans) looked
for ways to stabilize farmers' volatile commodity markets and to

[40] The East North Central includes Ohio, Indiana, Illinois, Michigan, and
Wisconsin; the West North Central includes Minnesota, Iowa, Missouri,
North Dakota, South Dakota, Nebraska, and Kansas; and in the West
South Central are Arkansas, Louisiana, Oklahoma, and Texas. The debt
held by life insurance companies is calculated from Horton et al., "Farm-
Mortgage Credit Facilities," pp. 222–4.
[41] Ibid., pp. 27, 30, 227–8.

Table 3.2. *Percent of farm mortgage debt held by major lenders, selected years, 1910-70*

Year	Life insurance companies	Commercial banks	Federal land banks[a]	Joint stock land banks	Individuals & other lenders[b]
1910	12.1%	12.7%	---	---	75.3%
1920	11.5	14.3	3.5%	0.7%	70.0
1925	19.6	12.1	9.3	4.5	54.5
1930	22.0	10.4	12.5	6.6	48.6
1936	15.0	6.6	39.2	2.7	36.6
1940	15.0	8.1	42.7	---	34.2
1950	21.0	16.7	17.3	---	45.0
1960	23.3	12.6	19.3	---	44.8
1970	19.9	11.9	22.8	---	45.4

[a]Federal land banks also include Land Bank Commissioner Loans.
[b]From 1940 to 1970, the Farmers Home Administration accounted for 0.5, 3.6, 5.6, and 7.7 percent of outstanding debt.
Sources: U.S. Department of Agriculture, *Agricultural Statistics, 1952* (Washington, D.C.: U.S. Government Printing Office, 1952), p. 721; and U.S. Department of Agriculture, "Economic Indicators of the Farm Sector: Income and Balance Sheet Statistics, 1983," ECIFS 3-3 (September 1984), p. 114.

improve farmers' sources of credit. Price regulation was proposed but rejected. Congress, however, did approve legislation to create public sources of credit.

In the wake of the credit crisis of the 1920s, Republicans and Democrats from agricultural states looked with renewed energy for ways to protect farmers from the effects of depressed markets. The most famous plan was the McNary–Haugen bill. It called for the creation of a government agency to buy cash crops so as to increase and stabilize prices. Excess stocks would be sold abroad, and the losses would be recovered, conveniently, through tariffs on imported commodities. Congress twice backed the bill, but President Calvin Coolidge balked at having the government fix prices and vetoed the bill each time.[42] Until Herbert Hoover took office in 1929, farmers received no long-term support to raise and steady commodity prices.

[42]Murray R. Benedict, *Farm Policies of the United States, 1790–1950* (New York: Twentieth Century Fund, 1953), pp. 207–38; Gilbert C. Fite,

Although price supports were rejected, Congress did pass two re-
markable pieces of legislation in 1916 and 1923. The first bill, the
Federal Farm Loan Act, established a nationwide farm mortgage
lending system. The United States was divided into twelve districts,
each with one federal land bank. The banks sold bonds on the open
market, just as any private corporation would in order to raise funds.
Farmers were encouraged to create cooperative loan organizations,
called national farm loan associations, to make use of these funds.
Federal land banks would assist these associations by providing initial
capital, which would be repaid gradually; the local associations
worked through land banks to offer individual farmers long-term
mortgages. Interest rates were set at a level no higher than the rate
obtained on the most recent bond offering plus one percentage point.
The intent of the federal lending system, then, was to obtain funds at
the best rates through national credit markets, and to lend these funds
as individual farm mortgages at the lowest interest rates over the
longest period of time (averaging some 30 years).

In addition to federal land banks, the 1916 act provided for so-
called joint stock land banks. These institutions, which were run by
private individuals, made long-term loans; they were required to pay
half the $250,000 minimum capital in cash, and could not sell tax-
exempt bonds until they had sold their entire stock subscription. This
part of the experiment had a short life. While joint stock land banks
made many loans between the years 1922 and 1927, and held 6.7
percent of all farm mortgage debt in 1929, most of them were liquidated in the 1930s. By 1939, joint stock land banks held just 1.2
percent of all farm mortgage debt.[43]

Shortly after World War I, Congress passed a second bill, the
Agricultural Credits Act of 1923, which provided for shorter-term
credit. This measure created a system of twelve Federal Intermediate
Credit Banks, which loaned funds to other credit agencies. Private

George N. Peek and the Fight for Farm Parity (Norman: University of
Oklahoma Press, 1954); John Mark Hansen, Gaining Access (Chicago:
University of Chicago Press, 1991).
[43] The average size of loans made by joint stock land banks was $6,922. This
sum was large when compared with the U.S. average, which ranged from
a low of $2,470 in 1935 to a high of $4,270 in 1920. Horton et al.,
"Farm-Mortgage Credit Facilities," pp. 16, 66–9, 124–31, 162; Murray,
Agricultural Finance; and L. J. Norton, Financing Agriculture (Danville,
Ill.: Interstate Press, 1938).

lenders, such as commercial banks, could then offer farmers intermediate credit.[44]

By 1929, federal lenders had become a presence in different markets, but none accounted for a large share of farm debt. Federal land
banks held the most, $1.2 billion, or 12.1 percent of all farm mort-
gage debt; as noted earlier, joint stock land banks held 6.7 percent.
The Federal Intermediate Credit Banks fared worse. Because they
required borrowing institutions to charge no more than 1.5 percent
above the discount rate, few creditors had asked for funds. As a
result, the banks advanced loans of just $95 million in 1929, a
negligible share of the shorter-term credit market.[45] Most farmers still
relied on private lenders, particularly local creditors.[46]

Technology and productivity reconsidered

In the years between 1920 and 1940, new types of scientific and
mechanical technology were introduced to the farm sector. Some
gains were recorded in the 1920s, but it was in the years after the
mid-1930s that farmers attained high rates of productivity growth.
There are two different ways to explain this pattern, and they single
out different – in part, contradictory – causes. One style of analysis
maintains that, given their competitive markets, farmers would have
adopted technology once a product lowered costs below that of its
existing substitute. Regardless of the cash expense involved, if the
item reduced costs, it should have been adopted. In order to account
for the pattern of farm productivity between 1920 and 1940, this line
of reasoning indicates that farmers either lacked new inventions until
1935 or that the technology failed to deliver cost savings until that
time.

[44] Among various studies of farm credit, see Horton et al., "Farm-Mortgage
Credit Facilities," pp. 12, 66–9; Murray, *Agricultural Finance*; and Norton, *Financing Agriculture*.
[45] For federal banks, see Horton et al., "Farm-Mortgage Credit Facilities,"
pp. 15–17, 222. For Federal Intermediate Credit Banks, see Wall, "Agricultural Loans of Commercial Banks," pp. 25–7; Murray, *Agricultural
Finance*, pp. 254–6.
[46] Roughly 7 percent of all federal land bank loans were used for farm
improvements including investments in equipment. See Horton et al.,
"Farm-Mortgage Credit Facilities in the United States," pp. 15–17, 94.

A different line of analysis is suggested by farmers' investment climate and the financial demands of technology. While new techniques raised productivity, they required additional cash outlays. The expense, of course, varied by product. Hybrid seed or chemical fertilizers, for instance, necessitated relatively small cash payments each year. Capital equipment, by contrast, called for large sums. Further, in the case of the tractor and harvesting machinery, the technology entailed fixed costs that could be better supported by employing extra land. In this way, the technology raised the question of whether a family should invest in land as well as machinery.

Viewed in isolation, these financial considerations need not have mattered. If, however, farmers considered problems of safety and credit in their investment calculus, then the trend in productivity could have been shaped in one of two ways. Relatively cheap inventions, available only after 1935, may have accounted for the productivity gains in the late 1930s. Alternatively, expensive types of technology may have been available in the 1920s, but farmers may have shunned investments because of the inventions' cash demands.

In an effort to decide which of these analyses is most useful, I focus on the diffusion of specific types of technology – the tractor, the mechanical corn picker, and hybrid corn – so as to determine whether farmers delayed investments. Here the threshold model is important because it can be used to determine whether the actual diffusion of a mechanical invention differed at all from the rate predicted on the basis of its cost savings. A related cost analysis is used for hybrid corn.

In Part II, I examine these inventions in the 1920s and 1930s for one region, the Corn Belt. I selected the Corn Belt because in this region I can single out questions dealing with family enterprises and their financial resources at a time when land patterns in the Midwest were relatively stable. Sharecropping, for instance, accounted for a large number of farms in the Midwest, but, unlike the South, harvests in the Midwest were not so labor-intensive and sharecropping did not restrict the size of farms in the same way. Farms operated by sharecroppers often matched or exceeded the size of farms that operators owned outright. Nor did the question of new settlement apply to the Midwest in the twentieth century (as it had in the case of reapers in the nineteenth century). The size of farms had increased slowly from 1890 to 1920. During the 1920s, the number of farms shrank slightly, while their average size increased by one to eight acres in each Corn Belt state. In the 1930s, the number remained relatively stable and the average size changed little.[47]

In this respect the Midwest was also different from parts of the Wheat Belt. Semiarid regions became noteworthy for their plow-ups in the 1920s and their droughts and dust bowls in the 1930s.[48] In these regions farmers grew little other than wheat, and most of their expenses (with the exception of their own labor) were cash outlays. Thus they did not have the same options as more diversified farmers to differentiate among cash and noncash outlays. East of the semiarid line, families engaged in more diversified agriculture, and they worked farms significantly larger than those found in the Corn Belt. But even these farmers suffered in the 1930s. The Dust Bowl cut a wide ring swinging south through western Kansas, western Oklahoma, and the panhandle of Texas, and then north again, slicing across the eastern corner of New Mexico and the eastern third of Colorado. There drought and erosion were the worst, and the "black blizzards" that followed afflicted these regions as well as those far beyond the immediate crisis area. These storms and their destruction of crops and livestock persisted through 1935, 1936, and into the late 1930s, creating unusual circumstances for the mechanization of wheat farms during the Great Depression.

[47] With the exception of Missouri, the average size of tenant farms exceeded the average of owner-operated farms from 1910 through 1940. Changes in farm size and the number of farms, and the average size of farms are calculated from U.S. Department of Commerce, *Thirteenth Census of the United States: 1910* (Washington, D.C.: U.S. Government Printing Office, 1913), Agriculture, vol. 5, pp. 68–9, 75; *Fifteenth Census of the United States: 1930*, Agriculture, vol. 2, part 1, pp. 400, 482, 566, 884, 978; *Sixteenth Census of the United States: 1940* (Washington, D.C.: U.S. Government Printing Office, 1940), Agriculture, vol. 1, part 1, pp. 426, 536, 650, and part 2, pp. 112, 232.

[48] The literature is extensive. For the emergence of wheat farming, see, for example, Shannon, *The Farmer's Last Frontier.* For the nature of farm organization in the Plains states, studies vary with the nature of farmland and region. For a sociological view, see Friedmann, "World Market, State, and Family Farm." On the Dust Bowl, see Donald Worster, *Dust Bowl: The Southern Great Plains in the 1930s* (New York: Oxford University Press, 1979). Two other studies include R. Douglas Hurt, *The Dust Bowl: An Agricultural and Social History* (Chicago: Nelson-Hall, 1981); and Michael E. Schuyler, *The Dread of Plenty: Agricultural Relief Activities of the Federal Government in the Middle West, 1933–1939* (Manhattan, Kans.: Sunflower University Press, 1989).

Whereas sharecropping in the Cotton South and the Dust Bowl in the Wheat Belt shaped technological change in the 1920s and 1930s, the Corn Belt presents a setting for studying the long-term financial ambiguities inherent in technology. On the one hand, midwestern farmers were well situated to absorb the ideas of "modern" farming. The two most important manufacturers, International Harvester and Deere & Company, were located in the Midwest. As we saw in the previous chapter, the region had excellent land grant universities by the 1920s. The University of Illinois started a program of farm management in the 1910s. There and at Iowa State University researchers conducted studies intended to discover how to raise farm efficiency, both in terms of the adoption of machinery and the practice of better "farm management." So too, farmers in the Corn Belt were among the first to obtain a large share of their credit from lenders outside their local communities, notably from life insurance companies. One would expect that the educational institutions along with the presence of manufacturers and centralized creditors favored rapid technological change in the Midwest.

Looking closely at developments in this region, one can see other factors at work, however. For although families responded to these incentives, they also confronted different financial messages in their commodity and credit markets. Whether they favored new techniques over old methods turned on answers to certain questions. For instance, how burdensome were the financial demands of a new technique? What alternatives did farmers have if they wanted to circumvent a conflict between safety and productivity? How widespread was the credit crisis of the 1920s? How did lenders and borrowers react to this crisis? Because midwestern farmers dealt with strong financial pressures, it is in their choices about adopting expensive technology – notably the tractor – that we can see how the climate for farm investment worked within competitive markets to shape the pace and pattern of technological change.

PART II. "Power Farming" in the Corn Belt, 1920–1940

4. The tractor factor

Starting in World War I and continuing into the 1920s, International Harvester launched a campaign to sell small dependable tractors to farmers in the Corn Belt. Until then horses had provided the power for every major task on a midwestern farm: they were used in plowing and disking fields, planting seed, cultivating row crops, mowing hay, and hauling in the harvest. To win farmers as customers, Harvester dwelled on the tractor's best asset, its power. In a 1929 advertisement, IHC reported that thanks to three types of power – drawbar, belt, and power take-off – its tractor "produced" greater profits by performing work more quickly and in a more timely fashion. The industry leader instructed farmers to become "masters" of mechanical power and warned that "the man who places his dependence on muscle power is sadly handicapped" (Figure 4.1).

Pursuing the theme of profits through power, Harvester gave detailed evidence in an advertisement that featured farmer Elza C. Lawson (Figure 4.2). Using his Farmall tractor and equipment, Lawson produced 100 acres of corn at 14.5¢ a bushel, or $7.23 an acre. Compared with the official government estimate of $16.33 for producing an acre of corn in the Midwest, Lawson had cut costs by more than half. The fine print explained that his cost savings translated into handsome profits of more than $2,000, or a return on his investment in land of 13.5 percent.

Harvester and other manufacturers convinced many farmers of the tractor's cost savings and related benefits, and sales rose at a brisk pace in the 1920s (Table 4.1).[1] But did all farmers profit from a

[1] While sales of tractors are not reported by region, the number of tractors per 100 crop acres charts the tractor's adoption in the Midwest. In the East North Central the ratio rose from 0.09 in 1920 to 0.43 in 1930, and in the West North Central it rose from 0.07 to 0.22. By 1940 the ratio had risen to 0.77 for the East North Central and to 0.40 for the West North Central. Martin R. Cooper, Glen T. Barton, and Albert P. Brodell, "Progress of Farm Mechanization," U.S. Department of Agriculture Miscellaneous Publication No. 630 (October 1947), p. 45.

Figure 4.1. "Be the Master of Mechanical Power," International Harvester Company advertisement. From *Bureau Farmer,* Ohio Edition, 6 (November 1930), inside front cover. Courtesy of the International Harvester Company Archives, Navistar International Transportation Company, Chicago, Illinois.

Figure 4.2. "For Utility and Economy no Tractor can Match a McCormick-Deering," International Harvester Company advertisement. From *Bureau Farmer,* Ohio Edition, 6 (May 1931), p. 2. Courtesy of the International Harvester Company Archives, Navistar International Transportation Company, Chicago, Illinois.

Table 4.1. *Number of tractors purchased by farmers in the United States, each year, 1910–39*

Year	Tractors purchased[a]	Year	Tractors purchased[a]	Year	Tractors purchased[a]
1910	3	1920	140	1930	116
1911	4	1921	65	1931	58
1912	7	1922	95	1932	25
1913	5	1923	108	1933	25
1914	11	1924	91	1934	65
1915	16	1925	113	1935	122
1916	19	1926	113	1936	165
1917	41	1927	133	1937	221
1918	84	1928	82	1938	151
1919	109	1929	137	1939	159

[a]Number of tractors purchased are in thousands.
Source: A. P. Brodell and R. S. Pike, "Farm Tractors: Type, Size, Age, and Life," U.S. Department of Agriculture, F.M. 30 (February 1942), p. 2.

tractor, as IHC's detailed calculations about Lawson might have led them to believe? And did all farmers who could have reduced costs, actually invest in the machine? Since answers to these questions depend on an abstract analysis of the tractor's cost savings, they prompt a third question: did farmers actually invest in tractors by this criteria? Individual answers apparently varied with the tractor's price, farmers' financial resources, and the options farmers elected in credit markets or in the world around them. The problems were not random, however, but varied systematically across the Midwest.

"Horseless" farms?

Prior to World War I, tractors were large, heavy, clumsy pieces of equipment. They carried larger-than-life names like Titan and Mogul, but these early machines reduced costs for just a small number of the very largest farms. Only with technological improvements did the machine seriously challenge horses, and, even then, technological improvements did not guarantee the tractor a place in every farmer's corn field.

In the 1920s, manufacturers made several technological improvements to tractors. Ford – thanks to his knowledge of mass-production techniques – introduced a smaller tractor. International Harvester developed a more versatile machine, first with the "power take-off," and second with its tricycle designed frame. "The square turn," a farmer from Illinois wrote in 1926, "is one of the best improvements that was ever put on a tractor; it enables one to get right up in the fence corners and there is no sliding sideways in loose ground."[2] In addition to these two changes, in 1927 Deere & Company introduced the "power lift" (which raised and lowered implements and reduced much physical strain for farmers). There were other small but important changes. Harvester, which claimed its Farmall was "built for years of service," equipped its machines with new air filters, throttle governors designed to keep speeds uniform, removable cylinders, and a better lubrication system; it also designed the machines so that the farmer had easy access to work on parts.[3]

With these changes the general-purpose tractor became more versatile and more reliable, and it offered – manufacturers claimed – a complete substitute to horses. Drawing on contorted images of slavery, IHC announced that by becoming masters of mechanical power farmers could be "emancipated" from the drudgery of fieldwork (Figure 4.3). To celebrate this "progress," Harvester reported that there were 1,000 horseless farms by the fall of 1929.

Although Harvester's Farmall, like other general-purpose tractors, represented a complete mechanical substitute for horses, few farmers – as Harvester's 1,000 figure indicated – relied solely on tractors. Most farmers never switched completely from horses to tractors because they preferred horses for planting corn, believing they did a better job; they also preferred horses to cultivate corn when the plants

[2] See "Tractor Does It All," John C. Blood Papers, Box 7, n.d., n.p., Illinois State Historical Library, Springfield, Illinois.
[3] For a detailed account of changes in the tractor, see R. B. Gray, *The Agricultural Tractor: 1855–1950*, part 2, rev. ed. (St. Joseph, Mich.: American Society of Agricultural Engineers, 1975); and Robert C. Williams, *Fordson, Farmall, and Poppin' Johnny: A History of the Farm Tractor and Its Impact on America* (Urbana: University of Illinois Press, 1987). Examples of Harvester's claim for better service are found in "Power Farming is More Pleasant and Profitable," John C. Blood Papers, Box 7, n.d., n.p., Illinois State Historical Library.

Figure 4.3. "The Great Emancipators," International Harvester Company advertisement. From *Bureau Farmer,* Ohio Edition, 5 (November 1929), inside cover. Courtesy of the International Harvester Company Archives, Navistar International Transportation Company, Chicago, Illinois.

were young and fragile.[4] Rather than decide between a tractor and a team of horses, most farmers opted to keep a large team of horses or to rely on a tractor and a smaller team.[5]

The question of how many horses to keep was tied closely to the value of the tractor when the farmer considered the most hectic stage of production: springtime plowing. Without a tractor, plowing created a temporarily large demand for horses. After the ground thawed, farmers had only a few weeks available to break and disk their fields. Plowing was also a time-consuming job: a single horse took a full ten-hour day to break one acre. Caught between the short time for breaking and disking and a horse's slow pace, farmers often found that they needed five if not six or more horses simply to plow their fields.[6]

One Illinois farmer worked his team of horses steadily from March to December, typically averaging 600 hours of labor every two weeks. But his tractor took over in March and April during the plowing season.[7] Without the tractor, the farmer would have needed five extra horses to do the plowing in the first two weeks of April. Even reshuffling plowing into late March and late April, the farmer would have needed two to three more horses.[8] Once this job was finished, the

[4] In a study of sixty-five farms in central Illinois, P. E. Johnston and J. E. Wills found that farmers relied almost entirely on tractors to plow and disk their farms. When it came time to plant fields, 83 percent of the farmers used their horses. See P. E. Johnston and J. E. Wills, "A Study of the Cost of Horse and Tractor Power on Illinois Farms," University of Illinois Agricultural Experiment Station Bulletin No. 395 (December 1933), p. 322.

[5] The following researchers tried to find farmers who relied solely on tractors, but could only obtain a few examples. L. A. Reynoldson, W. R. Humphries, S. R. Speelman, E. W. McComas, and W. H. Youngman, "Utilization and Cost of Power on Corn Belt Farms," U.S. Department of Agriculture Technical Bulletin No. 384 (October 1933).

[6] Nicholas Sargen identified this conflict between time and the working capacity of a horse or a tractor as the "capacity limit," where he defined capacity limit as the maximum number of acres that a tractor or team of horses could work given the amount of time available to complete a given task. See Nicholas Peter Sargen, *"Tractorization" in the United States and Its Relevance for Developing Countries* (New York: Garland Publishing, 1970).

[7] H. C. M. Case, R. H. Wilcox, and H. A. Berg, "Organizing the Corn-Belt Farm for Profitable Production," University of Illinois Agricultural Experiment Station Bulletin No. 329 (revised, June 1934), p. 301.

[8] These conclusions are reached as follows: five horses typically worked 10 hours a day, six days a week, for a total of 600 hours every two weeks. In the first two weeks of April, the tractor put in 600 hours of work, or the

extra horses were no longer needed. Indeed most farms required only three or perhaps four horses to perform other tasks.[9] The tractor's initial promise was one of quickly plowed fields, and the elimination of two and possibly three or four horses.

Had farmers shared these machines, they might have avoided this trade-off between a tractor and horses. But farmers rarely shared tractors (unlike the reaper). Two economic historians, Alan Olmstead and Robert E. Ankli, have noted: "There are few published accounts describing sharing schemes, but those that do exist suggest such practices were not very common and that they did not work well."[10] The University of Illinois's annual farm business reports on some fourteen hundred individual farms in 1929 supported this conclusion: farmers rarely shared tractors.[11] For prospective buyers who did not have the option of sharing, they had to ask: did they work farms large enough to profit by replacing two or more horses with a tractor?

The tractor's threshold, 1929

This question can be put in a formal economic framework, described in Chapter 3 as the threshold model. Faced with a new method of production, a farmer will want to adopt it provided the new technique is more efficient than the older substitute. Yet, depending on

equivalent time of a team of five horses. Between mid-March and early May, the tractor averaged almost 400 hours every two weeks, or the equivalent time of three horses.

[9] After plowing, threshing grain or putting away hay were the most time-consuming jobs, but in these cases a horse could cover an acre in just four hours, and just three or four horses could perform these jobs on time. Case et al., "Organizing the Corn-Belt Farm for Profitable Production," p. 289.

[10] See Robert E. Ankli and Alan Olmstead, "The Adoption of the Gasoline Tractor in California," *Agricultural History*, 55 (July 1981), p. 227.

[11] See University of Illinois Department of Farm Organization and Management, "Farm Account Summary Sheets, 1917–1947," Record Series 8/4/14, Box 1, University of Illinois Archives, University of Illinois at Urbana-Champaign. That these Illinois farmers did not share tractors is an assumption required for the analysis of the Illinois records, and one made by Robert Charles Graham in his dissertation. See Robert Charles Graham, "Diffusion during Depression: The Adoption of the Tractor by Illinois Farmers" (Ph.D. dissertation, University of Illinois, 1985). Also see Robert E. Ankli, "Horses Vs. Tractors in the Corn Belt," *Agricultural History*, 54 (January 1980), pp. 134–48; Warren C. Whatley, "Institutional Change and Mechanization in the Cotton South: The Tractorization of Cotton Farming" (Ph.D. dissertation, Stanford University, 1983), pp. 12–18.

the size of their farms, not all farmers will reduce costs by using the new method. Here the threshold model measures the two techniques' fixed and variable costs so as to determine the acreage or "threshold" beyond which farmers will save costs by employing the new technology.

The model singles out all costs associated with raising crops. Fixed charges include depreciation and interest for machinery, equipment, and horses; a portion of feed for horses, since horses needed some feed regardless of whether they worked; and repairs. Variable costs include the cost per acre of labor, feed, and fuel; these costs are calculated as the amount of work in hours per acre times the cost per hour. The operator's time in the fields is multiplied by the going wage rate; horses' time is multiplied by the cost of feed per hour; and the amount of fuel consumed is multiplied by the cost of fuel. Further, because the amount of fieldwork varied by crop, the amount of time per acre is weighted according to the proportion of land devoted to each crop; costs per acre are adjusted according to the distribution of crops.

Both fixed and variable costs are summed for each method of production and are expressed in per-acre rates. They lead to the equation: $VC_0/\text{acre} + FC_0/X \text{ acre} = VC_1/\text{acre} + FC_1/X \text{ acre}$. For the existing technique, VC_0 represents its variable costs per acre and FC_0 its fixed costs per acre. Similarly, VC_1 and FC_1 represent the variable and fixed costs per acre for the new technique. In the equation, variable costs per acre and total fixed costs are known. The equation is solved by finding the acreage (X) at which the cost of one technique equals that of the other. Beyond that acreage or threshold, the new technique will provide greater cost savings; farmers whose land exceeds the threshold acreage will profit by using the new technique. Farmers with fewer acres than the threshold should keep their existing source of power, namely horses.[12]

Could all farmers have reduced costs by buying a tractor? A tractor replaced at least two horses. I use two horses as a conservative estimate of the point at which the tractor became more economical. The trade-off is calculated for one choice between a team of five horses and a smaller team of three horses and a tractor, as well as for

---

[12] For a technical and mathematical discussion of this model, see Whatley, "Institutional Change and Mechanization in the Cotton South," pp. 12–18.

a second choice between six horses and a smaller team of four horses and a tractor.[13] The first case tested whether the tractor was more profitable on small to medium farms, the second case tested the tractor's profitability for larger farms.

In both cases, the tractor's competitiveness depended on its relative fixed and variable costs. These costs are detailed in Appendix A, and they result in the following differences. For fixed costs, the tractor and smaller team of horses required roughly $41 more than the original team of horses, primarily because a farmer paid interest and depreciation for the tractor. But for variable costs, the tractor reduced charges by roughly $0.63 per acre because the machine plowed and disked fields faster than a team of horses. As a farmer worked more acres, the tractor maintained its variable-cost savings per acre and its fixed costs per acre fell. Eventually, the tractor's total (fixed plus variable) cost per acre slipped below the per-acre cost of the team of horses.

In the case of six horses, farmers crossed the threshold at 67.5 crop acres. In the case of five horses, the tractor offered greater savings at 61.4 crop acres. Given that farmers devoted two-thirds of their land to crops on average, the threshold amounted to a farm size of roughly 100 acres. The threshold analysis indicates that the tractor was not profitable for all farmers, only for those whose farms exceeded 100 acres. In 1929, nearly half of all farms fell short of this mark, and therefore, those farmers had no reason to purchase tractors (Table 4.2).

The threshold model, however, can be used to reach a second conclusion. Census data indicate that in 1929 roughly 25 percent of

---

[13] The two cases are selected for the horses' relative capacity constraint. A farmer needed five horses beyond roughly 50 to 58 crop acres, and six horses beyond 63 to 73 crop acres. The number of horses varied with the number of crop acres on a farm. In three studies, the ratio of crop acres to horses on farms of less than 80 crop acres ranged from 12.5 to 14.5, and gave four horses a range of 50 to 58 crop acres; five horses would have been needed beyond that range, and six horses beyond 63 to 73 crop acres. For farms with 80 to 120 crop acres, ratios averaged 15 to 18 crop acres per horse. For six horses, this ratio amounted to 90 to 108 crop acres. John A. Hopkins, Jr., "Horses, Tractors and Farm Equipment," Iowa State College Agricultural Experiment Station Bulletin No. 264 (June 1929); Johnston and Wills, "A Study of the Cost of Horse and Tractor Power on Illinois Farms," p. 282; and Reynoldson et al., "Utilization and Cost of Power on Corn Belt Farms."

Table 4.2. *Percent of farms that passed the tractor's acreage threshold, and the percent of farmers with tractors, 1929*

State	Percent of farms above threshold[a]	Percent of all farmers with tractors
Ohio	40.8%	23.1%
Indiana	45.0	22.3
Illinois	62.6	30.9
Iowa	72.1	29.4
Missouri	52.3	9.3

[a]The threshold size was calculated to be 100 farm acres, and represents the acreage above which the tractor offered farmers more cost savings than did a team of horses. Calculations are explained in Appendix A.
Source: The data reporting farm size are found in U.S. Department of Commerce, *Fifteenth Census of the United States: 1930* (Washington, D.C.: U.S. Government Printing Office, 1932), Agriculture, vol. 2, part 1, county tables 2 and 12.

all farmers in the Corn Belt owned tractors (Table 4.2). In other words, the number of farmers owning tractors fell short of the number predicted on the basis of the machine's cost savings. In the two most important corn states, Illinois and Iowa, 63 and 72 percent of all farmers worked more than 100 acres. Still, only 30 percent of farmers in these two states owned tractors. Throughout the Corn Belt, for every farmer who owned a tractor there was another one who did not, even though he or she could have reduced costs and raised profits by investing in the machine.

This finding runs counter to our perceptions of economic self-interest. Under pressure to reduce costs and remain competitive, farmers should have purchased tractors in larger numbers. Unwilling to abandon self-interest, I find it necessary to ask two questions about the threshold analysis. First, does the model value inputs so as to determine accurately the tractor's relative competitiveness? Second, do the calculations make sense? I discuss both questions in Appendix A, but here is a summary.

In the threshold model all inputs are valued at their market rates. The tractor is valued according to its selling price in 1929; horses are valued according to prevailing market prices; feed is valued according to prices for hay and grains; labor is valued according to the market wage. Farmers, as we have seen, did not necessarily buy all items on the market. For instance, they often raised feed for horses on the farm. But the model takes into account the market value of all factors. Since markets existed for grains and since farmers could have bought or sold hay and oats on the market, the cost of feed in the model is calculated as the going market price times the amount of feed a team of horses consumed. This logic is also applied to the price of horses and labor.

In the case of labor, however, one might object to using a market wage rate. A farm operator need not have paid market wages for family labor. Labor markets did not always assure alternative jobs or, put another way, few children found jobs off the farm. In the language of economists, family members had a low opportunity cost. If the cost of labor is reduced, then the tractor's threshold will rise and the lag in its adoption will disappear. Unfortunately, this alteration in wages creates more problems than it solves. Although it may be used to explain the tractor's slow diffusion during the 1920s, it makes it more difficult to explain the tractor's subsequent diffusion in the 1930s. For the Great Depression, the opportunity cost of labor would have had to increase so as to reduce the tractor's threshold. But from 1929 to 1939, the opportunity cost of family labor fell: labor suffered high rates of unemployment in the 1930s, and in the Corn Belt, wages for farm labor dropped 25 to 35 percent between 1929 and 1939.[14]

There is a second and more important problem with this approach. Family labor needs to be considered in relation to the operator's own labor and within the context of the model. The model does not consider all farm activities; instead, it values time spent performing field jobs (plowing, disking, planting, and cultivating crops). In carrying out such tasks, one person worked with one source of power – either the tractor or a team of horses. Family members certainly helped with many farm activities, but it was the operator's responsibility to see these field tasks completed.[15] Put another way, as the head of the household, the farmer faced an opportunity cost by being under pressure to earn an income whether it be in farming or some

[14] For changes in farm wages by state, see U.S. Department of Agriculture, *Crops and Markets*, 19 (July 1942), pp. 150–1.
[15] See, for example, Lucy Studley, "Relationship of the Farm Home to the Farm Business," University of Minnesota Agricultural Experiment Station Bulletin No. 279 (July 1931).

other occupation. The market wage thus serves as an appropriate gauge of the farmer's labor within the context of the threshold model. In this regard, my calculations are not unusual. Existing threshold studies have used market rates to calculate all costs, including the cost of labor. I follow conventional practices when I value labor and other factors at market prices (Appendix A).

My second question about the threshold model concerns the specific calculations. I employ data that state and federal officials collected during the 1920s and 1930s. To assess my figures, I compare my calculations to those made in two different threshold studies, which are discussed in detail in Appendix A. Since I follow Warren C. Whatley's techniques for calculating the threshold, I compare my figures to his analysis of the tractor's threshold in the Cotton South in the 1920s. I also compare my figures to the one other study by Robert Ankli of the tractor's diffusion in the Corn Belt.[16] In the case of the South, Whatley reported a threshold of 83 acres; the difference between this finding and my estimate of 61–68 acres is accounted for by regional differences in wage rates. In the case of the Corn Belt, Ankli examined a farmer who replaced all horses and purchased both a tractor and a mechanical corn picker. Once his results are adjusted for a technical error, they indicate that the tractor's threshold amounted to 48 acres. This threshold is lower than mine, and suggests that the lag in the tractor's diffusion was even greater than I have concluded.

In brief, using the existing and accepted practices, I obtained an unexpected result: namely, that large numbers of farmers in the Corn Belt delayed purchases of tractors despite its cost savings. This conclusion, although counterintuitive, is corroborated by the independent findings of Whatley's and Ankli's studies.

Judging tractors

In the 1920s, half the farmers who could have profited from tractors did not make investments. To understand why farmers put off these investments, we can look first at the tractor's price. In 1929 the tractor's initial purchase set a farmer back roughly $1,000. Compared with the average of farmers' existing cash expenditures, the tractor

[16] Whatley, "Institutional Change and Mechanization in the Cotton South"; and Ankli, "Horses Vs. Tractors."

demanded a significant new outlay. Its annual cost for depreciation and interest, which made up fixed costs, totaled roughly $165, or $175 with added attachments. There were also operating costs (fuel, oil, and grease) along with annual repairs, which amounted to roughly $140.[17] Total charges came to roughly $315. By replacing two horses, a farmer could reduce the tractor's net cash demands from $315 to $295. But $295 still imposed a large outlay. In 1929, midwestern farmers spent on average $1,082 in cash for farm expenses, or $1,220 with taxes. At these levels the tractor's adjusted charges boosted existing cash expenses by 24 to 27 percent.[18]

The tractor's expense can also be considered in relation to the margin of cash farmers had available between receipts and expenditures. In Illinois, for instance, the gap between cash receipts and cash outlays (feed, fuel, hired labor, machinery, and electricity) amounted to roughly $1,080 in 1929.[19] This figure requires one qualification, however. It does not take into account the operator's living expenses. Although operators did not pay a cash wage to themselves, they did incur cash living expenses and they paid for these family expenses with income "left over" from their farm revenues after deducting cash outlays. Families – as we have seen – tried to avoid cash expenses by relying on resources from their farm. One important "noncash" good consisted of food raised on the farm. But families could not obtain all living expenses in this fashion. In other words, they needed to pur-

---

[17] Calculated from the U.S. Department of Agriculture, *Income Parity for Agriculture* (Washington, D.C.: U.S. Government Printing Office, 1940), part 2, sec. 3, p. 53, and sec. 4, p. 43.

[18] Farm costs and taxes are calculated using data for the five states in the Corn Belt. See U.S. Department of Commerce, *Fifteenth Census of the United States: 1930* (Washington, D.C.: U.S. Government Printing Office, 1932), Agriculture, vol. 2, part 1, county tables 11 and 12.

[19] Calculated as the difference between cash receipts and cash farm expenses. This margin varied by state. In Iowa, it was higher, averaging $1,685. But Iowa's farmers found that their cash resources were severely tested by burdensome debts. In this chapter, I also discuss the role of debts, and find that both debts and farmers' cash incomes were important to Iowa's farmers. In Ohio, Indiana, and Missouri the margin of cash averaged $500, or half the figure for Illinois. Illinois thus represents a middle case between Iowa and the other three states. For farm receipts, see the U.S. Department of Commerce, *Fifteenth Census of the United States,* Agriculture, vol. 3, part 1, county table 3. For cash farm expenditures, see the *Fifteenth Census of the United States,* Agriculture, vol. 2, part 1, county table 12.

chase some items, including part of their food, clothing, insurance, repairs for their home, and related expenses. Illinois officials who ran the state's farm management program set an operator's annual wage at $720. Even if a family's cash expenses did not amount to $720 – even if they amounted to a smaller sum of say $370 – this still reduced a farm's cash margin, and limited funds available for other farm improvements such as the purchase of a tractor. Considering the tractor's price along with their farm and home expenses, families could readily conclude that the tractor imposed a substantial new addition to their budgets.[20]

Despite its cash demands, the tractor should not have stopped farmers from purchasing it – at least, this was the message conveyed by two groups who gave their advice freely to farmers. One group consisted of implement manufacturers, the second of researchers at agricultural experiment stations and land grant colleges.

Manufacturers demonstrated the value of the tractor by fixing on the cost of production, when all costs were measured at their going market prices (as is the case in the threshold model). If for some reason farmers distinguished between cash and noncash outlays, then the tractor's savings would be smaller. But if they valued all inputs at market rates, then the tractor's savings would be substantial. Obviously this was the conclusion firms sought to draw.

Consider, for instance, International Harvester's advertisement featuring Elza Lawson (Figure 4.2). Lawson appeared to be enormously efficient because his costs amounted to $7.23 an acre as compared with the official cost of $16.33 per acre. Both studies valued all inputs

---

[20] It is difficult to obtain information on family expenditures. One study reported that for the year 1930 a family with comparatively small total (cash and noncash) expenditures valued at $885 devoted $372 to cash outlays. Another study reported that for the year of 1931 eight families with a median farm size of 146 acres spent $384 in cash. Gladys J. Ward, "Possible Farm-Home Adjustments Related to the Present Price Level," in "Illinois Agricultural Adjustment Conferences, November, 1931," and Paulena Nickell, "Financing the Farm Home," in "Illinois Agricultural Adjustment Conferences, September-October, 1932," Record Series 8/4/829, Box 1, University of Illinois Archives, University of Illinois at Urbana-Champaign. For the operator's wage, see the farm account summary sheets in University of Illinois Department of Farm Organization and Management, "Farm Account Summary Sheets, 1917–1947," Record Series 8/4/14, Box 1, University of Illinois Archives, University of Illinois at Urbana-Champaign.

at market rates. Lawson saved substantial amounts of time in the cost of labor. Had a farmer valued labor or horses in terms of the actual cash it took to cover these costs, then both studies would have reported lower costs, but the relative savings obtained by Lawson's tractor would have been smaller. Put another way, by using market rates to calculate the cost of labor, horses, and other inputs, manufacturers could more easily promote "power farming."

Experiment station scientists, like manufacturers, maintained that farmers should compare the market value of each input. One group noted that feed for horses was a "real cost." They contended that a market rate should be applied.[21] Similarly, agricultural researchers used a market wage to value labor time and labor savings.[22]

It is true, of course, that these officials were not tractor boosters. Agricultural advisers cautioned farmers that horseless farms were often discussed but rarely found. They maintained that based on relative cost savings, a tractor was not profitable for all farmers. But a farmer considering the purchase of a tractor, they said, should value all production costs at their going market prices.

At the same time that these researchers asked farmers to value costs according to market rates, they also recognized that farmers might hesitate to do so. Operators considered tractors and other factors — factors that manufacturers overlooked. That is, they contemplated the tractor's price while they also calculated the effects of unstable commodity prices. From that perspective, the tractor forced potential buyers to choose between their desire to raise productivity and their need for financial safety. The credit crisis of the 1920s complicated this problem not only for indebted farmers but for those who wanted access to credit.

The tractor's financial dilemma

Midwestern politicians, in their effort to win votes, devoted stump speeches to the question of financial safety. Lester Dickinson, a Re-

---

[21] Case et al., "Organizing the Corn-Belt Farm for Profitable Production," p. 296.

[22] See for example ibid., and P. E. Johnston and K. H. Myers, "Harvesting the Corn Crop in Illinois," University of Illinois Agricultural Experiment Station Bulletin No. 373 (September 1931), pp. 357–405. Economic historians have obtained data about market wages from these agricultural studies and have used the data in their threshold calculations. See, for example, Ankli and Olmstead, "The Adoption of the Gasoline Tractor in

publican representative from Iowa and a leader in bipartisan efforts to pass farm legislation in the 1920s, lamented time and again the difficulties farmers faced in predicting what the price of corn or wheat would be from one season to the next. There were many factors that might change markets to cause a slip or a more serious slide in prices. Dickinson instructed, "You don't know whether the Lord is going to send the drouth or sunshine or rain . . . nobody can tell." There were as well uncertainties off the farm: "There are too many influences on the outside of the front gate of every farm over which he [the farmer] has no control, that absolutely determine the revenue he is going to receive."[23]

Dickinson could have nailed down his point with quantitative data on corn prices. From 1890 through the 1920s, corn prices had varied nearly 20 percent from year to year, on average.[24] This variability created problems for Dickinson's home state of Iowa where prices had averaged seventy-two cents a bushel, in excess of farmers' average per-bushel cost of sixty cents. But in nearly a third of all months from 1921 to 1929 prices fell below the cost of production.[25] While monthly prices reflect seasonal variations, they nevertheless indicate that prices frequently dropped below a farmer's cost of production. More to the point, it was difficult for farmers to gauge when prices would fall or by what amount they would decline.

Volatile markets, however, did not necessarily spell disaster for Iowa and other Corn Belt farmers. Total revenues might slide below total costs, but unlike the USDA, farmers did not value all costs (land and labor included) on a full cash basis. From the farmer's perspective not all expenses took the form of cash payments.[26] The two most

California," pp. 218–20; Whatley, "Institutional Change and Mechanization in the Cotton South," p. 210.

[23] Lester Dickinson, "Address at Conference of National Association of Commissioners and Secretaries of Agriculture," given in Chicago in 1926, Lester Jesse Dickinson Papers, MsC 94, Box 1, pp. 1, 4, Special Collections Department, University of Iowa Libraries, Iowa City, Iowa.

[24] The figure is estimated for the years from 1921 to 1930. See Willard W. Cochrane and Mary E. Ryan, *American Farm Policy, 1948–1973* (Minneapolis: University of Minnesota Press, 1976), p. 385.

[25] Figures are reported for 108 months from 1921 to 1929. The standard deviation was seventeen cents a bushel. U.S. Department of Agriculture, *Yearbook of Agriculture, 1928* (Washington, D.C.: U.S. Government Printing Office, 1929), p. 1045. Iowa Department of Agriculture, "Average Prices Paid by Iowa Farmers" (mimeo, n.d.), n.p.

[26] For more detail, see U.S. Department of Agriculture, *Crops and Markets*, vol. 1, supplement 6 (June 1924), p. 176.

important items were labor and horses. Farmers obtained most of their labor from themselves and their family, and horses typically did not require large cash outlays. In brief, farmers could guard against the consequences of low prices by doing precisely what agricultural researchers instructed them *not* to do: they could value their home-grown resources according to the actual cash requirements rather than market rates. By favoring resources that entailed small cash payments and conserved cash, families could insulate themselves from the consequences of volatile prices.

Analyzing this strategy requires us to go beyond the threshold analysis in two ways. First, we should take into account all of the farmer's activities. The threshold analysis applied to field operations, but farmers earned an income from other activities (such as raising livestock) not captured by the threshold model. Second, we need to distinguish between cash outlays and other inputs. The fact that farmers chose to value items at less than their cash (market) value does not necessarily imply that the item had a low opportunity cost. Recall the case of feed. Farmers certainly could buy and sell feed. Given the logic of the threshold model, a farmer should have placed a market value on feed even if it was not actually purchased. But in practice, a farmer could choose (for reasons not having to do with "opportunity cost") to distinguish between items bought at market prices and paid for with hard-earned dollars and those raised on the farm that did not require a cash outlay.

This distinction between cash and noncash outlays became important when farmers considered purchasing a tractor. Comparing horses to tractors, Illinois researchers singled out the tractor's larger cash demands: "Of the total cost of keeping horses . . . only 5.8 percent was made up of cash expenses and 18.9 percent was for depreciation." For tractors, cash items amounted to 55.7 and depreciation to 31.8 percent of all costs. The authors continued:

> Whereas depreciation on a tractor represents a cash expenditure which was made at some previous time but which in the accounts is spread over the period when the machine is being worn out, much of the depreciation on horses does not represent an original cash outlay, since many of the horses were reared by the farm operators themselves.[27]

---

[27] Johnston and Wills, "A Study of the Cost of Horse and Tractor Power on Illinois Farms," p. 309.

Not surprisingly, farmers who assessed tractors in terms of their
cash rather than total costs found that the machine was relatively less
desirable. The threshold analysis helps us illustrate this dilemma. In
the original calculations all inputs are valued at their market rates. If
farmers chose to value noncash items at prices less than items they
paid for in cash, then the tractor's relative cost savings would shrink
and its threshold would rise. For instance, by reducing the fixed and
variable costs of feed by 25 percent, then the tractor's threshold
would double, and far fewer farmers would cross this line.

Agricultural bulletins written by researchers at land grant universities gave ample testimony that farmers evaluated the tractor on the
basis of cash, not total costs. To their chagrin, one group of researchers who had asked farmers to place a value on horse feed did so
precisely because they found farmers were reluctant to value feed at
market rates. As they complained: "Since a large part of the cost of
horse labor is for feed grown on the farm, the cost of horse power is
not usually appreciated." But they insisted that feed was a "real cost,"
and they had asked farmers to include this "cost as truly as if a cash
outlay had been required."[28]

In another study, two scholars examined the competitiveness of
mechanical corn harvesters – an invention which, like the tractor,
entailed large cash outlays. They concluded that in 1928 and 1929
mechanical harvesters were cheaper "when all cash costs plus the
value of labor, equipment, and power furnished by the farm were
considered." Yet they noted among the reasons for hand husking that
"it may often be done by the labor regularly employed on the farm,
thus saving cash expense."[29]

P. E. Johnston made the problem explicit. He published a circular
in which he supplied work sheets for farmers to calculate their cost of
production and to determine whether to invest in mechanical technology. Although the work sheets listed all expenses, including family
labor and horses, a farmer could easily skip in-kind items to arrive at
a purely cash comparison. Johnston expected this outcome: "The
individual farmer will probably be more interested in figuring his

Case et al., "Organizing the Corn-Belt Farm for Profitable Production,"
p. 296.
[29] Johnston and Myers, "Harvesting the Corn Crop in Illinois," pp. 402–3.
The mechanical corn pickers created a similar financial dilemma; this
experience is discussed in Chapter 6.

costs on an actual cash outlay basis than in figuring in as actual costs many items, such as those for family labor, horses, and wagons, which are already available on the farm."[30] Johnston's point came from experience. By 1930 he was coauthoring the state summary reports of the Illinois farm management program. His contacts with farmers over the years convinced him that many frequently judged machinery on the basis of cash rather than total costs. Determined to conserve cash, these farmers perceived the tractor as being more expensive than a team of horses – that is, more expensive than the threshold analysis indicated.

Farmers' investment climate for machinery and equipment

Could farmers circumvent the tractor's cash dilemma? The threshold analysis described a set of formal economic calculations farmers made each year as they organized production. Within this context, the tractor's cash outlays consisted of operating and fixed charges. But fixed charges (interest and depreciation) represented expenditures that a farmer did not necessarily pay each year. By finding ways to cover the initial price of a tractor, farmers could get by for a number of years with only paying operating expenses and repairs.

One strategy was to bargain. It is hard to imagine a farmer who did not know how to trade in old equipment for a lower price on new models. One dealer quipped: "No trade, no sale." He gave this answer to the Federal Trade Commission's survey of manufacturers' sales policies; the survey asked both dealers and farmers their views about the implement business from roughly 1928 to 1937.[31] Nearly all dealers reported that they took used machinery. An Ohio dealer

[30] P. E. Johnston, "Reducing Costs of Corn Harvesting," University of Illinois Agricultural Experiment Station Circular No. 396 (August 1932), pp. 14–15. Robert Ankli also noted this problem of cash in "Horses Vs. Tractors," pp. 147–9.

[31] The survey is taken with caution. There is no information about respondents' incomes or the size of their farms. They simply answered questions about buying equipment. Of the 16,000 surveys sent to farmers, roughly 2,000 were returned. Implement dealers submitted close to 1,500 reports. Reports are included in U.S. Federal Trade Commission, "Farm Machinery Investigations (1936)," Record Group 122, National Archives. The FTC's investigation was much larger and results were submitted as *Report on the Agricultural Implement and Machinery Industry*, 75th Congress, 3rd sess., House Document 702 (June 6, 1938).

accepted "any type of farm implements, horses, cows, pigs, even down to second handed ice boxes and stoves. One now even had an elephant he wanted to trade for farm machinery." Most dealers did not deal in pachyderms. Typical was one dealer who took "plows, disks, harrows, spreaders, cultivators, seeders, hay loaders, hay rakes, mowers, binders, corn binders, silo fillers, threshers, tractors." Another dealer simply wrote, "All kinds of farm equipment."[32]

From the farmers' perspective, two things emerge. First, bargaining paid off. For those individuals who answered the survey, trade-ins affected roughly half of their purchases. On implements, dealers often cut prices by 5 to 10 percent regardless of the age of the "trade-in," which is to say even if it was junk. Farmers may have traded horses for tractors, but dealers rarely stated that they took horses. Farmers also rarely mentioned using horses for trade-ins.[33] If they did not sell horses to implement dealers, then they sold them to professional breeders or to other farmers. What they earned for the extra horses, of course, depended on an animal's age and health. Two horses were valued at $158 in the late 1920s, and at that price, would have reduced a tractor's price by roughly 16 percent.[34]

Second, these savings had to be balanced against the cost of tractor-related machinery. When IHC described its Farmall as a "great emancipator," implicit was the assumption that farmers would purchase the "right" implements – a plow, a two- or four-row planter, a two- or four-row cultivator, a seven-foot Farmall-powered mower, and perhaps a harvester (Figure 4.3). These items added significantly to the basic investment in a tractor. One Illinois farmer who purchased a tractor in 1929 also bought a plow, harrow, and cultivator, for a total purchase of $1,225. The same farmer spent $583 for a mechanical corn picker in 1930, bringing the sum to $1,808.[35] Rarely did

[32] According to answers for Illinois, Iowa, and parts of other midwestern states, dealers consistently listed machinery and implements but rarely listed horses. "Farm Machinery Investigations," Record Group 122, Sch 3 Ohi 5 Hul 5, Box 1531; Sch 3 Ohi 5 Eis 5, Box 1531; Sch 3 Ill 5 Lan 5, Box 1502; and Sch 3 Ill 5 Edw 5, Box 1502, National Archives.

[33] Of sixty-eight cases involving tractors in Illinois, Indiana, and Iowa, fewer than five mentioned horses. Ibid., Sch 3 Ill 5 Sch 3, Box 1504.

[34] The average value of a horse in 1929 was $79, or $158 for two, as calculated for the five midwestern states. See U.S. Department of Agriculture, Yearbook of Agriculture, 1931 (Washington, D.C.: U.S. Government Printing Office, 1931), p. 890.

[35] Federal Trade Commission, "Farm Machinery Investigations," Record Group 122, Sch 5, Ill 5, Shu 5, Box 1547.

farmers buy mechanical harvesters in the late 1920s. They did, however, routinely spend $200 to $300 for implements, especially plows and disks, and sometimes cultivators.

The sum of $1,200 to possibly $1,800 was a large amount for most corn farmers. By the 1920s, real-estate mortgages averaged from $3,500 to $4,500.[36] Purchases of machinery and equipment therefore ranged from a quarter to half of a long-term loan. Mortgages, of course, were not intended to finance equipment, but they give a sense of the magnitude of the investments that were entailed in this machinery and equipment.

For this money, farmers often turned to lenders of short-term credit. Both implement companies and banks readily loaned farmers money, but the terms made the purchases still burdensome. For a $1,000 loan on a tractor and equipment, a farmer needed cash for three annual payments amounting to between $200 and $400, plus interest, plus the tractor's operating expenses. Once the loan was paid off, the farmer only had to cover operating costs for the next several years. But while the loan was in force, a farmer faced large cash payments totaling roughly $450 – that is, a 37 percent increase in cash outlays.[37]

In order to pay for the equipment, farmers could try to earn extra income. Those who lived near cities could take advantage of opportunities to acquire part-time jobs, take in boarders, perform special services such as sewing, or raise and sell perishable crops that otherwise would have been consumed at home. After studying families in Minnesota, one home economist reported that "Whether or not the commodities were produced for sale rather than home use it is impossible to state, but experience and observation have shown that many

---

[36] Iowa mortgages were often two to three times greater than mortgages in other states. Excluding Iowa, mortgages averaged $3,513 and $2,828 in 1925 and 1930, respectively. Donald C. Horton, Harald C. Larsen, and Norman J. Wall, "Farm-Mortgage Credit Facilities in the United States," U.S. Department of Agriculture Miscellaneous Publication No. 478 (1942), p. 162.

[37] Some farmers may have wanted to wait and save funds. That is, they could choose to pay the full bill when they picked out their machinery. Having paid in cash, a farmer only incurred the tractor's operating expenses. But to execute this option farmers needed $1,000 or more dollars. Some farmers may have had the cash, but others would have to save the funds. By waiting, they delayed purchases and missed potential savings in productivity.

farm families still deprive themselves of milk, cream, butter, broilers, and other desirable products because of the money that may be obtained from selling them."[38]

Most farmers did not pursue this strategy, however, if only because in the Midwest most farms were isolated. The 1930 Census reveals that in Illinois and Iowa more than a quarter of all counties reported that no one resided in urban places.[39] Even in counties with an urban population, many farmers did not earn much income off their farms. In a 1930 farm management report on 1,571 Illinois farms, labor earnings off the farm or miscellaneous earnings amounted to less than $100 each year, on average, or less than 5 percent of total earnings.[40]

Some farmers could try to recoup part of the cash expended on a tractor by reducing the need to hire labor. To do so, the machine had to displace hired labor that was employed in jobs for which a tractor saved time. Based on a detailed study of Illinois farms in 1930 and 1931, researchers concluded that this saving was elusive. "Undoubtedly," the authors wrote, "one man and a tractor performed a specific field job on a tractor farm in less time than one man and the average size of a team did a similar job on a horse farm, but this time saving was not reflected in a material reduction in the cost for man labor on the tractor farms." They added: "Apparently many farmers owning tractors had not made adjustments that would enable them to reduce the peak of labor requirements to the point where a smaller amount of hired labor would be needed."[41]

These authors nevertheless found a good reason to buy tractors. This was not for its annual cost savings, for they cautioned that "it must be remembered that cash operating costs are much higher with

---

[38] Studley, "Relationship of the Farm Home to the Farm Business," p. 6.

[39] In Iowa 30 of 99 counties and in Illinois 27 of 102 counties reported no urban residents. See U.S. Department of Commerce, *Fifteenth Census of the United States: 1930*, Population, vol. 3, part 1, county table 13, pp. 614–20, 767–73.

[40] In 1929 state summaries reported not "labor" but "miscellaneous" income. The results, however, were the same. For 1930, see University of Illinois Department of Farm Organization and Management, "Summary of Annual Farm Business Reports on One Thousand Five Hundred and Seventy-One Farms for 1930," M-287 (September 1931), n.p., "University of Illinois Farm Business Reports," Record Series No. 8/4/814, Box 3, University of Illinois Archives, University of Illinois at Urbana-Champaign.

[41] Johnston and Wills, "A Study of the Cost of Horse and Tractor Power," pp. 296, 297.

the tractors than with the horses." But they countered: "It must also be kept in mind that the individual farmer who plans his work well so that he can utilize the time saved by using tractors to farm more land or to care for more productive livestock has an opportunity to increase his net income over that of the farmer with horses only or who uses for leisure the time he saves thru [sic] operating with tractors."[42] As they suggested, farmers' investment patterns in the 1920s may have been more conservative than the tractor's cost analysis indicated they should be. By renting or buying extra land, say twenty acres, farmers could have crossed the acreage threshold and profited from mechanizing preharvest tasks. This entailed a larger financial commitment: $1,000 for a tractor and equipment, plus perhaps $3,000 for the extra land.

This strategy, however, would involve greater financial risk. In bad years, farmers might not cover their loans. If they ran into trouble, the creditor presumably would carry them through a season. But farmers had to be confident that this would happen and, in the 1920s, they were generally not optimists. Nor were their creditors.

The credit crisis of the 1920s

Thanks to a boom in real estate that colored the years during and especially after the First World War, farmers' capacity to invest in extra land – let alone to finance a tractor – rapidly deteriorated. Though the crisis was severe, not all farmers caught in the boom were speculators, nor were all indebted farmers carrying burdensome debts. To understand the extent to which the credit crisis created a barrier to investment, we need to ask: how was the burden of debt distributed among farmers?

The real-estate boom had its start with the sharp rise in crop prices during World War I. Between the outset of the war and 1920, the price of corn nearly doubled. When in the war's early years farmers could not readily adjust production to meet war demands, they bid up land values. Bidding accelerated after the armistice, as Glenn E. Rogers, head of Metropolitan Life's Farm Mortgage Department, explained:

[42] Ibid., p. 329.

When the war was over the return of the farmers' sons was a
sentimental spur for their parents to purchase additional land with
the money accumulated during the prosperous war years. Real estate brokers, country bankers, and other business men in rural
communities along with farmers took part in bidding up on farms.
This spiral had been innocently started by the farmers themselves.
Occasionally individual farms would be sold several times within a
period of a few months. . . . It was not uncommon for land in
Illinois and Iowa to sell for $400 to $500 per acre and . . . good
cornbelt farms in Illinois sold for as high as $700 to $800 per acre
in 1920.[43]

In each Corn Belt state land values jumped at least 70 percent between 1910 and 1920 (Table 4.3). The peak came in 1920. Within
two years, corn prices had dropped more than 50 percent, and, as
farmers' cash income collapsed, so did the price of farmland. William
Adcock, of Warren County, Illinois, reported that his farm had sold
for nearly $450 an acre in 1919, but when he purchased it in 1922, it
was down to $250 "for cash." He added that "if I was to put it on
the market today [1924] it would bring less than the purchase price
possibly $225 not more." In every state, farmers recounted Adcock's
tale, as land prices slid 35 percent in nominal terms, on average (40
percent in real dollars), by 1922.[44]

In the wake of the market's collapse, critics blamed farmers for
their "wild cat speculation." It was true that farmers took out substantial sums of debt. By 1920, the average indebted farmer carried
loans of $2,604 in Indiana, $5,379 in Illinois, and $9,358 in Iowa
(Table 4.3). It was also true, one survey indicated, that many farmers
used debt financing. Asking farmers to report how they purchased
their farms, researchers at Iowa State University found that among
1,400 Iowa farms sold in 1919, only 9 percent of the buyers paid cash
on the spot. Another 26 percent paid more than half the purchase
price in cash, leaving most farmers (65 percent) with a mortgage for

[43] Glenn E. Rogers, "Twenty-Five Years in the Farm Mortgage Investment
Field," pp. 2–3, in V.F. – Rogers, Glenn, (# 12 03 02), Metropolitan Life
Insurance Company Archives, New York, New York.

[44] For price changes, see U.S. Department of Agriculture, *Yearbook of Agriculture, 1929* (Washington, D.C.: U.S. Government Printing Office, 1929).
Peter Lindert has explained that real land values fell from 1914 through
1942. Peter Lindert, "Long-run Trends in American Farmland Values,"
Agricultural History, 62 (Summer 1988), pp. 54–7, 82–5.

Table 4.3. *Financial crisis among midwestern states, 1910-30*

State	Land value per mortgaged farm		Debt per mortgaged farm, 1920	Changes in farm debt		Debt as a percent of land value		Number of commercial bank suspensions, 1921-9	Number of farm foreclosures, 1926-9[a]
	1910-20	1920-30		1910-20	1920-30	1920	1930		
Ohio	74%	-19%	$2,812	60%	12%	31.3%	42.9%	57	13.6
Indiana	73	-38	2,604	43	5	24.0	40.2	114	21.3
Illinois	72	-33	5,379	23	15	25.4	43.8	132	18.8
Iowa	138	-43	9,358	83	3	27.0	48.5	529	29.2
Missouri	80	-35	3,147	44	3	28.8	45.4	295	25.6
U.S.	84	-22	3,356	163	6	29.1	39.6	5,712	17.0

[a]The U.S. Department of Agriculture began publishing data for farm foreclosures by individual states in 1926.

Sources: For changes in land values per mortgaged farm, see Lawrence A. Jones and David Durand, *Mortgage Lending Experience in Agriculture*, National Bureau of Economic Research (Princeton: Princeton University Press, 1954), pp. 80, 83; and U.S. Department of Commerce, *Fifteenth Census of the United States: 1930* (Washington, D.C.: U.S. Government Printing Office, 1932), Agriculture, vol. 2, part 1, p. 49. For borrowing data, see U.S. Department of Commerce, *Fourteenth Census of the United States: 1920* (Washington, D.C.: U.S. Government Printing Office, 1922), Agriculture, vol. 4, part 1, p. 47; and U.S. Department of Commerce, *Fourteenth Census of the United States: 1920* (Washington, D.C.: U.S. Government Printing Office, 1922), Agriculture, vol.-2, part 1, p. 49. For bank suspensions, see Board of Governors of the Federal Reserve System, *Banking and Monetary Statistics* (Washington, D.C.: National Capitol Press, 1943), p. 284. For farm foreclosures, see E. H. Wiecking, "The Farm Real Estate Situation, 1929-30," U.S. Department of Agriculture Circular No. 150 (November 1930), p. 41.

50 to 100 percent of the property's value. Iowa State's survey also considered the question of speculation. It found that 22 percent of the buyers reported that they bought farms to resell. They could be classified as speculators, as could the 30 percent of individuals selling land who reported that they did so to "realize a speculative profit."[45]

As for other farmers, 13 percent reported no clear motives, 44 percent of buyers intended to operate the farm, and another 20 percent purchased land with the intent of renting it or having it worked by relatives. In other words, they wanted to increase their productive capacity and anticipated profits from the higher farm prices. E. B. Carter, of Woodbury County, Iowa, fit this category. While he had owned 825 acres of "good Iowa land," and most of it clear, he said that he bought more land so that his "four boys" could go to work. After prices collapsed, Carter confessed in 1924, "[I am] in such horrible financial condition, [I] don't want to put it on paper unless prices get better."[46]

Writing to the Secretary of Agriculture in 1924, Irwin Ellsworth reported that conditions in his community were becoming poor: "Banks are foreclosing on farms, slowly but surely. Some good farmers failed to pay taxes. Not much is said publicly but if you watch the county paper you will observe notice of foreclosure." An Illinois farmer elaborated: "Merchants are unable to collect but partial payments on accounts. Local banks are extending time rather than to force foreclosures." He added: "Crop conditions and prices are such that not much relief will be had this season."[47]

Until 1926, the USDA did not report farm foreclosures by state. But the figures from that date show midwestern rates were quite high. Overall, foreclosures had climbed from 4 farms out of 1,000 in the

[45] O. G. Lloyd, a professor at Iowa State College, presented the survey findings at the annual meeting of the Iowa Farm Mortgage Association in 1920, and figures were reproduced in correspondence from a loan agent, Thomas F. Steele, to Connecticut Mutual Life Insurance Company, June 7, 1920, Docs. 1. Exec. / Pres. 7 (Robinson) / Investments – Farm Loans, Corporate Library, Connecticut Mutual Life Insurance Company, Hartford, Connecticut.
[46] Ibid. E. B. Carter to Secretary of Agriculture, July, 1924, in "Debt Abstracts," Record Group 83, Entry 105, Box 8, National Archives.
[47] Irwin Ellsworth to the Secretary of Agriculture, July 1924, and Homer J. Tice to the Secretary of Agriculture, July 1924, both in "Debt Abstracts," Record Group 83, Entry 105, Box 8, National Archives.

United States between 1914 and 1920, to 17 by the mid-1920s. In Iowa (the worst state), the figure was 27 foreclosures, in Missouri it was 22.5 farms; in Indiana and Illinois, 16 and 17 farms, respectively; in Ohio – the only midwestern state "below average" – foreclosures took place at a rate of 12 per 1,000 farms.[48]

Because foreclosures were so high, it was easy for contemporaries in the 1920s, as for scholars today, to conclude that the credit crisis devastated the Corn Belt. But looking at the makeup of indebted farmers, some contemporaries were more cautious. W. H. Brenton wrote of his county in Iowa in July 1924: "I made a survey of the farms ... being in our banking territory around Dallas Center. I took every farm in these ninety-two sections and classified them for indebtedness." Of 317 farms, he found 200 were "clear" of debt, and another 44 carried "light" loans. Another 58 farmers worked with "regular loans," which he defined as "loans heavier than light mortgages but loans that can be obtained readily from insurance companies." Finally, Brenton put 18 farms in the "heavy" category, and doubted an insurance company would refinance them. All in all, 73 percent of farmers in Dallas County carried light loans or no loans, and only 6 percent carried heavy mortgages.[49]

Two other surveys found that debts did not burden farmers equally but instead afflicted a significant minority. Reviewing four Iowa counties, one study found that roughly a third of the farmers carried small loans relative to their assets and only 3.5 percent of these borrowers eventually failed by the late 1930s. Another third carried moderate loans, and 9 percent of these farmers failed. A study of 827 indebted farmers in Illinois concluded that roughly half carried debts that amounted to less than 40 percent of the appraised value of their farms, and 93 percent of them serviced their debts without failing.[50]

[48] E. H. Wiecking, "The Farm Real Estate Situation, 1928–1929," U.S. Department of Agriculture Circular No. 101 (December 1929), pp. 45–6. Similar patterns emerged for farm bankruptcies. See David Wickens, "Farmer Bankruptcies, 1898–1935," U.S. Department of Agriculture Circular No. 414 (September 1936), pp. 4–6.

[49] W. H. Brenton to the Secretary of Agriculture, July 1924, in "Debt Abstracts," Record Group 83, Entry 105, Box 8, National Archives.

[50] Joseph Ackerman, "Factors Influencing Farm Lending Experience in Coles and the Six Adjoining Counties, Illinois, 1917–1933" (Ph.D. dissertation, University of Illinois, 1937); Aaron Nelson, "Experience of the Federal Land Bank with Loans in Four North Central Iowa Counties, 1917–1947" (Ph.D. dissertation, Iowa State University, 1949), pp. 38, 76, 78–81.

The ability of farmers to manage their loans was reflected in the experiences of centralized lenders, who did not incur severe delinquencies. Federal land banks reported that 6 percent of loans were delinquent as of 1929; life insurance firms reported problems in isolated counties for which "distressed assets" amounted to more than 10 percent of their farm investment in 1929 (Figure 4.4). But a number of farmers managed their loans successfully – a conclusion supported by events of the early 1930s. Despite the fact that corn prices fell more than 50 percent from 1929 to 1932, half of the borrowers either held debts small enough in size or drew on strong enough financial resources that they were able to remain current on their loans.[51]

The credit crisis was severe but selective. Most farmers were not indebted. The Census reported that, as of 1920, 60 percent of owner-operator farms carried no debt, and this figure went down to 55 percent by 1929.[52] Among those who were indebted, the case studies suggested that a majority could manage their loans, but that a large minority – perhaps a quarter or a third – were saddled with large debts relative to their assets.[53] Not only would they need cash of $300 to $400 for the tractor each year, but cash for interest payments that averaged from $540 in Iowa to $350 in Illinois and to $200 in Indiana, Ohio, and Missouri.[54] For these farmers, debts could readily bar investments in land and technology.

The credit crisis for creditors

While burdensome debts represented a barrier to increased productivity, this was not the only consequence of the credit crisis. In the same years that farmers acquired debts, centralized lenders, notably life

[51] See Table 5.1.
[52] The percentage of farmers indebted is based on the number of full owners and is the average of five midwestern states; state figures are reported in U.S. Department of Commerce, *Fifteenth Census of the United States: 1930*, Agriculture, vol. 2, part 1, p. 47.
[53] Nelson reported that a third of farmers carried large debts, large enough to cause nearly a quarter of the farmers to fail. Ackerman found that half the farmers in his study carried debts that amounted to more than 40 percent of assets; nearly a fifth of these farmers ultimately failed by the mid-1930s. See Ackerman, "Factors Influencing Farm Lending"; and Nelson, "Experience of the Federal Land Bank," pp. 38, 76, 78–81.
[54] U.S. Department of Commerce, *Fifteenth Census of the United States: 1930*, Agriculture, vol. 2, part 1, pp. 468, 550, 643, 963, 1064.

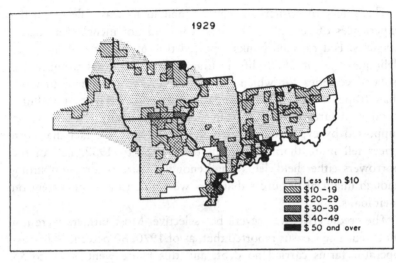

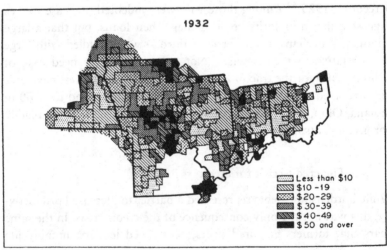

Figure 4.4. Distressed assets per $100 of farm investment in the Corn Belt by life insurance companies, 1929 and 1932. Unpublished information supplied by life insurance companies to Lawrence A. Jones and David Durand. Maps were originally printed in Lawrence A. Jones and David Durand, *Mortgage Lending Experience in Agriculture*, National Bureau of Economic Research (Princeton: Princeton University Press, 1954), p. 84. Courtesy of the National Bureau of Economic Research, Cambridge, Massachusetts.

insurance companies and federal land banks, acquired a larger share of loans previously held by local creditors (banks and private individuals). Presumably these centralized creditors provided some relief to farmers who refinanced loans. Yet, this shift among lenders was overshadowed by the impact of the crisis on lenders' ability or willingness to offer farmers credit.

Like farmers, banks were caught in the boom cycle during the war and immediate postwar years. Met Life's Rogers explained: "In the years after 1916, sharing the prosperity of the farmers, the deposits of rural banks had increased materially so that the bank executives were having trouble keeping their money at work." He added that it "was not uncommon" for rural banks to encourage farmers to make loans. Once markets collapsed, however, these banks often asked borrowers to refinance loans with other lenders. But Rogers concluded that this option posed problems when farmers turned to local creditors:

> Farmers with unencumbered farms who had been requested to liquidate their loans with the bank not infrequently went to a neighbor or to a retired farmer living in town and secured the funds from him. This resulted in the loan being paid at the bank but also caused the deposits in the bank to be lowered to the extent of the loan granted as in many instances both men were customers of the same bank.

Rogers suggested an alternative: "One of the easiest methods by which a country bank could liquidate a loan owed by a farmer whose farm was clear of encumbrance was to encourage that farmer to place a mortgage with an insurance company or with the Federal Land Banks."[55]

Outside lenders certainly took advantage of opportunities in local markets. Met Life first engaged in the business in 1917. By 1920 it had made $34.8 million in new farm loans, or four times the value of loans made in 1919, and its annual volume of new loans averaged roughly $36 million into the early 1920s. A similar pattern prevailed for Aetna. The Hartford company's new loans averaged $11 million in the war, up 19 percent over the prewar years. Between 1920 and 1924, new

[55] Rogers, "Twenty-Five Years in the Farm Mortgage Investment Field," pp. 2, 4. Rogers's analysis was supported by Norman J. Wall, "Agricultural Loans of Commercial Banks," U.S. Department of Agriculture Technical Bulletin No. 521 (July 1936), pp. 8–13, 17–18, 20.

loans jumped from $11 million to $16.3 million a year, on average.[56] Although federal lenders recorded few loans in 1920 and 1921 while waiting the outcome of a lawsuit, from 1922 on they expanded their loan portfolio.[57] As a result, centralized lenders more than doubled their share of outstanding farm mortgage debt between 1920 and 1929. By the end of the decade, insurance firms held 29 percent of mortgage debt in Illinois and 41 percent in Iowa; federal land banks held 7.4 percent in Illinois and 6.2 percent in Iowa. Joint stock land banks, aided by government initiatives but privately run, held 11.2 percent of the debt in Illinois, 7.3 percent in Iowa.[58]

These centralized lenders wrote loans with longer maturities and lower rates of interest than did either banks or private individuals (Table 3.1). With interest rates set at a point less than local rates and with twice the maturity (say of an eight- as compared with a four-year loan), a mortgage from a centralized lender eased the burden of debt and presumably freed up funds for other activities.

Aside from borrowers, Met Life concluded that this refinancing effort also helped banks:

> The Company has rendered a great financial service to the individual states in which we make farm loans . . . as under our direct operation it is claimed by our Correspondents and in fact hundreds of small local bankers . . . that the Metropolitan farm loan money made it possible for the banking doors to remain open. The procedure being that we made farm loans to individuals for an amount sufficient to permit them to discharge in whole or in part their

[56] Rogers, "Twenty-Five Years in the Farm Mortgage Investment Field," pp. 1, 3–5. For Aetna, see "A Record of Mortgage Loan Experience" (1948), p. 11, Record Group 42, Aetna Life and Casualty Company Archives, Hartford, Connecticut.

[57] For changes in the lending policy of federal lenders in 1921, see Wall, "Agricultural Loans of Commercial Banks," p. 19.

[58] Changes in outstanding debt for life insurance companies, federal land banks, and joint stock land banks are calculated for two regions, the East North Central and the West North Central. The share of debt held by life insurance firms increased from 10.5 to 19.8 percent in the East North Central, and from 20.9 to 34.5 percent in the West North Central between 1919 and 1929; for federal land banks, their share of debt increased from 0.9 to 9.1 percent in the East North Central, and from 1.5 to 7.9 percent in the West North Central in these same years. Regional figures for joint stock land banks were not given for 1919, but presumably they would be quite small. Data for individual states for 1929 and regional data are found in Horton et al., "Farm-Mortgage Credit Facilities," pp. 15–18, 222–3.

obligations held by local banks. By continuing the process in a local community very often the amount involved being around $50,000 divided by a number of individual borrowers made it possible for the local bank to keep open its doors and meet the banking needs of the community.[59]

Met Life's role merits scrutiny. It was possible that insurance firms and land banks refinanced secure loans and left local banks saddled with a larger proportion of weak loans. Or at least, their role may have been more ambiguous: helpful by injecting cash into local banks, but harmful by acquiring relatively secure loans and leaving local lenders tied to weak mortgages.

Regardless of the effect of these refinancing activities, commercial banks suffered high rates of suspension. Between 1921 and 1929 1,127 banks in the five midwestern states were suspended (Table 4.3). While the numbers of banks had increased during the First World War, and their decline in the 1920s should be seen relative to the earlier spurt, the surge in suspensions was important because it reduced sources of farm capital. Failed banks "immobilized" deposits that served as the basis of farm loans; they also worked against many farmers in good credit standing who were forced to find an alternative creditor. Some located credit with other banks, but others had to secure loans from lenders (such as implement dealers) who typically charged higher rates. As some banks suspended operations, others – wanting to restore confidence to their depositors – often became cautious. One official noted that "banks followed the policy of keeping an increasing proportion of their assets invested in readily liquidated securities purchased outside of the community."[60]

This phase of the crisis was not confined to banks. As local creditors reduced their loanable funds, so did centralized lenders. The speed of their decisions varied. Aetna reacted quickly. From 1925 through the late 1920s, Aetna cut the annual value of farm loans to roughly 70 percent of that of the first part of the 1920s. Met Life was more lenient. Its farm mortgage department maintained the volume of new farm loans at roughly $36 million a year through 1926, and at $30 million in 1927 and 1928. It was not until 1929 that the firm decided to reduce new farm loans because, as Rogers explained,

[59] "Farm Loan Division Organized 1917" (1927), p. 2, V.F. – Farm Loan Division (# 1), Metropolitan Life Insurance Company Archives.
[60] Wall, "Agricultural Loans of Commercial Banks," pp. 24–8.

"defaults and foreclosures gave no indication of an improvement in the farmers' situation."[61]

Just before the crisis started, land banks had been established with the hope that they would restructure credit markets. As public creditors entered the farm loan business, private lenders wondered aloud whether they would have to change their practices. In 1917 Connecticut Mutual cautioned that "some lenders are now accepting a seven- or ten-year period and of late the plan of a 20 year loan with annual amortization of the principal has been offered. This so-called amortization plan is offered by some lenders to meet possible and expected competition of the Federal Land Banks." But in the 1920s, lenders chose not to alter their policies. Based on a survey in 1924, the USDA concluded that most loans (65 percent) were still written for five years. Nearly 18 percent averaged fewer than five years, while 15 percent were for ten years and only 2.5 percent ran from eleven to thirty years. One USDA economist, David Wickens, reported similar results for 1929, stating that out of forty insurance companies, just four firms made loans for more than ten years.[62]

Clearly, the credit crisis of the twenties complicated the relations between borrowers and creditors. While insurance firms helped many farmers by refinancing loans with comparatively lower interest rates and longer maturities, all lenders experienced losses and reduced the capital available to farmers. In some regions, notably Iowa, banks simply failed, thereby restricting the capital for farmers or forcing them to obtain loans at higher rates from other lenders. Insurance firms, the experience of Aetna and Met Life suggested, were curbing their new farm loans in the late 1920s. Congress had hoped that federal land banks would improve the farm mortgage situation, but the crisis prevented the new banks from achieving these long-term goals. Now, the instability of commodity markets had disrupted private and public lenders, as well as farmers.

[61] Rogers, "Twenty-Five Years in the Farm Mortgage Investment Field," pp. 1, 3–6. For Aetna, see "A Record of Mortgage Loan Experience" (1948), p. 11.

[62] "Farm Loan Investments" (1917), p. 9, Docs 1. Exec. / Pres. 6 Taylor / Investments – Farm Loans, Corporate Library, Connecticut Mutual Life Insurance Company. David L. Wickens, "Farm-Mortgage Credit," U.S. Department of Agriculture Technical Bulletin No. 288 (February 1932), pp. 75–7, 88.

The tractor's threshold: Geographical patterns

Thus far we have examined the threshold using data for individual states. We need to look more closely at what was happening within each state, where there was a great deal of variation among individual farmers. Could these variations so alter the threshold as to eliminate the lag in the tractor's rate of diffusion? If so, then the problems of cash and credit would not have mattered.

Figure 4.5 maps the tractor's rate of adoption in each county of Illinois and Iowa.[63] In southern Iowa and southern Illinois, the proportion of farmers who adopted the tractor consistently fell short of state averages. By contrast, in north-central Iowa and in east-central Illinois, the tractor enjoyed a much warmer welcome, and close to half the farmers invested in the machine. In the five counties surrounding Chicago (Lake, McHenry, Kane, DuPage, and Will), large numbers of farmers purchased tractors. Although on average one in four midwesterners had purchased a tractor in 1929, in some areas less than one in eight owned the machine, while elsewhere as many as three out of five farmers bought tractors.

This pattern reflected different specialties of corn farming, which were themselves inspired by two environmental forces that limited farmers' production choices: soil quality and topography. In counties endowed with rich, dark soils and flat prairies, farmers pursued the most profitable enterprise: growing corn. But not all acres were so well endowed. In some areas the soil contained too much acid. Without liming the fields, harvests never yielded as much corn as the naturally fertile prairies. In other regions the land was too steep, and farmers had no choice but to pasture cattle on these hills. Some land had to be drained, and until farmers reclaimed the marshes, they too had to use their land for pasture.[64] These environmental factors were reflected in five subregions of the Midwest: the cash grain, western meat-feeding, mixed livestock, dairy, and pasture (Figure 4.6).

The cash grain areas, not surprisingly, possessed the richest soils

---

[63] For a discussion of regions in Illinois, see H. C. M. Case and K. H. Myers, "Types of Farming in Illinois," University of Illinois Agricultural Experiment Station Bulletin No. 403 (June 1934). For Iowa, see C. L. Holmes, "Types of Farming in Iowa," Iowa State College Agricultural Experiment Station Bulletin No. 256 (January 1929).

[64] Case and Myers, "Types of Farming in Illinois," especially pp. 154–206; Holmes, "Types of Farming in Iowa," pp. 116–66.

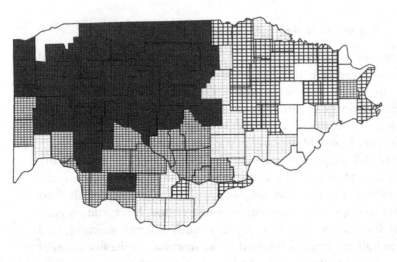

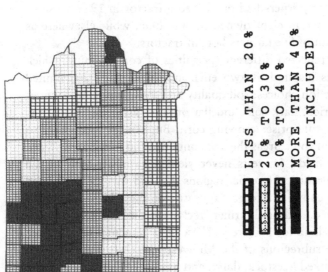

Figure 4.5. The tractor's rate of diffusion in Illinois and Iowa, 1929. Counties are shaded according to the percentage of farms with tractors. Calculations from data in the U.S. Department of Commerce, *Fifteenth Census of the United States: 1930* (Washington, D.C.: U.S. Government Printing Office, 1932), Agriculture, vol. 2, part 1, county tables 1 and 12.

LESS THAN 20%
20% TO 30%
30% TO 40%
MORE THAN 40%
NOT INCLUDED

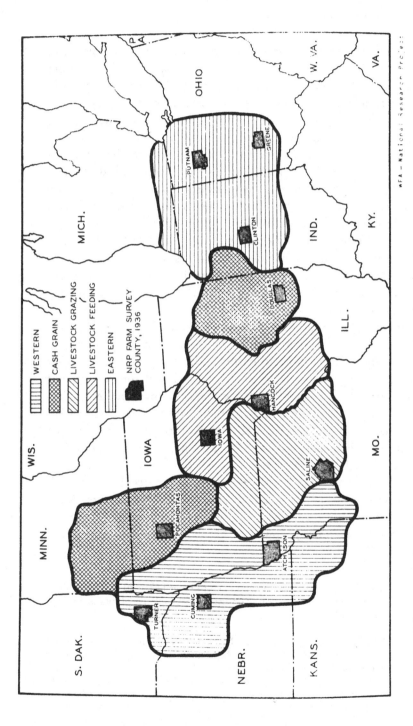

Figure 4.6. Subregions within the Corn Belt. (Shaded areas mark selected regions.) From Works Progress Administration, *Changes in Technology and Labor Requirements in Crop Production: Corn*, National Research Project No. A-5 (Philadelphia, 1938), p. 48.

and flattest prairies. Cash grain farmers devoted the vast majority of their land to crops and much of their cropland to corn.[65] Corn occupied roughly 40 percent of all farmland (half of all cropland). Farmers rotated oats into another 25 to 30 percent of their land so as to replenish acreage previously planted in corn. The rest was planted in hay, wheat, soybeans, or pastured to cattle and hogs.[66]

Of the four remaining areas, the western meat-feeding area was also endowed with fertile land. Dark alluvial soils flanked the Missouri River and its tributaries, and farmers in this part of the Corn Belt planted as much of their land in corn as those in the cash grain districts; they also planted small sections in hay, oats, wheat, or soybeans. Western land, however, was also hilly. Rather than plow under hills and risk soil erosion, farmers pastured cattle. They also devoted more time to raising hogs and purchased corn from the cash grain areas in order to feed their livestock. Farmers in the mixed-livestock area followed the same practice.

In the east, however, the soils were not as fertile and the land was more hilly than in the western areas. Mixed-livestock farmers devoted less land to corn and more to pasture. The so-called pasture region took its name from areas in southern Iowa and southern Illinois where soils were poor and the land was hilly. Farmers in these counties planted crops on slightly more than half their land. The rest went to grazing cattle. In the last area, the dairy region, farmers sowed roughly half their land in corn and oats. In counties near Chicago, farmers not only benefited from rich soils but also from urban markets. They specialized in fruits, vegetables, and especially dairy products. Dairy farmers had an added incentive to buy tractors. Aside from fieldwork, tractors could be used for "belt work" – that is, for providing stationary power to fill silos or operate feed grinders.[67]

---

[65] In Iowa the percentage of land in crops ranged from 70 to 85 percent of total farmland in the cash grain regions. See Holmes, "Types of Farming in Iowa."

[66] Ibid.

[67] Ibid., and Case and Myers, "Types of Farming in Illinois." For dairy farms, see "Illinois Agricultural Adjustment Conference 1928–1929 Facts assembled for use of Committee on: Mechanical Equipment, Drainage, and Farm Buildings" (October 1928), pp. 12–13, 15, Record Series 8/4/829, Box 1, University of Illinois Archives, University of Illinois at Urbana-Champaign.

Due to these geographic differences, the tractor had not one, but several thresholds throughout the Midwest. Recall that the tractor's farm-size threshold was defined as the number of crop acres above which the tractor reduced farm costs divided by the percentage of land devoted to crops: 100 farm acres for the entire Midwest. This was based on the assumption that farmers planted two-thirds of their land in crops, however, and that did not hold true in all parts of the Corn Belt. Farmers in the southern pasture areas planted fewer acres whereas cash grain farmers devoted more land to crops. As the percentage of land in crops fell, the tractor's acreage threshold rose. There is also a second qualification. The crop-acreage threshold itself varied in terms of the mix of crops. The most time-consuming and costly crop to raise was corn. As the proportion of cropland devoted to corn fell, the tractor's cost advantage declined relative to a team of horses. In areas where farmers planted less corn relative to all crops, and devoted a smaller portion of their land to crops, the tractor's threshold was much higher than 100 acres. Conversely, in cash grain areas, the actual threshold was less than 100 acres.

Even when the acreage threshold is calculated on a county basis, however, the lag in the tractor's rate of diffusion persists in both states (Figure 4.7). On average, only half of Illinois and Iowa farmers whose land surpassed the county-adjusted thresholds actually invested in tractors. Regional patterns also persisted. The highest percentage of farmers who both qualified to own and did own tractors farmed in east-central Illinois – that is, in the cash grain region. The tractor also fared well in urban counties, particularly those surrounding Chicago, but also St. Louis, Peoria, Moline, and Des Moines. In pasture regions of southern Illinois and southern Iowa, however, farmers were least likely to buy tractors. Midway between these extremes were the western meat-feeding, dairy (outside of Chicago), and mixed-livestock regions.

Both the rate of the tractor's diffusion and the relative lag in the invention's adoption followed certain regional patterns. Geographic factors explain, in large part, the first pattern – why proportionately more farmers in areas well-suited to raising crops bought tractors than farmers in other areas. Geographic distinctions, however, do not explain the second pattern – the lag in the tractor's rate of adoption. Even so, they are important because it is possible to account for the tractor's lag by explaining these regional differences.

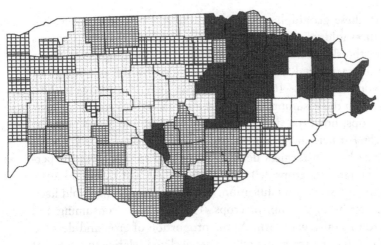
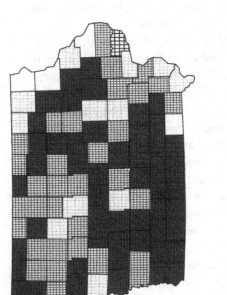
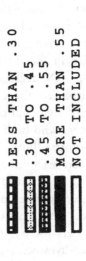

LESS THAN .30

.30 TO .45

.45 TO .55

MORE THAN .55

NOT INCLUDED

Figure 4.7. Lag in the tractor's adoption in Illinois and Iowa, 1929. The lag in the tractor's adoption is defined for each county as the ratio of the percentage of farmers whose land exceeded the acreage threshold but did not own tractors to the percentage whose land exceeded the threshold. Counties are shaded according to the lag in the tractor's rate of adoption. Calculated from data described in Table 4.4.

Quantitative evidence for regional variations

If the financial problems farmers encountered hampered their investments, as the evidence suggests they did, then farmers' cash needs or
their credit problems should account for the regional variations in
farmers' investment patterns. To examine this proposition, I ideally
would use information for individual farmers. But there is no consistent source for this information. Instead, I employ county-level census
data. Doing so, I must assume that experiences of individual farmers
varied systematically across different counties. No doubt, county-
level data cannot spot some distinctions in individual cases. Still, to
the extent that financial concerns took on geographic patterns, they
should identify differences in the tractor's diffusion among counties. I
explore this proposition for the two most important states, Illinois
and Iowa.

The test is constructed as a regression. The variable to be explained
is the lag in the diffusion of the tractor − the ratio of the percentage
of farmers who worked more land than the threshold yet who did not
invest in the machine to the percentage whose land passed the threshold. It is calculated as follows. First, because the threshold in each
county varied depending on the proportion of cropland devoted to
corn, a crop-acreage threshold is estimated for each county (following
the procedures outlined in Appendix A). Second, to obtain the farm-
size threshold, each county's crop-acreage threshold is divided by the
percentage of land in crops. Third, the percentage of farms that
passed each county's farm-size threshold is estimated. The Census
reports the number of farms that fell into such categories as 50 to 99
acres and 100 to 174 acres. I calculate the percentage of all farmers
that fell within each Census category (say 50 to 99 acres) and use this
information to estimate the percentage that passed the threshold.[68]

---

[68] I calculate a farm-size threshold as opposed to a crop-acre threshold
because the Census only reports the size distribution of farms by farm size,
not by crop size. To estimate the proportion of farms that passed a given
threshold, I first calculated the percentage of farms that passed a given
threshold based on an even distribution. For example, if the threshold is
75 acres, then I would add 50 percent of the farms in the category of 50
to 99 acres to the percentage of farms with more than 100 acres. It is
unlikely, however, that farms were evenly distributed. For this reason, I
recalculated figures in which I increased the proportion of farms that
passed the threshold by 20 percent so as to add or subtract a larger than
proportionate number of farms. For instance, if the threshold is 75 acres, I
added not 50 percent of the farms but 60 percent of the farms in this

Finally, the proportion of farmers whose land exceeded the threshold but did not own tractors is divided by the proportion of farms that exceeded the threshold. This indicates the lag in the tractor's adoption.

I examine several variables in an effort to assess the variation in the tractor's lag (Table 4.4). To take into account the conflict farmers faced between safety and productivity, I employ as a proxy the margin of cash between farmers' average earnings and their average cash expenses. The variable serves as a gauge of farmers' cash resources, and it varied a great deal across counties. At the low end, farmers' cash income averaged less than $500 (Table 4.4). For these midwesterners the tractor would have absorbed half the funds they had left each year. At the high end, some farmers earned more than $2,000 in cash after expenses. For these individuals, the tractor imposed a much smaller financial burden. One would expect the tractor's lag to vary inversely with farmers' average cash income.

In the case of Iowa, there is a second proxy, the variability of corn yields. This variable is far from ideal because it measures changes in yields rather than the volatility of farm income. But it gives a rough indicator of areas that were subject to more difficult growing conditions, and one might hypothesize that farmers who faced greater variations in their corn yields would be less likely to spend their money on tractors.

In some regions farmers may have been able to avoid these cash dilemmas by tapping other sources of income, and one proxy suggests itself: the percentage of individuals in a county that lived in urban places. The measure takes into account farmers who, by their nearness to urban centers, may have been able to sell farm goods in urban markets or find additional employment, and thus acquire the money for purchasing expensive equipment. This variable, like that for farm-

category. This method increases the proportion of farms that passed the threshold if the county's threshold was less than 100 acres and reduces the proportion of farms that passed the threshold if the threshold was greater than 100 acres. The revised figures reduce the lag where it is greatest and increase the lag where it is smallest, thus reducing variation among counties. Further, I use the case of six horses versus four horses and a tractor to calculate the threshold. This results in a lower estimate of the tractor's lag inasmuch as the threshold is slightly higher and the proportion of farms that passed the threshold is slightly lower than in the case of five horses versus three horses and a tractor.

ers' cash income, varied a great deal, ranging from a low of 0 percent urban to a high of 85 percent.

To capture the effects of burdensome debts, two proxies are added. One measures the percentage of farms that were mortgaged; the second is the ratio of average debts to the average value of farmland and buildings. Like other variables, these two measures varied among parts of the Midwest. In some areas, more than 60 percent of owner-operated farms were mortgaged and debts amounted to more than half the value of their land and buildings. In other areas, less than 40 percent of farms were mortgaged and debts amounted to 38 percent of farmers' assets (Table 4.4). One would anticipate that as either financial measure increased, farmers would be less likely to purchase tractors despite cost savings.

I use one last variable, the percent change in commercial bank deposits from 1920 to 1929. This categorical variable is based on information that was classified into two cases for an increase in deposits (0–50 and more than 50 percent) and three cases for a drop in deposits (0–25, 26–50, and 51–75 percent).[69] Insofar as declines in deposits are concerned, the variable captures financial problems communities faced as banks suspended operation or farmers withdrew deposits and the funds available for loans dwindled. But in cases where bank deposits increased, presumably the reverse followed: farmers were better able to obtain loans. Alternatively, if they did not actually borrow from banks, the change in bank deposits signaled that these farmers enjoyed a measure of prosperity and thus were better able to purchase equipment.

[69] The data differ somewhat for Iowa and Illinois. In the case of Iowa, no county reported an increase of deposits of more than 50 percent. By contrast, in Illinois, no county reported a drop in deposits of 51 to 75 percent. Of the remaining categories, the 95 counties in Iowa reported the following distribution: 19 cases for an increase in deposits of 0 to 50 percent; 49 cases for a decline of deposits of 0 to 25 percent; 21 cases for a decline in deposits of 26 to 50 percent; and 6 cases for a drop in deposits of 51 to 75 percent. In Illinois, the 91 counties reported the following distribution: 2 cases for an increase in deposits of more than 50 percent; 43 cases for an increase in deposits of 0 to 50 percent; 38 cases for a decline in deposits of 0 to 25 percent; and 8 cases of a decline in deposits of 26 to 50 percent. For the regressions, I have coded the data as a categorical variable. I did not organize the data; rather, the categories are based on data collected and reported in Lawrence A. Jones and David Durand, *Mortgage Lending Experience in Agriculture,* National Bureau of Economic Research (Princeton: Princeton University Press, 1954), p. 48.

Table 4.4. *Descriptive statistics for counties in Iowa and Illinois, 1929*

Variables[a]	Mean	Standard deviation	Minimum	Maximum
A. Iowa (95 counties)				
Percent of farms reporting tractors	31%	9.4	10%	53%
Crop acreage threshold	66 acres	8.5	47 acres	97 acres
Farm acreage threshold	101 acres	22.1	62 acres	165 acres
Percent of farms above farm threshold	70%	15.6%	24%	92%
Percent of farms above farm threshold that did not use tractors	55%	9.8	21%	78%
Cash margin	$1,685	$541	$242	$2,962
Percent of owner-operated farms that were mortgaged	59%	7.5	40%	76%
Ratio of debt to value of land	48.7	3.5	38.4	58.5
Percent of population in urban places	26%	23.5	0%	85%
Ratio of standard deviation to average yield, corn, 1900-29	0.188	0.0292	0.1288	0.2689
B. Illinois (91 counties)				
Percent of farms reporting tractors	34%	16.2	6%	65%
Crop acreage threshold	71 acres	10.8	55 acres	110 acres
Farm acreage threshold	106 acres	22.3	70 acres	163 acres
Percent of farms above farm threshold	59%	20.3	19%	91%
Percent of farms above farm threshold that did not use tractors	44%	22.4	-82%	81%
Cash margin	$1,080	$701	-$172	$2,457
Percent of owner-operated farms that were mortgaged	44%	8.4	22%	59%
Ratio of debt to value of land	43.0	5.8	29.0	63.4
Percent of population in urban places	33%	24.8	0%	85%

[a]The definition and sources of variables are as follows:

Notes to Table 4.4 (cont.)

The percentage of farms reporting tractors is the number
of tractors divided by the number of farms in each county.
See U.S. Department of Commerce, *Fifteenth Census of the
United States: 1930* (Washington, D.C.: U.S. Government
Printing Office, 1932), Agriculture, vol. 2, part 1, county
tables 1 and 12.

I calculate a crop acreage threshold for each county
because the threshold varies in relation to the percentage of
land devoted to corn. In particular, the threshold rises as
the percentage of land in corn falls. The method for
estimating each county's crop acreage threshold is described
in Appendix A. For each county, I adjusted the distribution
of crops according to the proportion of cropland devoted to
corn. See U.S. Department of Commerce, *Fifteenth Census of
the United States: 1930*, Agriculture, vol. 2, part 1, county
tables 1 and 5.

The farm acreage threshold is calculated as the crop
acreage threshold divided by the percentage of land in crops,
the latter being equal to the total number of crop acres per
county divided by the total number of acres in farmland. See
U.S. Department of Commerce, *Fifteenth Census of the United
States: 1930*, Agriculture, vol. 2, part 1, county table 1.

The lag in the adoption of the tractor is defined as one
minus the ratio of the proportion of farms with tractors to
the proportion of farms that passed the acreage threshold.
Calculations are discussed in the text. For the distribution
of farms, see U.S. Department of Commerce, *Fifteenth Census
of the United States: 1930*, Agriculture, vol. 2, part 1,
county table 2.

The average cash margin represents the average total
earnings per farm minus the average cash farm expenses. The
Census defines farm revenues as the value of "all products
(sold, traded, or used by operator's family)," but I
subtracted the value of goods consumed by the operator's
family so as to arrive at their actual cash earnings. "Farm
expenditures" are defined as payments for "feed, fertilizer,
farm labor (cash), farm implements and machinery, and
electric light and power." For farm revenues see the U.S.
Department of Commerce, *Fifteenth Census of the United
States: 1930*, Agriculture, vol. 3, part 1, county table 3.
For farm cash expenditures, see the *Fifteenth Census of the
United States*, Agriculture, vol. 2, part 1, county table 12.
Both total revenues and total cash expenditures are divided
by the number of farms reporting.

The percentage of farms mortgaged and the ratio of farm
debts to the value of farmland and buildings are reported in
U.S. Department of Commerce, *Fifteenth Census of the United
States: 1930*, Agriculture, vol. 2, part 1, county table 11.

(cont.)

Tables 4.5 and 4.6 report the results for Iowa and Illinois, respectively. For both states, the adoption of the tractor varied among counties according to its financial burden, the lag being greatest in those counties where farmers' average cash margins were lowest.[70] In Iowa, the second proxy, the variability of corn yields was not significant. But if the regression was run excluding the variable for farmers' margin of cash (Table 4.5, case 4), then the variable was significant at a 10 percent level of confidence. Of the two variables, farmers' margin of cash carried more explanatory power in the regressions. When it was excluded (Table 4.5, cases 3 and 4 for Iowa, and Table 4.6, case 5 for Illinois), the remaining variables held considerably less explanatory power in accounting for systematic variations in the tractor's lag.

[70] It is conceivable that in certain counties farmers' net cash incomes were higher simply because they worked larger farms on average and, as a result, obtained larger incomes from crops and livestock. To control for this possibility, I ran regressions in which I included average farm size and average farm size excluding woods and "all other" land. In these cases, proxies for average farm size were not significant. Alternatively, I divided farmers' cash income by farm size and by farm size excluding woods and other land. In both states, the adjusted variables remained significant.

Notes to Table 4.4 (cont.)

The percentage of a county's population in urban places is reported in U.S. Department of Commerce, *Fifteenth Census of the United States: 1930*, Population, vol. 3, part 1, county table 13.

The variability of corn yields is measured as the standard deviation of yields divided by the mean for the years 1900 to 1929. Data for individual counties is found in the Iowa Department of Agriculture, *Thirty-Fifth Annual Year Book of Agriculture* (Des Moines, Iowa, 1934).

Statistics are reported for 95 of 99 counties in Iowa and 91 of 102 counties in Illinois. For Illinois, I eliminated Cook County since it represents Chicago. For both states, I eliminated counties for which farmers devoted a small portion of their land to corn. In Iowa, Allamakee, Clayton, Davis, and Jackson were eliminated; in Illinois, Jo Davies, Perry, Monroe, Randolph, Union, and Washington were cut. I also eliminated four counties in Illinois for which very few farmers owned tractors. They were Hamilton, Hardin, Jefferson, and Pope.

Table 4.5. Estimated regression coefficients for counties in Iowa, 1929[ab]

Independent variables[c]	Case 1	Case 2	Case 3	Case 4
Cash margin	-0.0001 (-5.991)*	-0.0001 (-5.730)*		
Corn yield variability	-0.0015 (-0.005)	-0.0633 (-0.201)		0.5481 (1.709)***
Bank deposits -0-25%	0.0406 (1.899)***		0.0587 (2.401)**	0.0599 (2.476)**
Bank deposits -26-50%	-0.0123 (-0.471)		0.0131 (0.437)	0.0114 (0.387)
Bank deposits -50-75%	-0.0162 (-0.423)		0.0229 (0.537)	0.0203 (0.483)
Percent farms mortgaged	0.0066 (4.569)*	0.0068 (4.741)*	-0.0002 (-0.181)	0.0002 (0.143)
Debt/land value[d]			0.0094 (3.447)*	0.0089 (3.272)*
Percent urban	-0.0015 (-3.818)*	-0.0013 (-3.412)*	-0.0013 (-2.976)*	-0.0011 (-2.387)**
Adjusted R^2	0.41	0.37	0.25	0.26

[a]The dependent variable is the proportion of farms that passed the tractor's threshold but did not own a tractor.

[b]Findings are reported for 95 counties.

[c]The student $\underline{t}$-statistic appears in parentheses under the coefficient, such that: * denotes significance at a 99 percent confidence level, ** at a 95 percent confidence level, and *** at a 90 percent confidence level.

[d]If the variable, debt/land value, is included in cases 1 and 2, it is not significant.

Sources: See Table 4.4 and text.

Table 4.6. *Estimated regression coefficients for counties in Illinois, 1929*[a][b]

Independent variables[c]	Case 1	Case 2	Case 3[d]	Case 4[d]	Case 5[d]
Cash margin	-0.0002 (-6.282)*	-0.0001 (-4.517)*	-0.0002 (-6.874)*	-0.0001 (-6.761)*	
Bank deposits +0-50%	0.9359 (8.651)*				
Bank deposits -0-25%	0.9569 (8.686)*		0.0213 (0.706)		0.0215 (0.612)
Bank deposits -26-50%	0.8456 (7.007)*		-0.0908 (-1.738)***		-0.0658 (-1.084)
Percent farms mortgaged[e]					-0.0088 (-4.123)*
Debt/land value	0.0017 (0.582)	0.0087 (2.322)**	0.0012 (0.459)	0.0012 (0.461)	-0.0005 (-0.158)
Percent urban	-0.0018 (-2.692)*	-0.0029 (-3.518)*	-0.0018 (-2.914)*	-0.0016 (-2.733)*	-0.0024 (-3.538)*
Adjusted R²	0.61	0.27	0.42	0.40	0.24

[a]The dependent variable is the proportion of farms that passed the tractor's threshold but did not own a tractor.

[b]Findings are reported for 91 counties.

[c]The student t-statistic appears in parentheses under the coefficient, such that: * denotes significance at a 99 percent confidence level, ** at a 95 percent confidence level, and *** at a 90 percent confidence level.

[d]Regression excludes Lake and DuPage counties.

[e]If the variable, percent farms mortgaged, is included in the first four cases, it is not significant.

Sources: See Table 4.4 and text.

Farmers also made investments in response to their debt obligations. In Iowa, as proportionately more farms were mortgaged, proportionately fewer farmers invested in tractors (Table 4.5, cases 1 and 2). When the cash margin variable is dropped from the regression, the proxy for the ratio of debt to the value of land was significant in Iowa (Table 4.5, cases 3 and 4). In Illinois the ratio of debt to the value of farmland was significant, indicating that as the burden of debts increased, proportionately fewer farmers elected to invest in a tractor (Table 4.6, case 2). Aside from these variables, the urban proxy (the percent of individuals living in urban places) was significant in both states. It appears that farmers who lived near cities were able to offset lower farm incomes with other ventures.

Data for bank deposits indicated that while indebted farmers in both states suffered, farmers in Iowa suffered far more than those in Illinois. Nearly half of all commercial bank suspensions in the five Corn Belt states were in Iowa; Illinois reported 132 suspensions, or roughly 1 for every 4 in Iowa (Table 4.3). The problem of bank suspensions no doubt contributed to a sharp drop in bank deposits and, by implication, to a reduction in funds available for farm loans. Looking at the two states, nearly four in five counties in Iowa experienced a decline in deposits; in Illinois, by contrast, half the counties reported gains in deposits.[71] The problem of bank suspensions, and their concentration in Iowa, obviously reflected the distress of individual farmers. Debt levels were much higher, and borrowers experienced higher levels of foreclosure in Iowa than in other states (Table 4.3).[72]

To the extent that the credit crisis was far worse in Iowa than in Illinois, Iowa's farmers should have been slower to invest in the tractor. This proposition can be tested statistically by using a difference-of-means test (a test of whether differences in average values of variables for Iowa counties as compared with Illinois counties are statistically significant). I examined twenty counties from the north-central area of Iowa and the east-central region of Illinois. As reported in Table 4.7, the results indicate that the differences in the means of farmers' cash income or their locations near urban centers

[71] See n. 69.
[72] Jones and Durand reported a close correlation first between farm distress transfers and the number of bank failures and, second, between farm distress transfers and the decline in total deposits of commercial banks. Jones and Durand, *Mortgage Lending Experience in Agriculture*, pp. 45–6.

Table 4.7. *Difference-of-means test for selected counties in Iowa and Illinois, 1929*[a]

Variables	Difference of mean[b]	Is sign correct?	T-test probability
Lag in adoption of tractor	0.1587	Yes	0.00001
Cash margin	$90.65	No	0.3964
Percent farms mortgaged	13.2%	Yes	0.00001
Debt/value	5.2	Yes	0.00001
Percent urban	3.9%	Yes	0.5975

[a]Twenty counties each were selected from north-central Iowa and east-central Illinois. For Iowa, they were Boone, Butler, Calhoun, Dallas, Franklin, Greene, Grundy, Guthrie, Hamilton, Hancock, Hardin, Humbolt, Jasper, Marshal, Polk, Poweshiek, Story, Tama, Webster, and Wright. For Illinois, they were Bureau, Champaign, DeWitt, Douglas, Ford, Grundy, Iroquois, Kankakee, LaSalle, Livingston, Logan, McLean, Macon, Marshall, Menard, Piatt, Putnam, Tazewell, Will, and Woodford.
[b]Difference between the mean of values of selected counties in Iowa and counties in Illinois.
Sources: See Table 4.4.

were not significant. Instead, both the percent of farms mortgaged and the ratio of debt to the value of farmland had higher means in Iowa than in Illinois, and the differences in the means were statistically significant. Aside from this exercise, changes in bank deposits also indicate conditions were worse in Iowa. For in only one of the twenty counties in Iowa had deposits increased during the decade and in six counties deposits had fallen by more than 25 percent. In Illinois, the reverse held true. In only one county had deposits fallen by more than 25 percent; in six, deposits had increased during the decade. Although indebted farmers in both states suffered, the crisis was clearly worse in Iowa and, as such, played an important role in accounting for the tractor's greater lag there as compared with the situation in Illinois.

The experience of Illinois, though, was more complicated than the credit crisis alone indicates. Two counties (DuPage and Lake) reported an increase in deposits of more than 50 percent. Their experiences were distinctive because in the regression these two counties – and only these two – reported owning more tractors than was predicted by the threshold analysis. As a result, the variable for changes in commercial bank deposits exerts a major influence on the regression (Table 4.6, case 1). Why did farmers in these counties prosper so? The explanation is their proximity to Chicago. Each county's population grew dramatically in the 1920s: Lake's increased by 41 percent and DuPage's by 118 percent.[73] Other counties did not report such rapid population growth, and in both counties, their rapid growth no doubt contributed to the farmers' unusual prosperity.

Without the two counties (Table 4.6, cases 3, 4, and 5), the effect of bank deposits is less important, and the other variables are better able to account for the overall variation in the lag in the tractor's diffusion. In particular, the margin of cash between revenues and expenses proves decisive to the results. If it is excluded from the regression (Table 4.6, case 5), then the other variables have less explanatory value.

Variations in certain environmental factors – soil, topography – can explain why proportionately more farmers purchased tractors in some areas rather than others, but systematic variations in financial variables account for variations in farmers' reluctance to buy a tractor relative to its expected cost savings. For Iowa's farmers, the credit crisis was the most visible factor: the burden of debts and the prevalence of indebtedness in all likelihood accounted for much of the lag in the tractor's diffusion in Iowa, and were a major reason why the lag was greater in Iowa than in Illinois. Many farmers, however, were not indebted. For debt-free or indebted farmers, other factors shaped their investments. In both states, the margin of cash between receipts and expenses proved significant, as did the variable for bank deposits. Together, these factors tend not to assign the tractor's reception to one factor over another. Instead, they suggest that the mixture of these related financial conditions influenced farmers' decisions to delay investments in tractors.

Consequences for labor productivity

Inasmuch as farmers hesitated to buy tractors, how did their behavior affect farm productivity? A 1938 Works Progress Administration (WPA) study permits the calculation of the potential gains in labor productivity had all farmers who stood to reduce costs by adopting

[73] Calculated from the U.S. Department of Commerce, *Fifteenth Census of the United States: 1930*, Population, part 1, pp. 614–20.

tractors used them. The study reported three types of information: the number of hours a farmer spent raising an acre of corn in 1919 and 1929; the hourly rates for performing particular jobs such as plowing or planting; and the proportion of farmers who performed each task with either horses or tractors.[74]

For the 1920s, virtually all savings in the time a farmer spent raising and harvesting corn came in preharvest activities, which averaged 12 percent for the decade.[75] Of this 12 percent reduction in preharvest time, the tractor accounted for savings in plowing and disking.[76] To determine the potential savings in labor productivity under the proposition that all farmers who should have invested in tractors did so, new levels of productivity in 1929 were calculated based on the assumption that twice as many farmers invested in a tractor and they obtained twice the savings in plowing and disking cornfields. These extra savings amount to 0.70 hours per acre. If the potential savings are subtracted from total preharvest labor hours, then farmers would have reduced preharvest hours not by 12 percent but by 19 percent (i.e., from 10.4 to 8.4 hours per acre). Total (preharvest and harvest) hours would have fallen by 12 percent, as compared with the actual decline of 8 percent.[77] Had farmers matched their actual investments with the

[74] Works Progress Administration, *Changes in Technology and Labor Requirements in Production: Corn,* National Research Project Report No. A-5 (Philadelphia, 1938).

[75] The WPA reported statistics for five regions within the Corn Belt, which included cash grain, eastern, livestock feeding, livestock grazing, and western. Preharvest labor gains accounted for 100 percent of all gains in four out of five counties and accounted for 80 percent of all gains in the cash-grain region. Ibid., p. 62.

[76] For the 12 percent savings in preharvest labor, nearly all savings were associated with three jobs: plowing, disking, and cultivating. While the substitution of tractors for horses accounted for savings in disking and plowing, the tractor may have contributed as well to savings in cultivation. The WPA reported, however, that most savings in cultivation came from switching from a one-row to a two-row cultivator and that this switch occurred for both horses and tractors. By not including changes in time spent cultivating, my figures underestimate the tractor's potential savings. Ibid., table 10, p. 58, and table 11, p. 62.

[77] Based on the WPA survey, harvest hours averaged 5.70 hours per acre in 1919, and 5.66 hours per acre in 1929. Total hours spent raising and harvesting corn averaged 16.08 hours per acre in 1919, as compared with 14.82 hours per acre in 1929. If total labor hours are adjusted for the potential extra savings in plowing and disking, then the total number of hours for 1929 would have averaged 14.08 hours per acre, rather than the actual level of 14.82 hours per acre. Calculated from ibid., p. 62.

threshold model's predicted level, they could have obtained an extra 50 percent savings for the decade.

In the 1920s, farmers' efforts to respond to competition and adopt tractors were more discussed than realized. Certainly manufacturers appealed to the logic of competitive markets because they could best sell tractors by comparing the market costs of different inputs. Agricultural researchers also supported this approach if only because it fit their own strategy of encouraging farmers to adopt efficient technology. By following this advice, farmers found that the tractor offered important savings.

The threshold model permitted a direct calculation of the tractor's competitiveness as determined by its costs. These equations indicated that the tractor became more profitable than a team of horses at roughly 65 crop acres. Yet, farmers apparently did not base investment decisions simply on the issue of cost. Half of all potential buyers passed this threshold, but only a quarter of all farmers made investments.

Other factors had impinged on farmers' investment calculus during the 1920s, creating uncertainty or conflicting financial demands. Farmers sought to guard against volatile crop markets by favoring resources obtained on their farms without cash to "store-bought" items that had to be paid with cash. Creditors faced constraints that hampered their ability to meet farmers' investment needs. Once the consequences of the credit crisis were felt, moreover, both creditors and borrowers acted in ways that hampered investments. Large numbers of farmers, then, shunned the advice of manufacturers. Given their climate for investment, they acted conservatively – choosing safety over productivity. Enough did so that they missed a good part of the tractor's potential savings in labor productivity at this time.

5. Depressed markets and market regulation

After 1929, farmers in the Corn Belt became caught in a crisis caused by a combination of burdensome debts and ruinously low crop prices. To meet this emergency, President Hoover pushed through Congress a commodity stabilization plan, but that program was quickly engulfed by what turned out to be the worst depression in the history of the United States. After Franklin D. Roosevelt's new administration took office in 1933, it promoted legislation creating three new federal agencies: the Farm Credit Administration (FCA), the Agricultural Adjustment Administration (AAA), and the Commodity Credit Corporation (CCC). The FCA initiated an emergency debt-refinancing program designed to lower farmers' credit costs. The AAA set out to raise farm prices by reducing the quantity of each crop reaching its respective market. The CCC acted faster: it put cash into farmers' pockets immediately by creating a short-term loan system, in which farmers used their crops as collateral.

In 1933, each agency represented an experiment in public policy and might have survived no longer than the emergency. For although the collapse in crop prices certainly gave farmers the impetus to ask for bold legislation, others closely tied to the farm sector did not necessarily support these initiatives. Both the AAA and the CCC had to contend with politicians who wanted no part in subsidizing farm income. The FCA also needed the cooperation of private lenders, but banks and insurance companies did not at first expect to gain from the FCA's actions, particularly when the federal lender proposed to offer farmers lower (subsidized) rates of interest than the rates private lenders could provide. Eventually, however, even the opponents of federal intervention accepted this regulation after they realized how depressed the markets would be. As the three programs became institutionalized, they not only provided relief but also reshaped farmers' investment climate through the Depression and after the crisis had passed. How the regulation obtained this long-term role – that is,

136

how this political conflict worked itself out in the 1930s – is the subject of this chapter.

The crisis

In 1929, despite the crash of the stock market, most crop prices held steady. The price of corn, for instance, had lost only a few pennies from its 1928 average, standing at eighty cents a bushel in 1929. Conditions were worse in 1930, however, as corn dropped to sixty cents, and in 1931 the price tumbled to thirty-two cents. So too, between 1929 and 1932, the collapse in demand cut prices for cotton, wheat, rice, and oats by more than half.[1]

By 1932, the farmers' crisis had infected every related business activity. Implement dealers saw their business vanish. Whereas sales of tractors dropped slightly from 1929 to 1930, in 1931 sales skidded 50 percent, and fell another 57 percent to just 25,000 tractors, in 1932 and 1933 (Table 4.1). Sales at all implement manufacturers dwindled, and by 1932 all reported losses.[2] Deere & Company told its shareholders the obvious: "The reduction in profits ... was due to the abnormally low prices of farm products and the consequent impairment of the buying power of the farmer, who is our only customer."[3] The crisis likewise caught creditors, whose losses skyrocketed with farmers' loan delinquencies. Whereas federal land banks had reported 6 percent of mortgages delinquent in 1929, nearly half their borrowers were behind payments by 1932 (Table 5.1). Life insurance firms also suffered heavy delinquencies, and as all lenders faced losses, they proceeded to foreclose at an astonishing rate: with roughly two in five farms mortgaged, nearly 10 percent of mortgaged farms faced "distress transfers" (because of delinquency in taxes or interest) each year from 1930 to 1934.[4]

[1] U.S. Department of Agriculture, *Agricultural Statistics, 1957* (Washington, D.C.: U.S. Government Printing Office, 1958), pp. 2, 24, 35, 46, 72.
[2] Federal Trade Commission, *Report on the Agricultural Implement and Machinery Industry, Part II, Cost, Prices, and Profits,* 75th Congress, 3rd sess., House Document 702 (June 6, 1938), p. 606.
[3] Deere & Company, *Deere & Company Annual Report, 1932,* n.p.
[4] Donald C. Horton, Harald C. Larsen, and Norman J. Wall, "Farm-Mortgage Credit Facilities in the United States," U.S. Department of Agriculture Miscellaneous Publication No. 478 (1942), p. 39.

Table 5.1. Delinquency rates of farm mortgage loans, given as a percentage of loans outstanding, reported for ten life insurance companies, federal land banks, and Land Bank Commissioner loans, 1929-37

Lender	1929	1930	1931	1932	1933	1934	1935	1936	1937
Federal land banks[a]	6%	10%	23%	49%	49%	33%	27%	22%	21%
Land Bank Commissioner loans[ab]	--	--	--	--	1	10	18	19	23
Life insurance companies[c]									
Delinquent--less than 90 days	--	--	--	9	6	4	2	2	2
Delinquent--more than 90 days	--	--	--	29	32	24	18	12	9
Total delinquent	--	--	--	38	38	28	20	14	11
Nondelinquent	--	--	--	55	55	63	72	79	85
In foreclosure	--	--	--	7	7	9	8	7	4

[a]Federal lenders defined any loan as delinquent if interest or principal was unpaid. After 1932 loans that received extensions were included among loans defined as delinquent.
[b]Land Bank Commissioner loans were not made prior to 1933.
[c]Delinquencies were not reported for life insurance firms prior to March 1933; for 1932, the rate of delinquency for insurance companies was reported not in 1932, but in March, 1933.
Sources: For federal lenders, see Donald C. Horton, Harald C. Larsen, and Norman J. Wall, "Farm-Mortgage Credit Facilities in the United States," U.S. Department of Agriculture Miscellaneous Publication No. 478 (1942), pp. 100, 120. For life insurance firms, see Resumé of Farm Loan Experience, 1928-1937 (Farm Mortgage Conference of Life Insurance Companies, December 1939), p. 20, as reported in Raymond J. Saulnier, Harold G. Halcrow, and Neil H. Jacoby, Federal Lending and Loan Insurance, National Bureau of Economic Research (Princeton: Princeton University Press, 1958), table 25, p. 167.

Throughout the 1920s, politicians had debated how they could protect farmers from the effects of unstable or depressed markets. Although President Calvin Coolidge twice vetoed the McNary–Haugen bill for stabilizing commodity prices, his successor, Herbert Hoover, found a compromise in an associational approach to economic problems. In 1929 Hoover signed into law the Agricultural Marketing Act, which created the Federal Farm Board. The board put his associational approach to work in the form of centralized cooperatives whose job was to seek to stabilize prices by evening out the flow of commodities onto the market. It was assumed that over the long term markets would clear and that the board would only hold commodities off the market during the downturn of a price cycle. This voluntary approach for raising farm prices ran into various problems, the worst of which was a major decline in demand and prices, something far worse than a normal business cycle; with the onset of the Great Depression, the board collapsed under the weight of excess supplies.[5] When Roosevelt won the 1932 election, federal farm policy offered no effective solution to ruinously low prices.

Intent on exploring solutions, the University of Illinois brought together farmers and creditors in a conference held a few weeks after Roosevelt's victory.[6] Speaking for farmers, W. G. McCormick announced that borrowers could not pay their debts until the price of corn was restored to pre-Depression levels. Looking back to 1929, he reported that a farmer could have paid a $250 loan "with 500 bushels of corn," but "today it will take 2,500 bushels."[7] While McCormick exaggerated the decline, he nevertheless correctly identified the equation between corn prices and the "ability to pay" debts. Conference

[5] For Hoover's farm policy, see David E. Hamilton, *From New Day to New Deal: American Farm Policy from Hoover to Roosevelt, 1928–1933* (Chapel Hill: University of North Carolina Press, 1991). On the politics of farmers' access to government, see John Mark Hansen, *Gaining Access* (Chicago: University of Chicago Press, 1991). The mechanics of the McNary–Haugen Bill are detailed in Murray R. Benedict, *Farm Policies of the United States, 1790–1950* (New York: Twentieth Century Fund, 1953), pp. 207–38. Also see Gilbert C. Fite, *George N. Peek and the Fight for Farm Parity* (Norman: University of Oklahoma Press, 1954).

[6] "Papers Presented at the Farm Debt Conference," College of Agriculture, University of Illinois, Urbana, Illinois (December 1932), H. C. M. Case Papers, Record Series 8/4/20, Box 4, University of Illinois Archives, University of Illinois at Urbana-Champaign.

[7] Ibid., p. 2.

members asked whether creditors could reduce the size of mortgages in line with the fall in prices. Spokesmen for banks and life insurance companies said they would like to avoid foreclosures, since they did not want to own and operate farms; still, they could not scale back loans by some 50 percent. The director of the Federal Land Bank of St. Louis made the obvious point that federal "banks must borrow the money they lend." As such, federal lenders were obligated to pay interest on these borrowed funds "regularly and promptly," implying that banks could not simply write off farmers' bad debts without risking their own destruction. Private creditors also desperately needed a way out of the foreclosure crisis. One local banker said, "There is nothing to be gained these days by a dog-eat-dog policy," but he had no specific alternative to offer.[8]

As the Illinois conference revealed, farmers and creditors generally shared the view that private solutions would not work because the crisis had been created by an extraordinary collapse in the demand for crops. The conference participants identified two solutions, both beyond their power: to restore crop prices or to reduce the size of outstanding debts. Farmers lacked the market power to restore prices; creditors lacked the resources to reduce debts in line with the 50 percent drop in crop prices. Instead, it remained to the New Deal to fashion relief measures for both prices and credit.

1933: Experiments in credit, production, and price regulation

Since the federal government already had in place a public system of farm credit, one might have anticipated that the federal land banks provided a good measure of immediate relief. The land banks' past activities reinforced this expectation. By the end of the 1920s, they held 12 percent of the farm mortgages; but of greater importance, they had been especially active in areas where interest rates were high and alternative sources of credit relatively unavailable.[9]

Despite this promise, the banks did not accelerate their activities in the early 1930s. Two provisions in their 1916 charter held them back.

---

[8] Ibid., pp. 7, 11, 12.
[9] Among numerous studies, see Horton et al., "Farm-Mortgage Credit Facilities," pp. 12, 66–9; William G. Murray, *Agricultural Finance* (Ames: Iowa State College Press, 1941); and L. J. Norton, *Financing Agriculture* (Danville, Ill.: Interstate Press, 1938).

One provision defined the maximum size of a loan in terms of a farm's current market value. Farmers could not receive loans in excess of 50 percent of their farms' value plus 20 percent of the value of the buildings. Once the nominal value of farmland plunged after 1920, mortgages had often topped this 50–20 limit; the restriction prevented the most desperate farmers from turning to the federal land banks for aid. A second provision also constrained relief efforts. Under the original credit act, land banks obtained most of their funds through the sale of bonds on national credit markets. But after the 1929 Crash, bond prices dropped to such low levels that it was useless for member banks to issue new bonds. As a result, in the worst years of the foreclosure crisis – 1931, 1932, and 1933 – the land banks made less than half as many loans as they had averaged in the 1920s. Of all new public and private farm loans made in the early 1930s, public lenders accounted for less than 5 percent of the total.[10]

In an effort to refinance mortgages on a large scale, the new administration quickly consolidated and expanded its farm credit agencies. Executive Order 6084 created the Farm Credit Administration, which took charge of existing and new federal credit institutions. At the same time, the Emergency Farm Mortgage Act of May 12 made federal loans more generous. The maximum interest rate on mortgages was reduced from 6.0 to 4.5 percent.[11] Restrictions on the maximum size of a loan were also relaxed. Henceforth, property was assessed at its "normal" (not current) value, where normal was defined as the land's expected value when crops and livestock fetched parity prices – that is, prices that endowed farmers with the kind of purchasing power they had enjoyed in the years from 1909 to 1914. In 1933, a crop's parity price was easily 50 percent more than its current price, thus allowing for generous increases in the size of federally funded loans.[12]

[10] Farm Credit Administration, *Third Annual Report of the Farm Credit Administration* (Washington, D.C.: U.S. Government Printing Office, 1936), p. 121; Murray, *Agricultural Finance*, pp. 204–8; Horton et al. "Farm-Mortgage Credit Facilities," pp. 21–2, 88–9.

[11] Farm Credit Administration, *Second Annual Report of the Farm Credit Administration* (Washington, D.C.: U.S. Government Printing Office, 1935), pp. 18–19; Horton et al., "Farm-Mortgage Credit Facilities," pp. 78, 85, 89, 115. The Treasury subsidized rates by 0.5 to 2 points.

[12] In the next three years, more than 85 percent of all long-term loans offered through the FCA were used to refinance existing loans. See Farm Credit Administration, *First Annual Report of the Farm Credit Administration* (Washington, D.C.: U.S. Government Printing Office, 1934), p. 82; *Second Annual Report*, p. 97; and *Third Annual Report*, p. 19.

The act also authorized new, so-called Land Bank Commissioner loans. These loans were earmarked for farmers whose debts were so large that a single federal land bank loan would not be sufficient to refinance them. The loans were available as first or second mortgages with a rate of interest of 5 percent. A loan's term was typically ten years; and farmers were allowed to defer principal payments during the first three years.[13]

Besides these refinancing measures, the Farm Credit Act of 1933 revised federal lending procedures for intermediate loans. As noted in Chapter 3, the government already had established a set of twelve Federal Intermediate Credit Banks, but these organizations lent money only to other creditors, such as commercial banks, and not directly to farmers. Through the 1920s, few creditors sought their services, and the Federal Intermediate Credit Banks remained minor players in the farm credit market. To better supply intermediate credit, the act created the Production Credit Corporation. Through local organizations known as production credit associations (PCAs), the corporation loaned small sums directly to farmers at a rate of 5 percent.[14] Although less prevalent than the long-term loans, PCA loans served to help many farmers meet their short-term needs.[15]

By the end of 1933, the FCA had its entire emergency plan in place. Federal land banks and Land Bank Commissioner loans targeted farmers saddled with long-term mortgages. Interest rates were set at one point below the going market rate, first at 4.5 percent and later in 1935 at 3.5 percent. The terms were from ten to forty years. The legislation also made possible deferments on the principal of land

---

[13] In addition, in January 1934 the Federal Farm Mortgage Corporation was created and authorized to issue up to $2 billion in bonds whose proceeds would be used to supply funds for federal land bank or Land Bank Commissioner loans. Gladys L. Baker, Wayne D. Rasmussen, Vivian Wiser, and Jane M. Porter, *Century of Service: The First 100 Years of the United States Department of Agriculture* (Washington, D.C.: U.S. Government Printing Office, 1963), pp. 214–16; Horton et al., "Farm-Mortgage Credit Facilities," pp. 109–20.

[14] Murray, *Agricultural Finance*, pp. 252–60; W. I. Myers, "Permanent Sources of Cooperative Credit for Agriculture," *Mortgage Bankers Association of America 1935 Year Book* (Chicago: Mortgage Bankers Association, 1935), pp. 31–2.

[15] Aside from the Production Credit Corporation, Congress also created a credit system for lending to farm cooperatives. For a review of the different lending organizations, see Murray, *Agricultural Finance*, pp. 252–91.

bank loans for five years after 1933 and for Land Bank Commissioner loans for three years.[16]

As the FCA moved to refinance loans, Roosevelt sought to ensure that farmers had the "ability to pay" their mortgages. He signed into law his administration's basic price-control measure, the Agricultural Adjustment Act, on May 12, 1933. The act instructed the secretary of agriculture, Henry A. Wallace, to curb production and thereby raise prices of such "basic commodities" as wheat, cotton, corn, tobacco, rice, milk, and milk by-products.[17] The act listed several ways in which the secretary could cut production, but Wallace already had in mind a strategy, the so-called domestic allotment plan. Farmers were asked to sign contracts renting a portion of their land to the secretary of agriculture for a specified price per bushel of the crop normally grown there; farmers agreed, in turn, to leave that land fallow. For example, if a farmer rented 10 acres of land otherwise planted in corn at a rate of 50¢ per bushel and the average corn yield was 35 bushels per acre, then the government paid the farmer $175.[18]

When the act took effect on May 12, the new administration modified its plan. Because most farmers had already planted their fields, the AAA decided to pay farmers to plow under or otherwise

[16] In 1935 and subsequent years, Congress extended the emergency legislation. Starting in July 1935, the rate of interest on federal land bank loans was cut from 4.5 to 3.5 percent. For Land Bank Commissioner loans, interest rates began at 5 percent in May 1933, were reduced to 4 percent in July 1937, and were cut again to 3.5 percent in July 1940. This rate remained in effect into the war years. The 1935 act also extended the terms of Commissioner loans from a maximum of thirteen to forty years. The Farm Credit Act of 1937 made possible further deferments on Commissioner loans. Farm Credit Administration, *Third Annual Report*, pp. 20, 65–6; Horton et al., "Farm-Mortgage Credit Facilities," pp. 78, 90, 115–16, 119; U.S. Department of Agriculture, *Agricultural Finance Review*, 17 (November 1954), p. 88.

[17] In 1933 hogs were also included, but in later years only corn was counted as a basic commodity. In April 1934 Congress added seven other commodities: rye, flax, barley, sorghum, cattle, and peanuts. Potatoes were listed in August 1935. Edwin G. Nourse, Joseph S. Davis, and John D. Black, *Three Years of the Agricultural Adjustment Administration* (Washington, D.C.: Brookings Institution, 1937), p. 42.

[18] For the development of the domestic allotment program, see Richard S. Kirkendall, *Social Scientists and Farm Politics in the Age of Roosevelt* (Columbia: University of Missouri Press, 1967); and for the New Deal in general, see Theodore Saloutos, *The American Farmer and the New Deal* (Ames: Iowa State University Press, 1982).

destroy large parts of the potential 1933 harvests of such major crops as cotton, corn, and wheat. In the Cotton South, farmers contracted to plow under 25 to 50 percent of their cotton acreage at a price paid per pound of cotton on the average yield of each acre removed from production.[19] More than ten million acres were placed in contract – enough, the AAA hoped, to reduce supplies and boost cotton prices. In wheat states, farmers pledged to idle part of their acreage, but this plan was discarded when the Dust Bowl dramatically reduced the wheat harvest.[20] In the Corn Belt, because official forecasts for May and June predicted a small corn harvest, the AAA wrote no contracts. It offered some contracts to idle production of wheat, and launched a program to slaughter hogs with the hope of cutting excess pork supplies.[21]

As summer turned to fall, these measures failed to lift prices. In cotton states unusually good weather produced bumper yields despite the plow-under program, and cotton prices remained low. In the Midwest, early projections of a small corn harvest were replaced by August with forecasts of a large crop. Corn prices peaked in July and then fell. The hog slaughters tried to make up for sagging corn prices. Supplies shrank 10 percent, but this only gave political ammunition to Wallace's critics, who sported campaign buttons proclaiming "6,000,000 piglets Squeal, Hank Wallace's Raw Deal."[22] By early fall the AAA seemed hopeless to farmers, not so much for the unpopular hog-slaughter program as for its inability to raise their income. W. E. Crum, a country banker in Iowa, listed its failures: "We've tried reduction of surpluses by killing pigs and sows, by the wheat allotment plan, by paying bonuses for idle land." None worked. Crum explained that "the hog crop ... has been little affected. Farmers have sold some little pigs ... but others have bred more sows. I'm told there is more wheat sown in the county now than there was last year." Asking, "What else is there to do for the farmer?" Crum gave

[19] Saloutos, *The American Farmer and the New Deal*, pp. 67–8.
[20] Ibid., p. 75.
[21] Dennis Fitzgerald, *Corn and Hogs under the Agricultural Adjustment Act: Developments up to March 1934* (Washington, D.C.: Brookings Institution, 1934), pp. 4–6, 28–30.
[22] To make matters worse, the AAA intended to make its first installment of cash benefits to corn producers (who signed 1934 acreage reduction contracts) by December 1933. But in the early fall, the agency realized its own internal problems would keep it from meeting this deadline. Ibid., p. 57.

his answer: "Only one thing that I can see . . . is to give him a price for his products that will approximate the prices he was receiving when he went into debt."[23]

In succeeding weeks, the USDA sought to do as Crum asked. Secretary Wallace and his aides proposed another loan organization, the Commodity Credit Corporation, to assist corn and cotton farmers. The CCC established a fixed loan price per bushel of corn or per bale of cotton. The total amount of a loan equaled the CCC's loan price times the quantity of corn (or cotton) the farmer put up as collateral. Obtaining a loan was simple. An early memorandum announced: "Corn must be warehoused under seal on the farm[,] where State farm warehouse laws exist[,] and stored by producers in public warehouses in other states. The Warehouse certificate is to be the loan collateral." With the crop sealed and the certificate in hand, a farmer went directly to a local bank. Bank officers wrote a CCC loan and issued the farmer cash on the spot. Banks acted automatically because all CCC loans were backed by the U.S. government. Any farmer became eligible by signing a contract with the AAA restricting the amount of land under production for the next growing season. Officials made the loans relatively cheap. Including fees for sealing the corn, insurance, recording the loan, and an annual interest charge of 4 percent, a corn farmer would pay $25.68 for a loan of $450, or less than 3¢ a bushel.[24]

The CCC hoped this loan system would put cash into farmers' hands immediately. When an Iowa farmer received the first loan in late November, the *Des Moines Register* detailed the news in a front-

---

[23] G. W. Churchill, "A Country Banker's View of the Farm Problem," *Des Moines Register* (October 8, 1933), p. 7.

[24] Provisions for the 1933 loan were outlined in a memo entitled "Two Hundred Million Dollar Commitment for Loans on Corn," Office of the Secretary of Agriculture, Record Group 16, General Correspondence, 1933, Box 1816, Corn, pp. 1–2, National Archives, Washington, D.C. Estimates for the cost of a $450 loan and the cost per bushel were reported in "Summary of the 1933 Corn Loan Operation," Office of the Secretary of Agriculture, Record Group 16, General Correspondence, 1935, Box 2143, Corn 6, p. 3, National Archives. Evaluations of the CCC were found in this general correspondence. See, for instance, J. H. Lloyd, Director of the Department of Agriculture in Illinois, to Henry (Hank) Wallace, October 21, 1937, as well as instructions for completing a CCC loan application, Office of the Secretary of Agriculture, Record Group 16, General Correspondence, 1937, Box 2536, Corn 6, National Archives.

page story. Federal officials asserted that the CCC was "proof" that the government could get money to farmers. Under a headline "Cash Handed Over in 24 Hours," the article explained how the CCC loaned W. W. Eral of Pocahontas, Iowa, $585 "on a crib containing 1,300 bushels of corn" at a price of 45¢ a bushel. In order to show readers that Eral really had received this loan, it photographed each step of the application process. The last photo showed Eral outside his bank; the caption read: "Just to prove that the money he received on his government loan on corn was real, W. W. Eral of Pocahontas stopped long enough Friday afternoon to show the currency to several other Pocahontas county farmers" (Figure 5.1).[25]

In its effort to insure the cooperation of farmers like Eral, the CCC, as the *Des Moines Register* explained, wrote loans with a special "nonrecourse" feature: Eral's "corn is given as full security for the loan and if corn cannot be sold to net Eral 45 cents a bushel" by the time the loan expires, then Eral is free to have the corn "turned over to the Commodity Credit Corp. in full satisfaction of the obligation."[26] All farmers received this treatment. If, at the end of the loan period, typically twelve to eighteen months, the market price had not recovered, then the farmer could forfeit the crop and keep the money. Yet if the market improved, farmers stood to gain. Again the *Des Moines Register* took pains to explain this to readers: while "the crib on which the loan was granted is sealed until Aug. 1, 1934," Eral could reclaim the crop and sell it "prior to that time and then the loan becomes payable." Thus, "If corn is worth more than 45 cents, Eral gets the benefit of the increased price."[27] Like Eral, all farmers could meet their cash needs immediately; they could also wait for a chance to sell their crops at higher prices; and should prices decline, they had no fear of having to repay a loan at a lower market price.

By the end of 1933, farm relief depended in good part on the FCA, the AAA, and the CCC. Their introduction in 1933, however, gave no guarantee to their long-term survival let alone to their immediate role in providing relief. Each faced opposition, and their opponents initially cared more about the perceived problems of regulation than

[25] J. S. Russell, "Iowan Gets First U.S. Corn Loan," *Des Moines Register* (November 25, 1933), pp. 1, 4.
[26] Ibid., p. 4.
[27] Ibid. After the 1934 drought, the CCC expiration date for selling corn was extended from August 1, 1934, to January 1, 1935.

Figure 5.1. W. W. Eral of Pocahontas County, Iowa, displaying cash obtained from CCC loan in November, 1933. From "Iowan Gets First U.S. Corn Loan," *Des Moines Register* (November 25, 1933), p. 5. Courtesy of the *Des Moines Register*, Des Moines, Iowa.

about the need for relief. Some politicians, for instance, objected to subsidizing farm income whether through the AAA or the CCC. Private creditors objected to the FCA's loan policies. In normal times, their complaints would have compromised the legislation or killed it, as Coolidge's vetoes did in the 1920s. But the 1930s were not normal times. As they dealt with the consequences of the depressed markets, creditors and politicians alike found reasons to support the agencies in their relief efforts. Ironically, as these agencies acquired the ability to provide short-term relief, they obtained long-term roles in their respective markets.

1934–1936: Securing credit regulation

Implicit in the FCA's effort to mitigate the credit crisis was the assumption that private lenders would cooperate. Metropolitan Life, however, gave various reasons why lenders would not want to do so. Despite Congress's "good intentions," management told its correspondents that it feared that "every borrower of an insurance company will feel that he is entitled to a reduction of interest rate and to be placed on the same basis as the borrower of a Federal Land Bank." Management likewise objected to efforts to reduce the size of mortgages. Noting that "the executives of the Farm Credit Administration will do their utmost to bring about a scaling down of farmers' debts," they saw negative prospects for themselves, concluding: "Obviously, a scaling down of mortgages held by insurance companies . . . would not be a benefit." They also protested the FCA's subsidized interest rates, its extension of loan maturities, and its deferments of loan payments.[28] Unfortunately for the FCA, in order to refinance farmers, it needed creditors' support. It ultimately succeeded, once private lenders came to realize the consequences of delinquent farm loans.

Life insurance companies' troubles had their origin in the 1920s. Many firms invested as much as half their funds for mortgages in farm loans (Table 5.2). Although most of these loans remained in good standing during that decade, thousands became delinquent after 1929; and by 1932, insurance lenders suffered losses of more than 50 percent of their investments in several counties in midwestern states.[29] Inasmuch as farmers vigorously sought relief from burdensome debts by the early 1930s, their creditors also began to look for ways to avoid the losses associated with delinquent loans.

At first, farmers' and creditors' interrelated problems led not to cooperation but to conflict in the important case of state "moratoria" laws. In nearly every state where farm foreclosures rose sharply, legislatures either passed such laws or already had them in place.

[28] "Confidential Memorandum to Financial Correspondents, Branch Office Managers and Field Representatives" (1933) in V.F. Farm Loan Division (# 19 05 03), Metropolitan Life Insurance Company Archives, New York, New York.
[29] Lawrence A. Jones and David Durand, *Mortgage Lending Experience in Agriculture,* National Bureau of Economic Research (Princeton: Princeton University Press, 1954), p. 84. See also Figure 4.4.

Table 5.2. *Value of farm mortgages held by selected life insurance companies, 1933*[a]

Company	Value of farm mortgage loans[b]	As a percentage of all mortgage loans
Metropolitan	$139.8	10.3%
Prudential	185.1	18.0
Equitable (New York)	169.4	36.7
Northwestern	190.7	50.6
Travelers	55.9	59.4
John Hancock	146.8	56.6
Mutual Benefit	121.8	62.4
Aetna	43.9	67.4
Union Central[c]	117.7	80.0
Connecticut Mutual	31.8	58.4
Bankers Life	58.2	81.5
Equitable (Iowa)	44.3	87.5

[a]Data are reported for the twelve largest farm lenders among a total of twenty-six life insurance companies investigated by the Temporary National Economic Committee.
[b]Millions of dollars.
[c]In the New York Insurance report, Union Central is called Union Life.
Source: State of New York, *Seventy-fifth Annual Report of the Superintendent of Insurance. Part 2. Stock and Mutual Life Insurance Companies* (Albany, N.Y.: J. B. Lyon Printers, 1934), pp. 41–587.

Moratoriums prevented lenders from foreclosing delinquent borrowers' land for a period ranging from a few months in some states to four years in others. The laws were designed to give farmers a breathing spell. It was hoped that if farm foreclosures were halted for a limited period, markets would improve in the interim and farmers would be able to pay their creditors. Some insurance firms cooperated with state governments. Others, however, complained about such regulations.[30]

[30]Between 1932 and 1934, twenty-five states passed farm moratorium laws; eight more states already held lenient policies for farm foreclosures; and three more allowed courts room to be lenient in conducting farm foreclosures. Lee Alston argues that in response to the laws creditors reduced the funds available for farm mortgages. Lee J. Alston, "Farm Foreclosure Moratorium Legislation: A Lesson from the Past," *American Economic Review,* 74 (June 1984), pp. 446, 449, 451–6. For a map listing a slightly different mix of states that passed laws between 1930 and 1936, see

In Iowa, the conflict over moratoria laws produced a bitter struggle between Democrats and Republicans. The dispute accelerated when insurance firms (which held roughly 40 percent of outstanding farm mortgage debt in the state) tried to replace a 1933 moratoria bill farmers favored with their own weaker bill. Hostilities lingered so long that the Democrats were able to use the moratorium issue in the 1936 gubernatorial campaign. Under the slogan, "Come One! Come All! Watch Wil$on Sell the Farmer Short," Democrats charged that the Republican candidate, George Wilson, had earned legal fees of more than $30,000 from Bankers Life Insurance Company. He had voted to suspend insurance firms' "contracts with policy-holders until they could pay," and had voted against the farmers' version of the moratorium act (and for the insurance companies' version).[31] The Democrats' candidate, Nelson G. Kraschel, won the election.

As his victory indicated, the companies' strategy of weakening Iowa's moratoria law was risky. A less controversial strategy private lenders had initially favored involved plans to boost crop prices and farmers' incomes.[32] After a time, they considered another option: by cooperating with the FCA, they could win some relief for themselves as the agency brought relief to indebted farmers.

Metropolitan Life raised the issue of relief in 1933. The firm urged its agents to consider refinancing farmers' debts with the help of Land Bank Commissioner loans. Since this kind of loan could be used for a first mortgage of $5,000 or less, Met Life indicated that "any of our borrowers having a loan of less than $5,000 in default should be encouraged and assisted to make [an] application for a mortgage loan under this provision of the Act." It instructed agents to make similar provisions when Land Bank Commissioner loans were used as second mortgages, provided the firm did not have to agree "not to foreclose" on a second mortgage. Thus, for loans in default, Met

"Investigation of Concentration of Economic Power," U.S. Congress, Temporary National Economic Committee, *Hearings before the Temporary National Economic Committee, Part 28, Life Insurance Operating Results and Investments,* 76th Congress, 3rd sess. (February 12–16, 19–21, 26–9, and March 1, 1940), p. 14878.

[31] Campaign literature is found in Nelson George Kraschel Papers, MsC 174, Boxes 3 and 4, Special Collections Department, University of Iowa Libraries, Iowa City, Iowa.

[32] See for example "Higher Farm Prices Held Only Mortgage Situation Solution," *National Underwriter. Life Insurance Edition* (January 6, 1933), p. 1.

Table 5.3. *Proceeds of federal land bank and Land Bank Commissioner loans used to refinance farm mortgages held by life insurance companies and all lenders, May 1, 1933-January 1, 1937*

Lender	Federal loan proceeds used to refinance lenders 1933-7[a]	Outstanding farm mortgage debt held in 1933[a]	Federal proceeds as a percent of outstanding mortgage debt held in 1933
Life insurance companies	$305.8	$1,869.2	16.4%
All lenders[b]	1,504.2	8,638.4	17.4

[a]Millions of dollars.
[b]"All lenders" includes life insurance companies, commercial banks, individuals, federal banks, and other lending agencies.
Source: U.S. Congress, Temporary National Economic Committee, *Hearings before the Temporary National Economic Committee, Part 28, Life Insurance Operating Results and Investments,* 76th Congress, 3rd sess. (February 12-16, 19-21, 26-9, and March 1, 1940), p. 15505.

Life's agents were asked to consider the benefits of a federal loan program.[33]

Met Life and most other life insurance firms took part in the subsequent large-scale refinancing efforts. The Bureau of Agricultural Economics (BAE) estimated that federal agencies devoted $305.8 million, or 20 percent of their proceeds, from federal land bank and Land Bank Commissioner loans to the refinancing of mortgages held by insurance firms. Put another way, the federal proceeds served to remove 16 percent of all farm mortgages held by insurance firms in 1933 (Table 5.3). This figure underestimates the FCA's role. Since refinancing efforts addressed delinquent loans, by 1937 federal lenders had refinanced $305.8 million, or 40 percent of insurance firms' delinquent loans in 1933 (Table 5.1). For other creditors, federal agencies refinanced a similar proportion, 17 percent (Table 5.3). Unfortunately, records were not kept on overall rates of delinquency. If farmers were no more delinquent with commercial banks and individ-

[33] "Confidential Memorandum to Financial Correspondents, Branch Office Managers and Field Representatives" (1933).

uals than they were with insurance firms, then federal lenders provided substantial relief to these private creditors.

It is possible that federal agencies refinanced relatively good loans, but in 1940 Norman Wall, head of the Agricultural Finance Division of the Bureau of Agricultural Economics, testified before Congress that most federal loans went to refinance distressed loans.[34] Insurance representatives corroborated this conclusion. Speaking for Metropolitan Life (New York), Glenn Rogers stated that the FCA refinanced mortgages totaling $23.6 million and, of these, "close to $5,000,000 of our farm mortgages that were in good standing as to payment of interest, principal, and taxes at the time they were taken over." This left $18.6 million, or 80 percent, for delinquent mortgages. R. R. Rogers of Prudential, the second largest holder of farm loans, gave similar testimony, stating that the FCA assumed more than $18 million in farm loans. The committee asked Rogers: "Were most of the mortgages in bad shape or were there some that you considered adequate security?" He answered: "Some of them, possibly, but in most cases they were cases of dire need. It was a case where he owed storekeepers' bills, and so on, and it was a plan to refinance him, to start him off fresh."[35]

Northwestern Mutual, without the glare of congressional hearings, affirmed its own satisfaction with what was accomplished. M. J. Cleary, as president of Northwestern, the nation's largest farm lender among insurance firms, reported in 1938 that federal agencies had refinanced $67 million of the firm's farm mortgages. Northwestern had granted discounts on the principal in some cases and discounts on interest in most cases. Total discounts amounted to nearly $1.5 million on the $67 million investment. As Cleary explained, part of the refinancing was in the form of bonds that had increased substantially in value; should the company sell them, it would actually reap a net profit.[36]

[34] U.S. Congress, Temporary National Economic Committee, *Hearings before the Temporary National Economic Committee, Part 28, Life Insurance Operating Results and Investments*, p. 14879.

[35] Ibid., pp. 14996–7, 15047.

[36] "President Cleary's Message to Association," *Field Notes* (Milwaukee: Northwestern Mutual Life Insurance Company, 1938), p. 7. During the 1920s, the firm held 10 to 14 percent of the total farm investment made by life insurance companies. Harold F. Williamson and Orange A. Smalley, *Northwestern Mutual Life: A Century of Trusteeship* (Evanston, Ill.: Northwestern University Press, 1957), p. 212.

THOUSANDS OF APPLICATIONS

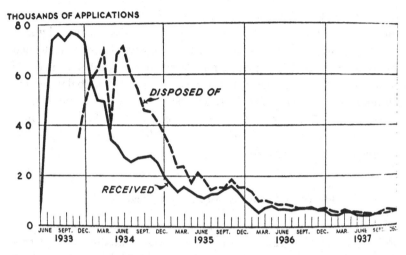

Figure 5.2. Receipts and disposals of mortgage loan applications for federal land bank and Land Bank Commissioner loans, 1933–6. (Not all disposals resulted in new loans.) Illustration from the Farm Credit Administration, *Fifth Annual Report of the Farm Credit Administration* (Washington, D.C.: U.S. Government Printing Office, 1938), p. 18.

Once private lenders began to work with the FCA, the public lender was able to refinance farm mortgages quickly. In its first year, it encountered delays and refinanced few loans, but in the next two years its pace quickened.[37] In 1934 alone it closed 496,501 loans (worth $1.28 billion) throughout the nation. In 1935, it closed 149,972 more loans, bringing the total amount loaned since its start to more than $2 billion. In its third annual report, the FCA concluded that its "emergency refinancing has largely been accomplished."[38] The experience of the next few years backed this claim. Figure 5.2, reproduced from the FCA's 1937 annual report, shows the pattern of

[37] By the end of 1933 federal land banks had closed a nationwide total of only 79,339 loans from among a half-million applicants. The FCA defended its slow start by asserting that it had less than three months to train appraisers as well as to set up an administrative network. The FCA blamed farmers too, saying that some farmers whose debts exceeded federal limits on the size of loans would have to ask the original lender to scale down the mortgage's interest rate or its principal. This took time. Still, excuses – even if some were valid – were no substitute for new loans. *Des Moines Register* (July 12, 1933), p. 1; *Des Moines Register* (August 10, 1933), pp. 1, 13; and *Des Moines Register* (August 13, 1933), p. 1. Farm Credit Administration, *First Annual Report*, p. 7.

[38] Farm Credit Administration, *Third Annual Report*, p. 8.

applications and disposal of applications (meaning processing either for or against the applicant) from 1933 to 1937. As one would guess, the volume of applications ballooned in 1933, while disposals leaped upward in 1934. But then applications and disposals trailed off through 1935. By the end of the year, the FCA had balanced the number of loans with disposals. Thereafter the level of applications (and disposals) remained relatively small. By December 1935, after thirty-two months of operation, the FCA felt it had accomplished its emergency refinancing effort.[39]

1934–1936: Securing price-support regulation

Like the FCA, the CCC faced opposition when it began operation in 1933. Neither Congress nor the White House initially assumed that the agency would have a long-term role in stabilizing crop prices. Indicative of this attitude was the CCC's charter: its authority to function as a government agency ran only from October 1933 to January 1935. But much like the FCA, the CCC was able to institutionalize its role in the agricultural system.

From the New Deal's earliest days, the Roosevelt administration had assumed that an agricultural recovery would be the basis of the industrial sector's return to prosperity. Federal officials held that farm prices had to be restored to parity – that is, to a level where farmers' ability to purchase nonfarm (industrial and service sector) goods matched their ability to buy these items during the prosperous years between 1909 and 1914. The administration's goal was to restore farmers' purchasing power to parity so that farmers could help provide the demand needed to pull American industry out of the Depres-

---

[39] In 1936, 84,030 applications were matched with 65,291 loans closed. In the next three years the number of applications, loans closed, and value of loans continued to shrink. See Farm Credit Administration, *Second Annual Report*, p. 9; *Third Annual Report*, p. 121; *Fourth Annual Report of the Farm Credit Administration* (Washington, D.C.: U.S. Government Printing Office, 1937), pp. 115, 121; *Fifth Annual Report of the Farm Credit Administration* (Washington, D.C.: U.S. Government Printing Office, 1938), pp. 115, 119, 155; *Sixth Annual Report of the Farm Credit Administration* (Washington, D.C.: U.S. Government Printing Office, 1939), p. 122; *Seventh Annual Report of the Farm Credit Administration* (Washington, D.C.: U.S. Government Printing Office, 1940), p. 140.

sion. However dubious this assumption was, it justified devoting special attention to farmers and their income.[40]

In 1933, the administration pinned its hopes of achieving parity on the AAA's acreage restriction programs. Unfortunately, this supply-side response encountered two problems. First, the AAA rarely succeeded in raising prices because its acreage restrictions failed most of the time to reduce production. For instance, although the number of acres planted in corn in the Midwest was cut 18 percent in the early 1930s and remained at this reduced level through 1939, yields rose and total corn production actually increased. Second, within two and a half years the AAA lost its major source of funding. In 1933 and 1934 it had relied on a special processing tax. But in January 1936, the Supreme Court ruled this tax unconstitutional, thereby forcing the AAA to depend on an annual congressional appropriation. Getting a large appropriation when Congress was already strapped for funds proved difficult, and the administration was compelled to consider alternative mechanisms for supporting farm income.

One option was the CCC. It attracted favorable press in the Midwest during the drought-ridden season of 1934. In 1933 many midwestern farmers had sealed their corn crop and taken out CCC loans. Instead of suffering from the drought, they reaped benefits: as the supply of corn dwindled, prices rose from forty-five to seventy cents and, in some places, to one dollar a bushel. To assess the program's outcome, reporters again interviewed the nation's first recipient of a CCC corn loan, W. W. Eral. He had just sold 1,300 bushels of corn he had pledged for his loan at the market price of seventy cents a bushel. This sum, Eral told reporters, was the "highest price paid for corn in this county since 1929." Having "signed up when I was nearly broke," the enthusiastic Eral urged that the CCC support system "be carried on indefinitely."[41]

[40] In hindsight this assumption is hard to swallow. By the 1930s America was largely an industrial nation. As such, the relatively small farm sector could not pull the rest of the economy out of the Depression. Albert U. Romasco, *The Politics of Recovery: Roosevelt's New Deal* (New York: Oxford University Press, 1983).

[41] Quoted in a newspaper article, "Eral Winds Up Loan on Corn," in Evans Scrapbook, 1933–6, Inventory Number 6, n.p., n.d., Rudolph Martin Evans Papers, MsC 74, Special Collections Department, University of Iowa Libraries, University of Iowa.

Thanks to Eral and like-minded farmers, Secretary of Agriculture Henry Wallace reaped his own political harvest. Writing from Des Moines, Iowa, one Democrat noted: "Henry is no longer being looked upon as a dreamer" because "the corn and hog program and the corn loan program are receiving more support out here than ever before. . . . Even the business men and bankers are now for the program." Wallace had been an early fan of the CCC, which he liked to call the "ever normal granary." In his 1934 book, *New Frontiers,* Wallace claimed that the CCC would benefit consumers and farmers alike because it could be "used to stabilize the corn price at a fair level, to keep it from going unduly low in years of low price and unduly high in years of high price."[42] Initially, Wallace was unusual insofar as he anticipated a major, long-term role for the CCC; but after a sequence of good and bad years in the 1930s, his ideas acquired wide support.

The largest, more conservative, and more influential farm lobbying group, the American Farm Bureau Federation, gradually accepted this position. In 1933 Earl Smith, then head of the Illinois chapter of the Farm Bureau, claimed he had suggested an emergency corn loan program to Roosevelt.[43] But beyond his claims, newsletters spoke little about the plan in 1933 or 1934. By 1935, however, the Farm Bureau had changed its mind. Typical was its story of an Illinois farmer, Alden Sutter. Sutter had stored his corn with the CCC in 1933 and, after the drought started, sold some at fifty-two cents and the rest at seventy-two cents a bushel. Generalizing from Sutter's experience, the story concluded: "Alden Sutter and his father were foresighted when they held . . . old corn until the corn loan was secured. But so were thousands of others. The point is that without the farm price-raising program . . . these things wouldn't have happened."[44] The Farm Bureau thought the CCC was the best mechanism to ensure fair prices for farmers, particularly where its membership was strong in the South

[42] Joseph S. Davis notes that Wallace had developed this idea "at least 10 to 15 years before he entered the Roosevelt Cabinet." See Joseph S. Davis, "The Economics of the Ever-Normal Granary," *Journal of Farm Economics,* 20 (February 1938), p. 8.

[43] Christiana McFadyen Campbell, *The Farm Bureau and the New Deal* (Urbana: University of Illinois Press, 1962), pp. 65–6.

[44] Sutter's story is reported in "Farm Program Is Restoring Prosperity . . . Read What Central Illinois Farmers Say about It," *Farm Bureau* (August–September 1935), p. 8.

and the Midwest. The president of the Farm Bureau, Ed. O'Neal, claimed he was in the odd position of supporting Wallace's price-support program when some of his presumed friends – members of Congress – balked over government price fixing.[45]

A number of members of Congress had raised questions about the plan's funding. Initially, the CCC appeared as vulnerable to cutbacks as the AAA. The agency had been granted the paltry sum of $3 million to carry out its operations, and like the AAA, it had returned to Congress, asking for new and larger sums of capital. The need for funding arose out of a faulty assumption. It was at first presumed that whenever the CCC made loans to farmers, the market price would rise above the loan rate before the loan period expired. Then farmers could sell their crop and pay off their loans. As it turned out, however, market prices all too often remained depressed. Once the loans expired, farmers simply forfeited the crop and kept the loaned money. That burdened the CCC with large stocks of corn or cotton (the two crops covered by the CCC), and created the agency's need for government money to recover its lost funds. Only Congress could allocate the money; and if Congress refused, the CCC would collapse.

Congress did not reject the agency's requests, however, as the first case revealed. Jesse Jones, chairman of the Reconstruction Finance Corporation (RFC), the CCC's parent corporation, handled the issue. Jones first requested funds in February 1936. The 1934 cotton crop, he explained, had created the problem.[46] The CCC had offered farmers 12¢ a pound for cotton in 1934, and farmers had taken out $300 million in loans. In 1935 market prices were still in a slump, and the CCC extended the farmers' loans into that year. The CCC decided against another loan extension for 1936, and with prices still low farmers forfeited the crop. This left the CCC obliged to pay $300 million it owed the RFC. It could choose between two solutions. It could, as Representative Thomas Ford proposed, simply liquidate its cotton stocks by selling them.[47] That would enable it to pay its debts,

---

[45] Campbell, *The Farm Bureau and the New Deal*, pp. 111–14.

[46] Jones was blaming the symptom, not the cause. To be correct, he should have blamed the CCC because it made a loan well above the going price of cotton.

[47] U.S. Congress, House, *To Enable the Commodity Credit Corporation to Better Serve the Farmers in Orderly Marketing, and to Provide Credit and Facilities for Carrying Surpluses from Season to Season*, 74th Congress, 2nd sess. (February 1936), p. 6.

but the increase in cotton supplies might send prices to ruinously low
levels. Jones feared this outcome, saying the action would "tear the
market to pieces."[48] He proposed a second solution: borrowing the
money. This could be difficult: "The Commodity Credit Corporation," Jones said, "owes $300,000,000 with $3,000,000 in capital.
That does not present a very good financial picture if you want to go
into the market and borrow money."[49] If, however, the RFC turned
debts of $97 million into capital stock, then the CCC's capitalization
would be $100 million and its debts $203 million. With this ratio, the
corporation should be able to borrow on the collateral of its cotton.
Jones asked the committee to convert one-third of the agency's debt
into capital.

Some senators rejected Jones's recommendation. They wanted to
put an end to the loan corporation. Senators Thomas Gore of Oklahoma and James Couzens of Michigan instructed:

GORE: Does this bill contemplate unwinding the whole business?
JONES: It will put us in a position where we can unwind. That is exactly
the purpose.
GORE: To get out of the business, it seems to me is the thing to do.
COUZENS: I think you [Mr. Jones] would be doing the smart thing if you
would ask us to repeal the section of the Reconstruction Finance
Corporation Act you have read instead of asking us to extend your
powers and authority with respect to lending.
GORE: I think any scheme that encourages farmers and makes it easy for
them to carry one crop over against another crop is fundamentally
unsound. It will bring disaster. That is what all of these things
have done.[50]

Jones agreed with the two senators that "unwinding the whole
business" was the ultimate goal, but he wanted them to wait until
the CCC could unwind without affecting prices. In 1936, as Jones
recognized, the economic and political consequences of letting prices
fall would keep senators like Gore and Couzens in check. As long as
demand for cotton and corn remained depressed, the CCC was too
important to eliminate. Jones's refinancing proposal was approved by

[48] Ibid.
[49] Ibid., p. 4.
[50] U.S. Congress, Senate, *To Increase R.F.C. Subscription to Capital Stock of
the Commodity Credit Corporation*, 74th Congress, 2nd sess. (February
1936), pp. 7–9.

Congress, and the CCC acquired a secure position in U.S. agricultural policy.

Congress acknowledged the growing consensus behind the CCC when in February 1938 it drafted new farm legislation. The Second Agricultural Adjustment Act explicitly instructed the CCC to set the loan rate of cash crops between specific parity ranges. Cotton and wheat prices were to vary between 52 and 75 percent of parity. Loan prices for corn were also set between 52 and 75 percent of parity (with the loan rate declining as the annual supply rose above its average).[51] The act further ordered the CCC not to unload accumulated stocks of commodities on the open market until prices had risen well above the original loan rates.

Technically, the Agricultural Adjustment Act of 1938 did not change the CCC's status. Until Congress granted it a charter in 1948, the agency remained a temporary organization. But politically, its status had risen dramatically between 1933 and 1938. In 1936, it had passed a severe political test when members of Congress concluded (some reluctantly) that they must continue funding the agency because abolishing it would mean "tearing the market to pieces." By 1937, the CCC was identified as the "heart" of efforts to sustain agriculture. As the Farm Bureau swung its weight behind the bill, Wallace convinced Congress to make the CCC the primary means of stabilizing farm prices and farm income.[52]

Regulation versus relief

By the mid-1930s, both the FCA and the CCC had won long-term roles in their respective markets. The FCA had refinanced most applicants by the end of that year. By 1936, the CCC was secure in its funding, and in February 1938 the Agricultural Adjustment Act gave this organization the lead role among the agencies established. Finally, the AAA remained as a partner with the CCC in seeing that

[51] Murray R. Benedict, *Can We Solve the Farm Problem?* (New York: Twentieth Century Fund, 1955), p. 255. Also on the 1938 act, see Michael W. Schuyler, *The Dread of Plenty: Agricultural Relief Activities of the Federal Government in the Middle West, 1933–1939* (Manhattan, Kans.: Sunflower University Press, 1989), pp. 183–200.

[52] Davis, "The Economics of the Ever-Normal Granary," p. 8.

production was limited as prices were raised. While these three agencies were providing an important measure of agrarian relief, their concept of "relief" had a narrow definition. The market-oriented programs supposedly addressed all farmers, including so-called marginal farmers who could not earn enough income – whether because of the amount or quality of their land – to support their families and to remain viable competitors. In practice, however, neither market-oriented policies nor special New Deal programs substantially aided these impoverished farmers, namely those most in need of relief.

According to government officials, even in the late 1930s 1.7 million farm families, accounting for perhaps 8 million persons, had less than $500 in annual earnings.[53] Many families had been caught in the Dust Bowl. In theory the AAA provided them with income for reducing acreage planted in wheat, but without crops all too often these farmers became migrants whom Route 66 would drop into California. Even without the Dust Bowl, rural poverty plagued many regions, especially in the South where farms were small and share-cropping common. In theory tenants received their share of AAA checks. But with administration left in the hands of local white and wealthy farmers, theory did not always see its way into practice.[54]

Congress, of course, created programs for farmers impoverished by special circumstances. In states afflicted by droughts and dust storms, the federal government provided emergency seed loans. The Shelter-belt Project also brought aid to hard-hit producers.[55] For all regions, the Resettlement Administration (created in 1935) and its 1937 successor, the Farm Security Administration (FSA), assisted marginal

[53] Schuyler, The Dread of Plenty, p. 179.
[54] On the Dust Bowl, see James Gregory, American Exodus: The Dust Bowl Migration and Okie Culture in California (New York: Oxford University Press, 1989); R. Douglas Hurt, The Dust Bowl: An Agricultural and Social History (Chicago: Nelson-Hall, 1981); Schuyler, The Dread of Plenty, pp. 163–82; Donald Worster, Dust Bowl: The Southern Plains in the 1930s (New York: Oxford University Press, 1979). For the South, see Pete Daniel, Breaking the Land: The Transformation of Cotton, Tobacco, and Rice Cultures since 1880 (Urbana: University of Illinois Press, 1988); Paul E. Mertz, New Deal Policy and Southern Rural Poverty (Baton Rouge: Louisiana State University Press, 1978). Theodore Saloutos also reviews rural poverty by region, in The American Farmer and the New Deal (Ames: Iowa State University Press, 1982), pp. 150–4.
[55] Saloutos, The American Farmer and the New Deal, pp. 192–207; Schuyler, The Dread of Plenty, pp. 81–225.

farmers. The Bankhead–Jones Farm Tenant Act of 1937 provided for special loans at 3 percent interest. But in all cases, a shortage of funds hampered relief. As of 1939, applications from tenant farmers for loans outnumbered approvals by a margin of 34 to 1. As for the FSA, by 1939 it had given some kind of assistance to more than 1.2 million farmers. In a survey of a quarter of these farmers, they reported substantial improvements but their gains came from a terribly low base: whereas their average income was $375 when they joined in the mid-1930s, it averaged just $538 in 1939. Moreover, the process of resettling poor areas, particularly the western section of the Great Plains and the Great Lakes cutover region, had fallen far short of expectations, and the core programs of the New Deal – the three market-oriented agencies – were clearly not reaching those most in need.[56]

The three regulatory agencies exerted more of their impact on those on the middle and upper rungs of the farm ladder. For these farmers, the regulatory agencies acted in unexpected ways that had little to do with relief and much to do with the questions of farm investment and farm productivity. Their goal was not to raise productivity. In fact, officials hoped that regulation could cut output so as to raise prices. But in reality the programs promoted increases in productivity by changing farmers' investment climate. Low prices, the culprit in 1933, represented one of the risks farmers had wanted to guard against. Burdensome debts also represented a barrier to long-term investment. Because government regulation altered the pattern of crop prices and the nature of credit markets, it transformed the climate for investment along these lines. Over the long term, these policies and programs would favor farmers who invested in land and labor-saving technology – the kind of investments that farmers most in need of relief were least able to make.

[56] Mertz, New Deal Policy and Southern Rural Poverty, pp. 206–20; Saloutos, The American Farmer and the New Deal, pp. 266–7; Schuyler, The Dread of Plenty, pp. 127, 170–82, 203–4, 212. For rural poverty in the South after 1940, see Daniel, Breaking the Land; and Bruce J. Schulman, From Cotton Belt to Sunbelt: Federal Policy, Economic Development, and the Transformation of the South, 1938–1980 (New York: Oxford University Press, 1991).

6. "If You'll Need a Tractor in 1936 You Ought to Order It Now"

In November 1935, International Harvester advertised its tractors not on the basis of low prices, as one might expect for the Great Depression. Instead, in a bold headline, IHC advised any farmer who wanted a tractor for next spring: "You Ought to Order It Now." Harvester explained: "One of the surprises of 1935 was the big demand that developed for new farm tractors. As early as January the flood of orders had reached a peak far greater than we could fill. Production went on at top speed, but it takes time to build the finely coordinated quality tractors of today. Thousands of farmers were greatly disappointed in not getting their tractors at the time they needed them most."[1] A few years earlier, in 1932 and 1933, prospects had looked grim for the industry's number-one firm. Harvester had reported losses for the first time in its history. But two years later Harvester earned $19.6 million and attributed much of its recovery to the tractor and farm implement markets.[2]

One might expect that the jump in tractor sales reflected a dramatic surge in farm income. Farm leaders in Congress were certainly trying hard to restore farm income to pre-Depression levels, if not to the more prosperous "parity" era prior to World War I (1909–14). After 1932 prices began rising, but in fact they never reached parity, nor even the levels of the 1920s. Nor did the recovery in prices necessarily provide better farm incomes. In 1934 and 1936, prices were boosted by two droughts that cut corn yields in half – roughly to sixteen bushels per acre. Higher prices therefore obscured the actual trend in profits, because as yields fell by 50 percent, per-bushel costs doubled. So a significant part of the earnings that the droughts had added in

[1] "If You'll Need a Tractor in 1936 You Ought to Order it Now . . .," International Harvester advertisement as printed in *Bureau Farmer*, 11 (November 1935), p. 9.
[2] International Harvester Company, *Annual Report, 1935*, p. 3.

the form of higher prices, they took back in lower yields and higher costs. Only in the Depression's last three years did the situation brighten. In 1937, 1938, and 1939, midwestern corn prices – backed by New Deal price supports – averaged fifty-four cents a bushel. Overall gross farm earnings in the Corn Belt increased 43 percent in the second half of the 1930s. But even with government payments included, this amount still fell short of the corresponding income for the late 1920s.[3]

Despite the trends in farm income, farmers invested in technology and achieved significant gains in productivity during the Depression (Table 6.1). Corn yields (land productivity) climbed more than 25 percent between 1929 and 1939. Labor productivity rose 18 percent, a rate that was at least two-thirds larger than the pace recorded for the 1920s (Appendix C).[4]

[3] Farm prices are calculated from the U.S. Department of Agriculture, *Agricultural Statistics, 1942* (Washington, D.C.: U.S. Government Printing Office, 1942), p. 66. Gross farm earnings are reported in U.S. Department of Commerce, *Statistical Abstract of the United States: 1930* (Washington, D.C.: U.S. Government Printing Office, 1930), p. 651; U.S. Department of Commerce, *Statistical Abstract of the United States: 1932* (Washington, D.C.: U.S. Government Printing Office, 1932), p. 603; U.S. Department of Commerce, *Statistical Abstract of the United States: 1934* (Washington, D.C.: U.S. Government Printing Office, 1934), p. 572; U.S. Department of Commerce, *Statistical Abstract of the United States: 1936* (Washington, D.C.: U.S. Government Printing Office, 1936), p. 603; U.S. Department of Commerce, *Statistical Abstract of the United States: 1938* (Washington, D.C.: U.S. Government Printing Office, 1939), p. 618; U.S. Department of Commerce, *Statistical Abstract of the United States: 1940* (Washington, D.C.: U.S. Government Printing Office, 1941), p. 670.

[4] In Appendix C, I consider other factors that affect my calculations for changes in labor productivity in the 1930s as compared to figures the WPA estimated for the 1920s. I find that by adjusting my estimates to exclude Missouri (so as to be consistent with the states used in the WPA calculations), labor hours fell by roughly 20 percent, or by almost twice the pace that was set in the 1920s. Had I also included an adjustment for the mechanical corn picker's usage rate from 1938 to 1939, harvest hours would have been smaller, and total labor savings would have been somewhat higher. Although the WPA includes some changes in productivity due to changes in farming practices (as opposed to mechanization), I am not able to include these factors. By altering figures in the 1920s and 1930s so as to compare the two on a similar basis (that is, to exclude factors other than mechanization in the 1920s, or to include factors other than mechanization in the 1930s) the rate of savings in the 1930s would have been more than two-thirds larger than the rate of increase reported for the 1920s. I discuss these issues in Appendix C.

Table 6.1. *Land and labor productivity in corn production, the Corn Belt, 1920-40*

Land productivity	Level of productivity			Change (%)	
	1918-19	1928-29	1938-39	1918/19-1928/9	1928/29-1938/9
Corn bushels per acre[a]	34.5	34.8	44.2	0.9%	27.0%

Labor productivity[b]	Level of productivity			Change (%)	
	1919	1929	1939	1919-29	1929-39
WPA	22.7	20.2	---	-11.0%	
Appendix C	---	12.38	10.18		-17.8%

[a]Corn yields are calculated as the average for yields in the five Corn Belt states. In reporting yields, I have taken the average of the last two years at the end of each decade. I do this because yields in 1919 and 1939 tended to be slightly high, while they were slightly off in 1929. If I only compared the last year of the decade, then the results would show a decline in yields of 9 percent from 1919 to 1929.
[b]Labor productivity is measured in hours spent raising an acre of corn. There is no single source for calculating labor productivity from 1919 to 1939. I calculate changes in productivity from 1919 to 1929 for four midwestern states -- Illinois, Indiana, Iowa, and Ohio -- based on data from a Works Progress Administration report. I calculate changes for the years 1929 to 1939 based on data in Appendix C.
Sources: Corn yields are reported in U.S. Department of Agriculture, *Yearbook of Agriculture, 1921* (Washington, D.C.: U.S. Government Printing Office, 1921), p. 512; U.S. Department of Agriculture, *Yearbook of Agriculture, 1931* (Washington, D.C.: U.S. Government Printing Office, 1932), p. 620; U.S. Department of Agriculture, *Agricultural Statistics, 1940* (Washington, D.C.: U.S. Government Printing Office, 1940), p. 47, and *Agricultural Statistics, 1941* (Washington, D.C.: U.S. Government Printing Office, 1942), p. 50. For changes in labor productivity, see Works Progress Administration, *Changes in Technology and Labor Requirements in Production: Corn*, Report No. A-5 (Philadelphia, 1938), p. 149, and my Appendix C.

The coming of New Deal regulation had coincided with this upturn in productivity. But it is not clear whether regulation contributed to these gains. Did regulation matter to the diffusion of technology? If so, had it simply created short-term incentives to increase output or had regulation substantially altered, if inadvertently, farmers' investment climate? The answer to both choices is yes, I will argue. But the process was both regulation- and technology-specific; where one finds a positive answer depends on the type of technology selected (hybrid corn, the mechanical corn picker, or the tractor) and on the kind of regulation (acreage controls, prices controls, or credit policies).

Interpretations of technology and regulation also vary in terms of land and labor productivity. For land productivity, the AAA created short-term pressures for farmers to raise yields on what land they kept in production. For labor productivity, by contrast, regulation exerted long-term changes in the climate for investment. The CCC altered the risk of losses in the future as long as price supports designed to raise farm income were set high enough to reduce price volatility and secure an important part of farmers' cost of production. Similarly, the FCA in refinancing farm loans created new conditions under which farmers borrowed money, conditions that made debt financing more profitable to a competitive farmer. Such policies had implications beyond farmers. They encouraged private creditors to alter the loans they made available to farmers. The regulation also offered a new element of confidence for implement manufacturers and their dealers.

Inasmuch as the CCC and the FCA initiated long-term changes in the relationship between farmers and their markets, how these changes played out in agriculture depended upon the manner in which certain specific questions are answered. First, did the new types of technology require substantial cash outlays? If not − if relatively inexpensive inventions were responsible for the productivity gains − then regulation would have been irrelevant. Second, did the New Deal effectively alter farmers' investment climate? Were CCC loan rates set high enough to cover cash expenses? Did the FCA, while refinancing thousands of loans, substantially alter the kind of loans these borrowers obtained? Finally, there is the question of timing. The CCC and the FCA secured long-term changes in commodity and credit markets only after 1933. Regulation could not have been responsible for the productivity gains, then, unless the gains came in the second half of the 1930s.

Raising corn yields: The AAA and hybrid corn

The AAA intended to restrict output so as to raise prices by removing crop acreage from corn production. But as one critic asked Secretary Wallace, "How do you know that they [farmers] are all honest?" adding, "perhaps some of them are as tricky as politicians and some government servants."[5] It would be easy for farmers to trick the AAA by simply setting aside their least fertile acres. Smaller acreage would be countered with higher corn yields. It is likely that the farmers Russell Lee photographed understood this perverse incentive as they snickered at the official presenting the latest soil conservation provisions (Figure 6.1).

Farmers had other reasons to grin. The acreage restrictions also brought about a second and stronger effect on yields. In 1936 when the Supreme Court ruled that the federal government could not pay farmers to restrict production, the court did not eliminate the possibility of paying farmers to plant certain crops. Hence the idea of soil conservation was hatched. The AAA paid farmers to plant "soil building" crops in place of "soil depleters," where the soil builders were defined as legumes and pasture crops, and the soil depleters included all the major cash crops, such as corn and cotton. By following the new program – that is, by adopting better conservation practices – farmers further increased yields. A WPA study reported that if farmers reduced the proportion of land planted in corn each year from 60 to 40 percent and planted soil-conserving crops instead, then average yields would increase 11 to 15 percent.[6] After 1933, farmers converted 18 percent of their total corn acreage to other crops; at this rate, the AAA programs contributed to roughly an 8 percent increase in corn yields.

That the AAA boosted corn yields did not mean, however, that it

[5] Letter to Henry Wallace, August 26, 1935, Office of the Secretary of Agriculture, Record Group 16, General Correspondence, 1935, Box 2143, Corn 5, National Archives, Washington, D.C.
[6] Works Progress Administration, *Changes in Technology and Labor Requirements in Production: Corn*, Report No. A-5 (Philadelphia, 1938), pp. 25–7.

Figure 6.1. Soil Conservation Meeting of Farmers in Livingston County, Illinois, 1937. Photo by Russell Lee. From 34–10464–D, U.S. Farm Security Administration Collection, Prints and Photographs Division, Library of Congress, Washington, D.C.

necessarily promoted the diffusion of the new land-saving invention, hybrid corn. The seed quickly acquired a reputation on its own for earning profits. In a 1936 advertisement, the DeKalb Agricultural Association promised that its "Winged Ear" corn would be a farmer's "Mortgage Lifter."[7] Experiments showed that this hybrid yielded "from 75 to 90 bushels per acre on good land." Even if DeKalb exaggerated, it was evident by the late 1930s from experiment studies that hybrids increased productivity. Prior to 1936, reports were mixed; their yields averaged perhaps 10 percent more than existing open-pollinated brands. By 1936, however, the Iowa station was

[7] "Winged Ear Corn," DeKalb Agricultural Association advertisement in *Prairie Farmer*, Illinois Edition (October 24, 1936), p. 40. This advertisement as well as the development of hybrid corn are reviewed by Deborah Fitzgerald, *The Business of Breeding: Hybrid Corn in Illinois, 1890–1940* (Ithaca, N.Y.: Cornell University Press, 1990).

reporting 30 percent gains, and by 1940, Illinois was reporting gains of 50 percent. A 1938 WPA study concluded that at the very least hybrids offered a 10 percent advantage over open-pollinated varieties; it speculated that maximum gains might amount to more than 35 percent, and average gains at least 20 percent.[8]

If farmers, like the one at a 1939 Hardin County, Iowa, cornhusking contest (Figure 6.2), could count on a simple gain of 20 percent in their corn yields, then hybrids would nearly sell themselves. A bushel cost a farmer about $7.75 and seeded seven acres, bringing the cost of planting eighty acres in hybrid corn to roughly $90.[9] But the 20 percent increase in yields translated into earnings that easily exceeded this cash expense. At the late Depression (1935–9) average price of 50¢ per bushel, a farmer would earn $300 more in revenues, or $210 in operating profits. To actually lose money, the going price of corn had to decline to a level where the extra revenues no longer offset the seed's initial cost. Hybrid corn was an unusual variable-cost item in this regard. Because it was so profitable, for farmers to actually lose money the market price of corn had to drop to 12¢ a bushel. Yet even in the worst years of the Depression, the price had sunk no lower than 32¢. Thus farmers could invest in hybrid corn knowing they would earn additional revenues at the harvest. Based on the average increase in yields of 20 percent and the average market price of corn of 50¢ a bushel, farmers earned a 200 percent return on their new investment.

As of 1936 farmers were planting only 5 percent of their cornfields with hybrids, but in the next four years, as researchers reported gains

[8] R. R. Copper, G. H. Dungan, A. L. Lang, J. H. Bigger, B. Koehler, and O. Bolin, "Illinois Corn Performance Tests 1940," University of Illinois Agricultural Experiment Station Bulletin No. 474 (January 1941), pp. 173–223; M. M. Rhoades and Joe L. Robinson, "The 1936 Iowa Corn Test," Iowa Agricultural Experiment Station Bulletin No. 355 (February 1937), pp. 185–240; Joe L. Robinson and M. M. Rhoades, "The 1935 Iowa Corn Yield Test," Iowa Agricultural Experiment Station Bulletin No. 343 (February 1936), pp. 149–98; Works Progress Administration, *Changes in Technology: Corn*, p. 16.

[9] Bryce Ryan and Neal Cross, "Acceptance and Diffusion of Hybrid Corn Seed in Two Iowa Communities," Iowa State University Research Bulletin No. 372 (January 1950), p. 668; hybrid corn prices are found in U.S. Department of Agriculture, "Prices Paid by Farmers for Seed," Statistical Bulletin No. 328 (1963), pp. 97–101. Ryan and Cross estimated the cost of open-pollinated seed averaged about fifty cents a bushel.

Figure 6.2. Examining hybrid corn at a corn-husking contest in Hardin County, Iowa, 1939. From 33–3434–M3, U.S. Farm Security Administration Collection, Prints and Photographs Division, Library of Congress, Washington, D.C.

ranging from 35 to 50 percent, the diffusion of hybrid corn rose sharply. By 1940, over 90 percent of all corn in Iowa was a hybrid, and two-thirds of all midwestern cornfields were planted with this seed.[10] If one assumes, as the WPA did, that hybrid corn raised yields by 20 percent on average, then (after adjusting for the percentage of land planted in hybrids), the new seed raised land productivity by 13 to 15 percent. If hybrid corn's advantage was as great as 25 or 30 percent, then it raised land productivity by 17 to 20 percent.

Together, hybrid corn and the AAA raised yields by 22 percent, and possibly by 25 percent. Hybrid corn was clearly more important: at least half and possibly two-thirds of the gains in land productivity derived from an invention that farmers adopted because it was cheap and its returns were high. One-third of the gains can be ascribed to a program that backfired – trying to restrict output but nevertheless giving farmers at least two tactics to boost yields on existing acreage.

If we focus on corn, then the results of regulation were that the AAA spurred gains in productivity, but it promoted the diffusion of hybrid corn only indirectly. Hybrid corn was exceptional because it was so profitable. As a result, market forces could best account for the seed's popularity. Can we draw the same conclusion about investments in machinery for changes in labor productivity?

Mechanical technology

The two major mechanical inventions in the 1930s were the mechanical corn picker and the tractor. Neither machine was as clearly profitable as the new seed. Their cost savings came in reducing labor time, a part of production that most farm families supplied themselves and did not value at market rates. Both machines were also expensive. Whereas hybrid corn could be purchased in small quantities each year, the capital equipment required a lump sum payment of $600 to $1,000.

[10]U.S. Department of Agriculture, *Agricultural Statistics, 1944* (Washington, D.C.: U.S. Government Printing Office, 1944), p. 39. For the distribution of seed, see the Works Progress Administration, *Changes in Technology: Corn*, p. 16. Zvi Griliches, "Hybrid Corn: An Exploration in the Economics of Technological Change," *Econometrica*, 25 (October 1957), pp. 501–22.

Few farmers had purchased the mechanical corn picker in the years prior to the Depression. The machine attracted attention in World War I, and again near the late 1920s. A few reports were optimistic about the harvester's use in the late 1920s, but actual practice fell short of this mark.[11] The WPA reported that the corn picker's diffusion had reached just 5 percent in 1929. In the early Depression, the survey found corn pickers "only in the Western Dairy, Corn and Small Grain Areas, and in these in limited numbers only. Even in the Corn Area, where this machine had the greatest acceptance, it was used in 1936 by only 5 percent of the growers surveyed."[12] By the late 1930s, however, more farmers had begun to use harvesters, and a USDA survey reported that 28 percent of the whole Corn Belt was machine harvested in 1938.[13]

Higher yields accounted for much of the machine's new popularity in the late 1930s. A mechanical picker cost a farmer no more to run through a field of 500 bushels of corn than through the same field of 1,000 bushels, so per-bushel harvesting costs fell in proportion to the increase in yields. In hand picking, by contrast, workers were paid a flat rate per bushel. As hybrids and the effects of the AAA boosted yields, they reduced a machine's cost per bushel, and in doing so, lowered a machine's per-bushel costs relative to the cost of hand picking.

By the late 1930s, corn yields had increased to an average of forty-five bushels per acre and made corn pickers very competitive with hand husking. Table 6.2 provides a simple acreage threshold for the corn picker based on its costs relative to hand husking. A farmer needed to plant 53 acres in corn in order to profit from the harvester. Or, with roughly 35 percent of a farm planted in corn, the threshold amounted to a total farm size of roughly 150 acres. This threshold indicated that substantial numbers of farmers should have used a mechanical picker, and records indicate that they did so. In Illinois, for example, 46 percent of the farms passed the acreage threshold

[11] See, for example, Jay Whitson, "Northern Iowa Adopts the Corn Picker," *Wallaces' Farmer*, 11 (November 18, 1929), p. 1408.

[12] Works Progress Administration, *Changes in Technology: Corn*, pp. 11, 87.

[13] U.S. Department of Agriculture, *Agricultural Statistics, 1940* (Washington, D.C.: U.S. Government Printing Office, 1941), p. 563. Sales are reported in Works Progress Administration, *Changes in Technology: Corn*, p. 108.

Table 6.2. *The mechanical corn picker's acreage threshold, 1937*[a]

Costs	Mechanical picker	Hand husking
Fixed costs		
Picker	$137.67	
Tractor	39.77	
Total	$177.44	
Variable costs per acre		
Labor	$0.68	$2.25
Fuel, oil, grease	0.23	---
Horses and wagon	0.34	2.38
Elevator	0.48	0.48
Total	$1.73	$5.11

[a]The mechanical corn picker's acreage threshold equals the number of acres above which a farmer will save money by adopting the mechanical harvester. To calculate the threshold, all costs are expressed in per-acre rates (as shown in the subsequent equations). The per-acre cost of hand picking is known once the yield, which is set at 45 bushels for the late 1930s, is multiplied by the per-bushel rate of 5¢. This leaves fixed costs as the only variable where per-acre costs are unknown. The equation is solved for the acreage where the harvester's fixed and variable costs equal the cost of hand picking an acre of corn, as follows:

Mechanical Corn Picker   Hand Husking
$177.44/x + $1.73 per acre = $5.11 per acre
x = 53 corn acres

Any farmer whose acreage exceeds the threshold of 53 corn acres will achieve cost savings by using the mechanical harvester.

The threshold varies with the yield. In 1937 the yield averaged 45 bushels per acre in the Midwest. Using a lower yield of 35 bushels per acre, labor costs drop to $1.75 per acre and the threshold rises to 62 corn acres. For a yield of 55 bushels of corn, labor costs increase to $2.75 per acre and the threshold drops to 46 corn acres.

Source: Costs for 1937 are found in M. P. Gehlbach, "Harvesting Costs Reduced by Use of Mechanical Corn Pickers," *Illinois Farm Economics*, 42 (November 1938), pp. 205-7.

in 1938 and 43 percent of the farmers used mechanical corn pickers. In Ohio 21 percent of the farms passed the threshold and 12 percent used harvesters. In Indiana 28 percent of the farms qualified and 22 percent used mechanical pickers. In Iowa roughly 50 percent of the farms exceeded the threshold, and given unusually low yields in selected counties, 35 percent harvested their corn with machines.[14]

By contrast, in the late 1920s the machine had not been so profitable. Whereas its cost savings translated into a threshold of 53 acres of corn in 1937, the threshold approached 70 corn acres or 197 total farm acres in 1929 (Table 6.3).[15] Fewer farmers stood to profit from investing in mechanical pickers in the 1920s. In Illinois, for instance, 46 percent of farmers passed the threshold in 1937, but in 1929 only a quarter did so. Similar proportions prevailed in Iowa.

These data, though, invite a second conclusion. Although the number of farms that passed the threshold was smaller in the late 1920s, the threshold analysis nevertheless indicated that a gap existed between the predicted and actual rates of adoption.[16] Overall, in 1929

[14] In Iowa 56 percent of the farmers technically passed the 150-acre threshold, but corn yields in 23 percent of Iowa's counties averaged less than 38 bushels in 1937 and 1938. Low yields disqualified three-quarters of farmers in these counties from the pool of candidates who could profit by adopting the corn picker. The Census reports the number of farms with 140 or more acres. I use this as a threshold to calculate the percentage of eligible farms. The mechanical corn picker's rate of diffusion would have been higher throughout the Corn Belt if conditions in Missouri had been different. Yields in Missouri averaged less than 30 bushels into the late 1930s, precluding many farmers from realizing cost savings and from investing in the machine. Less than 5 percent of the corn crop in Missouri was machine-harvested in 1938. The percent of farmland harvested with mechanical corn pickers is calculated from data in U.S. Department of Commerce, *Sixteenth Census of the United States: 1940* (Washington, D.C.: U.S. Government Printing Office, 1942), Agriculture, vol. 1, part 1, pp. 662, 682, and part 2, pp. 124, 142.

[15] Thirteen of the sixteen acres in the reduction of the machine's threshold between 1929 and 1937 were accounted for by the increase in corn yields from 35 to 45 bushels per acre. Aside from my calculations, another study (conducted for 1927 and 1928), revealed a similar threshold for the late 1920s. Using $4.32 per acre for the cost of hand husking, $168 for the mechanical corn picker's fixed costs, and $1.92 for its variable costs, the equation resulted in a threshold of 70 corn acres. Bert S. Gittins, "Will the Bang-Board Cease to Bang?" *Bureau Farmer,* Ohio Edition, 5 (November 1929), pp. 5, 28.

[16] In a separate study, the historian Allan G. Bogue similarly reported that data "suggest that there were significant savings involved in using the mechanical picker in the areas of Illinois and Indiana most dependent on the corn crop during the 1920s." Allan G. Bogue, "Changes in Mechanical and Plant Technology: The Corn Belt, 1910–1940," *Journal of Economic History,* 43 (March 1983), pp. 18–19.

Table 6.3. *The mechanical corn picker's acreage threshold, 1929*[a]

Costs	Mechanical picker	Hand husking
Fixed costs		
Picker	$141.11	
Tractor	53.20	
Total	$194.31	
Variable costs per acre		
Labor	$1.16	$2.38
Fuel, oil, grease	0.36	---
Horses	0.24	2.10
Wagon	0.05	0.14
Elevator	0.49	0.49
Total	$2.30	$5.11

[a]The cost of labor for hand husking is calculated at a wage of 6.8¢ a bushel times a yield of 35 bushels of corn per acre. The threshold is determined as follows:

     Mechanical Corn Picker   Hand Husking

     $194.31/x + $2.30/per acre = $5.11

     x = 69 corn acres

To determine the effect of changes in yields, I calculate the threshold for 1929 using a yield of 45 bushels per acre. The revised threshold equation is:

     Mechanical Corn Picker   Hand Husking

     $194.31/x + $2.30/per acre = $5.79 per acre

     x = 56 corn acres

     In calculating the threshold for 1929, I use changes in prices as reported in Appendix B, Table B.1. In the case of labor and fuel, I also adjusted the per-acre cost for a 20 percent estimated savings in time that resulted from improvements in the mechanical corn picker between the late 1920s and the late 1930s. In the case of horses, I split changes in their cost evenly between the cost of feed and changes in the price of horses. In the case of the mechanical corn picker, its price appears not to have changed in the 1930s. I have adjusted it in line with general equipment prices.

Sources: See Tables 6.2 and Appendix Table B.1.

a quarter of farmers could have profited from the machine, but only about 5 percent of them did so.[17]

One factor might help explain the machine's more rapid diffusion in the 1930s. Mechanical harvesters reduced part of a farmer's bill

[17]Works Progress Administration, *Changes in Technology: Corn*, p. 11.

for hired labor. This benefit no doubt varied in the Midwest, and was greater in regions where farmers devoted a large portion of land to corn – that is, the so-called cash grain regions. But these same incentives should have applied in the late 1920s as well as the late 1930s. Further, outside the cash grain counties, studies suggested that the corn picker was more likely to replace family than hired labor.[18] The case for market forces was therefore ambiguous. The machine became more profitable in the late 1930s and many farmers adopted it. But the machine had also been economical for a quarter of farmers in the late 1920s and fewer than 5 percent had adopted it.

Farmers' investment patterns indicated that other factors had shaped their purchases of mechanical corn pickers in the 1920s. Like the tractor, the mechanical harvester was expensive. A machine with two snouts sold for roughly $600, and to use it, a farmer first had to buy a tractor. Given the corn picker's cash demands, even in the 1930s farmers could have resisted this invention and clung to their pre-Depression strategy of conserving cash. But they did not do so. Farmers boosted investments and narrowed the gap between predicted and actual rates of adoption. Their behavior indicated that something had changed their investment calculus in the Depression. A similar change prevailed in the case of the tractor.

The tractor's rate of diffusion in the 1920s could be explained only in part by relative cost savings. As of 1929, 30 of every 100 farms in Iowa and Illinois had tractors. By standards of relative efficiency, this rate should have been twice as high; another 30 percent of farms passed the tractor's acreage threshold. In the course of the Depression, farmers substantially closed the gap between the tractor's actual and predicted rates of diffusion. Overall, the number of tractors on midwestern farms increased 68 percent, from 25 to 42 per 100 farms. In 1939, the threshold predicted that 50 to 60 percent of all Illinois and Iowa farms should employ tractors based on the machine's cost savings, and 52 and 55 percent of farmers owned tractors (Table 6.4). Two factors – technology and prices – exerted significant but

[18] Custom harvesting suggests a similar line of analysis, being available in the 1920s and the 1930s. Bogue reports that custom harvesting accounted for 12 percent of acreage picked by mechanical harvesters from 1929 to 1931. See Bogue, "Changes in Mechanical and Plant Technology," p. 19. Also see P. E. Johnston and H. H. Myers, "Harvesting the Corn Crop in Illinois," University of Illinois Agricultural Experiment Station Bulletin No. 373 (September 1931), pp. 364–5, 402–3.

Table 6.4. *Percent of farms that passed the tractor's acreage threshold, and the percent of farmers with tractors, 1939*

State	Percent of farms above threshold[a]	Percent of all farmers with tractors
Ohio	38.2%	35.6%
Indiana	43.3	37.1
Illinois	61.1	51.8
Iowa	71.5	55.3
Missouri	51.5	16.4

[a]The threshold size was calculated to be 100 farm acres, and represents the acreage above which the tractor offered farmers more cost savings than did a team of horses. Calculations for changes in the tractor's threshold between 1929 and 1939 are described in Appendix B.
Source: Data reporting farm size are found in U.S. Department of Commerce, *Sixteenth Census of the United States: 1940* (Washington, D.C.: U.S. Government Printing Office, 1942), Agriculture, vol. 1, parts 1 and 2, state tables 1 and 11.

contradictory effects on the tractor's competitiveness (Appendix B). Technological improvements made possible large cost savings. The most talked-about item was the pneumatic tire. Rubber tires claimed to take the "jolt" out of driving and offered substantial gains in traction and pulling power.[19] In an advertisement directed at implement dealers (Figure 6.3), Firestone stated that its "Ground Grip Tire" provided "greater traction, greater drawbar pull and rolls easier than steel lugged wheels." The payoff, Firestone reasoned, was a 25 percent savings in time and fuel. Firestone may have been somewhat optimistic, but I nevertheless have used this estimate in calculating changes in the cost of labor and tractor inputs, fuel expenses, and total variable costs. If we judge by those calculations, rubber tires cut a farmer's variable costs per acre by 8 percent (Appendix B).

Other improvements in tractors made them more reliable and longer-lasting. In 1929, farmers surveyed in Iowa expected tractors to last roughly eight years. By 1939, a tractor lasted perhaps thirteen

[19] G. S. Conrad, "Farmers Tell Why They Like Air-Tired Tractors," *Farm Implement News,* 56 (September 9, 1935), p. 26.

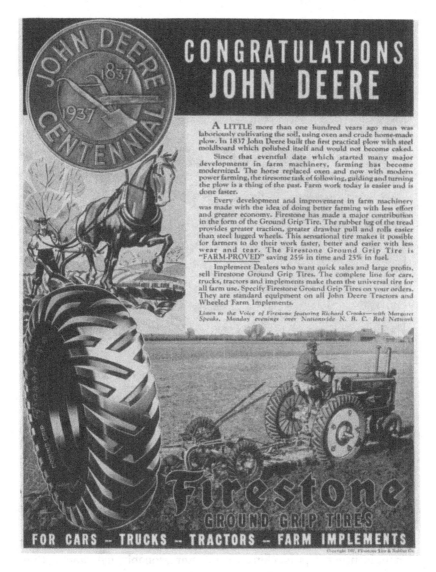

Figure 6.3. "Firestone Ground Grip Tires," Firestone Company advertisement. From *Farm Implement News,* 58 (January 14, 1937), p. 7. Courtesy of the Bridgestone-Firestone Company, Nashville, Tennessee.

Figure 6.4. A Farmall tractor, 1939. Courtesy of the International Harvester Company Archives, Navistar International Transportation Company, Chicago, Illinois.

years. This gain, plus a reduction in interest rates for calculating rental fees, caused a farmer's annual fixed charges (in 1929 prices) to drop 8 percent (Appendix B).[20]

These technical improvements were striking because they were visible changes as indicated in Harvester's 1939 tractor (Figure 6.4). But they would only be important of course if a nonvisible factor – tractor prices – were not too high. Farmers, however, charged that manufacturers kept machinery prices unreasonably high, and in 1936

---

[20] Aside from these technological changes, farmers could have replaced two-row cultivators with four-row implements in the 1930s. Four-row cultivators, however, were expensive. Whatley places the cost at $266.88 for a new cultivator, or $41.90 for an annual rental fee. As a result, the four-row cultivator raised the tractor's threshold above its 1929 level. Warren C. Whatley, "Institutional Change and Mechanization in the Cotton South: The Tractorization of Cotton Farming" (Ph.D. dissertation, Stanford University, 1983), p. 207.

Congress asked the Federal Trade Commission (FTC) to investigate the implement industry.[21] The FTC reported that "from 1929 to 1933, the reduction in farm equipment prices was slight; few articles were cut more than 10 percent. . . . Most of the reductions ranged from 8 down to less than 1 percent and a few items increased in price." The FTC further indicated: "There was a general increase in prices of farm implements and machines from 1933 to 1935 . . . . So extensive was this upward movement of the prices of farm equipment that the prices of a majority of . . . equipment in 1935 were above their prices in 1929." This upward trend continued for 1936 and 1937, but a small reprieve came at the end of 1938 and in 1939. In June, 1938, Harvester announced price reductions for tractors and implements; Deere & Company announced some reductions in 1939.[22]

Whether manufacturers' high prices mattered to the tractor's profitability depended on the movement of other prices between 1929 and 1939 (Table B.1, Appendix B).[23] By increasing 14 percent in the 1930s, the price of horses improved the tractor's comparative cost savings. But against this shift, nearly all other prices had little effect or changed in ways that reduced the tractor's competitiveness. The cost of two very large inputs, feed and labor, fell 32 and 27 percent, respectively. Each reduced the costs of both tractor and horse farms, but reduced costs relatively more on the farms that used only horses (Appendix B). Taking into consideration the direction and relative weight of these different prices, their movement largely canceled the cost savings of technological improvements. In other words, the tractor's threshold fell just a few acres. In 1929 the tractor became profitable at roughly 65 crop acres; in 1939 it became profitable at roughly 59 crop acres (Appendix B).

The figure for 1939, though, represents a generous estimate of the threshold. Aside from prices and technology, the AAA's acreage

[21] U.S. Congress, Temporary National Economic Committee, *Report of the Federal Trade Commission on Agricultural Implement and Machinery Inquiry*, Monograph No. 36, 76th Congress, 3rd sess. (1940), p. 226.

[22] Ibid., pp. 232–57.

[23] For a detailed theoretical analysis of the marginal effects of individual inputs needed to raise or lower a tractor's threshold, see Whatley, "Institutional Change and Mechanization in the Cotton South," especially pp. 125–32.

restriction program – a program that most farmers took part in – also changed the threshold. As farmers diverted land from the cash crop, corn, to other crops, they changed the cost of production. Corn was the most labor-intensive crop, and the tractor's cost advantage came in reducing time and labor, especially time spent raising corn. By joining the AAA program and reducing corn acreage by 15 to 25 percent and redistributing land to other crops, costs for tractor and horse farms declined. But farmers with horses cut costs faster. Set asides raised the tractor's threshold to 68 acres, or enough to cancel out the small reduction in the threshold associated with changes in prices and technology (Appendix B).

Still, even without the effect of the AAA, other factors suggest that the threshold of 1939 had changed little from 1929; in other words, 59 acres for 1939 represents the low side. It is unlikely that the tractor's service life in 1939 amounted to thirteen years. Shortening the tractor's life to twelve years (and excluding any effect from the AAA), the 1939 threshold would have risen above its 1929 level (Appendix B). Similarly, the calculations for the price of feed, fuel, and the tractor reflect an average of trends in the Midwest and the nation at large. Had calculations been made only with figures for the Midwest, then the 1939 threshold would have exceeded its 1929 level (Appendix B). Individual farmers no doubt made rough calculations. But to conclude that the tractor's threshold declined, farmers needed to be generous in their thinking about prices and the expected life of a tractor. Taking a slightly more cautious stand about any one of these items – prices, the tractor's life, or the effects of the AAA acreage restrictions – a farmer found that the tractor's threshold failed to drop in the 1930s or actually rose above its 1929 level. On net, then, there was no significant new reason to invest in the tractor. Yet, in the 1930s, many farmers purchased tractors and by and large closed the gap between the tractor's predicted and actual rates of adoption.

The investment patterns of these farmers were surprising. For given the ambiguous market forces and given the daily reminders that they labored in the worst depression on record, many farmers nevertheless made sizable financial commitments for labor-saving technology. Something had renewed farmers' confidence about making investments, and this, I argue, was New Deal regulation.

The New Deal's obvious consequence was relief. The CCC and

the AAA directly raised farm income. The FCA refinanced indebted farmers. These effects were short-term. But inasmuch as relief came in the form of market controls, regulation could exert long-term changes in the climate for farm investment. Such changes were both price- and credit-specific. The CCC could create a measure of stability if its loans were high enough to reduce the fear that prices would slide below farmers' costs. The FCA could change credit markets so as to encourage the competitive farmer to employ loans with long terms and low rates of interest.

Short-term changes in income, long-term changes in prices

Both the AAA and the CCC sought to raise farmers' incomes, partisan supporters hoped, to the level of parity. Neither agency met this goal. Instead, as the New Deal provided some immediate income relief, it altered the long-term pattern of crop prices. Here the primary agent was the CCC.

Immediately, officials discovered that they needed to raise prices in order to win farmers' political support. To receive a CCC loan, each farmer was required to sign up for the AAA acreage-restriction programs. Since the AAA depended on farmers' individual and voluntary participation, the administration could only win their support if it paid better-than-market prices. As one official reported in 1934: "It was recognized that the plan would fail unless these payments were large enough to insure the participant that his income not only would compare favorably, but would be larger than the income under the plan to a non-participant whose corn-hog enterprise was of similar size."[24]

Officials took steps that directly boosted farmers' incomes. The CCC supported corn prices in the late 1930s at 150 to 160 percent of the low levels experienced in 1932 and 1933. The AAA contributed directly to farmers' earnings, accounting for roughly 5 to 6 percent of

[24]U.S. Department of Agriculture, Agricultural Adjustment Administration, *Agricultural Adjustment: A Report of Administration of the Agricultural Adjustment Act May 1933 to February 1934* (Washington, D.C.: U.S. Government Printing Office, 1934), pp. 123–4. That the CCC was identified with the AAA is noted, for example, in Walter W. Wilcox, *The Farmer in the Second World War* (Ames: Iowa State College Press, 1947), p. 26.

their total cash income by the late 1930s. Between 1932 and 1936, these changes (plus the partial rebound in prices of wheat and soybeans) doubled farmers' cash income.

After 1935, farmers' cash income increased by only small amounts. This disappointed partisan supporters. They wanted prices raised to parity, but the CCC never came close: from 1933 to 1939, support prices averaged only 64 percent of parity and the highest rate, set in 1939, equaled only 75 percent of parity.[25]

The CCC, it turned out, was more successful in reducing the risk of cash losses than it was in meeting relief expectations. This new element of security came in relation to farmers' cost of production. From 1922 through World War II the USDA conducted surveys in which farmers were asked to estimate their production costs, in *cash*, for all preharvest tasks, the harvest, transportation to market, fertilizers, manure, seed, crop insurance, overhead, and storage, and to calculate "charges for labor of the farmer and his family and a charge for the use of the land on a cash rental basis."[26] The surveys showed that as corn prices tumbled after 1929 farm costs fell too, albeit at a slower pace. By the middle to late 1930s, farm costs averaged about 85 percent of the totals recorded in the 1920s. In the years 1935 to 1939, it cost farmers in Iowa and Illinois 43¢ a bushel to produce corn, and farmers in Ohio, Indiana, Michigan, Wisconsin, and Minnesota 60¢ a bushel.

Given these costs, the CCC granted very generous loans. For the Depression's last five years, its loans averaged 52¢ per bushel, or 98 percent of the cost of production for Illinois and Iowa farmers, and 87 percent of production costs for farmers in nearby states (Table 6.5).[27] The CCC therefore guaranteed farmers that they would be

---

[25] Calculated from U.S. Congress, House, *H.R. 4972 superseding H.R. 4694 to continue the Commodity Credit Corporation as an agency of the United States, to maintain its capital unimpaired, to increase its borrowing power, and for other purposes*, 77th Congress, 1st sess. (May–June 1941), p. 207. The AAA's share of farmers' cash income is calculated from U.S. Department of Agriculture, *Agricultural Statistics, 1940*, pp. 547–50.

[26] U.S. Department of Agriculture, *Crops and Markets*, 1 Supplement 6 (June 1924), p. 176. Annual results are reported in this journal and in the U.S. Department of Agriculture, *Yearbook of Agriculture* and *Agricultural Statistics*.

[27] These estimates include the effects of one drought year, 1936. Excluding this year, the CCC loans averaged 111 percent of Illinois and Iowa production costs and 91 percent of production costs in the other states.

Figure 6.5. "Ever-Normal Granary" seal on Corn-Crib, Grundy County, Iowa, 1939. From 34–28299–D, U.S. Farm Security Administration Collection, Prints and Photographs Division, Library of Congress, Washington, D.C.

Table 6.5. *Cost of production of corn and the CCC loan prices for states in the Corn Belt, 1932-40*

Year	Cost/acre ($/acre)	Yield (bushels)	Cost/bushel ($/bushel)	Loan price ($/bushel)
A. *Iowa and Illinois*				
1932	$15.33	42.6	$0.36	$ ---
1933	14.93	34.7	0.43	0.45
1934	17.38	24.6	0.71	0.55
1935	18.62	38.2	0.49	0.45
1936	19.04	23.1	0.82	0.55
1937	21.53	45.9	0.47	0.50
1938	21.15	45.3	0.47	0.57
1939	22.12	52.0	0.43	0.57
1940	22.47	47.8	0.47	0.61
B. *Ohio, Indiana, Michigan, Wisconsin, and Minnesota*				
1932	16.59	36.9	0.45	---
1933	16.27	31.3	0.52	0.45
1934	19.50	27.0	0.72	0.55
1935	21.81	38.4	0.57	0.45
1936	21.19	26.9	0.79	0.55
1937	23.71	40.9	0.58	0.50
1938	23.69	40.1	0.59	0.57
1939	24.69	47.7	0.52	0.57
1940	24.73	38.2	0.65	0.61

Sources: U.S. Department of Agriculture, *Agricultural Statistics, 1944* (Washington, D.C.: U.S. Government Printing Office, 1945), p. 46; and *Agricultural Statistics, 1952* (Washington, D.C.: U.S. Government Printing Office, 1952), pp. 680-1.

able to recoup all or nearly all production expenses even when family labor was evaluated at its cash or market value.

Prior to the Depression, farmers had obtained security by conserving cash, but that recourse was no longer compelling. With the coming of the CCC, they could be more confident that prices would not fall very far. That is, they could feel safe knowing that the price of corn would not fall to levels that would make investments unprofitable. This encouraged farmers to invest in variable-cost inputs such as chemical fertilizers (even if the input was not as profitable as hybrid corn). They could also better invest in expensive machinery since the CCC offered them a higher, steadier cash price to cover these new expenses.

Politicians clearly understood this outcome. Scott Lucas, a Democratic congressman from Illinois, who drafted agricultural legislation, reasoned: "The loans act as a floor under prices and prevents [sic] excessive slumps in price levels. It is an absolute protection against such catastrophes as the farm price collapse of 1932." In his bid for the U.S. Senate in 1938, Lucas campaigned on this theme. In one speech, he declared: "Certainly the corn loan feature of the Agricultural Adjustment Act is an element of stabilization which can not be overlooked by any interested farmer. Cooperating farmers will get not less than 46 cents per bushel in the way of a loan, and in my humble opinion history will repeat itself if corn should go below that price. Ultimately those who bin their corn and take advantage of the government loan will be money ahead." Writing to Henry Wallace in 1939, James A. Farley quoted a campaigner in Rushville, Indiana: "Be assured Sec. Wallace's corn loans have done a tremendous amount of good as an effective price-pegging suggestion. Corn down at our corn belt corner is nearing the loan figure of 57 cents. If those loans had not been granted corn would be selling around 25 cents per bushel and all farmers know that."[28]

One politician, Representative Frederick Biermann of Iowa, caught this change of heart when in 1935 he asked local aides to gauge his chances of reelection. From Decorah, Iowa, Allen Wise reported, "I believe people are in a fairly good frame of mind. Hartvig Engbretson says it has been an exceptionally good year for the sale of farm machinery, and that instead of taking notes, he is being paid cash." Warren F. Miller of Independence, Iowa, claimed his community was prospering since each farmer "is selling his hogs for around nine dollars and his corn for 75 cents." He added, "It is not only the farmer, but business in every line has improved so much."[29]

Because corn farmers could only use CCC loans provided that they

[28] Farley was the postmaster general and chairman of the Democratic National Committee. For Lucas, see "Bond County Speech," September 15, 1938, Box 42, Folder 0542, and "Speech at Roseville," August 26, 1938, Box 42, Folder 0544, Scott Lucas Papers, Illinois State Historical Library, Springfield, Illinois. James A. Farley to Henry A. Wallace, January 20, 1939, Office of the Secretary of Agriculture, Record Group 16, General Correspondence, 1939, Box 2997, Corn 2 (loans), National Archives.

[29] Allen Wise to Frederick Biermann, July 3, 1935, MsC 128, Box 3, #1582, and Warren F. Miller to Frederick Biermann, June 27, 1935, MsC 128, Box 3, #1579, Frederick Elliot Biermann Papers, Special Collections Department, University of Iowa Libraries, Iowa City, Iowa.

signed AAA contracts, they signaled their attitude toward the new market supports when they voted on the AAA. In 1934, after the AAA's first year, they approved the program by just a 3-to-2 margin. In 1935, however, their sentiments improved. At an Iowa fair, one reporter quizzed "42 farmers picked at random in the hog barns." Asked what to do if the Supreme Court "knocked out" the AAA, thirty-two said it should be reinstated: "If the act's unconstitutional, let's make it constitutional."[30] Their comments reflected the upturn in the AAA's overall approval rating, which jumped to a 13-to-2 approval margin in 1935. Between 1934 and 1937 corn farmers increased the number of acres of cropland under contract from 53 million to 108 million acres (roughly two-thirds of all midwestern cropland).[31]

In a 1937 study, the Bureau of Agricultural Economics assessed the CCC's role. It noted that in years of low prices, notably 1933, farmers took advantage of the loans. Yet in years of higher prices, such as 1934 when the drought halved corn yields, few farmers took out loans. Their behavior prompted officials to ask, "if farmers were not expected to take advantage" of CCC loans in a given year, "why initiate a corn loan plan"? The BAE answered that a loan price offered protection against unforeseen events: "Such a loan would act as a bumper, preventing any severe price decline which might otherwise occur if the business situation became worse or the market failed to gauge correctly all of the factors in the situation."[32]

[30] Memo to Mr. Pierce from *Wallaces' Farmer and Iowa Homestead,* August 31, 1935, Office of the Secretary of Agriculture, Record Group 16, General Correspondence, 1935, Box 2143, Corn 6, National Archives.

[31] U.S. Department of Agriculture, Agricultural Adjustment Administration, *Agricultural Adjustment in 1934: A Report of Administration of the Agricultural Adjustment Act. February 15, 1934 to December 31, 1935* (Washington, D.C.: U.S. Government Printing Office, 1936), pp. 87–117; U.S. Department of Agriculture, Agricultural Adjustment Administration, *Agricultural Adjustment 1933 to 1935. A Report of Administration of the Agricultural Adjustment Act May 12, 1933 to December 31, 1935* (Washington, D.C.: U.S. Government Printing Office, 1936), pp. 165–83; U.S. Department of Agriculture, Agricultural Adjustment Administration, *Agricultural Adjustment, 1937–1938: A Report of the Activities Carried on by the Agricultural Adjustment Administration* (Washington, D.C.: U.S. Government Printing Office, 1939), p. 39.

[32] See study entitled "Corn Loans" sent by A. M. Mach of the Bureau of Agricultural Economics to Secretary of Agriculture, Henry Wallace, October 22, 1937, Office of the Secretary of Agriculture, Record Group 16,

Short- and long-term changes in credit markets

As the CCC was creating greater stability in commodity markets, the FCA was altering the ability of farmers to employ credit. Part of the change came purely as short-term relief. Here all three market-oriented programs contributed to a quick and sharp contraction of debts. But these short-term effects were only one part of the New Deal's consequences for credit markets. In the early 1930s, the FCA gained a large share of the farmers' mortgage market and, in doing so, exerted long-term changes in sources of credit – changes that contributed to investments in expensive technology.

By raising farm income, the AAA and the CCC mitigated the effects of burdensome debts. In 1933, interest fees had swelled from a little more than 7 percent of farmers' cash income in 1929 to 11 percent.[33] Acreage controls and price supports (plus the partial rebound in prices of other commodities) boosted farm income to twice its level during 1932 and 1933. This effectively cut the burden of interest from 11 to 7 percent of income in the Depression's last few years.

For many indebted farmers, income relief was not enough. They needed debt relief, and the FCA's program to refinance loans helped them get "on a permanent basis."[34] Both reductions in the rate of interest and the amount of debt outstanding made possible a 42 percent cut in farmers' annual interest fees. Overall, average rates (public and private combined) in the Corn Belt fell from 5.8 percent in 1929 to 5.0 percent in 1936. Much of the decline came from efforts in Congress to cut rates on federal loans. Representative Guy M.

General Correspondence, 1937, Box 2536, Corn, p. 4, Record Group 16, National Archives.

[33] Cash income for individual states is reported in U.S. Department of Commerce, *Statistical Abstract of the United States: 1932*, p. 603; U.S. Department of Commerce, *Statistical Abstract of the United States: 1934*, p. 572; U.S. Department of Commerce, *Statistical Abstract of the United States: 1936*, p. 603; U.S. Department of Commerce, *Statistical Abstract of the United States: 1940*, p. 670. Interest charges are reported by individual states in Donald C. Horton, Harald C. Larsen, and Norman J. Wall, "Farm-Mortgage Credit Facilities in the United States," U.S. Department of Agriculture Miscellaneous Publication No. 478 (1942), pp. 49, 239–41.

[34] See Frank A. O'Connor to Nelson G. Kraschel, October 4, 1934, Nelson George Kraschel Papers, MsC 174, Box 1, Special Collections Department, University of Iowa Libraries.

Gillette congratulated his Iowa colleague, Biermann, for his "loyal and painstaking efforts as chairman of the sub-committee on refinancing farm indebtedness" to lower interest rates on federal land bank loans to 3.5 percent. This low rate, in itself, accounted for three-quarters of the decline in interest rates in the Corn Belt and, lower average rates brought about a 15 percent drop in farmers' annual interest expense.[35] The rest of the decline resulted from a $1 billion drop in the amount of debt outstanding between 1930 and 1939. The FCA helped bring about this reduction by scaling down 16 percent of all loans in 1934 and 20 percent of all new loans in 1935.[36] It also encouraged private lenders to scale down farm debts so that some borrowers could qualify for federal loans.

In Iowa, a state hit very hard by the debt crisis, Governor Kraschel reported a rapid decline in farm debts. A debt advisory council had been created in 1933 to supervise debt adjustments. In his campaign literature, Kraschel noted that, from 1933 to 1938, "the committee has scaled down more than $25,000,000 in farm debts to less than $19,000,000 and millions more have been adjusted through private lender–borrower agreements." By the end of 1938 Kraschel concluded that the debt crisis had diminished to the point that no special advisory council was needed. Writing to one member, he explained that the number of foreclosures was small: "I am advised there are less than 2,000 moratorium cases of record. . . . The progress made in the last six years and the fact that the Farm Security Administration can carry on the work makes it unnecessary, it seems to me, to continue the Iowa Farm Debt Advisory Council."[37]

[35] Guy M. Gillette to Frederick Biermann, May 18, 1936, Frederick Elliot Biermann Papers, MsC 128, Box 5, #2622, p. 5, Special Collections Department, University of Iowa Libraries. I calculated changes in outstanding debt, interest rates, and interest charges for the five midwestern states from Horton et al., "Farm-Mortgage Credit Facilities," p. 59, 220–1, 228, 240–1.

[36] Farm Credit Administration, Second Annual Report of the Farm Credit Administration (Washington, D.C.: U.S. Government Printing Office, 1935), p. 4; and Farm Credit Administration, Third Annual Report of the Farm Credit Administration (Washington, D.C.: U.S. Government Printing Office, 1936), p. 7.

[37] A campaign bulletin, "Mr. Farmer:" details changes in farm debts; see Nelson George Kraschel Papers, MsC 174, Box 4, Special Collections Department, University of Iowa Libraries. For Kraschel's elimination of the debt advisory committee, see Nelson G. Kraschel to Ray Murray, December 19, 1938, MsC 174, Box 6, Nelson George Kraschel Papers, Special Collections Department, University of Iowa Libraries.

Iowa's recovery typified other midwestern states. Farm foreclosures for the Corn Belt peaked in 1933 and were cut in half by 1935 and in half again (to 13 foreclosures per 1,000 farms by 1938).[38] Whereas in 1933 interest charges had taken 11 percent of farmers' cash income, by 1936 this burden dropped to less than 5 percent. For the remainder of the Depression, farmers spent less than 5 percent of their income for interest. A comparison with U.S. figures suggests that farmers in the Corn Belt carried an interest burden in the late 1930s that was just one point above the rate farmers had held in the prosperous period prior to World War I.[39]

From 1933 to 1935, then, the New Deal brought about an important reduction in the burden of debt. This relief, no doubt, provided a short-term boost for investments. But in providing relief, the FCA also initiated long-term changes in public and private sources of credit.

In 1934 and 1935 lenders turned over thousands of loans to federal agencies: the federal land banks and Land Bank Commissioner loans accounted for 74 percent of all new loans recorded in 1934, and 44 percent in 1935. By 1936 federal lenders held nearly 40 percent of outstanding farm mortgage debt.[40] This in itself would not necessarily matter, but in assuming the loans federal lenders set new competitive standards. Federal land banks reduced interest rates to 3.5 percent in

[38] By 1938 out of every 1,000 farms, foreclosures averaged 8.8 in Ohio, 10.6 in Indiana, 11.0 in Illinois, 11.3 in Iowa, and 22.6 in Missouri. For 1933 to 1935, see B. R. Stauber, "The Farm Real Estate Situation, 1935–36," U.S. Department of Agriculture Circular No. 417 (October 1936), pp. 26–7; for 1938, see M. M. Regan, "The Farm Real Estate Situation, 1936–37, 1937–38, and 1938–39" U.S. Department of Agriculture Circular No. 548 (October 1939), pp. 32–3. For the point that federal programs reduced farm failures, see also Ronald R. Rucker and Lee J. Alston, "Farm Failures and Government Intervention: A Case Study of the 1930's," *American Economic Review*, 77 (September 1987), pp. 724–30.

[39] Figures for the cash income of individual states are not available for the years before 1929. Prior to 1929 gross income rather than cash income was reported for individual states. Gross income includes the cash value of farm products consumed on the farm. To the extent that the value of farm products consumed on farms remained constant between 1910 and 1940, gross income acts as a good measure of the trend in cash income. Trends in gross income among Corn Belt states follow the national trend in cash income. See U.S. Department of Commerce, *Statistical Abstract of the United States*, various issues.

[40] Federal land banks' market share includes the holding of Land Bank Commissioner loans. Horton et al., "Farm-Mortgage Credit Facilities in the United States," pp 53, 112.

standards. Federal land banks reduced interest rates to 3.5 percent in 1935 and offered amortized loans for substantial terms of up to forty years. Paul Bestor of Prudential Insurance Company acknowledged this: "It should be said that the present basis of their competition has been due largely to the pressure of the emergency situation which confronted agriculture."[41] According to Bestor, private lenders had wanted relief from their dog-eat-dog days of 1931 and 1932. Although the FCA helped private lenders, it had created a new kind of competition.

Private creditors responded in different ways. Some firms opted to make fewer loans. Northwestern Mutual Life, the largest lender in the 1920s, made this choice.[42] Other firms, however, decided to offer loans at terms similar to federal land banks. Aetna was one example. The Hartford insurer had slowed its volume of farm loans in the late 1920s and drastically cut them in the early 1930s. In 1935, it closed just $0.5 million in new loans. But after that date, it returned to the market, closing $2.5 million in 1936 and $3.6 million in 1937. Further, Aetna cut its rate of interest sharply, from 6.3 percent in 1932 to 4,8 percent in 1936 and 3.5 percent in 1938 (Table 6.6). The firm also offered long-term amortized loans, under a new program begun in 1934. It reported that these loans were highly successful; only 1 in 300, it estimated, became delinquent in subsequent years.[43]

[41] Paul Bestor, "The Financing of Agriculture," *Proceedings of the Thirtieth Annual Meeting of the American Life Convention* (Chicago: October 7–11, 1935), pp. 58–9.

[42] Its historians, Harold F. Williamson and Orange A. Smalley, observed: "During the late 1930's the renewed interest of other insurance companies, particularly Prudential, and the competition of federal and other private lending agencies, made funds available on terms more satisfactory than Northwestern was willing to offer. The result was the continuous contraction of the farm loan account." Harold F. Williamson and Orange A. Smalley, *Northwestern Mutual Life: A Century of Trusteeship* (Evanston, Ill.: Northwestern University Press, 1957), p. 265.

[43] Aetna's shift to long-term loans and their low delinquency rate is noted in "In Light of Experience," in "Marketing Materials, 1930s–1945," p. 3, Record Group 42. For Aetna's new loans in 1936 and 1937, see Mortgage and Farm Loan Department, "1937 Annual Report," in "Annual Reports – 1937 Annual Report," p. 1, Record Group 42. Loans from the 1920s are reported in "A Record of Mortgage Loan Experience," p. 11, Record Group 42, Aetna Life and Casualty Company Archives, Hartford, Connecticut.

Table 6.6. *Average rates of interest for new farm mortgage loans, federal land banks, and selected life insurance companies, 1932, 1934, 1936, and 1938*

	Rate of interest charged for new loans			
Lender	1932	1934	1936	1938
Federal land banks	5.6%	4.5%	3.5%	3.5%
Life insurance companies[a]				
Metropolitan	5.5	5.1	4.4	4.4
Prudential	5.7	5.3	4.8	4.7
Equitable (New York)	5.5	5.3	5.1	4.6
Northwestern Mutual	5.3	5.1	4.6	4.1
Travelers	b	b	b	b
John Hancock	5.6	5.6	5.2	4.9
Mutual Benefit	5.3	4.0	4.2	4.4
Aetna	6.3	5.1	4.8	3.5
Union Central	6.2	5.5	5.3	5.4
Connecticut Mutual	5.6	5.1	4.9	4.7
Bankers Life (Des Moines)	5.2	5.8	4.8	4.6
Equitable of Iowa	b	b	b	b
Average for 10 firms	5.6	5.2	4.8	4.5

[a]The twelve firms are selected as those which held the largest value of farm mortgages in 1929.
[b]There was no record of new interest rates for farm mortgages.
Sources: For federal land banks, see Donald C. Horton, Harald C. Larsen, and Norman J. Wall, "Farm-Mortgage Credit Facilities in the United States," U.S. Department of Agriculture Miscellaneous Publication No. 472 (1942), p. 60; for life insurance companies, see U.S. Congress, Temporary National Economic Committee, *Hearings before the Temporary National Economic Committee: Part 10-A Life Insurance Operating Results and Investments of the 26 Largest Legal Reserve Life Insurance Companies Domiciled in the United States 1929-1938*, 76th Congress, 3rd sess. (February 12, 1940), p. 163.

Other insurance firms followed Aetna's strategy for interest rates. Whereas in 1932 they had charged 5.6 percent for loans, on average, by 1938 average rates had dropped to 4.5 percent (Table 6.6). No doubt part of private lenders' actions reflected general changes in credit markets. Insurance firms, for instance, reported similar declines in interest rates charged for urban loans.[44] But it was also possible that while firms reduced rates in urban markets (where they had experienced fewer troubled loans), they might not have dropped rates as much in farming.

What the historical record makes clear is that private lenders specifically cited federal land banks for increasing competition. Starting in 1935, trade association meetings regularly addressed what mortgage bankers called their "chief competitor." C. G. Worsham of Connecticut General Life confessed, "I used to always say that when interest rates got to five per cent on farm homes, I would not make loans, but we were forced down and had to make loans at five per cent." Worsham expected that "we will have to continue this in the future."[45] At the 1938 meeting of the Mortgage Bankers Association (its Silver Jubilee), Deane W. Trick of Bankers Life (Des Moines, Iowa) defended the federal land banks' role, saying in the emergency most would agree that the FCA's efforts were not "excessive or unnecessary." But as a creditor, Trick felt "cornered by Uncle Sam."[46] To better compete, he reported that private lenders were adjusting their lending tactics. Interest rates had fallen; and, though low by the standards of the 1920s, he suggested rates might not be too low to earn a return.[47] He also reported that "the term of the farm loan has lengthened, in some instances, from a year to a generation." As Trick said:

> The Federal Land Banks should be given credit for starting this movement. Long term loans were almost an unknown quantity . . .

[44] The same life insurance firms cut rates of interest for urban loans between 1932 and 1938 by amounts similar to cuts in rates for farm loans. It is possible in urban markets insurance firms also responded to new federal lenders. For interest rates, see U.S. Congress, Temporary National Economic Committee, *Hearings before the Temporary National Economic Committee: Part 10-A Life Insurance Operating Results and Investments of the 26 Largest Legal Reserve Life Insurance Companies Domiciled in the United States 1929–1938*, 76th Congress, 3rd sess. (February 12, 1940), p. 197.

[45] Other bankers were more resentful. E. H. Lougee announced that resolutions had been passed, all of which could be condensed to say that the federal government should "get the hell out of the business." See *The Mortgage Bankers Association of America 1936 Year Book* (Chicago: Mortgage Bankers Association, 1936), pp. 188, 196.

[46] Deane W. Trick, "Farm Mortgage Facts and Fancies," in *The Mortgage Bankers Association 1938 Year Book* (Chicago: Mortgage Bankers Association, 1938), pp. 110–19.

[47] Ibid., p. 115.

before 1916. Under the old five year term the maturity date was too often just a renewal date; now it seems sound to provide the borrower with a gradual repayment plan lengthened out to coordinate with his income.[48]

Trick's observation was corroborated by William G. Murray, a specialist in agricultural finance, who testified that in the 1930s "the long-term amortized loan had grown in popularity."[49]

What the federal land banks were for long-term credit markets, PCAs were for shorter-term markets. One Illinois farmer, Carl Peterson, recalled how a PCA altered his own investment outlook. Peterson ran into trouble obtaining credit in the early 1930s. He had held a loan through a bank that failed and the new bank refused to extend him credit. The farmer, however, tapped a second source. As he said: "I wasn't going to have too much trouble about it. They had started a new Production Credit Association in Jacksonville . . . so I went over there. . . ." Peterson continued: "I . . . told them my troubles and so after he talked to me awhile and wanted to know what I had and how much land I had rented. . . . So, they said, 'Yes, we'd loan you all the money you want.' . . . So I'd just go over there and borrow maybe four or five hundred dollars or whatever I thought I would need."[50]

Not all farmers were as fortunate as Peterson, and it is not possible to generalize from Peterson's experience to all farmers. Had he not been renting land from his family, the PCA might not have lent Peterson funds. Or had his existing debts been higher, the PCA might have turned him down. Still, what was important in his case was his sense that the federal system gave him new options in obtaining credit.

During the Great Depression, the FCA and the CCC introduced

[48] Ibid., p. 124.
[49] In the 1941 edition of his book, *Agricultural Finance,* Murray repeated this point and listed Prudential as one of the lenders that had increased its farm mortgages and had begun to offer longer-term amortized loans. See William G. Murray, *Agricultural Finance* (Ames: Iowa State University Press, 1941), pp. 154–5; U.S. Congress, Temporary National Economic Committee, *Hearings before the Temporary National Economic Committee, Part 28, Life Insurance Operating Results and Investments,* 76th Congress, 3rd sess. (February 12–16, 19–21, 26–9, and March 1, 1940), p. 14894.
[50] Carl Peterson Memoir, Sangamon State University (1988), vol. 2, p. 102, Sangamon State University *Archives,* Springfield, Illinois.

long-term changes in credit and commodity markets, and two indicators suggest that the short- and long-term effects of regulation were beginning to be felt. One was the farmers' rapid rate of investment. Their willingness to invest in technology went beyond tractors to capital expenditures in general. Table 6.7 records farmers' cash receipts and capital expenditures between 1930 and 1939. In most regions of the Corn Belt, farmers saw their cash receipts decline.[51] But in all regions capital expenditures increased. As manufacturers' records indicate, the increase in capital expenditures reflected purchases of expensive items. Sales of tractors and corn pickers in the late 1930s exceeded those of the late 1920s by more than 40 percent.[52] For every 100 corn-producing farms, the number of tractors doubled between 1929 and 1939 (Table 6.7). A second indicator of the effects of regulation was provided by those who stood to profit from farmers' new investment patterns – implement manufacturers and their dealers.

Farm investment: Manufacturers' perspective

When equipment markets began to recover in 1935, manufacturers could well have responded to this upturn with caution. For one thing, they resented the effects of New Deal labor legislation on their costs of production. By 1937 IHC had raised wages over levels for 1929, and by 1939, Caterpillar reported that its wage rates had risen above pre-Depression levels.[53] For a second, manufacturers had cause for concern about farmers' cash income. Their customers had just been overwhelmed by the crisis of 1931–3. Although farm incomes rose from the terrible years of 1932 and 1933, after 1935 increases in

[51] The one exception was the poorest region where farm income in 1939 averaged half the income of the next poorest region. Farmers in this region earned half the income of the next poorest region in 1929.

[52] For the years 1936 to 1939, the number of tractors sold averaged 174,000 per year, as compared with 116,000 for the years 1926 to 1929. For mechanical corn pickers, sales jumped from 8,730 machines, on average, between 1927 and 1929 to 15,451 units per year in the late 1930s. For tractors, see Table 4.1. For mechanical corn pickers, see U.S. Department of Agriculture, *Agricultural Statistics, 1941* (Washington, D.C.: U.S. Government Printing Office, 1941), p. 565.

[53] Document No. 2156, International Harvester Company Archives, Navistar International Transportation Corporation, Chicago, Illinois. Caterpillar Company, *Annual Report, 1939*, p. 9.

Table 6.7. *Capital expenditures, cash receipts, and the diffusion of the tractor in the Corn Belt, 1930-9*

Farm type	Capital expenditures[a][b]			Cash receipts			Tractors per 100 farms	
	1930	1939	Change (%)	1930	1939	Change (%)	1930	1939
Hog-beef-raising	$501	$655	31%	$1,261	$1,373	9%	20	40
Hog-beef-fattening	890	1,115	25	5,144	4,074	-21	44	80
Hog-dairy	810	1,020	26	2,945	2,574	-13	26	54
Cash grain	927	1,198	29	3,533	3,550	1	44	80

[a]Government payments included.
[b]Expenditures include cash outlays for machinery and farm buildings.
Source: U.S. Department of Agriculture, "Costs and Returns to Commercial Family-Operated Farms by Type and Size, 1930-1951," Statistical Bulletin No. 197 (November 1956), pp. 22-9.

farmers' cash income were small. If manufacturers anticipated that sales would follow the trend in farm income, then they should have anticipated a short recovery and adopted a cautious strategy.

Instead, they responded enthusiastically, linking their optimism about machinery sales to the consequences of New Deal regulation. In the most obvious sense, they understood that without the New Deal farmers' incomes would shrink and so would their sales. In early 1936, the Supreme Court made manufacturers jittery when it declared the AAA unconstitutional. But they took heart, noting that the Court had not invalidated the CCC loan system.[54] The president of the 1935 Iowa Implement Dealers' Convention pursued this theme, stating that the corn loan had been the most helpful of the income-support activities: "Due to the better prices for farm products and the aid rendered by the government, our customers have regained confidence. Manufacturers and jobbers tell us that dealers are no longer buying on the hand-to-mouth plan, but are placing orders for larger quantities than they have for several years."[55]

Regulation was important as well for supplying cash as it exercised its long-term effect on market prices. Speaking to an audience in Minnesota, a sales manager at Harvester, J. L. McCaffrey, reported in 1939: "The significance of these corn loans is that they represent 36-cent corn in Minnesota on which 57 cents is obtained by the farmer, with the difference between these two figures representing cash he may use for purchases or other purposes."[56] Fifty-seven cents was the CCC's loan rate for 1938 and 1939. McCaffrey's point was that a minimum price of fifty-seven cents, guaranteed by the CCC, assured farmers a margin of cash above levels they would otherwise expect (the thirty-six-cent corn). This difference, McCaffrey reasoned, provided critical funds for investment in machinery.

Manufacturers also singled out the consequences of credit policies. Speaking at the convention of the Farm Equipment Institute, Harry G. Davis saw the credit programs as more than just relief. Referring to both short- and long-term credit, Davis stated: "These associations

---

[54] "Passing of the AAA," *Farm Implement News,* 57 (January 16, 1936), p. 22.

[55] "Iowa Implement Dealers' Convention," *Farm Implement News,* 56 (January 17, 1935), p. 22.

[56] J. L. McCaffrey, "Don't Sell Agriculture Short!" *Farm Implement News,* 60 (March 23, 1939), pp. 32–4.

are in a position to make loans to farmers for any agricultural purposes including the purchase of machinery and equipment. In fact,
their literature emphasizes that they will loan money to purchase
equipment." He continued: "It would seem that dealers could make
excellent use of the facilities afforded by the local credit association
operating in their respective territories. When the farmer applies for
credit to the dealer, he might be referred to the production credit
association and there obtain a loan which would enable him to pay
cash."[57] Davis urged dealers to exploit this new option.

The market leader, IHC, acquired confidence about future sales
and invested accordingly. By 1938 it was spending close to $10
million in capital expenditures for trucks and tractors, or nearly as
much as it spent in the prosperous year of 1929.[58] Harvester also
increased its expenditures for "engineering and development" by
more than 35 percent between 1929 and 1939.[59] By the end of the
Depression, a National Research Council survey showed that in 1940
IHC's research staff of 1,802 was more than double that of 1933
(747 persons) and nearly three times that of 1927 (617 persons).[60]

In his history of Deere, Wayne G. Broehl, Jr., concluded that in the
1930s machinery companies "began to receive the fruits of farmers'
renewed optimism stemming from the New Deal legislative initia-

[57] Harry G. Davis, "State of the Farm Equipment Industry," *Farm Implement News,* 56 (November 21, 1935), p. 26.

[58] Calculated from annual reports for International Harvester.

[59] See "Indexes of Engineering and Development Expense Compared to United States and Canadian Sales of Machines and Repairs, 1913–1937," and "IHC United States Sales, Excluding Motor Trucks, Compared with Cash Farm Income," both in Document No. 2156, International Harvester Company Archives.

[60] In 1927, IHC reported 27 chemists, 51 engineers and designers, and 539 other personnel; in 1933, it claimed 20 chemists, 181 engineers and designers, and 546 other individuals. By 1940, categories were more re-fined: 93 chemists, 33 metallurgists, 70 physicists, 102 engineers, 302 layout men and draftsmen, 66 road engineers and field mechanics and testers, 805 mechanics, 108 technical individuals, and 223 other persons. See National Research Council, "Industrial Research Laboratories of the United States," Bulletin No. 60 (Washington, D.C.: U.S. Government Printing Office, 1927), p. 60; National Research Council, "Industrial Research Laboratories of the United States," Bulletin No. 91 (Washington, D.C.: U.S. Government Printing Office, 1933), p. 102; National Research Council, "Industrial Research Laboratories of the United States," Bulletin No. 104 (Washington, D.C.: U.S. Government Printing Office, 1940), pp. 151–2.

tives."[61] Without regulation, management knew, sales would have been smaller. Now, too, they could take advantage of FCA credit to boost sales. Knowing that, International Harvester, as the industry's largest firm, responded enthusiastically to the upturn after 1935, expanding capital outlays and funding for research. Regulation had been a new factor that had clearly altered the investment setting for the machinery companies as it had altered the climate for farmers.

Regulation and changes in productivity

Overall, in the 1930s land productivity increased by 27 percent and labor productivity increased by at least 18 percent. These gains reflected farmers' investments in technology, especially hybrid corn, the tractor, and the mechanical corn picker. Moreover, these gains in productivity were recorded in the second half of the 1930s – that is, in the years after regulation took effect. Farmers adopted hybrid corn after 1934. For tractors, their sales had slumped to just 25,000 units in 1932 and 1933, but doubled to 65,000 units in 1935 and averaged 174,000 units annually for the next four years (Table 4.1). Mechanical corn pickers showed a similar pattern. Compared with sales of 1,845 units in 1935, numbers had climbed to 13,546 units by 1937 and to 16,044 units by 1938. Overall, farmers' capital expenditures increased from 25 to 30 percent between 1930 and 1939 (Table 6.7).[62] If calculations for productivity gains are made for the years when farmers invested in technology, that is, from 1934 to 1939, then gains are large. Corn yields increased at a 4.9 percent annual rate. Labor savings were also substantial – representing a 3.6 percent annual rate of growth – and indicative of trends for the years after the Depression.

Farmers, then, had achieved these gains in productivity *after* regulation took effect. But the consequences of regulation differed from the

---

[61] Wayne G. Broehl, Jr., *John Deere's Company: A History of Deere & Company and Its Times* (New York: Doubleday, 1984), p. 527.

[62] For the mechanical corn picker, the USDA did not report a census of sales of most farm equipment for 1932 to 1934 presumably because sales were so low. Still, compared with sales in 1929, when manufacturers sold 8,620 corn pickers, sales in 1931 were down to 3,243 pickers and in 1935 totaled 1,845 units. U.S. Department of Agriculture, *Agricultural Statistics, 1941*, p. 565.

case of hybrid corn to that of labor-saving machinery. Regulation played only a small role in the diffusion of hybrid corn. The seed's unusually high level of profitability (as reflected in dramatic increases in yields) clearly brought about most of its rapid adoption. Farmers raised yields as well by reducing marginal land or by rotating crops. Here the AAA was at work, though it had created perverse short-term incentives to raise yields as a way to circumvent the intent of the legislation.

In the case of labor productivity, by contrast, regulation played a critical role by reshaping farmers' investment climate. The two most important labor-saving inventions had been the tractor and the mechanical corn picker. Appendix C reports the data needed to calculate the effect of these inventions on productivity between 1929 and 1939. The estimate is made in terms of the tractor's contribution to preharvest productivity, and the mechanical corn picker's contribution to harvest productivity. The results indicate that on average the tractor reduced preharvest labor hours by 16 percent, from 6.6 to 5.6 hours, and the mechanical corn picker reduced average harvest hours per acre by 20 percent, from 5.8 to 4.6 hours.[63] Total labor hours declined 18 percent during the decade.

Because my calculations are based on the two major inventions, tractors and harvesters, I also consider the effect of improvements in equipment, notably the use of four-row cultivators (Appendix C). Cultivators increased preharvest labor savings perhaps from 16 to as much as 21 percent. Even so, tractors and harvesters by themselves would have accounted for most of the gains in productivity. Changes in investment patterns directly associated with the coming of New Deal regulation were responsible for the majority of savings in labor productivity.

Farmers bought expensive technology in the 1930s, and their investment patterns can be explained only in part by market factors. For the tractor, changes in technology as well as changes in certain prices made the machine more competitive. But as the threshold model revealed, changes in other prices along with the AAA countered these savings. On net, there were no new incentives to buy

[63] These estimates are made including pneumatic tires. In Appendix C, I also estimate preharvest labor without the diffusion of pneumatic tires. In this case, preharvest labor drops not by 16 percent but by 14 percent.

tractors in the 1930s. Although market forces no doubt were important, they alone could not explain this change in farmers' investment patterns.

Instead, farmers' willingness to invest turned in large part on the long-term changes initiated by the New Deal farm policy. For in providing relief, New Deal policies encouraged farmers, their lenders, and their manufacturers to alter their strategies for buying and selling farmland and machinery. The FCA provided relief, and advanced better terms for farm loans. Private lenders responded by reducing interest rates and considering efforts to lengthen the terms of loans. Implement manufacturers and their dealers realized that both credit policies and price supports helped sell their machinery. As their customers found that they were no longer compelled to choose safety over productivity and that they could better utilize credit, they invested in tractors and other expensive labor-saving machinery and equipment.

In the 1930s when farmers in the Corn Belt began to respond to the effects of regulation, they attracted little fanfare. The number of midwestern farms as well as their average size changed little in the Depression decade.[64] But starting in the 1940s and continuing for the next three decades, the diffusion of technology marked both an extraordinary exodus of family farmers and the striking increase in the size of a shrinking number of farms. Those operators who survived changed in other ways – "progressive" farmers relied more and more on machinery, paid their bills in cash, acquired and maintained larger debts. Their changes were part of a complex process that gave rise to secular gains in productivity. This process began in the late 1930s and would continue into the 1940s, 1950s, and 1960s, shaped by policies originally designed for the Great Depression.

[64] In Ohio, the number of farms actually rose by 7 percent to 233,783 farms; in Indiana the number rose 2 percent to 184,549 farms. In Illinois and Iowa, the number fell 1 percent to 213,439 and 213,318, respectively. In Missouri, the number remained nearly the same at 256,100 farms. The average size of farms fell between 1930 and 1940 from 98 to 94 acres in Ohio, and from 108 to 107 acres in Indiana. The average farm size rose in other states, but by small amounts. In Illinois the average farm size jumped 3 acres to 145 acres in 1940, in Iowa the average farm increased by 2 acres to 160 acres, and in Missouri, 3 acres were added to the average farm size, bringing it to 136 acres by 1940. U.S. Department of Commerce, *Sixteenth Census of the United States: 1940* (Washington, D.C.: U.S. Government Printing Office, 1940), Agriculture, vol. 1, part 1, pp. 426, 536, 650; and part 2, pp. 112, 232.

PART III. A legacy for New Deal regulation

7. Regulation, competition, and the revolution in farm productivity

The large gains in productivity that farmers in the Corn Belt had recorded in the late 1930s characterized much of the farm sector in the years after the Great Depression. For several decades farmers stunned economic observers with their capacity to raise productivity. Writing as late as 1980, a reporter for the London *Economist* proclaimed farming to be "America's biggest business, with a workforce as large as that of steel, car and transport industries put together. It is also the most successful part. . . . Farm labor productivity has increased tenfold in the past 50 years."[1]

In *The Last Farmer*, Howard Kohn described in personal terms what a tenfold jump in labor productivity could mean. He depicted the new farmer in his neighbor, Don Reuger:

> During twenty years Don had enlarged and modernized the Reuger farm operation. It was the envy of anyone who attempted to do likewise. At age twenty-two, Don had been the Michigan Young Farmer of the Year. For every phase of the farm season, plowing, harrowing, planting, spraying, cultivating, harvesting, he had purchased mechanically superior equipment, the basis of championship agriculture.[2]

With his modern equipment, Reuger set a goal of operating 1,000 acres. Howard Kohn's father, by contrast, relied on old machinery and never enlarged his farm beyond the 120 acres his own father had owned.[3] Although they were an unlikely pair, when Kohn became too old to manage his land by himself, he put his front eighty in crop-shares with the younger farmer. It was a handshake agreement but held an implicit clause: if they still were partners when Kohn died,

---

[1] Tony Thomas, "The Technocrats," *Economist*, 274 (January 5, 1980), American Farm Survey, p. 3.
[2] Howard Kohn, *The Last Farmer* (New York: Harper and Row, 1988), p. 26.
[3] Ibid., p. 28.

Reuger would have the first chance to buy the land. Howard Kohn remembered the two farmers working one evening. His father was in the back forty, Reuger in the front eighty:

> Pulling a five-bottom plow, Don was seated inside the air-conditioned cab of a late-model, eight-wheeled John Deere tractor, trailing diesel smoke. Superweight machines, unaffordable unless used on a large scale, were a strange sight on the Kohn farm. My father was pulling a two-bottom plow with a Massey-Ferguson 220. . . . It was purchased in 1966, before tractors were glamorous and when fresh air was thought unavoidable in farming. . . . My father was running it slower than the John Deere. Don had a schedule to meet; he would stay past midnight, headlights blazing, until the front eighty was entirely turned over. The two tractors moved back and forth – folklore confronting progress – the prelude, you might have guessed, to an inevitable falling-out between the two drivers.[4]

Reuger and Kohn reflected two sides of the productivity revolution that transformed American farming after the Great Depression. Farmers like Reuger knew the formula for their success: they invested in new fertilizers and pesticides; they bought efficient machinery; and they reduced labor and machinery costs by buying or renting more land. In doing so, these farmers reduced production costs per acre, increased profits, and achieved sharp gains in productivity. Reuger's story was that of a minority of farmers. For each one who increased his or her efficiency and acreage, there were several others who left farming.[5] Kohn hung on longer than most, but he too eventually quit. Between 1950 and 1960 one-quarter of all farms in the United States disappeared; in the next decade, another quarter disappeared. Even for those who still farmed, most did not depend on agriculture for

[4] Ibid., p. 27.
[5] The number of farms in the United States peaked in 1921 at 6,511,000. During the 1920s, this number declined by 2.5 percent, and in the 1930s the number fell by 3.5 percent to 6.1 million farms. In the 1940s, however, the pace quickened and the number fell by 11.7 percent to 5.4 million farms. Then, during the 1950s more than 25 percent of all farms disappeared, leaving 3.96 million farms in 1960. In the 1960s, another quarter of all remaining farms disappeared, and finally, during the 1970s, the number declined by 17.5 percent, leaving 2.43 million farms in the United States in 1980. U.S. Department of Agriculture, *Agricultural Statistics, 1975* (Washington, D.C.: U.S. Government Printing Office, 1975), p. 417; U.S. Department of Agriculture, *Agricultural Statistics, 1984* (Washington, D.C.: U.S. Government Printing Office, 1985), p. 375; U.S. Department of Commerce, *Historical Statistics of the United States: Colonial Times to 1970* (Washington, D.C.: U.S. Government Printing Office, 1975), p. 457.

their main source of income. By 1978 of all individuals who called themselves farmers, 66 percent earned more than half their total income by commuting to work. Just 34 percent (roughly 911,000 farmers) still earned most of their income from working in the fields.[6]

Farm regulation had much to do with the pace and shape of this revolution in productivity. The original intent of regulation changed little after World War II. As in the Great Depression, farm leaders faithfully prodded regulators to shore up prices and to lower the cost of credit. If this goal seemed simple enough from the farmers' partisan perspective, the consequences of regulation were often unintended and contradictory. Most surprising were the effects on prices. Despite the lobbyists' best efforts, prices (adjusted for inflation) fell steadily from the end of World War II through the 1960s. Yet, as long as they did so, regulation created a financial climate that supported rapid investment in land and technology. This did not mean that regulation did away with competition. From the farmers' individual perspective, they had always worked in highly competitive markets and still did so after the coming of the New Deal. Regulation, however, shifted the terms of this competition: farmers who undertook risks associated with investments in chemicals, biological inputs, machinery, and land were more likely to survive and more likely to account for gains in productivity. The prelude to this postwar era was the exceptional period of "high" prices in World War II.[7]

Farmers and farm policy in World War II

Farm regulation had been created in the 1930s to meet an emergency related to low prices and burdensome debts. World War II ended this emergency. But despite the surge in farmers' income, the system of regulation was not dismantled. Memories of World War I haunted farmers. As prices rose in the 1910s, farmers had sought to expand production and reap profits by buying new farmland. Many borrowed to do so, and after prices collapsed in the early twenties, they

[6] See J. B. Penn, "Economic Developments in U.S. Agriculture during the 1970s," in D. Gale Johnson, ed., *Food and Agricultural Policy for the 1980s* (Washington, D.C.: American Enterprise Institute, 1981), pp. 21, 24; and U.S. Department of Agriculture, "Farm Income Statistics," Statistical Bulletin No. 627 (October 1979), pp. 52, 59.

[7] In the 1980s farmers' prosperity gave way to another credit crisis. I discuss this episode in the Epilogue.

were hard pressed to meet their interest payments. Worried that high prices in World War II would again collapse sometime after the war, farmers demanded protection. If Franklin D. Roosevelt's administration wanted dramatic increases in farm output, farmers asked that it take steps to prevent a potential new crisis. Given this wartime agenda, the Commodity Credit Corporation and the Farm Credit Administration assumed new roles.

The CCC still set minimum prices, but it established maximum prices as well. To limit inflation, price ceilings were fixed at 100 to 110 percent of parity. Price floors, however, were not far behind, being pegged at 90 percent of parity. In September 1942, Roosevelt asked Congress to continue this support after the war by recalling the First World War's legacy: "The farmer, instead of looking forward to a new collapse in farm prices . . . should be able to look forward with assurance to receiving a fair minimum price for one or two years after the war."[8] A few weeks later Congress passed the Price Stabilization Act of 1942, which provided that the CCC support all basic commodities at a rate equal to 90 percent of parity for two years after the war ended. These parity rates translated into high prices: whereas the CCC initially loaned farmers forty-five cents for corn in 1933, and offered fifty-seven cents in 1938 and 1939, by 1942 its support equaled eighty-three cents; two years later it reached ninety-eight cents. Cotton and wheat prices showed similar patterns; compared with prices in 1939, cotton nearly doubled by 1942 and wheat increased 80 percent.[9]

Prices represented one ingredient in a potential credit crisis. But farmers could better protect themselves by avoiding debts altogether. The FCA took this route. It asked farmers to think twice before assuming new loans. Speaking to Ohio bankers in 1944, Norman Wall, head of the Division of Agricultural Finance at the Bureau of Agricultural Economics, told private creditors that "great care must be exercised in the extension of credit to avoid contributing to inflationary tenden-

[8] President's Message to Congress, September 7, 1942. House Miscellaneous Reports IV, 77th Congress, 2nd sess., p. 2472.

[9] Crop prices are found in U.S. Department of Agriculture, *Agricultural Statistics, 1952* (Washington, D.C.: U.S. Government Printing Office, 1952), p. 680. For public policy, see Bela Gold, *Wartime Economic Planning in Agriculture* (New York: Columbia University Press, 1949); Walter W. Wilcox, *The Farmer in the Second World War* (Ames: Iowa State College Press, 1947).

cies." He added, "Bankers, through their loan policy, will thus be in a position to influence materially economic developments."[10]

Bankers and insurance firms cooperated.[11] Equitable Life Assurance Society, for instance, distributed a cartoon advertisement to its loan correspondents. The 1947 cartoon tracked land values for the two world wars, and revised the Mother Goose rhyme "Jack and Jill" so that Jack represented farmers in World War I, Jill farmers in World War II. It read: "Jack and Jill went up the hill to buy a farm on credit, Jack fell down and broke his crown; – is Jill for that fate headed?" Equitable hoped not. The ad cautioned: "Buy yourself a farm if you wish . . . pay what you think it is worth to you. But, for your own peace of mind and future security, *be sure that your loan will be within your means when money may come harder than it does now!*"[12]

There was reason for optimism. Whereas interest rates had averaged 6.1 percent in 1919, they were only 4.5 percent in 1944. Given this reduction, annual fees "were at least 25 percent below the charges on the same amount of debt in 1919." Because more debt was held by "federally sponsored and large centralized lending institutions than was the case after World War I," the BAE predicted that should a period of "economic strain" materialize, these lenders could better assist farmers than could individual lenders. Moreover, in the 1940s farmers were avoiding debt financing. In fact, outstanding farm mortgage debt fell by $2 billion between 1939 and 1946, and as late as 1949 remained $1.7 billion below its 1939 level.[13] So too, the barometer of farmers' financial health, the rate of farm foreclosures, fell swiftly throughout the war years and reached an all-time low by 1946 (Figure 7.1).

[10]Norman J. Wall, "Agricultural Credit in Wartime" (April 13, 1944), Record Group 83, Entry 224, Box 16, p. 4, National Archives, Washington, D.C.

[11]Wilcox notes the American Bankers Association's cooperation in *The Farmer in the Second World War*, pp. 309–11. For credit, also see Gold, *Wartime Economic Planning*, pp. 268–81.

[12]Equitable Life Assurance Society (New York), *Farm Loan News* (July 1947), back cover, Record Group 7, Equitable Life Assurance Society Archives, New York, New York.

[13]U.S. Department of Agriculture, Bureau of Agricultural Economics, "Wartime Changes in the Financial Structure of Agriculture," Miscellaneous Publication No. 558 (February 1945), pp. 24–5. Changes in farm mortgage debt are calculated from U.S. Department of Agriculture, *Agricultural Statistics, 1952* (Washington, D.C.: U.S. Government Printing Office, 1952), p. 721.

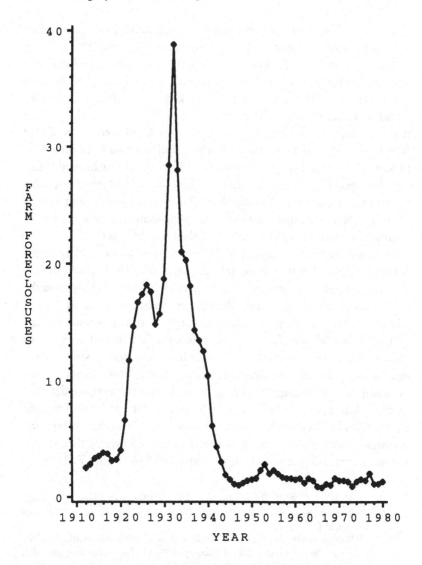

Figure 7.1. The number of foreclosures per 1,000 farms, 1912–80. The U.S. Department of Agriculture stopped collecting data after 1980. Data are from the following sources: for 1912 to 1954, U.S. Department of Agriculture, "Major Statistical Series of the U.S. Department of Agriculture," Agriculture Handbook No. 118 (1957), vol. 6, p. 11; for 1955 to 1966, U.S. Department of Agriculture, *Agricultural Statistics, 1967* (Washington, D.C.: U.S. Government Printing Office, 1967), p. 517; for 1967 to 1980, U.S. Department of Agriculture, *Agricultural Statistics, 1981* (Washington, D.C.: U.S. Government Printing Office, 1981), p. 421.

Inasmuch as farmers curtailed debts sharply in World War II, did this mean that they had skirted a land boom? Apparently not. Compared with the years spanning World War I, in the 1940s, at least 25 percent more farms were sold voluntarily each year, on average (Figure 7.2). And although land values had begun at a lower base than had been the case in the 1910s, prices doubled in the 1940s.[14] Despite their reduction of outstanding debt, farmers had sustained the largest exchange of farmland to date.

How did they finance it? The BAE's Norman Wall answered this question in terms of farmers' income. "Slightly over half of the farms reported sold in 1943," he stated, "represented cash sales, while down payments averaged just under two-fifths of the purchase price."[15] The surge in farmers' cash income permitted this outcome. Whereas in the years 1915–19 farmers' net income amounted to $7.0 billion, on average, for the ten-year period 1939–48 farmers' net income averaged $10.9 billion. In other words, farmers in the 1940s earned 50 percent more income over twice the time period. They were better able therefore to both curtail mortgage debts and to devote extra dollars to savings or to investments in new land.[16]

World War II did not produce a credit crisis. Farmers, in a sense, were able to have their cake and eat it too. Commodity markets produced unusually high prices and the CCC backed these high prices during the war. Further, farmers lobbied for and received extensions to price supports. Congress instructed the CCC to operate on the downside of commodity markets: that is, to support prices. As a result of trends in prices and credit, these farm buyers consolidated land, but escaped foreclosure.

Market subsidies, market stability: The CCC

After World War II, the FCA continued to sponsor its system of short- and long-term credit agencies. These organizations ran smoothly and

---

[14] Land values in the 1940s amounted to 75 percent of their "peak" value in 1921, or roughly 60 percent of the real value of land prices in the 1910s. Peter Lindert, "Long-run Trends in American Farmland Values," *Agricultural History*, 62 (Summer 1988), pp. 49–50.

[15] Wall, "Agricultural Credit in Wartime," p. 4.

[16] Ibid., p. 5. Changes in farm income are calculated from U.S. Department of Agriculture, "Farm Income Statistics," Statistical Bulletin No. 627, pp. 31, 38.

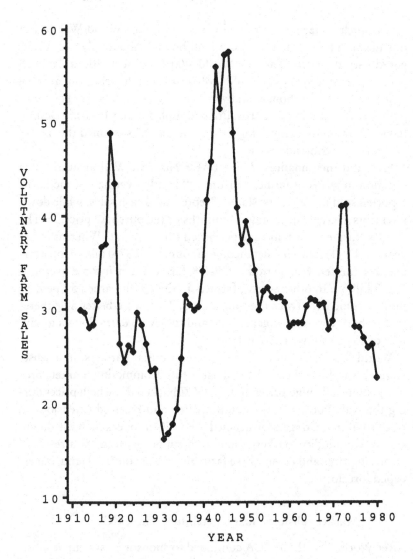

Figure 7.2. Number of voluntary transfers per 1,000 farms, 1912–80. The U.S. Department of Agriculture stopped collecting data after 1980. Data are from the same sources as in Figure 7.1.

attracted little public attention.[17] The same could not be said of price controls. The CCC, along with the acreage-restriction programs administered by the USDA, attracted a host of complaints from consumers because they subsidized farm income and artificially raised prices. Farmers, on the other hand, complained that the CCC had not done enough to stop prices from falling. Ironically, it was in response to this secular trend in falling prices that the government's supports worked to create a stable climate for investment.

Farm leaders should probably not have been as concerned as they were about falling prices. As farmers raised productivity, they reduced the amount of resources – land, labor, and capital – needed to raise crops, and in turn, the cost of production. If costs fell as fast as prices did, then operating income remained unchanged. Not all farmers, of course, were able to reduce costs fast enough, and many eventually were forced to quit. Still, other farmers were able to raise productivity, reduce costs, and continue to profit. Falling prices should have been associated with increases in productivity.

Many farm leaders found this economic outcome hard to swallow. A BAE survey conducted in 1944 revealed farmers' concern about prices. Officials asked, "What do you think would happen to prices in general if price control programs were done away with right after the war?" Roughly a third of farmers expected prices would fall. Others gave qualified answers, stating that prices would rise and then fall or that some prices would rise and others would fall. "[A]mong farmers who do express their attitude toward expected changes, by far the larger number are apprehensive about what would happen if price regulations were removed immediately after the war." The BAE found that in the Corn Belt and in the South, farmers worried most about deflation: "While a few speak of the inflationary period immediately after the last war, . . . more simply remember the low farm prices of the early 1920's and the depression years of the 30's, and consider that there is danger of a similar slump after this war if controls are not maintained." In California's Central Valley, the BAE found that more farmers expected an initial period of inflation, but this too worried them. One farmer was quoted as saying: "Things might shoot away

[17] For the FCA's record, see for instance, Farm Credit Administration, "1917–1957: Years of Progress with the Cooperative Land Bank System," Circular E-43 (January 1957).

out of sight. Prices went higher right after the other war than during the war. We have to have control until things get normal."[18]

Farmers and their organizations lobbied vigorously for an extension of controls. These efforts kept price supports at 90 percent of parity through 1954. Thereafter supports were lowered. In 1955 Congress dropped loan rates to 82.5 percent of parity; in 1956 cotton and wheat supports were lowered to 75 percent of parity and corn to 65 percent. These rates continued through the rest of the 1950s.[19]

Even with the shift to more flexible price supports, Congress consistently held loan rates above market prices. Consider Figure 7.3. From 1948 through the end of the 1950s, each crop's loan rate equaled or exceeded the crop's market price. The one exception occurred in 1951 and 1952 when wartime demands lifted market prices above loan rates. Because the government's loan rate so often exceeded market prices, farmers frequently allowed their loans to expire and forfeited crops to the CCC. By 1959 the agency owned 25 percent of a year's production of corn, a third of a year's supply of cotton, and more than half of a year's harvest of wheat (Table 7.1).

As surpluses accumulated, they forced regulators to fashion alternative strategies for stabilizing and subsidizing farm income. In 1961 the Kennedy administration instructed the CCC to reduce its loan rates to market levels. Farmers still received guaranteed minimum price supports for their crops, only at lower levels. A second provision asked the USDA to cut production with large-scale acreage restrictions. Harkening back to the Depression, the government paid farmers to idle 20 to 50 percent of their land devoted to cash crops. Those who signed such restriction contracts were paid a per-bushel rate that kept their total price per bushel (i.e., the CCC support price plus

[18] U.S. Department of Agriculture, Bureau of Agricultural Economics, "Farmers View the Postwar World" (September 25, 1944), pp. 34–5, Record Group 83, Entry 207, Box 9, #85, National Archives.

[19] For farm policy in World War II, see Wilcox, *The Farmer in the Second World War*; Gold, *Wartime Economic Planning*. For the immediate postwar years, see Allen J. Matusow, *Farm Policies and Politics in the Truman Years* (Cambridge, Mass.: Harvard University Press, 1967), and for postwar years in general, see Willard Cochrane and Mary Ryan, *American Farm Policy, 1948–1976* (Minneapolis: University of Minnesota Press, 1976); U.S. Department of Agriculture, "History of Agricultural Price-Support and Adjustment Programs, 1933–84," Agriculture Information Bulletin No. 485 (December 1984).

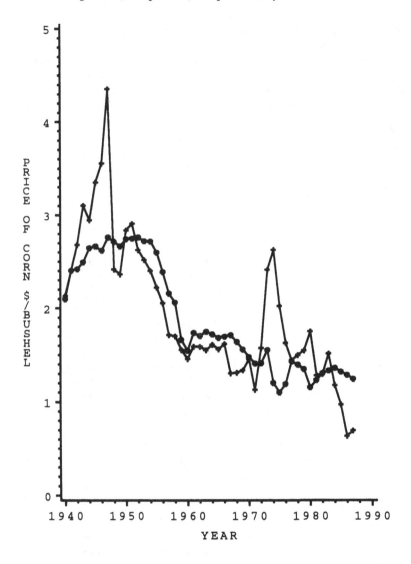

Figure 7.3A. Government support prices and market prices for corn, 1942–
87. * denotes the government support price; + the market price. Prices are
deflated based on the consumer price index. Beginning in 1974, the government support price is reported as the target price; prior to that date it is the
CCC loan price. Data are from these sources: U.S. Department of Agriculture, *Agricultural Statistics, 1952* (Washington, D.C.: U.S. Government Printing Office, 1952), pp. 680–1; *Agricultural Statistics, 1967* (Washington,
D.C.: U.S. Government Printing Office, 1967), pp. 2, 17, 23, 28, 35, 42, 74,
76, 161, 168; *Agricultural Statistics, 1988* (Washington, D.C.: U.S. Government Printing Office, 1988), pp. 1, 7, 30, 37, 61, 63; and *Agricultural
Statistics, 1990* (Washington, D.C.: U.S. Government Printing Office, 1990),
pp. 7, 38, 63.

Table 7.1. *Quantities of corn, cotton, and wheat owned by the CCC, 1949-87*

Year	Corn (million bushels)	Cotton (1,000 bales)	Wheat (million bushels)
1949	76	3,712	162
1950	399	98	271
1951	389	3	136
1952	280	236	132
1953	362	236	448
1954	606	1,805	749
1955	758	8,014	889
1956	984	6,662	840
1957	1,118	4,030	756
1958	1,168	1,616	777
1959	1,235	7,583	1,109
1960	1,471	5,028	1,133
1961	1,412	1,467	1,130
1962	1,045	4,705	1,045
1963	849	5,955	982
1964	835	7,793	712
1965	530	10,155	572
1966	156	8,389	216
1967	138	1,247	109
1968	261	135	100
1969	296	2,221	168
1970	215	2,077	283
1971	144	[a]	372
1972	140	[a]	267
1973	70	[a]	139
1974	6	[a]	15
1975	[b]	0	[b]
1976	[b]	[a]	[b]
1977	4	[a]	48
1978	101	[a]	50
1979	260	[b]	200
1980	242	[b]	196
1981	280	[b]	187
1982	1,150	397	192
1983	202	158	188
1984	225	123	378
1985	546	767	602
1986	1,443	73	830
1987	835	3	283

[a]Less than 50,000 units.
[b]Less than 500,000 units.
Sources: U.S. Department of Agriculture, *Agricultural*

acreage payments) above the going market price. In 1961 Kennedy tested his new farm program on feed grains (mostly corn, grain sorghum, and barley). In 1962 Congress added wheat to the plan; and in 1964, under the direction of President Lyndon B. Johnson, cotton was included. These crops remained under the Kennedy–Johnson program until the early 1970s, when world demand and farm prices rose sharply.[20]

Price supports and acreage controls led to huge subsidies. For the 1950s, the CCC supplied extra income through its high loan rates. If farmers had released crops stored at the CCC, prices no doubt would have fallen. Given the inelastic demand for crops, an increase in supply would have caused a proportionately larger decline in prices. For the 1950s and early 1960s, depending on one's assumptions about price elasticity, the price-support programs raised actual prices by at least 15 percent and perhaps as much as 50 percent.[21] For the rest of the 1960s, government regulation subsidized income through the acreage-restriction program. Table 7.2 lists the loan price and acreage payments for the three major commodities, corn, cotton, and

[20] Cochrane and Ryan give elaborate details for each year that the program was in effect. They review feed grains and wheat. See Cochrane and Ryan, *American Farm Policy*, pp. 189–98, 210–19.

[21] Reports include G. E. Brandow, "Policy for Commercial Agriculture, 1945–1971," in L. Martin, ed., *A Survey of Agricultural Economic Literature* (Minneapolis: University of Minnesota Press), vol. 1, pp. 249–50; Frederick Nelson, "An Economic Analysis of the Impact of Past Farm Programs on Livestock and Crop Prices, Production, and Resource Adjustments" (Ph.D. dissertation, University of Minnesota, 1975); and Daryll Ray and Earl Heady, "Simulated Effects of Alternative Policy and Economic Environments on U.S. Agriculture," Iowa State University Center for Agricultural and Rural Development Report No. 46T (Ames, March 1974); U.S. Congress, Joint Economic Committee, *Economic Policies for Agriculture in the 1960's – Implications of Four Selected Alternatives*, 86th Congress, 2nd sess. (December 1960); U.S. Congress, Senate, Committee on Agriculture and Forestry, *Farm Program Benefits and Costs in Recent Years*, 88th Congress, 2nd sess. (October 1964).

Notes to Table 7.1 (*cont.*)

Statistics, 1972 (Washington, D.C.: U.S. Government Printing Office, 1972), p. 623; U.S. Department of Agriculture, *Agricultural Statistics, 1983* (Washington, D.C.: U.S. Government Printing Office, 1983), p. 464; and U.S. Department of Agriculture, *Agricultural Statistics, 1990* (Washington, D.C.: U.S. Government Printing Office, 1990), pp. 7, 38, 63.

wheat. In each case, the USDA offered substantial increases in the crop's effective price. From 1963 through 1972, diversion payments boosted corn prices by 17 to 30 percent, wheat prices by 33 to 55 percent, and cotton prices by 45 to 75 percent.[22] These acreage payments represented substantial bonuses. Between 1961 and 1973, for every five dollars a farmer logged in as net farm (pretax) income, one came from the government. Even if one adds dollars earned off the farm, government payments were still significant and accounted for one out of every nine dollars of income.[23]

Subsidies, though, did not mean prices remained stable or even rose. Instead, looking at crop prices in the years since World War II, what stands out is regulation's effect in determining a pattern of falling prices. Despite the postwar supports, prices (adjusted for inflation) gradually drifted downward, and the total declines were quite large: from the close of World War II to the late 1960s, prices of corn, cotton, and wheat fell more than 50 percent (Figure 7.3).[24] Prices of other crops including rice, oats, soybeans, and sorghum fell more than 40 percent.[25]

What the politicians achieved was a soft landing: while prices fell, they never collapsed, and year-to-year variations were small. Consider Table 7.3. In the 1920s, prior to the coming of regulation, crop prices had varied 13 percent from one year to the next. With the crash of 1929 and the boom of prices during World War II, the variability of crop prices rose in the 1930s and 1940s. After the 1940s, however, the variance was sharply reduced: in the 1950s and 1960s, prices fluctuated little more than 3 or 4 percent from one year

---

[22] As diversion payments increased so did farmers' rates of participation. Of all eligible corn farmers, 40 to 60 percent enlisted; 50 to 70 percent of all wheat farms were placed under contract; and a spectacular rate of 80 to more than 90 percent of all cotton farms were contracted in those years. Participation rates are reported for individual years in U.S. Department of Agriculture, *Agricultural Statistics,* various issues. The data are also found in Cochrane and Ryan, *American Farm Policy,* pp. 188, 209, 226.

[23] Bruce L. Gardner, "Consequences of Farm Policies during the 1970s," in D. Gale Johnson, ed., *Food and Agricultural Policy for the 1980s* (Washington, D.C.: American Enterprise Institute, 1981), p. 59.

[24] One exception was the price of tobacco. Tobacco, however, was subject to different types of regulation, which reinforced labor-intensive methods of farming.

[25] Gardner, "Consequences of Farm Policies during the 1970s," pp. 48–60.

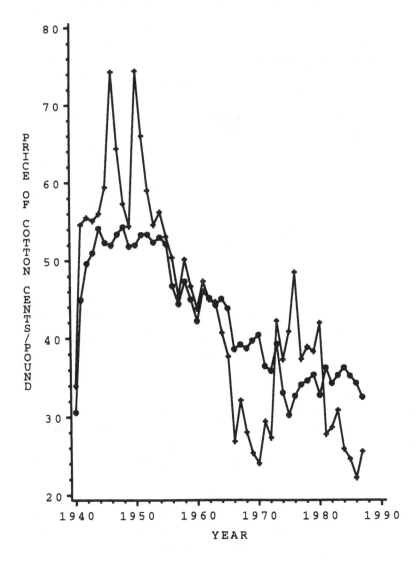

Figure 7.3B. Government support prices and market prices for cotton, 1942–87. * denotes the government support price; + the market price. Prices are deflated based on the consumer price index. Data are from the same sources as reported for Figure 7.3A.

218   A legacy for New Deal regulation

Table 7.2. *Government support prices and government payments for acreage restrictions per unit, 1963-72*

Year	Wheat		Corn		Cotton	
	CCC price ($/bu.)	Acreage payment ($/bu.)	CCC price ($/bu.)	Acreage payment ($/bu.)	CCC price (¢/lb.)	Acreage payment (¢/lb.)
1963	$1.84	---	$1.07	$0.18	31.72¢	---
1964	1.30	$0.43	1.10	0.15	29.30	3.50¢
1965	1.25	0.47	1.05	0.20	28.25	4.35
1966	1.25	0.65	1.00	0.30	20.21	9.42
1967	1.25	0.60	1.05	0.30	19.47	11.53
1968	1.25	0.58	1.05	0.30	19.69	12.24
1969	1.25	0.69	1.05	0.30	19.71	14.73
1970	1.25	0.75	1.05	0.30	20.15	16.80
1971	1.25	0.54	1.03	0.32	20.00	15.00
1972	1.25	0.47	1.01	0.40	20.85	15.00

Sources: U.S. Department of Agriculture, *Agricultural Statistics, 1967* (Washington, D.C.: U.S. Government Printing Office, 1967), pp. 17, 42, 76; and U.S. Department of Agriculture, *Agricultural Statistics, 1980* (Washington, D.C.: U.S. Government Printing Office, 1980), pp. 7, 37, 63.

to the next. By that time the CCC had closed the gap between market and loan prices, as Figure 7.3 indicates, and assured farmers that the market price would be no worse than the loan rate. It not only subsidized farm income but also offered farmers a measure of stability.

When the Bureau of Agricultural Economics surveyed farmers in 1944, it had asked them to explain their "desire for continued price regulation even in normal times." The officials summarized the responses by saying: "Wide fluctuations of prices endanger the farmer. If prices fall sharply, he must take a loss. Even rising prices are looked on with suspicion by many farmers, because they fear these prices must be followed by a slump." When asked about the future of prices, roughly 75 percent of farmers expected the government to "step in" if prices fell sharply. A Corn Belt farmer said: "We are much better off to go along on a fairly stable level with controls to knock off the peaks and prevent the severe dips. These really hurt us. If the

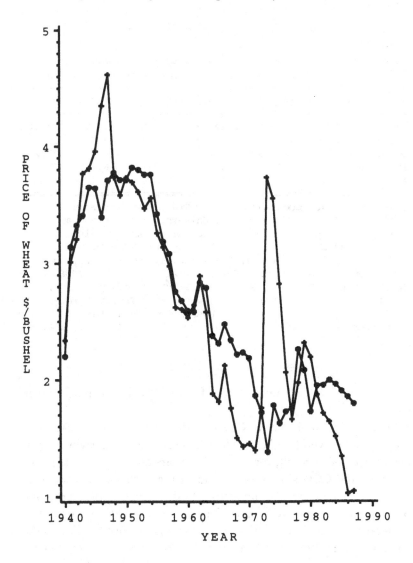

Figure 7.3C. Government support prices and market prices for wheat, 1942–87. * denotes the government support price; + the market price. Prices are deflated based on the consumer price index. Data are from the same sources as reported for Figure 7.3A.

Table 7.3. *Year-to-year changes in prices of agricultural commodities, 1921-80*

Crop prices	Average absolute percent change from previous year					
	1921-30	1931-40	1941-50	1951-60	1961-70	1971-80
Corn	18.6%	33.0%	22.5%	6.0%	7.0%	23.0%
Cotton	27.2	20.3	19.9	5.9	9.7	19.6
Wheat	17.8	24.9	16.1	3.3	10.7	27.2
Soybeans	11.2	33.7	20.7	5.1	6.9	21.5
All crops	13.1	18.5	13.9	3.7	3.4	13.5

Sources: Willard Cochrane and Mary Ryan, *American Farm Policy, 1948-1973* (Minneapolis: University of Minnesota Press, 1976), p. 385; and U.S. Department of Agriculture, *Agricultural Statistics, 1976* (Washington, D.C.: U.S. Government Printing Office, 1976), pp. 1, 29, 57, 128; U.S. Department of Agriculture, *Agricultural Statistics, 1988* (Washington, D.C.: U.S. Government Printing Office, 1988), pp. 1, 30, 61, 124, 403; U.S. Department of Agriculture, *Agricultural Statistics, 1990* (Washington, D.C.: U.S. Government Printing Office, 1990), pp. 1, 31, 61, 121, 454.

extremes can be eliminated the farmers [will be] much more secure."[26]

In the years after World War II, politicians kept the CCC on a short leash, preventing the problem farmers feared – a swift slide in farm prices. As a result, for twenty-five years after the war, as prices dropped, the CCC slowed and steadied the decline. Price supports (and acreage controls) continued to subsidize farmers with handsome bonuses to their annual incomes. But the programs also gave farmers a greater measure of security than they had enjoyed prior to the coming of regulation, encouraging the "progressive" farmers to continue to make investments in the postwar years. This stable environ-

[26] Answering yes were 73 percent of Corn Belt farmers, 87 percent of farmers in the Southeast, and 74 percent of farmers in the Central Valley (California). See U.S. Department of Agriculture, Bureau of Agricultural Economics, "Farmers View the Postwar World" (September 25, 1944), pp. 30–1, 36–7. For the Corn Belt farmer, see "Farmers' Appraisal of Post-War Problems. Selected Interviews" (February 21, 1944), p. 6, Record Group 83, Entry 207, Box 9, #85, National Archives.

ment was especially important, given the changes that took place in credit markets.

Competition in credit markets

The rivalry with private lenders that the FCA initiated in the 1930s persisted long after the Depression had ended. As creditors pursued their competition, they introduced new loans and provided farmers – whether it was public or private funds – with more attractive terms than they had received prior to the 1930s.[27]

Not all private lenders criticized their public counterparts. At the Illinois Bankers' annual meeting in 1963, O. E. Anderson chastised his fellow bankers in a talk, entitled "You Can't Grow Corn in a Bank Lobby." "Many of you might agree with me," Anderson began, "that the short-sightedness of bankers in the 1920s left both politicians and farmers absolutely no other choice than to bring about the passage of legislation permitting the creation of Federal Land Banks, . . . production credit associations, and other governmentally operated or sponsored sources of credit." Anderson also reminded bankers of federal relief efforts in the 1930s:

> Perhaps some of you may remember, if you're old enough, that even happier than the farmer over this trend of events were the banker, the insurance company executives, the individual lenders, and businessmen in general. You can't do business with a man today if he is in danger of losing his farm tomorrow, and many bankers and many

[27]During the early postwar years, the National Bureau of Economic Research sponsored several studies about farm credit. See Harold G. Diesslin, *Agricultural Equipment Financing*, Occasional Paper No. 50 (New York: National Bureau of Economic Research, 1955); Donald C. Horton, *Patterns of Farm Financial Structure: A Cross-Section View of Economic and Physical Determinants*, National Bureau of Economic Research (Princeton: Princeton University Press, 1957); Lawrence A. Jones and David Durand, *Mortgage Lending Experience in Agriculture*, National Bureau of Economic Research (Princeton: Princeton University Press, 1954); R. J. Saulnier, *Costs and Returns on Farm Mortgage Lending by Life Insurance Companies, 1945–1947*, Occasional Paper No. 30 (New York: National Bureau of Economic Research, 1949); R. J. Saulnier, Harold G. Halcrow, and Neil H. Jacoby, *Federal Lending and Loan Insurance*, National Bureau of Economic Research (Princeton: Princeton University Press, 1958). Also see E. L. Baum, Howard G. Diesslin, and Earl O. Heady, *Capital and Credit Needs in a Changing Agriculture* (Ames: Iowa State University Press, 1961).

insurance executives were ... happy to have them [farm loans] refinanced through agencies organized or sponsored by the government.[28]

Still, Anderson had cause for concern with government-sponsored competition. He asked "Are we any smarter today?" In his assessment, banks still were "losing out in the competition for farm credit." They were losing to federal lenders.[29] Certainly public creditors still offered attractive loans. While the Treasury had stopped subsidizing interest rates on mortgages of federal land banks after 1944, the public lenders offered the lowest rates of interest at 4.1 percent until 1955 and 5 to 5.4 percent until 1970.[30] They also set the longest terms for repayment, averaging 25 to 35 years (Table 3.1). In short-term credit markets, production credit associations set competitive terms with interest rates that ranged from 5 to 6 percent.[31] This competition worried many bankers. Asked in a national survey about new sources of competition, 46 percent of all banks reported increased competition for agricultural loans during the late 1950s and early 1960s, and half attributed this competition to federal lenders (PCAs and federal land banks).[32] William A. McDonnell, president of a St. Louis bank, complained that "a banker on his chair is no match for a P.C.A. man on his toes."[33]

[28] O. E. Anderson, "You Can't Grow Corn in a Bank Lobby," *17th Annual Illinois Bankers Agricultural Credit Conference: A Digest of Proceedings,* April 3 and 4, 1963, pp. 22–5, Record Series 8/4/823, Box 1, University of Illinois Archives, University of Illinois at Urbana-Champaign.

[29] Ibid.

[30] During the Great Depression, Congress instructed the Treasury Department to reimburse the FCA for reducing interest rates by one point. Using these subsidies, the FCA lowered interest rates to 3.5 percent. Congress eliminated the subsidies on July 1, 1944. Aaron G. Nelson and William G. Murray, *Agricultural Finance* (Ames: Iowa State University Press, 1960), pp. 383–4.

[31] In the 1940s, interest rates averaged 4 percent; in the next two decades most PCAs set rates at 5 to 6 percent, but a few set rates above 6 percent. For the years from the 1930s to the late 1950s, see U.S. Department of Agriculture, "Major Statistical Series of the U.S. Department of Agriculture," Agriculture Handbook No. 118, vol. 6 (1958), pp. 30–1.

[32] American Bankers Association, Agriculture Committee, *Trends in Agricultural Banking: Report of Year-End 1962 Agricultural Credit Situation Survey* (New York: American Bankers Association, 1963), pp. 5–6.

[33] William A. McDonnell, "Agricultural Credit by Correspondent Banking," in American Bankers Association, *Proceedings of the National Agricultural Credit Conference – 1956* (St. Louis, December 10–12, 1956), p. 46.

McDonnell may have been too pessimistic, however, because by the 1950s and 1960s, private creditors were indeed on their toes, developing tactics to regain their share of the farm loan business. The earliest (and perhaps most aggressive) response came from the Equitable Life Assurance Society. In the late 1930s and early 1940s Equitable had been concerned about competition. In its 1942 annual report, the Farm Mortgage Department had singled out federal lenders as its "principal competitor," given the land banks' "standard loan of 34 1/2 years." The report also outlined how the Treasury Department, by subsidizing land banks' interest rates in the early 1940s, allowed the banks to offer rates that were slightly lower than Equitable's.[34]

The Farm Mortgage Department, however, was not closed out of the market. Equitable initiated important changes in its farm loans. It first began to emphasize long-term amortized loans – that is, loans comparable with the federal land banks' long-term loans. The manager of the Farm Mortgage Department, Nils Olsen, saw these loans as especially important. "Our field offices will promote the long-term amortized loan. We believe it can be sold to many borrowers even at the higher rate [of 4.5 percent]. Ability to make straight loans where necessary at 4 percent, and higher commissions on amortized loans, are counted on strongly to assist in this program."[35]

Equitable used two provisions to give flexibility to this basic loan. The first one allowed farmers to make payments on their loans "in any amount at any time if funds were from farm income." The privilege granted farmers more flexibility because in prior years Equitable had permitted prepayment of loans only in the amount equal to 20 percent of principal and only on specific interest-due dates. The next year Equitable announced a second provision, the "Prepayment Reserve Plan." Farmers could make extra payments on loans that would be held in a special account. The payments would be applied to interest due on the loan, but if the borrower encountered problems in meeting the loan's subsequent fees then the borrower could withdraw funds from the special account and use them to pay both interest and principal on the loan. This too provided flexibility: farmers could accumulate extra funds in years of prosperity to be used in

---

[34] Farm Mortgage Department, *Annual Report, 1942*, p. 7, Record Group 4, Equitable Life Assurance Society Archives.

[35] Amortized loans are detailed in Farm Mortgage Department, *Annual Report, 1939*, p. 5, Record Group 4, Equitable Life Assurance Society Archives.

years of low prices or poor harvests. In the Farm Mortgage Department's 1942 annual report, the new manager, R. I. Nowell, expressed that, "with the 4 percent amortized loan, the Farm Income Privilege and the Prepayment Reserve Plan the Equitable offers the best farm loan available today."[36]

Equitable also worked closely with commercial banks. The insurance firm had long-standing ties to banks, but it created a new program intended to improve this cooperation. This strategy was possible because local banks and insurance firms competed in different parts of the farm credit market. Most banks concentrated on short-term loans, and even for mortgages, their loans typically carried maturities of four to seven years (Table 3.1). By contrast, insurance firms offered longer-term loans, and for this reason, Equitable pioneered a new partnership with banks in 1943 through a program entitled the "Approved Mortgage Plan."[37]

The plan established a contract that took a similar form for each bank that worked with Equitable. A bank's officers first reviewed the application and, if they approved it, sent it to Equitable. Equitable's staff likewise reviewed the application. If they too approved it, then the bank and Equitable entered a long-term agreement. Technically, the bank would write a five-year loan, but it would hold the loan for two years during which time it received full interest. Then the loan was assigned to Equitable. Equitable recalled the experience of one banker, Harry Swanzey of Joliet, Illinois. Swanzey reported that once the loan was assigned to Equitable, Equitable would receive "3/4 of 1% of the unpaid balance of the commission," but his bank would

[36] Farm Mortgage Department, *Annual Report, 1941*, p. 7, and *Annual Report, 1942*, p. 7, Record Group 4, Equitable Life Assurance Society Archives. R. I. Nowell outlined the importance of the "Farm Income Privilege" program in "The Use of Credit for Farm and Home Improvement," address at the Institute of Rural Affairs, Virginia Polytechnic Institute, Blacksburg, Virginia (August 1950), p. 4, kept with *Farm Loan News* (August 1950), Record Group 7, Equitable Life Assurance Society Archives. For the "Prepayment Reserve Plan," also see Eli Ferguson, "The Modern Farm Loan," paper given in New York (November 16, 1948), p. 5, kept with *Farm Loan News* (December 1948), Record Group 7, Equitable Life Assurance Society Archives. For Nowell's comments, see Farm Mortgage Department, *Annual Report, 1942*, p. 7.

[37] Farm Mortgage Department, *Annual Report, 1943*, p. 7, Record Group 4, Equitable Life Assurance Society Archives.

continue to service the loan and receive a service fee from Equitable. The farm borrower would have a long-term amortized loan, typically running thirty-six or forty years, which allowed the borrower a "pre-payment privilege of any amount at any time, provided it is from agricultural income."[38]

Many bankers profited from Equitable's plan. Again, Equitable quoted Swanzey: "There are times when the usual bankable real estate loan will not meet the farmer's needs – times when a maturity longer than the bank can give is necessary. It is such loans – and many good ones – that have been going to the Federal Land Banks." With Equitable's plan, Swanzey felt that his bank could "give a complete loan service to agriculture. . . . There is nothing a federal agency has to offer that we cannot do." An Arizona banker, L. W. Fletcher, echoed Swanzey. Fletcher estimated that "of the applicants for farm loans, 75% wanted and needed financing for a period in excess of 10 years. . . . The majority of these would run in the neighborhood of 20 years." Since his bank was limited to ten-year loans, Fletcher could offer "full service" by working with insurance firms like Equitable.

Fletcher chose this route for a second reason: "We had been forced to direct our customers to other agencies, particularly the Federal Land Bank, which, in our area, has its land bank agency and PCA in the same building. In other words, we were sending business away, as the PCA group really worked over loan prospects when they got in the office." Fletcher wanted his own ties to long-term loans; Equitable gave him this option. In entering the contract, Fletcher identified one drawback: "The plan under which we are operating requires that the

[38] R. I. Nowell, then head of Equitable's Farm Mortgage Department, sent a clipping from the *Wall Street Journal* (December 20, 1943) to the Bureau of Agricultural Economics. The clipping describes the plan. See Bureau of Agricultural Economics, Record Group 83, Entry 224, General Correspondence, 1917–46, Box 16, National Archives. Equitable quoted parts of a speech Harry Swanzey gave at the Mid-Western Credit Conference of the American Bankers Association; he was quoted in "Agricultural Lending," *Farm Loan News* (January 1948), pp. 3–4; other reviews of the program include "A Banker Goes Farming," *Farm Loan News* (May 1947), pp. 6–7; "Organizing a Bank's Farm Loan Department," *Farm Loan News* (April 1952), pp. 6–7, Record Group 7, Equitable Life Assurance Society Archives; and R. Carlyle Buley, *The Equitable Life Assurance Society of the United States 1859–1964* vol. 2 (New York: Meredith, 1967), pp. 1117–18.

loans be assigned to Equitable at the expiration of two years." But he noted: "While we, of course, would like to carry them longer, we realize that there had to be some concession on our part to enable us to handle these long-term loans." This concession paid off: "Since entering into this contract with Equitable, we have produced a greater volume of loans on farm property . . . than our principal competitor, the Federal Land Bank, during the same period."[39]

While Equitable is the best documented case, other lenders initiated similar tactics. In its 1941 annual report, Equitable's Farm Mortgage Department found that its Farm Income Privilege provision "has been very well received by brokers and farmers . . . Competitors are disturbed by our action, and the President of at least one company has imitated the letter."[40] In its 1944 Annual Report, the department referred to its Approved Mortgage Plan, noting that "the Prudential Insurance Company announced a plan which copied after the Society's and late in the year Aetna Insurance Company announced a somewhat modified version."[41] By 1945 Aetna had introduced nearly all of Equitable's special features. A brochure informed potential borrowers that more than half of Aetna's loans were made "on the long-term full amortization basis." Farmers were given what Aetna called the "Any-Day Prepayment Privilege." Like Equitable's "Farm Income Privilege," Aetna's plan allowed farmers to make interest payments "at any time regardless of the interest date." Finally, Aetna offered farmers its "Reserve-Building Feature." Like Equitable, Aetna would allow farmers to accumulate extra payments in a special fund.

[39] For Harry Swanzey's review, see "Agricultural Lending," *Farm Loan News* (January 1948), pp. 3–4. L. W. Fletcher is quoted from his account, in *Bankers Monthly* (March 1947), as it was reprinted in "Loans for Six Months or Forty Years Make a Complete Loan Service," *Farm Loan News* (April 1947), pp. 6–7, Record Group 7, Equitable Life Assurance Society Archives.

[40] Farm Mortgage Department, *Annual Report, 1941*, p. 7.

[41] Farm Mortgage Department, *Annual Report, 1944*, p. 5, Record Group 4, Equitable Life Assurance Society Archives. In a 1954 speech, R. I. Nowell, head of Equitable's farm loan business, suggested that Equitable patterned its partnership plan with banks on a model that Aetna had begun in the early 1940s. Early records do not indicate this pattern, but if correct Nowell's remarks suggest that other firms were working along similar lines to develop new lending practices. For Nowell's speech, see R. I. Nowell, "Bank-Insurance Company Agreements," in American Bankers Association, *Proceedings of the National Agricultural Credit Conference – 1954* (Memphis, 1954), pp. 40–3.

The money could be called on in lean years to meet interest or principal payments.[42]

Insurance firms profited from this arrangement, and banks did so as well. Banks also maintained long-standing arrangements among themselves, with smaller, country banks working with city correspondents. In a 1964 credit survey, the American Bankers Association (ABA) found that 60 percent of banks used insurance companies to obtain outside mortgage funds. Country and city banks also entered partnerships. Country banks worked with correspondent or city banks when the size of a potential loan exceeded their lending limits. In credit surveys from the 1960s, the ABA found that correspondent banks handled at least half of the loans that were in excess of a smaller bank's loan limits.[43]

By the mid-1950s Equitable's Farm Mortgage Department took stock of the consequences of its lending policies. Nowell, head of Equitable's Farm Mortgage Department, reported that the company's farm loan investment had increased 350 percent from 1946 to 1954, or nearly five times that of other insurance firms. Equitable had become the nation's leading farm creditor (among insurance companies) in 1954, and it remained one of the nation's largest in subsequent years. Between 1954 and 1967, the value of its outstanding farm loans jumped from $293 million to $746.6 million.[44]

Overall, both insurance firms and commercial banks regained an edge in the farm loan business, as measured by their market share. In long-term markets, insurance firms' share rose from 15 percent of outstanding farm mortgage debt in 1940 to 20–25 percent in the

[42] See "In the Light of Experience," in "Marketing Materials 1930s–1945," Record Group 42, Aetna Life and Casualty Company Archives, Hartford, Connecticut.

[43] Banks' practice of working with insurance companies was especially prevalent in the Corn Belt. American Bankers Association, *Trends in Agricultural Banking: Report of Midyear 1964 Agricultural Credit Situation Survey* (New York: American Bankers Association, 1964), p. 9. American Bankers Association, *Agricultural Banking Developments 1962–1967* (New York: American Bankers Association, 1967), pp. 6, 14, 30.

[44] Equitable held $61 million in farm debt in 1946. R. I. Nowell, "Bank–Insurance Company Agreements," pp. 40–3. For 1946, see "Equitable Farm Loan Leadership," *Farm Loan News* (April 1952), p. 5; for 1954, see "Farm Loans by the Equitable Life Assurance Society of the United States 1954," *Farm Loan News* (March 1955), pp. 4–5; for 1967, see *Farm Loan News* (April 1968), p. 2, Record Group 7, Equitable Life Assurance Society Archives.

1950s and 1960s (Table 3.2). The banks' share of mortgage debt jumped from 8 to 12 percent over the same period. Federal land banks lost market share, as their stake fell from 43 percent in 1940 to 23 percent in 1970. For non–real estate debt, banks boosted their share of the market from 31 percent in 1940 to 49 percent in 1970. PCAs also increased their share from 5 to 22 percent in the same years. Private individuals and other lenders (such as dealers) lost out – their share fell from 49 to 25 percent between 1940 and 1970. In long-term markets, private individuals and "other" lenders also played a smaller role. Since the Depression their share rarely ran above 40 percent.[45]

As private lenders like Equitable regained their markets, they made the farm loan business highly competitive. Aetna, after "considerable soul searching," dropped out of the farm loan business in 1948. In subsequent years the firm reviewed its decision, but found that the market was simply too competitive to warrant reentry. Writing in 1965, Vice-President E. H. Warner concluded that the firm had three strikes against it: it had no trained staff; it would be at a disadvantage in acquiring a large enough volume of loans in a given geographic area to earn reasonable profits; and interest rates might be no better than rates for city loans. He advised that "we should remain out of the farm mortgage loan business."[46]

When these markets became highly competitive, they worked to the farmer's benefit. One advantage was reflected in the flexibility of loans. Under Equitable's special provisions, farmers could accumulate extra funds to help secure them through a few years of low prices or poor harvests. Equitable's Nowell noted that by 1950 farmers had $5 million in the prepayment reserve plan.[47] A second favorable change had been the shift to long-term, amortized loans.[48] Farmers were also better served insofar as "institutional" replaced individual lenders.

[45] Figures for short-term markets are calculated from U.S. Department of Agriculture, "Economic Indicators of the Farm Sector: Income and Balance Sheet Statistics, 1983," ECIFS 3–3 (September 1984), p. 116. For long-term markets, see Table 3.2.

[46] E. H. Warner, Vice-President, to Crampton Trainer, Senior Vice-President and Treasurer, March 5, 1965, and Crampton Trainer, "Farm Lending," April 7, 1965, "Correspondence – Historical Data," Record Group 42, Aetna Life and Casualty Company Archives.

[47] R. I. Nowell, "The Use of Credit for Farm and Home Improvement," pp. 4–5, Record Group 7, Equitable Life Assurance Society Archives.

[48] "In the Light of Experience," pp. 6–7.

Nowell explained in a 1950 speech: "Private mortgages, as a rule, are for short periods and usually come due in a lump sum or carry excessive amortization. Interest rates vary widely. I have heard of some non-interest bearing loans, but often the rate is higher than charged by banks or insurance companies."[49]

In this postwar setting, larger numbers of farmers were able to obtain loans on more favorable terms. In comparison to loans made in the years prior to the Great Depression, after World War II credit markets worked to farmers' advantage. In the 1920s only one in twelve farm loans was written for ten or more years, and interest rates averaged more than 6 percent. After World War II, by contrast, one in two farm real-estate loans averaged fifteen years or longer. These loans carried interest rates that in nominal terms were a point less than those of the 1920s, and once adjusted for inflation were nearly half that of the 1920s.[50] The annual financial burden of the loans was roughly halved.

Throughout the postwar years, competition between public and private creditors remained intense because most private lenders did not quit. For the basic terms of loans, private lenders copied their public counterparts. But they also introduced new tactics. Equitable's Approved Mortgage Plan was an important innovation because it established new ties between private lenders, enabling them to scoop new business from public banks. This rivalry worked to the competitive farmer's advantage. A farmer was better able to obtain credit on attractive terms, and in the years after World War II, farmers readily assumed new debts.

Financial demands for farm technology

From the end of World War II to 1970, farmers doubled and tripled crop yields while they reduced the amount of labor to one-third the time spent in 1930 (Table 7.4). These gains in productivity had been accomplished with large investments in fertilizers, pesticides,

[49] Nowell, "The Use of Credit for Farm and Home Improvement," pp. 4–5.
[50] In the 1920s, with no inflation, the rate of interest averaged 6 percent. In the 1950s and 1960s, once the 3 percent rate of inflation was factored into credit rates, the lenders' real rate of interest dropped to 4.5 percent. Inflation is measured in terms of the consumer price index for the years 1914 to 1939, and the implicit GNP price deflator for the period since 1940. *The Economic Report of the President, 1986* (Washington, D.C.: U.S. Government Printing Office, 1986), p. 257.

Table 7.4. *Indexes and rates of growth of land and labor productivity, selected years, 1910-80*

| A. *Index of land and labor productivity* | | | | | |
Items	1910	1930	1940	1970	1980
Crop production per acre	56	53	62	104	117
Labor hours of farm work	325	330	295	90	65
Output per hour of labor	14	16	20	112	190
B. *Compound rates of growth*				
Items	1910-30	1930-40	1940-70	1940-80
---	---	---	---	---
Crop production per acre	-0.3%	1.6%	1.7%	1.6%
Labor hours of farm work	0.1	-1.1	-3.9	-3.7
Output per hour of labor	0.7	2.3	5.9	5.8

Sources: For 1910 to 1970, see Donald D. Durost and Evely T. Black, "Changes in Farm Production and Efficiency," U.S. Department of Agriculture Statistical Bulletin No. 561 (September 1970), pp. 17, 32, 44; for 1970 to 1980, see U.S. Department of Agriculture, "Economic Indicators of the Farm Sector: Production and Efficiency Statistics, 1982" ECIFS 2-5 (February 1984), pp. 20, 34, 47.

fungicides, hybrid seeds, and farm machinery and equipment. So large in fact were investments that farmers more often than not changed the financial structure of their operations, which is to say they increased their financial leverage.

At the 1963 conference of Illinois bankers, B. L. Hauenstein profiled one livestock farmer who expanded his operation between 1948 and 1963.

> This farmer is 42 years old and owns 480 acres. In 1948 he had a net worth of $13,300. His livestock operation consisted of 10 dairy cows, 5 sows, and 30 steers on feed. Today he is feeding 1,200 to 1,500 cattle, he produces about 1,600 hogs. The labor force consists of the owner-operator, one full-time hired man, a half-time man, and two school-age boys. He has invested $175,000 in cattle sheds, machine sheds, cement hog house, elevator for grain storage, silos, harvestores, and a new home. Today he has a net worth of more

Table 7.5. *Investments in technology, selected years, 1910-80*

A. Investments in technology[a]					
Item	1910[b]	1930[b]	1940[b]	1970[b]	1980[b]
Fertilizer	$805	$862	$880	$5,571	$11,083
Lime	27	49	172	226	495
Pesticides	c	c	151	2,286	3,858
Machinery[d]	1,463	1,242	1,784	10,971	14,463

B. Compound rates of growth				
Item	1910-30	1930-40	1940-70	1940-80
Fertilizer	0.3%	0.2%	6.3%	6.5%
Lime	3.0	13.3	0.9	2.7
Pesticides	c	c	9.5	8.4
Machinery	-0.8	3.7	6.2	5.4

[a]Millions, 1982 dollars.
[b]For 1910 prices are deflated using the consumer price index, and for other years using the GNP implicit price deflator.
[c]No information.
[d]Machinery represents capital expenditures for motor vehicles and other machinery and equipment less automobiles.
Sources: U.S. Department of Agriculture, "Farm Income Situation," FIS-207 (July 1967), pp. 56, 62; U.S. Department of Agriculture, "Major Statistical Series of the U.S. Department of Agriculture," Agriculture Handbook No. 118 (1958), pp. 37, 40; and Board of Governors of the Federal Reserve System, *Agricultural Finance Databook* (December 1984), pp. 11, 13.

than $300,000. Capital investments have enabled him to expand to a large, efficient farming business.[51]

This Illinois farmer seemed exceptional, but general statistics indicated that even on average farmers invested in new resources at unheard-of rates. From 1930 to 1970, farmers increased their consumption of fertilizers and pesticides (adjusted for inflation) six times. Their use of machinery jumped nine times (Table 7.5).

With these purchases, farmers operated more on a cash and credit

[51]B. L. Hauenstein, "Pitfalls and Pleasures of Intermediate Credit," in *17th Annual Illinois Bankers Agricultural Credit Conference: A Digest of Proceedings,* April 3 and 4, 1963, p. 27, Record Series 8/4/823, Box 1, University of Illinois Archives, University of Illinois at Urbana-Champaign.

basis than they had in the past. One observer wrote in 1953, "Only a few years ago the farmer produced . . . his own feed, fertilizer, power, and many of his other necessities. . . . Today, however, the farmer purchases much of his food; he buys gasoline and electric power; and he buys his feed and commercial fertilizer."[52] Statistics charted this trend. As shown in Figure 7.4, the proportion of inputs purchased rather than obtained on the farm began rising in the late 1930s and continued to increase throughout the postwar era. By boosting the proportion of purchased items, farmers raised the proportion of each year's gross earnings to cash outlays. Whereas in 1946 farmers spent half their gross income on cash expenses, by 1970 the figure was up to 67 percent (Table 7.6).

Farmers also used more credit. In 1963 Robert Tootell, governor of the Farm Credit Administration, reported a study showing that "a higher proportion of an increasing capital investment is coming from credit. This is primarily because capital accumulation from farm income is too slow in this rapidly changing farm economy. Technology is moving so fast that one must adjust quickly or perish."[53] Subsequent trends substantiated his assessment. Between the end of World War II and 1970, farm mortgage debt, adjusted for inflation, increased at a 5 percent compound rate of growth, reaching $26 billion in 1970.[54] Even for operating expenses farmers often borrowed money. In a survey of Illinois and Iowa members in the early 1960s, the Iowa Farm Bureau reported that more than half the respondents said that they used credit to purchase at least some part of three variable inputs, gasoline, fertilizer, and feed.[55] The Farm Bureau represented the nation's more influential and wealthier farmers, and it is noteworthy that these farmers answered in this fashion. Overall,

---

[52] Homer J. Livingston, "Banking's Responsibility to Agriculture," in American Bankers Association, *Proceedings of the National Agricultural Credit Conference – 1953* (Chicago, November 16–18, 1953), p. 17.

[53] Quoted in Hauenstein, "Pitfalls and Pleasures of Intermediate Credit," April 3 and 4, 1963, p. 27.

[54] U.S. Department of Agriculture, "Economic Indicators of the Farm Sector: Income and Balance Sheet Statistics, 1983," ECIFS 3–3 (September 1984), p. 112.

[55] Iowa Farm Bureau Federation, "Farm Bureau Credit Study," no date, MS-105, Box 6, Folder 10, pp. 5, 9–10, Department of Special Collections, The Parks Library, Iowa State University, Ames, Iowa. Information in the survey was compared with data from the 1960 census, indicating that the study was made in the early 1960s.

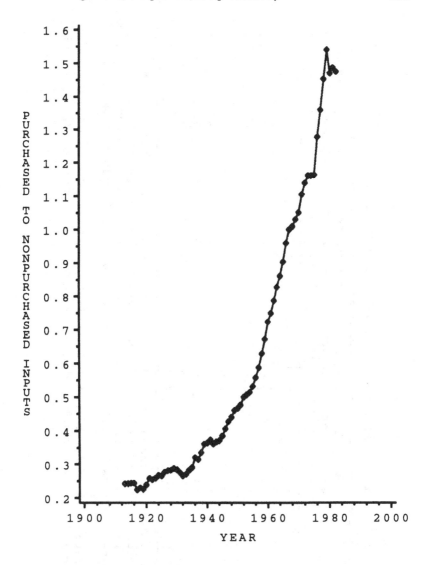

Figure 7.4. Ratio of purchased to nonpurchased resources, 1913–82. Data from U.S. Department of Agriculture, "Economic Indicators of the Farm Sector: Production and Efficiency Statistics, 1980," Statistical Bulletin No. 679 (January 1982), pp. 64–5; and U.S. Department of Agriculture, "Economic Indicators of the Farm Sector: Production and Efficiency Statistics, 1983," ECIFS 3–5 (February 1985), p. 57.

Table 7.6. Measures of financial leverage for U.S. agriculture, 1946-89

Year	Total farm debt[a]	Gross cash income[a]	Interest as a percent of gross cash income	Total debts as a percent of total assets	Cash expenses as a percent of gross cash income
1946	$38.1	$131.8	1.4%	8.0%	48.9%
1950	45.6	120.4	1.9	9.0	55.8
1955	55.5	109.7	2.7	11.0	59.2
1960	72.5	113.1	3.6	12.9	63.4
1965	105.9	124.9	4.7	16.2	65.2
1970	116.2	130.4	5.9	17.5	66.5
1975	143.3	153.0	6.7	16.6	67.4
1980	194.6	167.2	10.9	17.0	76.1
1985	160.1	142.3	11.3	23.0	70.1
1989	108.6	142.4	7.9	16.7	67.0

[a]Farm debt and gross cash income are deflated using the GNP implicit price deflator. Figures are reported in 1982 dollars. Interest expense includes payments for real-estate and non-real estate debt. Farm income is cash receipts plus government payments plus other farm-related cash receipts. Figures are calculated excluding operators' households.

Source: U.S. Department of Agriculture, "Economic Indicators of the Farm Sector: National Financial Summary, 1990," ECIFS 10-1 (November 1991), pp. 14, 17, 20, 23, 61.

non—real estate debt rose at nearly a 6 percent compound rate of growth or at a pace faster than that for real estate.[56] By 1970 farmers held nearly twice the total debt, adjusted for inflation, that they had held in the 1920s (at the time of the previous credit crisis).[57]

Although aggregate statistics signaled the importance of credit in financing investments, not all farmers chose this strategy. Recall the Michigan farmer, Frederick Kohn (who was described at the outset of this chapter). When his son pictured him as different from Don Reuger, it was not just a question of age or an affinity for small farms. Howard Kohn repeatedly makes clear that his father, in the language of economists, was risk averse, and this risk aversion was reflected in the older farmer's concern about cash. He never bought a new machine unless he paid the total cost, up-front, in cash. He never kept a checking account, but would withdraw cash directly from his savings. In a similar vein, he kept meticulous account of his cash outlays. His son noted that the father could track his costs (using receipts) over a fifteen-year period. It was not simply Frederick Kohn's preference, but his conservative financial strategy that kept him a small-time farmer.[58]

Because Kohn refused any debt, he was more extreme than most farmers. Still, the question of debt financing proved a crucial force dividing small from large operations. Tom Bauer, a Missouri corn-hog farmer, illustrated how a small farmer could profit from using debt financing. Bauer started his own farm in the early 1960s. His father had always shunned debt, always rented land, and, as a result, left the son no land to inherit. Tom Bauer's wife complained that by paying rent the father had made his landlord "rich." The younger couple decided to borrow money to buy land. The Bauers cultivated careful relations with their lenders. Over time they gained the respect of the local bank president; Tom Bauer also served on the board of the county PCA. Using these credit sources, the Bauers found them-

[56] U.S. Department of Agriculture, "Economic Indicators of the Farm Sector," ECIFS 3–3 (September 1984), p. 112.
[57] Calculated from U.S. Department of Agriculture, "Economic Indicators of the Farm Sector: National Financial Summary, 1984," ECIFS 4–3 (January 1986), pp. 69, 71; and U.S. Department of Agriculture, "Major Statistical Series of the U.S. Department of Agriculture," vol. 6, Agriculture Handbook No. 118 (October 1957), pp. 16–17, 26–7. Figures are deflated using the consumer price index.
[58] Kohn, The Last Farmer, p. 99.

selves almost always in debt, but they accumulated 337 acres to their own name in twenty-five years. They also rented land, allowing them to maintain an operation of roughly 1,000 acres in the 1980s.[59]

The contrast between farmers like Frederick Kohn and Tom Bauer can be used to characterize a general pattern. By the 1970s, the USDA classified farmers who earned more than $40,000 in sales each year as "commercial" farmers. Table 7.7 indicates that in 1975 the majority of farmers (88 percent), however, fell below this line and were known as "part-time" farmers. Part-timers accounted for 23 percent of all food produced in the country, and many were too small to reap the productivity savings associated with the larger farms.[60] The distinction between the two types of farmers was not only one of size but also one of finances. Small farmers typically relied on outside income rather than a mortgage to sustain their enterprises. As farms increased in size, however, operators were more likely to leverage their operations. Debt-asset ratios among these large operators were two and three times those for smaller farms (Table 7.7). Farmers with larger operations also devoted a greater share of cash earnings to cash outlays. Whereas those with sales of less than $40,000 spent 56 to 60 percent of cash receipts for cash outlays, farmers with more than $100,000 in sales spent from 80 to 86 percent of cash receipts for cash outlays.[61]

By the 1970s, fewer than a quarter of all farms accounted for three-quarters of farm output in the United States. These farmers who accounted for most of the output also were responsible for most of the gains in productivity. They had attained these gains because they had exploited incentives inherent in New Deal regulation: they took advantage of credit markets and used debt to expand operations; they

[59] Tom Bauer is a fictional name for a Missouri farmer Richard Rhodes spent a year interviewing for his book, *Farm: A Year in the Life of an American Farmer* (New York: Simon and Schuster, 1989). While Rhodes changed the names of people and places to protect their privacy, he states "Events and dialogue are authentic." For a discussion of Bauer's early use of credit, see pp. 22, 41–2.

[60] Using unpublished data the USDA collected, J. B. Penn reported that in order to obtain 90 percent of the economies of scale farmers in most regions of the country needed to work more than 200 acres or earn more than $40,000 in sales. See Penn, "Economic Developments in U.S. Agriculture," p. 44.

[61] Ibid., p. 34.

Table 7.7. Value of farm sales, off-farm income, and debt-to-asset ratios by the size distribution of farms, 1975

Sales class	Percent of farms in sales class	Gross cash farm income[a]	Percent of income in farm sector	Off-farm income as a percent of total income	Ratio of debts to assets
$1-5,000	44.5%	$2,445	2.7%	105%	4.5
$5,000-39,999	37.3	18,127	20.0	72	11.2
$40,000-99,999	12.5	22,514	24.8	23	18.6
$100,000 & over	5.7	47,621	52.5	11	27.9

[a]Millions.

Sources: For the debt-to-asset ratio, see U.S. Department of Agriculture, "Balance Sheet of the Farming Sector, 1978, Supplement No. 1," Agriculture Information Bulletin No. 416 (October 1978), p. 35; for all other items, see U.S. Department of Agriculture, "Economic Indicators of the Farm Sector: National Financial Summary, 1984," ECIFS 4-3 (January 1986), pp. 40, 43, 46-7.

also exploited the safety inherent in regulated commodity markets as they boosted the ratio of cash expenses to cash receipts.

The reverse was also true: regulation had favored large operators. This was apparent in the case of set-aside payments. Subsidies were based on the percentage of land taken out of production. Although each farmer received the same treatment, at the aggregate level subsidies offered much larger sums of cash to big-time operators than to small ones. The cumulative sums proved important because investments in expensive items, such as tractors and combines, demanded large payments. Although set-asides applied equally to all operators based on their individual reductions in acreage, the programs served to increase the financial capabilities of larger operators relative to their smaller counterparts.[62]

Critics explained that this outcome was not inevitable. Farm families populated regions characterized by the cash crops corn, cotton, and wheat. But among these family farms, productivity gains did not necessarily require the kind of size distribution of farms that materialized in the postwar years. USDA sources indicated that, as of 1979, to obtain 90 percent of all economies of scale in most regions farmers needed to work more than 200 acres or earn more than $40,000 in sales. But this did not mean working farms with $100,000 in sales. The USDA reported that on wheat, corn, cotton, and peanut farms, operators could obtain 90 percent of possible productivity savings with sales of $60,000 or less or with fewer than 450 acres.[63] It was possible to attain gains in productivity without having agriculture increasingly dominated by a small number of very large farms. That a more equal distribution did not persist reflected, in part, the financial character of the productivity revolution.

Gains in productivity, then, were closely tied to a distinctive set of financial patterns. Farmers, the statistics indicated, had taken on more

[62] See, for example, Marty Strange, *Family Farming: A New Economic Vision* (Lincoln: University of Nebraska Press, 1988), pp. 191–200. A summary of the mixed effects of different farm programs for the 1980s is provided in U.S. Congress, Office of Technology Assessment, *Technology, Public Policy, and the Changing Structure of American Agriculture*, OTA-F-285 (Washington, D.C.: U.S. Government Printing Office, 1986), pp. 123–34, 163–85.
[63] Unpublished data collected by the USDA and reported in Penn, "Economic Developments in U.S. Agriculture," p. 44. For an example of the critics, see Strange, *Family Farming: A New Economic Vision*, pp. 78–103.

risk in the postwar years. Trends showed a steady rise in the proportion of cash devoted to expenses. Even operators in categories of small farms devoted larger portions of their total receipts to cash outlays than had been true of farmers in the 1930s or early 1940s. Yet as regulation provided incentives to invest, these incentives worked more effectively for large operators. Not all farmers who eventually became large started in this category. The Bauers testified to the ability to survive and accumulate land in the postwar years even though they had no land to begin their enterprise. They, however, willingly used debt financing to expand. Over time, no matter how a farmer increased in size, this size offered certain advantages. In the case of subsidies, larger operators could use their lump-sums of cash better to finance payments for land and machinery. They also boosted their debt holdings relative to their assets, and increased the percentage of their cash earnings spent for cash outlays. This financial strategy had made possible the kind of productivity gains that caused the *Economist* to rate farming the nation's "number one" industry.

Farm foreclosures and regulation

If farmers consumed such large quantities of debt, did they pay a price in terms of their risk of failure? Speaking to the ABA's National Agricultural Credit Conference in 1967, the president of the Federal Reserve Bank of St. Louis, Darryl Francis, thought they would. He said:

> Farm credit risks have probably increased. Major fluctuations in farm income could formerly be absorbed by the farm family, since family labor and other nonpurchased materials constituted the major portion of farm production expense. Now, however, purchased inputs total more than four-fifths the value of all farm inputs and three-fourths the value of all farm product sales. The farmer has thus moved into the category of a businessman. His margin from operations has declined. His capital and credit demands are high in relation to net returns. He can now go bankrupt.[64]

Despite Francis's observations, neither farmers nor their creditors experienced high rates of failure. Indeed, the rate of failure remained remarkably low. The USDA indicated that from the end of World

[64] Darryl R. Francis, "Maneuverability of Funds for Agriculture," in American Bankers Association, *National Agricultural Credit Conference – 1967* (St. Louis, November 12–14, 1967), pp. 4–5.

War II through the 1970s, fewer than 2 farms in 1,000 were fore-closed on average each year (Figure 7.1). This rate is less than rates recorded in any previous era, including the years before World War I – the farmers' self-proclaimed "golden era." Nor was this trend a statistical fluke. Individual lenders reported remarkably few prob-lems. Life insurance companies, for example, reported that only 0.2 borrowers per 1,000 farm loans were foreclosed each year, on aver-age, between 1959 and 1970. Banks did not report foreclosures, but for the 1960s the ABA reported few delinquencies in its surveys; as it stated in its 1968 report, "during the past five years farm loan delinquencies have remained at a low level – generally at about 1 per cent of the total volume of farm loans outstanding."[65]

Farmers escaped foreclosure because they managed to balance the li-ability of debts with more valuable assets. If debts exceeded the value of a farm, then the owner was technically insolvent. Even without in-solvency, if a farmer acquired so much debt that interest payments ex-ceeded operating profits, then the farmer was forced into bankruptcy. Farmers encountered this problem in the early 1920s when farm prices and farmers' income plummeted. Unable to meet interest payments, many borrowers had no choice but to declare bankruptcy. Others were foreclosed. One factor that distinguished the financial climate in the years after World War II from the credit crisis of the 1920s was the role of prices. Whereas in the 1910s and 1920s the trend in farm assets, particularly land, closely trailed that of prices, this relationship re-versed itself after World War II thanks to the combined effect of farm-ers' productivity gains and New Deal regulation.

Both gains in productivity and government programs boosted land prices in the years after World War II. A farm's profitability – mean-ing its expected earnings – largely determined its value. In technical terms, a property's present value equaled the average of the sum of

---

[65] For delinquency rates by banks, see American Bankers Association, *Trends in Agricultural Banking: Report of Midyear 1968 Agricultural Credit Survey* (New York: American Bankers Association, 1968), p. 10. For life insurance companies see Table E.1. The USDA also reported information in its series, "Farm-Mortgage Lending." See, for example, U.S. Depart-ment of Agriculture, "Farm-Mortgage Lending," ARS 43-68 (December 1957), p. 3; U.S. Department of Agriculture, "Farm-Mortgage Lending," FML-14 (May 1965), pp. 2, 8–9; U.S. Department of Agriculture, "Farm-Mortgage Lending," FML-28 (June 1972), pp. 2–3, 8–9; U.S. Department of Agriculture, "Farm-Mortgage Lending," FML-30 (June 1973), pp. 2–3, 10–11.

future earnings divided by a discount rate.[66] Both price-support and acreage-restriction programs increased farm earnings and, in turn, raised land values. In the case of price supports, the CCC accounted for at least 10 and perhaps 20 percent of the price of major crops in the 1950s. If the discount rate remained constant, a given percent increase in farm income translated into a corresponding increase in the value of an acre of land. In the case of acreage diversions, payments were capitalized directly into the value of land. Between 1960 and 1965, for example, payments for an acre of corn increased by $1.54 per acre. Capitalizing the funds at a 15 percent rate, they added $10.27 to an acre of farmland and accounted for roughly a third of the increase in the value of farmland between 1960 and 1965.[67]

By its direct effect on farm income, regulation changed the pattern of land values. It is true, of course, that other factors affected the rising trend in values, notably gains in productivity. My point, however, is that, by boosting farm income, the price supports and government diversion payments accounted for significant increases in the average value of farmland during the years after World War II.[68] As a result, the risk of holding debts rose slowly. While debts tripled in real dollars, the ratio of debts to assets doubled only once between 1946 and 1970 (Table 7.6).

[66] John E. Reynold and John F. Timmons, "Factors Affecting Farmland Values in the United States," Iowa State University Agricultural Experiment Station Research Bulletin No. 566 (February 1969), pp. 333–4.

[67] Ibid., p. 329. In a simulation analysis that tested how a number of variables could explain the trend in land values from 1933 to 1965, government payments played a large role. The simulation indicated that a $1 increase in government payments brought about a $12 increase in land values between 1956 (when the program was started) and 1965. In a later study, the simulation was carried through to 1972; in this case, a $1 increase in government payments brought about a $22 increase in land values. Ibid., pp. 340–1; and Rulon D. Pope, Randall A. Kramer, Richard D. Green, and B. Delworth Gardner, "An Evaluation of Econometric Models of U.S. Farmland Prices," Western Journal of Agricultural Economics, 4 (July 1979), p. 117.

[68] Peter Lindert assessed different factors that contributed to the startling rise in real land values after 1942. Lindert, "Long-run Trends in American Farmland Values," pp. 45–85. Aside from Lindert, many other scholars have concluded that government payments and other factors were capitalized into the value of farmland. See, for example, two early studies: Robert Herdt and Willard Cochrane, "Farm Land Prices and Farm Technological Advance," Journal of Farm Economics, 48 (1966), pp. 243–63; Ray and Heady, "Simulated Effects of Alternative Policy and Economic Environments on U.S. Agriculture."

Of course annual interest fees also posed a risk. Mortgages demanded regular interest payments, and farmers' margin of cash between receipts and outlays was shrinking. As the president of the Federal Reserve Bank of St. Louis specifically noted, credit risks increased because purchased inputs consumed a larger percentage of profits. Given the smaller margin of cash income, farmers with debts were more at risk of failure should their cash receipts suddenly decline. This possibility, however, did not materialize in the twenty-five years after World War II. Prices of course fell, but they did not decline rapidly or severely. Instead, prices fell gently from one year to the next, let down slowly by government price supports. As detailed in Figure 7.3, price supports guided market prices and provided the stability that had been lacking in previous eras. For several years after the Second World War, the gap between farmers' cash outlays and receipts was shrinking, but, due to regulation, farmers had a high degree of certainty that their revenues would cover expenses each year.

Such low rates of foreclosure are surprising, all the more so because thousands of farmers gave up during this period. Their lives tell us that low rates of foreclosure did not always signal financial health. What happened to farmers who eventually quit? It is difficult to piece together their varied experiences, and I cannot speculate on the welfare of tenants because in some regions, notably the South, they frequently were forced off the land. Whether they located better-paying occupations is difficult to say.[69] But for those who borrowed from bankers, the ABA credit surveys give us a hint of what hap-

[69] Few studies have examined what happened to individuals who left farming in these years. Peter Lindert and Jeffrey Williamson charted general changes in the distribution of income and wealth. Their evidence indicates that part of the trend toward less inequality in the distribution of income in the 1930s and 1940s occurred with the redistribution of income to the bottom tier of earners; they also cite as one element in this process the technological gains within agriculture. Although they suggest that in these general terms the gains in farm productivity were associated with a short and rare period of a leveling in the distribution of income, it is not clear what happened to individuals who left from different rungs on the farm ladder. See Jeffrey G. Williamson and Peter H. Lindert, *American Inequality: A Macroeconomic History* (New York: Academic Press, 1980). For an analysis of cultural changes within southern farming, see Pete Daniel, *Breaking the Land: The Transformation of Cotton, Tobacco, and Rice Cultures since 1880* (Urbana: University of Illinois Press, 1985).

pened. In surveys conducted between 1962 and 1968, bankers anticipated that between 3 and 4 percent of farm borrowers would "discontinue business" in any given year because of "financial pressures."
Over the course of a decade this amounted to a large number, perhaps
30 percent of farm borrowers. Why would farmers go out of business? Bankers cited a "profit squeeze" or "price–cost squeeze," noting the large capital requirements needed to remain in farming. This
analysis suggested that small farms were particularly handicapped
because their size prevented them from accumulating the needed capital for optimal amounts of land or machinery. In its 1965 survey, the
ABA found that of those farms likely to discontinue, "74 per cent of
them currently have gross incomes of under $10,000."[70]

Still, to go out of business did not mean going bankrupt or being
foreclosed. A farmer could, as the USDA called it, "voluntarily" sell a
farm. Its figures indicated that many farmers took this route. While
the rate of farm foreclosures dropped to less than 2 per 1,000 farms
per year (Figure 7.1), voluntary sales averaged 30 per 1,000 farms
each year throughout the postwar years, and 46 per 1,000 farms (or
4.6 percent of farms each year) in the 1940s (Figure 7.2). What was
distinctive about these sales was that they occurred in an era of rising
land prices. In previous eras, large numbers of transfers had been
associated with financial crises. In the 1920s and 1930s, farmers sold
or lost their land in periods of falling land values. But as we have
seen, in the postwar years both gains in productivity and government
subsidies were capitalized into the price of land. Although the farmers' profit squeeze may have forced them to quit, they could earn
profits from the sale of their farms.

The experience of those who gave up by selling their farms was
illustrated in the life of Frederick Kohn. The Michigan farmer had
worked his 120 acres and maintained a tight budget. The family

[70] American Bankers Association, *Trends in Agricultural Banking: Report of
Midyear 1965 Agricultural Credit Situation Survey* (New York: American
Bankers Association, 1965), p. 10. Also see American Bankers Association,
*Trends in Agricultural Banking: Report of Midyear 1962 Agricultural
Credit Situation Survey* (New York: American Bankers Association,
1963), p. 5; American Bankers Association, *Trends in Agricultural Bank-
ing: Report of Midyear 1963 Agricultural Credit Situation Survey* (New
York: American Bankers Association, 1963), p. 6; American Bankers As-
sociation, *Trends in Agricultural Banking: Report of Midyear 1968 Agricultural Credit Situation Survey*, p. 6.

earned a profit of roughly $3,000 in cash each year. His son tells us that the father hung on as long as he did because he was so thrifty. Yet because his farm was small, it lacked the earning power to enable one of his children to carry on the enterprise and raise his or her own family. Although Kohn had several children, none took over the land. Instead, he sold out. He picked his buyers carefully. He refused Don Reuger; he turned down advances from oil firms that wanted to drill near Midland, Michigan, in the 1980s; finally, he sold his land to two Korean War veterans. The profits funded his retirement.[71]

For several decades after the mid-1930s, New Deal regulation modified commodity and credit markets so as to create a climate conducive to investment in land and technology. In credit markets, competition between federal and private lenders worked to make credit available to farmers on terms far better after 1935 than they had been prior to 1930. For commodities, price regulation shored up sagging markets. In one sense, this regulation subsidized farm income and farm investments. But price supports also offered a measure of safety for the added financial risk farmers assumed in credit markets.

For some twenty-five years after World War II, this mix of regulation and competition created a dynamic among farmers in which a small number survived but most quit. The economist Joseph Schumpeter had expected the destruction of firms as part of the process of economic growth. Here, the experience of agriculture compared to Schumpeter's idea of a creative–destructive cycle. Those who resembled the "creative" cycle had logged large gains in productivity through investments in chemicals, machinery, equipment, and land. The "destructive" phase was embodied in the thousands of farmers who exited the industry.

This analogy is not precise, however. Schumpeter attributed creative–destructive cycles to the role of the entrepreneur, but in the case of agriculture, market conditions and regulation governed the timing. Schumpeter also pictured the destructive cycle as following the creative cycle, but in agriculture rapid investment by some and the exit of many other farmers proceeded together. Finally, Schumpeter anticipated that the destructive cycle would entail high levels of failure. But in agriculture, ironically, this sorting-out process was

[71] Kohn, *The Last Farmer.*

"quiet." Farmers who increased their financial leverage avoided failure because they balanced larger debts with more valuable assets. The CCC also offered them protection by stabilizing commodity markets. The majority of farmers, the numbers tell us, charted a different course with their livelihoods. A large number funded smaller farm operations with the help of nonfarm jobs. Most farmers ultimately quit, however. Although these farmers in all likelihood had found it too difficult to earn profits to sustain their farms, many of those who owned land "voluntarily" sold it. Regulation had shaped these outcomes as well. For unlike previous eras when farmers were forced to sell in a crisis characterized by falling land values, in the postwar years farmers sold out in years when land values were rising. By historical standards, the exodus was unusual: unusual because it occurred so quickly and because it was accompanied with so few bankruptcies or bitter foreclosure auctions. For those who would have preferred not to quit, this trade-off between speed and financial stress may not have offered much solace. Regulation had shaped a dynamic set of market conditions, spurring a large and effective investment in technology but the speedy exit of smaller, more cautious, or less affluent farmers.

8. Conclusion

The revolution in farm productivity occurred in one of the most competitive industries in the United States economy. There existed at all times a large number of evenly matched producers who earned their living in markets in which none exercised control over prices. The one way to remain profitable, presumably, was to adopt technology so as to reduce costs. The nature of research sustained these relationships. Public research institutions and private manufacturers, International Harvester and Deere & Company included, readily disseminated information about their products. Since no one farmer had special control over this knowledge, all faced the continued pressure to adopt new techniques so as to reduce costs and remain profitable. So too, a drop in market prices did not necessarily alter this cost-based formula. Even if low prices created losses, farmers may have benefited from buying new techniques that could cut costs and reduce the amount of their losses.

Although this explanation is intuitively appealing, I have concluded that the revolution in farm productivity cannot be explained simply in terms of the desire to reduce costs borne out of competitive markets. This is not to say competition played no role, because it did of course. But competition gives only a partial answer insofar as it focuses on the cost side of a farmer's enterprise and on short-term market pressures. The experience of U.S. farmers revealed that the sources of productivity growth were more complicated. Focusing on farmers' investment climate, I have concluded that competitive markets prompted high rates of productivity growth not prior to 1930 but after the introduction of New Deal regulation in the Great Depression.

Implicit in the role of competition, I have argued, is the assumption that given competitive pressures, farmers readily financed investments in land, machinery, and biological and chemical inputs. This logic did not hold for all farmers in the 1920s, however. Although the competitive nature of markets no doubt created incentives to adopt cost-saving technology, markets also exerted their influence on farmers' long-term investment outlooks; the key factor here was the uncertain process by which supply and demand set prices each year.

The existence of volatile prices did not automatically hamper investments in productivity-enhancing equipment. Institutions farmers used to organize production or to obtain credit mediated between these market risks and their investment strategies. It was possible that in other industries, given the structure of the firm or sources of credit, such market risks might not have mattered. In agriculture, they did. The consequences of unstable prices, along with farmers' reactions and creditors' policies, created an investment climate that did not translate competitive pressures into the quick adoption of technology and high rates of productivity growth.

The experience of farmers in the Corn Belt illustrated this tension. The tractor represented the most important investment a farmer could make in the 1920s. Manufacturers promoted the machine on the basis of its potential cost savings – savings that according to advertisements were quite large if farmers valued all inputs at market prices. Still, the tractor had drawbacks. It consumed substantial sums of cash, enough in fact to raise an investor's total cash outlays by roughly 25 percent on average. Based on the competitive nature of markets, these cash demands should not have stopped them. The threshold model indicated that on the basis of cost savings, roughly half the farms in the Corn Belt passed the tractor's threshold and would have profited from using it in the 1920s. Yet actual investments fell short of this mark: nearly one in two farmers whose land passed the threshold shunned tractors.

Qualitative evidence located the cause of this lag in a set of financial patterns for which the tractor's cash demands created barriers to investment. One barrier centered on the conflict between safety and productivity. By favoring resources obtained on the farm, farmers reduced the probability that a slip or slide in prices would force them to lose money. Yet, as agricultural researchers noted, this strategy tempted farmers to judge the tractor on the basis of cash instead of total costs, and, as a result, the machine appeared less desirable than its relative cost savings indicated.

Credit markets did not offer much relief to this conflict over cash. In the most obvious sense, a large minority of farmers – some speculators, some young operators who had the bad luck to start their farms in these years – had been buckled under by the nominal swings in crop prices and land values associated with World War I and the immediate postwar years. With or without outright failure, such debts had precluded many individuals from making additional cash outlays for new equipment. Beyond this crisis, farmers complained about long-standing problems. Critics found that creditors set maturities for all types of loans too short to suit many farmers. Yet for their part, private creditors also were handicapped by other concerns. Because banks depended on deposits from their rural farming communities, their ability to make loans varied with farmers' incomes. Insurance firms were not as vulnerable to these local conditions, but they limited loans in response to other factors, including the expected returns for farm versus city loans and their receipt of premiums. Congress hoped that the introduction of public lenders, especially federal land banks, would improve lending conditions. But results were mixed for the 1920s. Few private lenders changed their policies, and few midwestern farmers obtained federal land bank loans.

Quantitative evidence supported this account of farmers' investment climate. Although the tractor received a poor reception throughout the Midwest, in some areas a farmer's reluctance to buy a tractor despite its cost savings was greater than in others. But what was striking about this geographic variance was that the lag in the tractor's adoption varied systematically with farmers' financial problems: their margin of cash between receipts and outlays, the variability of corn yields, the relative burden of debts, the proportion of indebted farmers, and the relative deposit holdings of commercial banks.

In the 1920s, then, farmers failed to adopt the most important invention at optimal rates. During that decade actual gains in productivity, I estimated, fell a third short of their potential, thus suggesting that financial conditions had exerted a serious influence on investment patterns as well as the rate of productivity growth.

With the onset of the Great Depression, Franklin D. Roosevelt's administration established regulatory programs to contain the effects of the crisis. Some policies addressed those most in need of assistance, but these programs remained underfunded. Instead, the programs that exerted the most influence on the farm sector were the three market-oriented programs, administered by the AAA, the CCC, and the FCA. Inasmuch as these programs addressed the crisis, they were intended to be temporary. There were other reasons to expect the programs to remain short term. Many members of Congress opposed market controls or income subsidies; private lenders objected to subsidies to federal creditors. In normal times, these opponents may well have prevailed. But the 1930s were not normal times. Under the severe market conditions, these opponents found reasons to support the programs. The regulatory agencies, then, not only provided relief, but also acquired long-term roles in farmers' commodity and credit markets.

In terms of relief, the effectiveness of the regulation was mixed. By refinancing many indebted farmers, the credit policies eased the burden of debts. But in terms of farmers' incomes, the CCC did not raise prices to the partisan goal of parity. Further, while farm income recovered from the terrible lows of 1932 and 1933, after 1936 farmers' cash income changed little. To the extent that this relief carried over to farm productivity, the role of the AAA backfired. Farmers lifted corn yields by restricting their most marginal land or by rotating "soil conserving" for "soil depleting" crops. Thus, in terms of their relief effort, my conclusion fits with the conventional wisdom. Regulatory programs, in an effort to raise prices and farm income, created perverse incentives for farmers to raise corn yields.

This is not the whole story, however. Although relief was only partially effective, I have argued that the programs became a mechanism for changing farmers' long-term investment climate. The CCC had been designed to put cash in farmers' hands immediately. More significantly, as it provided cash, it offered farmers a new source of long-term security against the annual ups and downs of commodity markets: its loan rate guaranteed farmers a price for their corn and set the price high enough to cover the vast majority of their production expenses on a cash basis. Farmers no longer needed to fear a sudden drop in the price of their cash crop, nor did they have to be so wedded to a strategy of conserving cash.

The FCA, primarily through federal land banks, offered farm borrowers mortgages with rates of interest subsidized by Congress and with maturities running much longer than those common prior to 1930. Between 1933 and 1935, these banks assumed a large share of the farm mortgage market and exerted a major influence on the kinds of loans private lenders offered farmers. Commercial banks and life insurance companies resented this competition and correctly pointed to federal lenders' special subsidies. Yet despite this inequity, they found that they had either to offer loans on similar credit terms or to see their borrowers do business with these public lenders. From the farmers' perspective this was a positive outcome. Borrowers could choose from a larger variety of lenders, and they often were able to obtain loans on better terms – both lower rates of interest and longer maturities.

Aside from farmers, one other party understood that they clearly could profit from these regulatory changes. Implement manufacturers and their dealers spotted the immediate effects of the AAA and the CCC in providing extra cash. In 1935, dealers had welcomed this relief when they pointed to the upturn in their own sales. But manufacturers saw long-term consequences as well. Dealers were urged to take advantage of government credit policies to help sell tractors; and officials at Harvester linked the importance of stable prices to farmers' ability to invest in equipment. Harvester, the industry's leader, demonstrated its optimism by increasing its staff and spending on research at a rate far in excess of the trends in farmers' cash income.

Although there were no clear incentives to buy tractors in the late 1930s over the late 1920s, farmers quickened purchases of tractors at the same time that they asked Congress to investigate manufacturers' high prices. They boosted investments in other items, such as mechanical harvesters, and, overall, their capital expenditures increased 25 percent, contributing to large gains in productivity. For the Depression decade, productivity in the Corn Belt rose at a rate that was at least two-thirds higher than that of the 1920s. For the second half of the 1930s (that is, for the years after regulation took effect), labor gains averaged 3.6 percent a year and signaled the high rates of the next four decades.

This blend of competitive and financial incentives persisted long after the Depression ended. For nearly forty years, farmers changed the structure of their farm operations as they came to rely far more on items purchased off the farm – seed, fertilizers, pesticides, herbicides, tractors, trucks, combines, and assorted implements. With this change in the structure of the farm, there also came a shift in its financial character: farmers increased their exposure to fluctuations in farm income by devoting a larger portion of their annual earnings to cash expenses. They also acquired short- and long-term debt at unusually rapid rates throughout the postwar years. Creditors supported these financial strategies. The FCA continued to sponsor credit agencies that made available long- and short-term loans on generous terms. Under Equitable Life Assurance Society's leadership, insurance companies introduced new tactics to compete more effectively with public creditors. Their strategies enabled them to regain market share, and in doing so they provided much larger numbers of farmers with more attractive loans – ones with greater flexibility, along with better rates of interest and longer maturities.

Although one might have anticipated that the accumulated debt would have caused a new round of farm foreclosures, this outcome did not materialize – at least as long as prices nudged downward. As price supports and productivity gains were capitalized into land values, rising land values balanced the surge in debt. Similarly, because price supports slowed and stabilized the trend in crop prices, they helped insure that while farmers maintained a smaller margin of safety between cash receipts and outlays, this margin would hold steady. In a period of gently falling prices, regulation shaped a set of conditions that promoted a financial climate suited to rapid gains in productivity. Compared with the era prior to the coming of the New Deal when farmers recorded less than a 1 percent gain in labor productivity per year, the period after 1935 saw the rate jump to more than 4 percent.

The conclusion reached in this study is counterintuitive, and one might be tempted to say that agriculture was an exceptional case. Certainly, this was true with respect to competition. Unlike some cases of regulation, such as the airlines industry, regulation did not restrict entry or exit in the case of farming. And in general, unlike railroads, telecommunications, and airlines, agriculture distinguished itself by its high level of competition. But it is precisely this unusual matchup between competition and regulation, I have found, that enables the experience of agriculture to serve as a useful inquiry into the relationship between market structure and sources of productivity growth. At one level, this case study has reached the conclusion that there has been no "yellow brick road" to mark the ties between regulated or unregulated markets and the pursuit of productivity. Both periods of regulated and unregulated markets had drawbacks. This has been easy to see in the case of market regulation, less so in the case of unfettered markets. But beyond this negative conclusion,

I have argued that the interpretation of regulation and sources of productivity depends upon one's perspective – whether one takes a short-term (static) or a long-term (dynamic) perspective.

To date, regulation has typically been analyzed for its static effects, as determined through the economic principle of competitive equilibrium. It is judged as inefficient when government programs fix prices above or below the equilibrium that would have prevailed in a free market. As measured by this standard, agricultural regulation fared poorly. There is no doubt that in the 1950s the CCC held prices well above market levels. These high prices resulted in excess supplies (Table 7.1). In the 1960s, the CCC lowered its support levels but regulation still interfered with market forces. In this decade the USDA restricted the supply of cash crops in order to raise prices. For some twenty-five years after World War II, then, regulation misallocated resources – raising prices and creating excess supplies or restricting production and artificially lifting prices.

As stated, this analysis is compelling. Farm surpluses have been quite large, and I do not mean to belittle these costs. In fact, my analysis suggests the conclusion that farm policies, particularly income supports, were constructed in a way to invite constant criticism. In periods of falling prices, large subsidies rightly angered taxpayers; conversely, in years of rising prices, consumers faced higher food prices, as was true in World War II and the 1970s. Like almost all kinds of government regulation, farm policies have been and remain controversial.

Although I do not dispute this conclusion, I find it limited because of the underlying static perspective. The framework is useful for estimating the costs of regulation in any given year. It is less suited, however, to a study of different patterns of investment and productivity because these historical events have entailed change not in any one year, but change over time.

My study, by contrast, was designed to assess the dynamic consequences of regulation. By looking at farmers' investment calculus, my analysis indicated that there existed a trade-off between short-term efficiency, as defined by the notion of competitive equilibrium, and long-term gains in productivity. In the years prior to the introduction of regulation, the farm sector was intensely competitive; by this standard, farm markets were efficient. But at the same time, markets set prices in ways that posed risks. In response, farmers and their creditors fashioned an investment climate in which farmers, despite their competitive markets, delayed purchases of expensive technology. At the aggregate level, farmers lowered the pace of technological diffusion below the rate expected on the basis of the tractor's cost savings.

The introduction of regulation marked a new era for competition. In the short run, price supports no doubt reduced market efficiency because the CCC set loan rates above the going market price. Yet regulation altered the dynamic interplay between technology, commodity markets, creditors, and manufacturers so as to encourage farmers to respond to competition with investments in expensive technology. These investments were directly associated with the accelerated rate of growth of productivity.

Balancing short- and long-term consequences, the record of farm regulation is no doubt ambiguous. But once again this is not the whole story. The experience of the farm sector prompts questions for how Americans judge regulation when it is considered in relation to productivity. Americans place a high premium on productivity growth for obvious reasons: gains in productivity have been crucial for the growth of per capita income and thus for their standard of living. But regulation is suspect in popular minds – being feared for hampering productivity by restricting the competitive process. The case of agriculture called this proposition into question. For whereas in the short run farm policy fulfilled popular fears, in the long run it promoted productivity because it altered the nature of farmers' investment climate and thus farmers' willingness or ability to respond to market pressures. To the extent that Americans value productivity growth, then, that this brand of regulation had promoted the kind of gains they wanted.

The analysis comes full circle in the 1980s. If the agricultural sector seemed unusual because farmers sustained such a long era of technological change, the outcome was not inevitable. Productivity gains in agriculture had been the product of particular market and institutional relationships. Inasmuch as New Deal regulation had mitigated market risks, this outcome mattered only insofar as regulation altered institutions playing an important role in shaping farmers' investment climate. As it turned out, these relations were by no means constant. Ironically, regulation had been created with the intent of mitigating or preventing the kind of market collapse that had characterized the Great Depression. When markets set new patterns in the

1970s – that is, when markets met the intent of the New Dealers and lifted prices – regulation no longer provided the same climate for investment. Instead, those who had profited from regulation and achieved gains in productivity became mired in a new financial crisis.

Epilogue: The credit crisis
of the 1980s

In 1980 the *Economist* had "applauded" American agriculture, but in just a few years the U.S. farm sector had entered its worst crisis since the Great Depression. From 1979 to 1983 gross farm income (in real dollars) fell 23 percent. By 1983, land values had fallen 30 percent from their 1980 high.[1] Yet neither farm mortgages nor interest charges fell in line with income. Instead, in words all too reminiscent of the 1920s and the 1930s, farmers complained about "low" prices and "ruinous" debts.

Americans responded in several different ways to farmers' complaints. Some denied that a crisis actually existed, arguing farmers were crying wolf in the 1980s, just as they had in four previous decades. Others focused on the plight of small farmers. According to this reading of the crisis, small farmers were the ones particularly hurt in the market crash because size determined a farmer's chance of survival. A third group blamed lenders – both public and private creditors – for enticing farmers to borrow more money than they could ever hope to repay. Finally, a fourth explanation held federal regulation accountable for the crisis, maintaining that regulation had tempted farmers to take out loans and expand production, thereby making a crisis inevitable. Although each of these views has an element of truth, no one explanation is convincing. Instead, I argue that the crisis can best be understood in terms of the shifting relationship between New Deal regulation and the nature of farmers' commodity and credit markets.

For those who wanted to discount the importance of the new crisis, there was ample evidence that farmers had repeatedly foretold

[1] Board of Governors of the Federal Reserve System, *Agricultural Finance Databook* (December 1984), table 112, p. 4; and Lawrence Shepard, "The Farm Debt Crisis: Temporary or Chronic?" *Contemporary Policy Issues,* 4 (January 1986), pp. 65, 68; U.S. Department of Agriculture, "Farm Real Estate Market Developments," CD-89 (August 1984), p. 10; U.S. Department of Agriculture, "Economic Indicators of the Farm Sector: National Financial Summary, 1987," ECIFS 7-1 (October 1988), pp. 9, 19.

disaster over the past four decades. One skeptic checked back issues of daily newspapers to discover that farmers had proclaimed almost every year after 1950 "the worst" year since the Great Depression.[2] Farmers' representatives in Congress had been guilty of exaggerating their plight. In February 1985, for example, Representative E. Thomas Colen of Missouri warned a House subcommittee hearing: "Farmers are faced with such high interest rates . . . and low rates of return on their products that they are reliving the Great Depression of the 1930s." The point of this message differed little from a warning made twenty years earlier in a report of the House Agriculture Committee: "Hundreds of thousands of our most progressive farmers will find their debt positions intolerable and will be forced into bankruptcy." This 1965 report, in turn, recalled the words of Senator Allen Ellender of Louisiana. Ellender, protesting President Harry S Truman's attempt to cut government price supports, opined: "This is not the time to lower prices farmers receive, particularly when farm income is already at an all-time low." Regardless of the decade, then, farmers and their representatives had consistently complained about low income, burdensome debts, and the threat of a crisis like the one of the 1930s.[3]

President Ronald Reagan reasoned much like these critics. He placed agriculture first in his list of budget cuts with a proposed reduction of $38.8 billion for price supports between 1986 and 1990. The only program that came close to this proposed four-year reduction was medicare, with estimated cost savings of $32.5 billion.[4] As late as 1985, the president refused even to hear out farmers and their allies.[5] When Secretary of Agriculture John L. Block submitted the Agricultural Adjustment Act of 1985 to Congress, he asked for lower loan prices, not for credit aid. Congress, he advised, should return farmers to free, unregulated markets as quickly as possible.[6] Reagan's

[2] Gregg Easterbrook, "Making Sense of Agriculture," *Atlantic Monthly*, 256 (July 1985), p. 77.

[3] Ibid., pp. 77–8.

[4] Lawrence R. Klein, "Federal Policy Created Farm Crisis," *Los Angeles Times* (February 26, 1985), part 4, p. 3. Also see Robert Pear, "President Plans Sharp Cutbacks in Farm Budget," *New York Times* (December 24, 1986), pp. A1, D16.

[5] "Let Them Eat Cowcake," *Economist*, 294 (March 2, 1985), p. 23.

[6] Peter T. Kilborn, "Veto is Likely If Farm Bill Is Too Costly, Aide Says," *New York Times* (October 25, 1985), p. B11; Keith Scheider, "Farm Bill: Its Impact," *New York Times* (December 6, 1985), p. A16. Also see "Food and Agriculture," *Economic Report of the President, 1984* (Washington,

indifference so angered one Missouri senator that the congressman likened the president to Marie Antoinette – telling farmers who had no bread to eat cake – and prompting the *Economist* to title a story "Let Them Eat Cowcake."[7]

This time, however, statistical studies verified the seriousness of the crisis. The USDA stopped reporting farm foreclosures after 1980, but other lenders did report their own measures of farm failures. Banks, for example, indicated that by June 1984 one-third of all borrowers (or one-sixth of all farmers) were "loaned-up" to the practical limit. Between 2 and 3 percent of all farms went bankrupt by the end of the year. Life insurance firms reported similar figures, finding that by 1986 more than 2 percent of borrowers were foreclosed (Table E.1).[8] In a new survey taken in January 1985, the USDA backed up these private figures. It discovered that one in eight farmers was in serious financial trouble, with debts exceeding 40 percent of assets and a negative cash flow.[9]

As the dimensions of the crisis became clearer, one newspaper after another ran stories about family farmers who were in financial trouble. *Newsweek*, for example, reported the story of Keith Schipper, a farmer who had worked in a factory and borrowed money to buy 280 acres of choice Iowa farmland. Schipper, however, had bad luck. In the three years after he signed the mortgage, poor weather de-

D.C.: U.S. Government Printing Office, 1984), pp. 122–44, and "Income Transfers to Agriculture," *Economic Report of the President, 1986* (Washington, D.C.: U.S. Government Printing Office, 1986), pp. 129–58.

[7] The article did not name the senator. See "Let Them Eat Cowcake," p. 23.

[8] It is tempting to compare these figures with those from the 1920s and 1930s; taking the figures at face value, one could conclude that the two crises were of comparable magnitude (although the recent crisis has been much shorter). Yet this comparison is, at best, only suggestive. The USDA series, which ran until 1980, is not calculated on the same basis as that reported by private lenders. There is a second problem. The very nature of the two crises differed insofar as the size distribution of farms had changed in the intervening years. Whereas a small percentage of farmers accounted for the vast majority of production by the 1980s, a much larger percentage of farmers accounted for the same share of production in the 1920s and 1930s. If one wants to focus on those farmers who were vital to the production of crops and livestock, then rates of foreclosure would need to be adjusted for the size distribution of farms in each period.

[9] U.S. Department of Commerce, *Statistical Abstract of the United States: 1986* (Washington, D.C.: U.S. Government Printing Office, 1985), p. 643; U.S. Department of Agriculture, "Financial Characteristics of U.S. Farms, January 1985," Agriculture Information Bulletin No. 495 (July 1985), pp. 19–22.

Table E.1. *Annual rates of farm failures as reported by lenders, 1959-90*

Year	Commercial banks: bankruptcies per 1,000 farms[a]	Life insurance companies: number of loans foreclosed per 1,000 farm loans	USDA: foreclosures per 1,000 farms
1959-69	b	0.2	1.3
1970-9	b	0.3	1.3
1980	b	3.0	1.3
1981	b	5.0	b
1982	8	2.0	b
1983	11	3.8	b
1984	26	6.4	b
1985	38	14.6	b
1986	42	27.2	b
1987	33	28.6	b
1988	22	15.6	b
1989	20	8.6	b
1990	b	3.3	b

[a]Commercial banks were surveyed for bankruptcies by the American Bankers Association; bankruptcies are reported for June of the year given. The number of foreclosures by life insurance companies is reported for the year given.
[b]No information.
Sources: For banks, see U.S. Department of Agriculture, "Agricultural Outlook," AO-157 (October 1989), pp. 18-20; and U.S. Bureau of the Census, *Statistical Abstract of the United States: 1991* (Washington, D.C.: U.S. Government Printing Office, 1991), p. 651. For insurance companies, the data were supplied by the American Council of Life Insurance, *Investment Bulletins*, various issues. For USDA foreclosure rates, see Figure 7.1.

stroyed his crops. By February 1985, the farmer was $405,000 in debt and on the brink of foreclosure.[10]

Family farmers of course failed, but they typically did not run small operations. Most small farmers had already been forced out of the business because of their size. Those that remained relied on jobs off the farm to sustain their modest operations, and they typically held small amounts of debt (Table 7.7). By contrast, medium and large

[10]John McCormick, "Bitter Harvest: Reagan Is Clashing with Farmers over Budget Deficits and amid Warnings the Farm-Belt Crisis Is Worsening," *Newsweek* (February 18, 1985), p. 52.

Table E.2. *Percentage of farms by sales class with debt-to-asset ratios of 40-70, 71-100, and more than 100 percent, January 1, 1985*

| | Debt-to-asset ratios | | |
Sales class	40-70%	71-100%	100+%
$1-10,000	5.8%	1.9%	0.9%
$10,000 - $19,999	8.1	3.5	3.0
$20,000 - $39,999	10.4	4.2	4.0
$40,000 - $99,999	16.8	6.0	4.6
$100,000 - $249,999	20.7	7.6	4.7
$250,000 - $499,999	23.6	8.9	5.8
$500,000 & over	21.1	8.6	6.1
All farms	11.6	4.3	3.0

Source: U.S. Department of Agriculture, "Financial Characteristics of U.S. Farms, January 1985," Agriculture Information Bulletin No. 495 (July 1985), p. 8.

farmers were far more leveraged and they were the ones who bore the brunt of the crisis. The USDA found that while commercial farms represented one-third of all farms, their operators held half of all farm debt and accounted for half of all financially troubled farmers. Whereas less than 6 percent of part-time farmers (those with less than $40,000 in sales) carried debt-to-asset ratios of more than 70 percent, 12 percent of commercial farmers were this highly leveraged (Table E.2). For its 1985 survey, the USDA reported that while less than 10 percent of noncommercial farmers experienced financial stress (with debts amounting to more than 40 percent of assets and negative cash flow), roughly 20 percent of all commercial farmers fell into this category.[11] It was not size as much as the burden of debts that determined which farmers were likely to fail.

For this reason, many farmers blamed bankers for their crisis. Dale and Brenda Mantooth of Rushville, Indiana, sued their credit agent, claiming he had acted as "more than a lender, advising them in 1978 to borrow some $200,000 and build a new hog facility."[12] One sixty-

[11] U.S. Department of Agriculture, "Financial Characteristics of U.S. Farms, January 1985" (July 1985), p. vi.
[12] Laurent Belsie, "Farmers' Lender 'Overreacted' but Claims Are Common for Delinquent Borrowers," *Christian Science Monitor* (November 26, 1985), p. 3.

three-year-old farmer, Dale Burr of Hills, Iowa, was so overwhelmed by his debts that in December 1985 he murdered his banker, John R. Hughes. Burr, who then shot himself, owed the banker $924,000.[13]

Although creditors did not make friends out of their borrowers, it proved difficult to make that charge stick. David Stockman told Congress in a 1985 Senate hearing: "For the life of me I cannot figure out why the taxpayers of this country have the responsibility to go in and refinance bad debt that was willingly incurred by consenting adults."[14] Stockman's insensitivity toward farmers was well known, but he nevertheless hit on an important point. Farmers had entered their agreements voluntarily. One could blame bankers only if one assumed farmers were too gullible not to make their own decisions. Furthermore, why would lenders have made so many loans if they knew such loans would ruin farmers? Banks were only as healthy as the individuals to whom they lent their money. If these individuals went broke, lenders often did as well. In the 1980s, failures of agricultural banks ballooned from one in 1981 to a high of seventy-five in 1987; at this peak year, nearly one in seven farm banks was classified as vulnerable to failure.[15] Among life insurance companies, farm loans had become a sore subject in the late 1980s as delinquency rates climbed to more than 14 percent of the amount of loans (compared to 3 percent for nonfarm loans).[16]

Like private lenders, public creditors (whose fortunes turned solely on farm loans) found themselves desperate for relief. By September 1985, the Farm Credit Administration reported that $11.1 billion, or

[13] Kevin Klose, "Killings, Suicide Echo Farm Crisis," *Washington Post* (December 11, 1985), pp. A1, A16; A. James Rudin, "Farmers in Crisis," *New York Times* (February 26, 1987), p. A27.

[14] Reported in Ed Magnuson, "Real Trouble on the Farm," *Time* (February 18, 1985), p. 24.

[15] There are two definitions of agricultural banks. The Federal Reserve System defines agricultural banks as those with a ratio of agricultural to total loans in excess of the unweighted average for all commercial banks at the date of comparison. The Federal Deposit Insurance Corporation uses a slightly different definition resulting in fewer agricultural banks. It defines a farm bank as one in which agricultural loans account for 25 percent or more of all bank loans. I use the first definition. See U.S. Department of Agriculture, "Agricultural Income and Finance," AFO-44 (February 1992), pp. 14, 52; for vulnerable farm banks, see U.S. Department of Agriculture, "Agricultural Outlook," AO-141 (May 1988), p. 24.

[16] U.S. Department of Agriculture, "Agricultural Income and Finance," AFO-32 (February 1989), p. 28.

15 percent of all its loans were uncollectible. Nine of the FCA's thirty-seven district banks reported that their problem loans exceeded their capital.[17] These troubles brought a dramatic change in investor confidence in the entire system of public farm credit. For the years prior to 1985, USDA officials reported that "the FCS [Farm Credit System] was one of the safest and most stable segments of the financial community. FCS bonds and notes were often priced to yield returns roughly the same as Treasury bills and notes – at rates reflecting the expectation of no risk to the lender." But with revelations of such large loan delinquencies and losses, officials found that "in the summer of 1985, the situation changed significantly. The rates of FCS bonds rose markedly from Treasury bond rates, reflecting increased concern in the financial community over the safety of FCS bonds." Public lenders ultimately received a bailout (from the Agricultural Credit Act of 1987) in the form of a loan of up to $4 billion. The act also tried to create a more efficient administration by consolidating divisions. Of these changes, the most important required that federal land banks and Federal Intermediate Credit Banks be merged to form Farm Credit Banks.[18]

Both private and public lenders suffered tremendous losses in the 1980s. They may well have been overly zealous in making loans to farmers. But they made these loans with the anticipation of earning profits, not incurring such large financial problems. In this sense, creditors were not the sole or primary source to blame.

If creditors were not to blame, some Americans (often lenders themselves) held federal regulation responsible. Edward Guay, chief economist of the life insurance company Cigna, wrote to the *Wall Street Journal*:

> Congressional actions with respect to the Farm Credit System, price supports and tax subsidies ... are the source of the farm credit

[17] Robert Hershey, Jr., "Farm Debt Aid Is Said to Emerge," *New York Times* (October 31, 1985), pp. D1, D8; Charles F. McCoy, "Out of Options: Farm Credit System, Buried in Bad Loans, Seeks Big Bailout," *Wall Street Journal* (September 4, 1985), pp. 1, 16; Charles F. McCoy, "Farm Credit System Reports 3rd-Period Loss. Deficit Totals $522.5 Million, and More Loan Troubles Predicted Through 1987," *Wall Street Journal* (October 24, 1985), p. 2.

[18] U.S. Department of Agriculture, "Agricultural Outlook," AO-119 (May 1986), pp. 24–5; and U.S. Department of Agriculture, "Agricultural Outlook," AO-139 (March 1988), p. 23. Also see Robert N. Collender,

crisis. Congress encouraged the abuse of credit on an overwhelming scale, encouraged overproduction by setting price supports above the world market levels, and provided such massive credit that it triggered a credit binge. . . . The farm crisis was caused on Capitol Hill, not on Constitution Avenue.[19]

Guay echoed the thoughts of David Stockman and other critics who argued that regulation had set farm prices too high and the price of capital too low. As a result, Stockman maintained, too many farmers had too much debt, and this had made agriculture inefficient. The credit crisis represented a necessary "shake out" – a poison pill to take out all those inefficient farmers.[20]

Farm regulation no doubt had set price supports high. Yet this did not in itself warrant the conclusion that regulation was responsible for the crisis. One problem was the supposed tie between inefficiency and failure. Farmers who were comparatively less efficient, the so-called noncommercial farmers with less than $40,000 in sales, were not the ones going broke in record numbers. Instead, commercial farmers – those who worked hundreds of acres – were failing. They were often heavily indebted, but they were not inefficient as the budget director had charged. Not only had they sustained an unusually high rate of productivity growth in comparison to other industries within the United States, but as of the early 1980s, American farmers produced more food per acre than farmers in any other country except Japan.[21] The economist and Nobel Prize winner Lawrence Klein wrote: "Agriculture . . . cannot be accused of lagging in a technological sense. . . . We should be doing everything possible to sustain this highly efficient sector of our economy."[22]

It is important to recall that in the ten years prior to the credit crisis (1972 to 1981), world demand – not government regulation – had raised farm prices. Farm programs consumed less than $2 billion per year on average in this period as compared with an average cost of

"Changes in Farm Credit System Structure," in "Agricultural Income and Finance," AFO-44, pp. 37–44.

[19] "Blame Congress," *Wall Street Journal* (November 14, 1986), p. 31.

[20] Hedrick Smith, "Stockman Insists U.S. Will Not Rescue Farmers from Credit Crisis," *New York Times* (February 14, 1985), p. A28.

[21] *State of the World 1987: A Worldwatch Institute Report on Progress toward a Sustainable Society* (New York: Norton, 1987), p. 142.

[22] Klein, "Federal Policy Created Farm Crisis," p. 3.

$10 billion per year from 1982 to 1989.[23] Hence, the cost of agricultural programs had risen only after the crisis started. How could price-support programs cause a crisis if they had played small roles in the preceding decade? Or put another way, farm regulation had been in existence for some fifty years. Farmers had acquired debts at a rapid rate for most of these years. Why was it suddenly in the 1980s that the programs produced a credit crisis? What had made debts suddenly unbearable after 1981?

Part of the answer can be found in the relationship between regulation and farmers' markets in the twenty-five years after World War II. During that era, FCA-sponsored credit agencies, no doubt, had stimulated debt financing, but farm policies, taken together, had also helped prevent credit problems. First, there had been little difference between market and regulated prices, and hence little opportunity for a new crash in prices. Second, by subsidizing prices, regulation bolstered farm income as well as the value of farmland. While farmers increased their debts, they balanced interest payments with earnings, and debts with assets.

What was important about the CCC was its relationship to the trend in prices. Congress originally had instructed the agency to shore up low prices. As a result, the agency stabilized markets as long as prices tended to fall. When prices met the goal implicit in farm legislation – that is, when a sharp increase in demand boosted prices – the CCC did not act to raise its loan rate. This condition did not matter if prices and farm income kept rising. But should markets become volatile they could prompt serious swings in exports, farm income, and the value of land. Once markets retreated, so could land prices and farm income – so much so that farmers could not service their debts. It was this sequence of volatile market events that characterized the 1970s, the decade preceding the farm crisis.

A boom in exports ushered in a new era of expanding markets in the early 1970s. A glance at Figure E.1 shows the inverse relationship between the value of the U.S. dollar in foreign exchange markets and U.S. agricultural exports. As the value of the dollar declined in rela-

[23] Keith Schneider, "Cost of Farm Law May Be $35 Billion," *New York Times* (July 22, 1986), p. A15. U.S. Department of Agriculture, "Economic Indicators of the Farm Sector: National Financial Summary, 1990," ECIFS 10-1 (November 1991), p. 18.

Exchange value   Exports (billions of dollars)

Figure E.1. Exchange value of the U.S. dollar and U.S. agricultural exports, 1967–84. From G. Edward Schuh, "International Agriculture and Trade Policies: Implications for the United States," in Bruce L. Gardner, ed., *U.S. Agricultural Policy: The 1985 Legislation* (Washington, D.C.: American Enterprise Institute, 1985), p. 58. Reprinted with the permission of The American Enterprise Institute for Public Policy Research, Washington, D.C.

tion to other currencies, farmers were able to sell more grain and related cash crops. From 1972 to 1975, the dollar plummeted to half its 1970 value, and from 1977 to 1981, it fell by half again. At the same time, exports of farm commodities boomed: between 1970 and 1975 total farm exports, adjusted for inflation, doubled, and in the next five years exports rose 30 percent, reaching $48.1 billion (or 30 percent of cash receipts) in 1980.[24]

[24] Exports are reported in 1982 dollars. U.S. Department of Commerce, *Statistical Abstract of the United States: 1988* (Washington, D.C.: U.S. Government Printing Office, 1987), pp. 617, 626.

In response to the market's upturn, the Nixon administration, under pressure about rising consumer prices for food, cut back government programs. First, acreage controls were largely phased out. Folklore has it that Earl Butz, then the secretary of agriculture, beckoned farmers to plant from "fence row to fence row." Anyone leery of price jumps he instructed to look for a new line of business.[25] Second, under the Agriculture and Consumer Protection Act of 1973, CCC loan rates were reduced while a new support mechanism, known as target prices, was introduced. According to the new plan, if market prices fell below target prices, farmers received a deficiency payment equal to the difference between the two prices. The CCC's loan system was kept in place, but loan rates were set below market prices to encourage farmers to rely on the market. In practice, both the CCC loan rates and the target prices remained below market prices during the early 1970s and at the end of the decade (Figure 7.3).[26]

As a result, the government's role in markets diminished. One indicator was the amount of crops farmers forfeited to the CCC. During the 1970s it held fewer than 100 million bushels of corn and wheat and less than 500,000 bales of cotton each year on average, or less than a fifth of the levels of the 1950s and 1960s (Table 7.1). Government payments also declined. From the start of the USDA's stringent acreage control program in 1961 through 1972, government payments had averaged 5.4 percent of gross cash income. But from 1973 until 1981, payments averaged 1.4 percent.[27] Finally, the statistics showed a new dependence on foreign markets, with one out of every three farm acres planted for export in the late 1970s. Corn exports tripled in the 1970s and by 1979, 30 percent of the crop was sold abroad. By that date, 60 percent of the wheat crop left our ports.

[25] Tony Thomas, "The Technocrats," *Economist,* 274 (January 5, 1980), American Survey, p. 13.

[26] Other crop prices also became volatile but the pattern of volatility varied among crops. See Bruce L. Gardner, "Consequences of Farm Policies during the 1970s," in D. Gale Johnson, ed., *Food and Agricultural Policy for the 1980s* (Washington, D.C.: American Enterprise Institute, 1981), pp. 50–4. For legislation, see U.S. Department of Agriculture, "History of Agricultural Price-Support and Adjustment Programs, 1933–84," Agriculture Information Bulletin No. 485 (December 1984).

[27] The USDA reports CCC stocks in *Agricultural Statistics, 1983* (Washington, D.C.: U.S. Government Printing Office, 1983), p. 464. For government payments, see U.S. Department of Agriculture, "Economic Indicators of the Farm Sector," ECIFS 7-1, p. 14.

Half of the soybean and rice crops, and one-third of the cotton crop were shipped to foreign markets.[28]

As farmers came to rely more on foreign markets and less on government price supports, they prospered. While farm debts jumped 23 percent from 1970 to 1975, they caused only a small change in farmers' financial leverage because farmers' income had increased. For the years from 1972 to 1976, net cash income (in constant dollars) averaged $56.8 billion, or 30 percent above levels for the years from 1965 to 1971.[29] In 1975 interest payments accounted for 6.7 percent of farmers' income, up slightly from 5.9 percent in 1970 (Table 7.6). Under these conditions, farm foreclosures remained flat, in line with the very low rates from the 1950s and 1960s (Figure 7.1).

While farmers prospered for the rest of the 1970s, the makings of a crisis began to appear in the second half of the decade. Prices became more volatile during the 1970s. As Figure 7.3 shows, prices for several crops more than doubled between 1971 and 1973. In 1974 and 1975, prices dropped to the government support level; in the late 1970s, prices rose again. Farmers' net cash income also became more volatile. After having risen in the early 1970s (1972–6), net cash income dropped 25 percent to $42.4 billion in the next four-year period (1977–80).[30] Despite falling cash incomes, farmers boosted debts by a whopping 36 percent between 1975 and 1980 (Table 7.6). Farmers may have needed larger loans in order to purchase land. Or, given that their net cash income had dropped 25 percent between the early and late 1970s, they may have wanted to accelerate their annual increases in debts so as to maintain their cash flow and high levels of capital expenditures.[31]

[28] G. Edward Schuh, "U.S. Agriculture in an Interdependent World Economy: Policy Alternatives for the 1980s," in D. Gale Johnson, ed., *Food and Agricultural Policy for the 1980s* (Washington, D.C.: American Enterprise Institute, 1981), p. 159. The case of corn is discussed in U.S. Department of Agriculture, "Agricultural Outlook," AO-85 (March 1983), p. 23.

[29] Figures are calculated from U.S. Department of Agriculture, "Economic Indicators of the Farm Sector," ECIFS 7-1, pp. 8, 19.

[30] Two-thirds of this $14.4 billion decline was due to higher production costs and one-third to higher interest payments. Ibid., pp. 16, 18, 19.

[31] While net cash income fell $14.4 billion between 1972–6 and 1977–80, farmers' annual increase in total debts jumped from $15.6 billion per year in the first period to $23.3 billion per year in the second period. Capital expenditures roughly matched the increases in debts. For 1972–6 capital expenditures averaged $20.2 billion per year, and for 1977–80, capital expenditures averaged $23.4 billion per year. Ibid., pp. 10, 19.

Regardless of the reason, the new debt was poorly timed and in just a few years two events precipitated an "unexpected downturn." The first shock was interest rates. The FCA boosted rates on new federal land bank loans from 8.4 percent in 1978 to 12.3 percent in 1982. Overall average interest rates on outstanding real-estate debts jumped from 7.4 percent in 1978 to 9.7 percent in 1982. As farmers increased their debts and as interest rates rose, annual interest charges (in constant dollars) increased 55 percent between 1978 and 1982.[32] The dollar gave these farmers a second shock: in 1981 and 1982 its value rose sharply relative to foreign currencies, and as a result, exports plummeted in the early 1980s. Farmers' net cash flow was not far behind, as it fell 44 percent from 1979 to 1983.[33] As exports and profits fell, land values collapsed. From 1980 to 1987, the real value of an acre of farmland skidded 50 percent from $956 to $481.[34]

Farmers passed their troubles along to those closely tied to the farm community. For lenders, farmers' cash-flow problems translated into greater rates of delinquency. Life insurance companies, for instance, reported that in 1985, 15 percent of loans were delinquent.[35] Delinquency was all too often a short stop – particularly for commercial farmers – on the way to bankruptcy or foreclosure (Table E.1).[36] As

[32] The USDA reports interest rates for new FCA loans and outstanding debts in *Agricultural Statistics, 1988* (Washington, D.C.: U.S. Government Printing Office, 1988), pp. 428–9; and it reports annual interest charges in "Economic Indicators of the Farm Sector," ECIFS 7-1, pp. 16, 19.

[33] Farmers' cash flow includes their net cash income, changes in outstanding debt, changes in liquid reserves of operators, and net rent to nonoperator landlords. Figures are reported before capital expenditures are deducted. Capital expenditures also fell sharply, from $23 billion per year in the late 1970s to $13 billion per year for the early 1980s. U.S. Department of Agriculture, "Economic Indicators of the Farm Sector," ECIFS 7-1, pp. 3, 10, 19.

[34] In 1980 exports (in 1982 dollars) peaked at $48.1 billion. Exports fell 24 percent to $36.6 billion in 1982, and fell 38 percent to $22.9 billion in 1986. U.S. Department of Commerce, *Statistical Abstract, 1988*, p. 626. See U.S. Department of Agriculture, "Economic Indicators of the Farm Sector," ECIFS 7-1, pp. 8, 10, 19, 62; and for an analysis of land values, see Lindert, "Long-run Trends in American Farmland Values," *Agricultural History*, 62 (Summer 1988), pp. 75–8, 83–4.

[35] U.S. Department of Agriculture, "Agricultural Income and Finance," AFO-44, p. 13.

[36] The USDA reported somewhat different rates for loans in the process of foreclosure by life insurance companies as compared with the rates reported in Table E.1. For December of the year given, the numbers per 1,000 in the process of foreclosure were as follows: 1980, 1.7; 1981, 2.8; 1982, 6.3; 1983, 8.9; 1984, 17.5; 1985, 28.6; 1986, 38.4; 1987, 30.2;

their financial health deteriorated, farmers restricted capital outlays for machinery and equipment. From 1979 to 1982 farmers reduced purchases of tractors 31 percent to $2.6 million; in 1985, outlays had slipped to $1.9 million; and in 1986, expenditures reached a new low of just $1.5 million, or less than half the level recorded in the late 1970s. Purchases of farm equipment showed similar trends: expenditures fell 37 percent from 1979 to 1982, and slipped another 36 percent by 1985.[37]

After the crisis started, farm policies helped mitigate its effects. Regulators raised price supports, and the government's target price remained well above market prices for the 1980s (Figure 7.3). By the late 1980s, participation rates were quite high: more than 75 percent of the base acreage of corn, more than 80 percent of wheat acreage, and close to 90 percent of cotton acreage were enrolled to take advantage of the price supports. These producers also received hefty payments through new acreage controls: from 1983 to 1989, direct government payments amounted to 7.1 percent of farmers' gross cash income, as compared to 1.4 percent in the years between 1973 and 1980.[38]

At the same time that regulation bolstered farmers' cash earnings, credit conditions eased. Following trends for the entire economy, both public and private lenders lowered interest rates. Commercial banks, for instance, cut interest rates for short-term farm loans from 14 to 15 percent in 1983–4 to 11 percent in early 1987; rates remained at this level until slipping below 10 percent in 1991. Long-term rates also fell. From their highs in the early 1980s of 14 to 15 percent, interest rates were down to roughly 10 to 11 percent in the late 1980s.[39] Along with lower interest rates, farm debt also declined;

1988, 26.0; 1989, 13.0; 1990, 11.3; 1991, 12.9. For 1980 to 1987, see U.S. Department of Agriculture, "Agricultural Income and Finance," AFO-32 (February 1989), p. 29; for 1988 to 1991, see "Agricultural Income and Finance," AFO-48 (February 1993), p. 27.

[37] Figures are calculated in nominal dollars and are reported in U.S. Department of Agriculture, "Economic Indicators of the Farm Sector," ECIFS 10-1, p. 42.

[38] For direct government payments, see ibid., p. 18. For participation rates from 1986–7 to 1991–2, see U.S. Department of Agriculture, "Agricultural Outlook," AO-180, p. 52.

[39] U.S. Department of Agriculture, "Agricultural Outlook," AO-131 (June 1987), p. 31; U.S. Department of Agriculture, "Agricultural Income and Finance," AFO-44, pp. 10–11.

adjusted for inflation, total farm debt fell from $160 billion in 1985 to $109 billion four years later. With smaller debts and lower interest rates, farmers found interest fees more manageable: interest had consumed 11 percent of farmers' cash income in 1985, but the burden was 8 percent in 1989 (Table 7.6).

Aside from these adjustments, many federal land banks tried to shorten the crisis by reversing what officials called the " 'wait for the bottom' psychology of the land market." In the St. Paul district, the federal land bank launched a special program in late 1986 intended to draw out those farmers who had maintained ample financial resources. The bank offered farmland with mortgages that carried large down payments but low interest rates. The special program lasted only 60 days but sold nearly 400,000 acres, or more than half of all the land held by the district bank. Officials maintained that the program did not depress markets inasmuch as the land sold, on average, for 4 percent more than it had been appraised. They concluded that "the psychological lift provided by this inventory reduction program appears to have strengthened one of the softest land markets in the United States." Officials further took heart in the program's imitation: "In response to the FLB [federal land bank] land sale, a number of commercial banks in the four States [sic] of the St. Paul district have independently begun similar land sale programs."[40]

By 1990, the outlook for farmers as well as for their creditors had improved considerably from the bleak days of 1985 and 1986. For life insurance firms, delinquencies as a percent of outstanding loans had peaked in 1986 at 17.0 percent, but had fallen to 4.2 percent in 1990; for commercial banks, delinquencies fell from 7.3 percent in 1985 to just 1.9 percent in 1990; and for the farm credit system delinquencies dropped from 14.4 percent of all loans in 1986 to 5.4 percent in 1990.[41]

As this perspective on the 1970s and 1980s suggests, regulation had not caused the crisis in the way that some critics charged. Certainly by the middle of the 1980s, price supports and direct government pay-

[40] U.S. Department of Agriculture, "Agricultural Outlook," AO-131, pp. 32–3.

[41] For the Farmers Home Administration (which held 8.3 percent of farmers' real estate debt in 1980), its delinquency experience was disastrous. Delinquencies amounted to more than 40 percent of outstanding loans from 1983 through 1990. See U.S. Department of Agriculture, "Agricultural Income and Finance," AFO-44, p. 13.

ments ran at high levels, and it was easy to read these high levels of government support back into the 1970s as a cause of the crisis. But to recall, price controls had been relatively small in the 1970s. So too, the store of crops left with the government had fallen to all-time lows in the 1970s. Instead, it was the return to more prosperous conditions, with market prices rising above government supports, that had initiated the volatile conditions of the 1970s.

The government's farm policies were poorly structured to deal with this type of market problem. Since the 1930s farmers supported programs to guard against the consequences of low prices. Neither they nor public officials sought to stabilize markets on the upside. Indeed the implicit goal in the 1930s was to protect farmers until markets improved. With the exception of World War II, market "improvements" were hard to come by. Only in the 1970s did prosperity return, but rising markets brought their own problems: farmers leveraged themselves to take advantage of the prosperity, but many could not service their debts when markets retreated in the 1980s. Regulation then mitigated depressed markets, but it did not contain the consequences of the expanding and volatile markets that caused farmers such financial grief in the 1980s.

It was ironic that the crisis crippled far more large than small farmers. Small farmers had already paid a price. Having taken on nonfarm jobs in previous years, part-time farmers could take consolation in knowing that they did not rely on debts to finance their modest enterprises. In the end, their salaried occupations offered them security against the vagaries of unstable prices and interest rates. For commercial farmers, however, the results were devastating. They took advantage of the capital gains inherent in land values and interest rates in the 1970s. But having increased their leverage, many of these farmers could not make their mortgage payments once interest rates shot up and farm income slipped in the early 1980s. The long-term role of regulation must have rudely disappointed these operators. The regulatory incentives of the 1950s and 1960s had created stable markets in which they leveraged their farms and produced astonishing gains in productivity. But in the 1970s, regulation – it turned out – was not well suited to addressing volatile markets. The relationship between finances and productivity proved a difficult one, too difficult for many commercial farmers, under these market conditions.

APPENDIX A The tractor's threshold, 1929

I employ the threshold model to ascertain the expected rate of diffusion for the tractor based simply on the machine's cost savings. In this appendix, I report fixed and variable costs for horses and for tractors. I use these figures to estimate the threshold for two cases: one in which a farmer kept six horses or used four horses and a tractor; and a second case in which a farmer kept five horses or used three horses and a tractor. After determining the crop-acreage threshold, I discuss the model and my calculations in relation to two other threshold studies.

For fixed costs of mechanical inputs, including the cost of the tractor, farm implements, and a wagon (Table A.1), I employ a valuation formula Warren C. Whatley developed.[1] This method entails two steps: first, I determine the retail price of each piece of equipment; second, I calculate the annual rental cost of each item as the retail price times the rental rate. The rental rate is determined as follows: $R(r,d) = r(1-e^{-rd})^{-1}$, in which the rental rate, R, depends on the interest rate, r, and the service life of the equipment, d. The annual cost of each item varies with respect to interest rates and the item's life expectancy. I set the interest rate at 7 percent. The life of the tractor equaled eight years, and the life of implements ranged from eight to twenty years (Table A.1).

Depending on the size of the farm and the size of the team of horses, a farmer might want to invest in different sizes of equipment. Table A.2 reports the average size of equipment needed to raise corn with the four different types of power, namely six horses, five horses, four horses and a tractor, and three horses and a tractor. The table shows that farmers used roughly the same size of equipment with all four arrangements. Farms with tractors could have used larger equipment, especially in the case of cultivators. A tractor could pull

---

[1] Warren C. Whatley, "Institutional Change and Mechanization in the Cotton South: The Tractorization of Cotton Farming" (Ph.D. dissertation, Stanford University, 1983), p. 206.

271

Table A.1. *Calculations for the annual fixed cost of the tractor, equipment, wagon, and horses, 1929*

Item	Retail price	Years of service[a]	Rental rate[b]	Annual cost
Tractor[d]	$1,000	8	.1632	$163.20
Standard equipment				
Plow, 2-bottom[e]	110	9	.1498	16.48
Plow, 3-bottom[e]	150	9	.1498	22.47
Disk, 8 ft.[f]	75	8[c]	.1632	12.24
Disk, 28 x 16 ft.[g]	100	8[c]	.1632	16.32
Harrow[e]	40	20	.0929	3.72
Manure spreader[e]	160	14	.1121	17.94
Specialized equipment: corn				
Corn planter, 2-row[e]	80	15	.1077	8.62
Cultivator, 2-row[e]	115	15	.1077	12.39
Corn sheller[e]	215	18	.0977	21.01
Specialized equipment: hay				
Mower, 5 ft.[e]	80	15	.1077	8.62
Rake, 11 ft.[e]	65	14	.1121	7.29
Loader, 8 ft.[e]	140	20	.0929	13.01
Racks[f]	30	10[c]	.1391	4.17
Specialized equipment: small grains				
Seeder, broadcast[e]	57	16	.1039	5.92
Drill, 11 ft.[f]	200	10[c]	.1391	27.82
Binder[e]	230	14	.1121	25.78
Wagon[e]	132	12[c]	.1232	16.26
Horse[h]	79	11[c]	.1304	10.30

[a] Service life is reported in years.
[b] Rental Rate = $r(1 - e^{-rd})^{-1}$, where the interest rate, r, equals 7 percent, and the service life, d, varies according to figures listed in the table.
[c] I estimated the number of serviceable years.
[d] The price of the tractor represents the average for the years from 1926 to 1929. U.S. Department of Agriculture, *Income Parity for Agriculture* (Washington, D.C.: U.S. Government Printing Office, 1940), part II, sec. 3, p. 53.
[e] J. B. Davidson, "Life, Service, and Cost of Service of Farm Machinery," Iowa State College Agricultural Experiment Station Bulletin No. 260 (June 1929), pp. 274-5.
[f] John A. Hopkins, "Horses, Tractors and Farm Equipment," Iowa State College Agricultural Experiment Station Bulletin No. 264 (June 1929), p. 401.
[g] Federal Trade Commission, *Report on the Agricultural Implement and Machinery Industry, Part II, Cost, Prices, and Profits*, 75th Congress, 3rd sess., House Document 702

Notes to Table A.1 (cont.)

(Washington, D.C.: 1938), p. 1150.
hThe cost of a horse is estimated as the average value of
horses in 1929 for the five midwestern states. The service
life is estimated at 11 years. Since horses were not used
when they were young, their service life began in their third
or fourth year. U.S. Department of Agriculture, Yearbook of
Agriculture, 1931 (Washington, D.C.: U.S. Government Printing
Office, 1931), p. 890.

Table A.2. *Corn equipment and farm size, 1929*

Operation	Three horses & a tractor	Four horses & a tractor	Five horses	Six horses
Plow	28 ft.	28 ft.	24-28 ft.	28 ft.
Disk	10	10	9	10
Harrow	20	20	18	20
Plant	All used 2 horses with a 2-row planter.			
Cultivate	All used 3 or 4 horses with a 2-row cultivator.			

Source: John A. Hopkins, "Horses, Tractors and Farm
Equipment," Iowa State College Agricultural Experiment
Station Bulletin No. 264 (June 1929), pp. 393-6.

four- or even eight-row cultivators. But the Works Progress Administration (WPA) discovered in a survey that most farmers used two-row
cultivators in the 1920s, and the vast majority of farmers who owned
tractors still relied on horses to cultivate their crops.[2] It is true that
farmers with tractors paid more for plows and disks. These items
raised annual equipment charges by roughly $10.07, representing a 5
percent increase in total equipment charges.

For horses, fixed charges are estimated in the same way. The average price of a horse in the Corn Belt was $79. With eleven years of
service, this translated into a cost of $10.30 per horse (Table A.1). Of
the remaining fixed charges, feed is included because horses were fed
whether they worked or not. I assume that farmers devoted 70 percent of their feed simply to keeping horses. The remaining 30 percent

[2] The percent of tractor-drawn cultivators increased from 1 to 5 percent in
the 1920s. Works Progress Administration, *Changes in Technology and
Labor Requirements in Production: Corn,* National Research Project No.
A-5 (Philadelphia, 1938), table 10, p. 58.

Table A.3. *Fixed costs for six horses, five horses, four horses and a tractor, and three horses and a tractor, 1929*

Item	Six horses	Four horses & a tractor	Five horses	Three horses & a tractor
Equipment[a]	$185.01	$195.08	$185.01	$195.08
Tractor	---	163.20	---	163.20
Wagon	16.26	16.26	16.26	16.26
Horses				
($10.30 each)	61.80	41.20	51.50	30.90
Horse care[b]				
($10.35 each)	62.10	41.40	51.75	31.05
Tractor repairs	---	17.29	---	17.29
Feed[c]				
($54.38 each)	326.28	217.52	271.90	163.14
Total	$651.45	$691.95	$576.42	$616.92

[a]Equipment charges (reported in Table A.1) include the annual cost of plows, disks, harrows, manure spreaders, corn planters, cultivators, corn shellers, mowers, rakes, loaders, racks, seeders, drills, and binders.
[b]Horse care includes cost of labor, bedding, shoeing, veterinary bills, and harness less credits for manure and a colt fee.
[c]The cost of feed represents 70 percent of the annual cost of feed per horse.
Sources: For the tractor, equipment, wagon, and horses, see Table A.1. For tractor repairs, horse care, and feed, see L. A. Reynoldson, W. R. Humphries, S. R. Speelman, E. W. McComas, and W. H. Youngman, "Utilization and Cost of Power on Corn Belt Farms," U.S. Department of Agriculture, Technical Bulletin No. 384 (October 1933), pp. 30, 39.

of the feed bill was drawn when horses worked and is reported as a variable cost.[3] Horse care (the cost of labor, bedding, shoeing, veterinary bills, and harness less credits for manure and a colt fee) came to $10.35 per horse. The last item, tractor repairs, amounted to $17.29. Each cost is reported in Table A.3, and they are totaled for each of the four types of farms.

[3]Here I am following the example of Robert E. Ankli, who divided the cost of feed into fixed and variable parts. See Robert E. Ankli, "Horses Vs. Tractors in the Corn Belt," *Agricultural History*, 54 (January 1980), p. 143.

Table A.4. *Hours per acre spent raising and harvesting an acre of corn, oats, wheat, hay, and soybeans, 1929*[a]

Crop	Six horses[b]		Four horses & a tractor[b]		
	Labor	Horse	Labor	Horse	Tractor
Corn	15.2	40.4	11.2	17.6	2.8
Oats	6.0	11.9	6.0	4.8	1.3
Wheat	10.9	26.0	8.1	8.2	2.4
Hay	6.4	8.2	6.4	8.2	---
Soybeans	11.1	28.2	10.2	18.8	1.8

[a]Adjustments for the case of five horses and three horses and a tractor are reported in Tables A.7 and A.8.
[b]Hours per acre for labor, horses, and a tractor.
Sources: For corn, oats, wheat, and hay, see L. A. Reynoldson, W. R. Humphries, S. R. Speelman, E. W. McComas, and W. H. Youngman, "Utilization and Cost of Power on Corn Belt Farms," U.S. Department of Agriculture Technical Bulletin No. 384 (October 1933), pp. 52-4. For soybeans, see H. C. M. Case, R. H. Wilcox, and H. A. Berg, "Organizing the Corn-Belt Farm for Profitable Production," University of Illinois Agricultural Experiment Station Bulletin No. 329 (revised, June 1934), p. 288.

Variable costs are calculated in three steps. First, I record the amount of time spent raising particular crops (Table A.4). Second, I estimate the proportion of land devoted to individual crops and multiply these weights by the amount of time required to raise each crop. The weighted time needed to raise each crop is tallied, and the sum amounts to the time spent raising an "acre" of crops (Table A.5). Finally, the total hours per acre are multiplied by the hourly cost of each variable-cost item. Total labor hours are multiplied by the wage rate; total tractor hours by the per-hour operating fees (fuel, oil, and grease); and total horse hours by the cost of feed measured at a per-hour rate. Table A.6 reports the hourly fees and the variable costs. Adjustments for the case of five horses as compared with three horses and a tractor are made in Tables A.7 and A.8.

To calculate the acreage threshold, all costs are expressed in per-acre rates, as shown in the following equations. The per-acre variable costs remain constant while fixed costs decline as the acreage in-

Table A.5. *Distribution of crops and weighted work hours per acre, 1929*[a]

| Crops | Percent of total | Six horses[b] | | Four horses & a tractor[b] | | |
		Labor	Horses	Labor	Horses	Tractor
Corn	52%	7.90	21.01	5.82	9.15	1.46
Oats	23	1.38	2.74	1.38	1.10	0.30
Wheat	10	1.09	2.60	0.81	0.82	0.24
Hay	9	0.58	0.74	0.58	0.74	---
Soybeans	6	0.67	1.69	0.61	1.13	0.11
Total	100%	11.62	28.78	9.20	12.94	2.11

[a]Hourly rates (hours per acre) are calculated by multiplying the rates given per crop in Table A.4 by the crop's percentage share of the land. Adjustments for the cases of four horses and three horses and a tractor are reported in Tables A.7 and A.8.
[b]Weighted hours per acre for labor, horses, and a tractor.
Source: For the distribution of crops, see P. E. Johnston and J. E. Wills, "A Study of the Cost of Horse and Tractor Power on Illinois Farms," University of Illinois Agricultural Experiment Station Bulletin No. 395 (December 1933), p. 315.

creases. The equation is solved for the acreage where the tractor's total cost per acre equals that of a team of horses.

	Team of Four Horses & *a Tractor*
Team of Six Horses	
$\$651.45/X + \$4.29/\text{acre}$	$= \$691.95/X + \$3.69/\text{acre}$
$X = 67.5 \text{ acres}$	

	Team of Three Horses & *a Tractor*
Team of Five Horses	
$\$576.42/X + \$4.40/\text{acre}$	$= \$616.92/X + \$3.74/\text{acre}$
$X = 61.4 \text{ acres}$	

This finding is surprising inasmuch as a threshold of roughly 65 crop acres indicates that farmers delayed investments in tractors despite the machine's cost savings. It therefore prompts questions as to whether my threshold analysis is in keeping with existing practices.

Table A.6. *Variable costs per acre, 1929*

Variable costs[a]	Six horses	Four horses & a tractor	Five horses	Three horses & a tractor
Feed[b]	$0.979	$0.440	$1.016	$0.444
Labor	3.312	2.622	3.386	2.662
Fuel, oil, grease	---	0.629	---	0.629
Total	$4.291	$3.691	$4.402	$3.735

[a]Variable costs (dollars per acre) are determined by the estimated number of hours spent by horses, tractors, and farmers (given in Tables A.5, A.7, and A.8) times the cost per hour. For the three inputs, the costs per hour are as follows: feed, $0.034; labor, $0.285; fuel, oil, grease, $0.298.
[b]The cost of feed is set as 30 percent of total feed cost, or $23.31. This amount is divided by 691 hours, as estimated to be the number of hours a horse worked.
Source: Hourly wage rates are found in L. A. Reynoldson, W. R. Humphries, S. R. Speelman, E. W. McComas, and W. H. Youngman, "Utilization and Cost of Power on Corn Belt Farms," U.S. Department of Agriculture Technical Bulletin No. 384 (October 1933), p. 29, n. 4; operating costs for tractors as well as the number of hours a horse worked each year are reported in the same source, pp. 30, 39.

Two specific questions are relevant. First, does a market wage apply to labor? Second, are the specific calculations reasonable?

One might object to the threshold model insofar as farmers did not always pay market rates for family labor. Spouses and children faced few job prospects and thus held a low opportunity cost. It is not possible to determine their exact opportunity cost. But it is possible to arbitrarily pick a low opportunity wage so as to reduce the cost of labor, raise the tractor's threshold, and eliminate the lag in its diffusion. Although this revised accounting may explain the tractor's rate of diffusion during the 1920s, it is suspect in at least two ways. First, it makes it more difficult to explain the tractor's subsequent diffusion in the 1930s. To explain the tractor's adoption in the 1930s, the opportunity cost of labor would have had to increase so as to reduce the tractor's threshold. But between 1929 and 1939 the opportunity cost of family labor (and wage rates) fell. One signal was the surge in

Table A.7. *Adjustments to hours per acre spent by five horses, as compared to six horses, in raising crops, 1929*

A. *Increase in hours per acre spent plowing, disking, and harrowing for corn*

Operation	Five horses[a]		Six horses[a]	
	Horse[b]	Labor[b]	Horse	Labor
Plow	11.81	2.15	10.50	1.81
Disk	3.09	0.60	2.29	0.45
Harrow	1.09	0.22	1.08	0.22
Total	15.99	2.97	13.87	2.48

B. *Adjustments to hours and costs per acre for a team of five horses[c]*

	Horses	Labor
Adjusted hours	40.4 + 2.12 = 42.52	15.2 + 0.49 = 15.69
Weighted share	52% of 42.52 = 22.11	52% of 15.69 = 8.16
Total hours[d]	22.11 + 7.77 = 29.88	8.16 + 3.72 = 11.88
Cost per acre[e]	$1.016	$3.386

[a]Hours per acre for labor, horses, and a tractor.
[b]The increase in horse hours per acre: 2.12 hours; percent change in hours: 15.3%; the increase in labor hours per acre: 0.49 hours; percent change in hours: 19.8%.
[c]The increase in time associated with five horses came in the three jobs: plowing, disking, and harrowing fields. For other jobs, farmers would have used five or fewer horses.
[d]Corn and other crops.
[e]The cost per acre for horses amounts to $0.034 times 29.88 hours, or $1.016; the cost per acre for labor amounts to $0.285 times 11.88 hours, or $3.386.
Source: For performance rates, see John A. Hopkins, "Horses, Tractors and Farm Equipment," Iowa State College Agricultural Experiment Station Bulletin No. 264 (June 1929), pp. 393-6.

unemployment that topped 20 percent in the Great Depression. It is true that New Deal agencies provided temporary jobs, but the net effect in rural areas was small. Fewer than 5 percent of all farmers in Iowa and Illinois were on relief, and fewer than 7 percent of all rural youths.[4] Apparently, the New Deal programs did not raise the

[4]For the number of persons on relief, see Works Progress Administration, *Workers on Relief in the United States in March 1935* (Washington, D.C.: U.S. Government Printing Office, 1938), vol. 1, pp. 334–5, 370–1. To

opportunity cost of family labor for substantial numbers of farmers. Perhaps more to the point, farm wages in the Corn Belt fell 25 to 35 percent between 1929 and 1939.[5]

Even without considering the subsequent trend in the tractor's diffusion, there is a second and more serious problem with the revised accounting: it does not make sense given the nature of the operator's labor and the purpose of the model. The model does not consider all farm activities; instead, it values time spent performing field jobs (plowing, disking, planting, and cultivating crops). In carrying out such tasks, one person worked with one source of power – either the tractor or a team of horses. Family members certainly helped with chores, but it was the operator's responsibility to see these field tasks completed.[6] Put another way, as the head of a household, the farmer faced an opportunity cost insofar as he or she was under pressure to earn an income whether it be in farming or some other occupation. The market wage, then, serves as an appropriate gauge of the farmer's labor within the context of the threshold model.

In using a market wage, my study fits with many existing studies. In his analysis of the tractor's diffusion in the Corn Belt, Robert E. Ankli used a market wage of 30¢ an hour for horse and tractor farms. Warren Whatley in his study of the tractor in the Cotton South used a market wage for the tractor driver of 20.8¢ an hour and a wage of 15.5¢ for day labor. (My wage rate compares favorably with Whatley's lower rate for day labor given the regional differences.) Nicholas Sargen in his study of the tractor in the Wheat Belt likewise used market rates for preharvest and harvest labor. And for their study of the tractor in California, Alan Olmstead and Robert Ankli used a market wage of 35¢ an hour for a tractor driver and 25¢ an hour for manual labor. Unlike the Cotton South or California, the driver did

calculate the ratio of farmers on relief to all farmers, I obtain the number of all farmers from the U.S. Department of Commerce, *Fifteenth Census of the United States: 1930* (Washington, D.C.: U.S. Government Printing Office, 1932), Agriculture, vol. 2, part 1, pp. 568, 648, 886, 968. For youths, see Bruce L. Melvin, "Rural Youth on Relief," Works Progress Administration Research Monograph No. 11 (1937), pp. 69, 74.

[5] For changes in farm wages by state, see U.S. Department of Agriculture, *Crops and Markets*, 19 (July 1942), pp. 150–1.

[6] See, for example, Lucy Studley, "Relationship of the Farm Home to the Farm Business," University of Minnesota Agricultural Experiment Station Bulletin No. 279 (July 1931).

Table A.8. *Adjustments to hours spent by three horses and a tractor, as compared to four horses and a tractor, in raising crops, 1929*

A. *Increase in time spent cultivating corn and cutting wheat*

Operation	Three horses & a tractor[a]		Four horses & a tractor[a]	
	Horse	Labor	Horse	Labor
Cultivating corn[b]	2.34	0.82	2.33	0.59
Cut wheat[c]	4.33	1.10	3.20	0.86

B. *Adjustments to Hours and Costs per Acre for Three Horses and a Tractor*

	Horses	Labor
Adjusted hours		
Corn	0.01 + 17.6 = 17.61	0.23 + 11.2 = 11.43
Wheat	1.13 + 8.2 = 9.33	0.24 + 8.1 = 8.34
Weighted share		
Corn	52% of 17.61 = 9.16	52% of 11.43 = 5.94
Wheat	10% of 9.33 = 0.93	10% of 8.34 = 0.83
Total hours[d]	13.06	9.34
Cost per acre[e]	$0.444	$2.662

[a]Hours per acre for labor, horses, and a tractor.
[b]The increase in hours for horses in cultivating corn: 0.1; percent change: 0%; the increase in hours for labor in cultivating corn: 0.23; percent change: 39%.
[c]The increase in hours for horses in cutting wheat: 1.13; percent change: 35.3%; the increase in hours for labor in cutting wheat: 0.24; percent change: 27.9%.
[d]Corn, wheat, and other crops. Total hours for horses amount to 9.16 + 0.93 + 2.97 = 13.06; total hours for labor amount to 5.94 + 0.83 + 2.57 = 9.34.
[e]The cost per acre for horses equals $0.034 times 13.06 hours, or $0.444; the cost per acre for labor equals $0.285 times 9.34 hours, or $2.662.
Source: See Table A.7.

not earn a special wage in the Midwest. Here my method is in keeping with Ankli's. But the point is that in all these studies, the economic historians used market wages to value all labor needed to calculate the tractor's threshold.[7] With respect to the model's valuation of

[7]Ankli, "Horses Vs. Tractors," pp. 143–4; Whatley, "Institutional Change and Mechanization in the Cotton South," p. 210; Robert E. Ankli and Alan L. Olmstead, "The Adoption of the Gasoline Tractor in California,"

inputs, then, I followed existing procedures, and, in doing so, these practices have produced this unusual conclusion.

Alternatively, one may question the specific calculations needed to arrive at the acreage threshold. Because the threshold is central to my argument, it is important to be confident of the individual cost components. A change in the cost of an item may either raise or lower the final threshold. In the case of the original team of six horses, an increase in the cost of horses, feed, or labor – three items used more on these farms – will tend to reduce the competitiveness of this method and lower the threshold. By contrast, an increase in the cost of the tractor, its operating fees, or equipment will reduce the competitiveness of the tractor technology and raise the threshold. Furthermore, the calculations are sensitive. An upward adjustment in labor costs of 10 percent lowers the threshold by 11 percent. In assessing my estimates, one would like them to be somewhat conservative. It is safer for the threshold to be a bit high and to underestimate the extent of the lag in the adoption of the tractor than for the threshold to be too low and to indicate falsely that farmers were slow to adopt the machine. To assess my choice of figures, I offer two measures of sensitivity. First, I compare my figures with the figures used by Warren Whatley in his study of the diffusion of tractors in the South and the estimates of Robert Ankli in his study of the Corn Belt.[8] I chose Whatley because I have followed his valuation method in calculating many of my own figures. I chose Ankli because he specifically studied the diffusion of tractors in the Corn Belt during the 1920s. Second, because Ankli and I both assess the Corn Belt, I compare my final threshold calculation with the one Ankli reached.

In comparing my choice of figures with Whatley's and Ankli's selections, I first consider variable costs and then fixed costs. In the case of variable costs, three items are relevant: wages, fuel, and feed. My choice for the wage rate is 28.5¢ per hour. Whatley's rate, by contrast, is significantly lower than mine, at 15.5¢ per hour. Still, Whatley's rate applies to southern farm workers who labored for significantly lower wages during the 1920s. If one compares the wages

Agricultural History, 55 (July 1981), p. 220; Nicholas Sargen, "Tractorization" in the United States and Its Relevance for the Developing Countries (New York: Garland Publishing, 1979), pp. 143, 145.
[8] See Whatley, "Institutional Change and Mechanization in the Cotton South"; and Ankli, "Horses Vs. Tractors."

reported in *Crops and Markets* (where Whatley obtained his wage rate), then southern farm wages should be 45 percent less than farm wages in the Midwest.[9] Ankli's wage rate for midwestern labor is 30¢ per hour, or roughly 5 percent higher than mine. In the case of operating costs, primarily fuel, the figures are very similar: 30¢, 28.7¢, and 29.8¢ per hour for Ankli, Whatley, and myself, respectively. Finally, for feed costs, my rate is 3.4¢ per hour, or 0.4¢ higher than Ankli's rate, and is 1.6¢ less than Whatley's rate of 5¢ per hour.[10] In comparison to Ankli, while my labor costs are somewhat low and the feed costs a bit high, the two charges cancel out each other.[11]

In the case of fixed costs, five items affected the final threshold: horses, horse care, feed, the tractor, and farm equipment. The first three may be grouped together since these items were calculated as a fee per horse times the number of horses. In my calculations, I charged $20.65 for the rental cost of horses plus horse "care," and $54.38 for feed, bringing the total cost to $75.03 per horse. Ankli's cost is a bit higher. His estimate is $19.50 for horse costs and $56.00 for feed, or a total cost of $75.50 per horse. Whatley's estimates are

[9] In *Old South, New South,* Gavin Wright presents figures that indicate that farm wages in the South were perhaps 50 percent less than farm wages in the Midwest during the 1920s. If his analysis is correct, then one would expect to find a large gap between my wage rate and Whatley's. For the five midwestern states, *Crops and Markets* reported that the average annual wage, based on four months, was 27.8¢ per hour. With this wage rate, my crop threshold rises two acres, from 68 to 70 acres. Whatley reports a threshold that is nearly 20 acres higher than mine, or 83 crop acres. The difference, however, can be explained by the lower wage rates found in the South. For the southern threshold, see Whatley, "Institutional Change and Mechanization of the Cotton South," p. 109. For Wright's figures on wages, see *Old South, New South: Revolutions in the Southern Economy since the Civil War* (New York: Basic Books, 1986), p. 66. Also see U.S. Department of Agriculture, *Crops and Markets,* 6 (1929), pp. 53, 120, 251, 496.

[10] Ankli takes 30 percent of a total feed bill of $80, or $24, and divides the figure by 800 hours to obtain a per-hour cost of 3¢ per hour. Ankli also states that the figures were slightly less for the case of an ordinary (six) horse farm – $77.68 for the total feed bill and 691 hours. In my calculations I take 30 percent of $77.69 per horse, or $23.31, and divide the figure by 691 hours to obtain the per-hour cost of 3.4¢ per hour. See Ankli, "Horses Vs. Tractors," p. 143 and n. 36.

[11] If I adjust my rates relative to Ankli's – that is, raise labor wages from 28.5¢ to 30¢ per hour, raise fuel charges from 29.8¢ to 30¢ per hour, and lower feed costs from 3.4¢ per hour to 3¢ per hour – then the threshold rises slightly from 68 to 71 acres.

not directly comparable because farmers in the South used mules, not horses. His cost for mules alone is $12.94 per mule, as compared with roughly $19.00 per horse in the Midwest. His estimate for feed is $56.15 per horse. This latter figure, however, assumes that 50 percent of the feed bill was a fixed cost, whereas Ankli and I assume that 70 percent of the feed bill was a fixed cost. If Whatley's variable cost rate is adjusted from 5¢ per hour to 3.5¢, so that it is comparable to my own variable feed cost, then his fixed cost for feed rises from $56.15 to $73.05 per mule, and his total fixed cost for mules rises from $69.09 to $85.99 per mule. Whatley's rate would then be roughly $11 higher than my charges per animal. All of this is to say that my estimate for horse costs is a bit lower (meaning more conservative) than Ankli's and is clearly lower than Whatley's.

For the two remaining items, the tractor and farm equipment, my estimate for the tractor is slightly higher than Ankli's estimate. I value the cost of the tractor (including repairs) at $180.49; Ankli estimates the fixed cost of the tractor at $184.20.[12] In the case of the tractor's farm equipment (including the wagon), however, we differ in our two estimates: I estimate equipment costs at $211.34, Ankli at $293.98. This difference in equipment charges can be explained in terms of the kind of farms we consider. Ankli examines a case in which the farmer relied solely on a tractor for every farm operation. He therefore includes the cost of a corn picker for harvesting and charges for other types of equipment that the tractor would have used. By contrast, I consider a more restrictive case in which the farmer used a tractor to plow and disk fields, but kept a small team of horses to perform most other tasks.[13] In my case, then, I do not assume that the farmer used a corn picker to harvest, nor do I assume that the farmer purchased some of the equipment that Ankli must assume a farmer did in order to use the tractor. To make our estimates comparable, I would need to subtract the cost of the corn picker (roughly $69) from Ankli's

[12] The net difference in fixed costs for sources of power – that is, for horses and the tractor – comes to $2.77, and raises the threshold by roughly five acres. This comparison, though, is not precise since Ankli assessed a case in which tractors were driven longer hours and would be expected to incur higher repair charges.

[13] My assumption is in line with the results found in a survey conducted by the Works Progress Administration. Roughly 35 percent of farmers reported using a tractor to plow and disk land in 1929. By contrast, the vast majority of farmers relied on horses for other operations, such as planting and cultivating the land. See Works Progress Administration, *Changes in Technology: Corn*, p. 58.

estimate of equipment charges for a tractor and substitute equipment that horses would have used rather than a tractor for some other operations. Under these conditions, Ankli's adjusted equipment charges are roughly the same as (or perhaps higher than) mine.[14]

It is more difficult to compare my estimates for equipment and the tractor with Whatley's. In the case of equipment (and wagon), my costs are higher: $211.34 for the method employing a tractor versus $146.63 for Whatley's technique that relies solely on a tractor. This comparison indicates that my costs are more conservative than Whatley's, but I suspect that my figures are higher because farmers employed more machinery in the Corn Belt than in the South. In the case of the tractor, Whatley's figure is the higher and more conservative estimate. His estimate for the cost of the tractor and its repairs is $272.41, whereas my estimate is $180.49. Whatley's higher charges derive from two factors: larger annual rental fees for the tractor, and larger repair charges. Whatley's higher charges, however, may be due in good part to the use of the tractor in the South. Whatley considers a case in which farmers relied solely on a tractor and used the tractor 5.16 hours per acre. By contrast, I consider the case in which farmers kept some horses when they bought a tractor, and therefore used a tractor for comparatively fewer hours per acre. In calculating the rental fee for the tractor, I use a life expectancy, based on a survey taken in the 1920s, that was eight years or two years longer than the

[14] Ankli does not state the cost of each item. His source, Davidson, estimated the annual cost of a corn picker to be roughly $69 in 1929. If this cost is subtracted from Ankli's equipment charges, then our figures are $14 apart. But Ankli also had roughly $28 extra in equipment charges for the tractor given that the machine was used for several operations. These extra charges can be seen as different pieces of equipment that he listed for the tractor when used in place of a team of six horses. Such items included a side delivery rake (rather than a dump hay rake for the team of horses), a ten-foot binder (rather than an eight-foot binder), a four-row check planter (rather than a two-row check planter), and a sixteen-inch plow (rather than a fourteen-inch plow). Because I assume a case in which farmers used a tractor mostly for plowing and disking, my calculations do not include some of these extra pieces of equipment. If half of these extra charges are subtracted from Ankli's estimate for equipment, then our figures for equipment are the same. If two-thirds of the extra costs are subtracted, then his estimate would be nearly $5 less than mine. For estimates of the cost of the corn picker, see J. B. Davidson, "Life Service and Cost of Service of Farm Machinery," Iowa College Agricultural Experiment Station Bulletin No. 260 (June 1929), p. 275. For Ankli's list of equipment, see Ankli, "Horses Vs. Tractors," p. 143.

life expectancy used by Whatley. While my interest rate was slightly higher (and more conservative) than Whatley's and while we use similar retail prices ($1,000 versus $1,014), the difference in life expectancy results in a $35 difference between our two annual rental charges, and accounts for two-fifths of the difference between Whatley's and my own charges for the tractor. In the case of repairs, one would expect repairs to increase as the vehicle performed more jobs and was driven for more hours. While one cannot determine the difference precisely, one would expect Whatley's repairs to be higher than mine.

To summarize, this comparison of fixed and variable costs was intended to determine whether my figures provide a reasonable estimate of the final acreage threshold. In the case of variable costs, my estimates are roughly the same as Ankli's. Compared with Whatley's estimates, the one major difference is his lower wage rate. The *Crops and Markets* surveys, however, indicated that wages in the South were much lower than midwestern farm wages. In the case of fixed costs, my estimates for horses are almost the same as Ankli's and more conservative than Whatley's estimates. For equipment, my figures are similar to Ankli's, once his figures are adjusted for the corn picker and other special equipment farmers who relied only on a tractor would have required. Compared with Whatley's, my equipment figures are more conservative, although the figures may reflect different types of farming. Finally, for the tractor, my estimate is similar to Ankli's, but was lower and less conservative than Whatley's. I attribute this latter discrepancy to the use of the machine in the South, both in terms of its life expectancy and its annual repairs. This comparison of my study to Ankli's and Whatley's suggests that my choice of individual figures was reasonable, and a threshold of 61–68 acres is not too low.

Having compared the cost components for the threshold equation, we are left with one last consideration: a comparison of my threshold of 65 crop acres and the threshold Robert Ankli calculated in his study of the Corn Belt. Ankli considered a hypothetical case in which a farmer relied solely on a tractor. He compared this method of production with two others: first, a small farm with three horses and, second, a large farm of six horses. After estimating his thresholds, Ankli concluded that "it was profitable to switch from a small team to a tractor at 47.6 acres. Finally, at 126.5 or more acres, the cost-

conscious farmer should have switched from a general purpose tractor to a large-team operation."[15] Ankli, however, made a small but
critical error in calculating the threshold between a tractor and a large
team of six horses. It appears that he omitted the cost of "other
items" ($19.50) per horse in calculating the total fixed cost of a large
team of horses. He calculated the total cost of the team of horses as
the feed cost of $56.00 per horse times six horses, rather than $56.00
plus $19.50 per horse times six horses.[16] Once the fixed costs are
determined as $75.50 per horse times six horses, then the team does
not become profitable until a farmer works more than 418 acres.
With this correction, Ankli's analysis indicates that any farmer who
worked more than 47.6 acres or less than 418 acres could have
reduced costs with a tractor. Since very few farmers worked more
than 418 acres in 1929, the important figure is the threshold of 47.6
acres.[17] This revised threshold is roughly 17 acres lower than mine
and indicates that proportionately more farmers should have adopted
the tractor in the 1920s.

To conclude, Ankli's results are valuable and support my own
threshold analysis. Together, our studies indicate that over a range of
investment decisions – whether to buy a tractor and still employ
horses, or to switch completely to a tractor – the tractor was the
more efficient technology for farmers who worked more than 65
crop acres.

[15] Ankli, "Horses Vs. Tractors," p. 144.
[16] Ibid., pp. 143–4.
[17] If the calculations are made for five horses, rather than six, the revised
threshold is 228 acres. Few farmers would have worked more than 228
crop acres; the important figure is still the lower figure of 48 crop acres.

APPENDIX B The tractor's threshold, 1939

Between 1929 and 1939, both changes in prices and changes in technology altered the tractor's threshold. Changes in technology lowered the tractor's cost, while changes in most prices raised its cost. The important question, however, is how much did the tractor's threshold rise or fall in response to prices and technology? In this appendix, I report the consequences of technological improvements and changes in prices. This leaves one last factor to consider, the Agricultural Adjustment Administration's acreage restriction programs.

Technological improvements reduced both the tractor's fixed and variable costs. In the case of fixed costs, several small improvements lengthened the life of a tractor and, in turn, reduced its fixed costs. In 1929, farmers had expected tractors to last roughly eight years; using the rental formula in Appendix A, the tractor's fixed cost amounted to $163.20. For 1939, the service life had increased to roughly thirteen years and the effective interest rate for calculating the rental fee had declined from 7 to 6 percent. The combined effect of these changes caused the tractor's fixed cost to drop 32 percent to $110.80.[1]

In the case of variable costs, pneumatic tires reduced time plowing and disking by perhaps 25 percent. If this rate applied to all time spent on a tractor, then a tractor's hours would have dropped from 2.11 to 1.58, and variable costs (in 1929 prices) would drop from $3.69 to $3.38 per acre.

While technological improvements reduced a tractor's cost, changes in prices eliminated most of these savings. Table B.1 lists the changes in various prices between 1929 and 1939. A change in the price of each item mattered both in terms of the direction of the change and its magnitude. Minor inputs could only exert a significant shift in the threshold if they experienced a dramatic change in their prices. For

---

[1] The lower interest rate for calculating the rental rate also applied to other items – equipment, wagons, and horses. The cost of wagons declined by the same amount for all four cases. The decline in the cost of a pair of horses roughly matched the amount of the decline for equipment. In effect, one canceled the other.

Table B.1. *Changes in prices of farm resources,
1929-39*

Input	Change in prices (%), 1929-39
Equipment[a]	-2.5%
Wagon[a]	-2.5
Tractor[b]	+7.4
Horses[c]	+14.4
Horse Care[d]	-26.5
Labor[d]	-26.5
Feed[e]	-32.2
Fuel, oil, grease[f]	-19.2
Tractor repair[g]	+13.3

[a]For prices of equipment (including the wagon), see Iowa
Department of Agriculture, "Prices Paid by Iowa Farmers for
Commodities used in Production," *Fortieth Annual Yearbook*
(Des Moines, 1939), p. 553. In measuring equipment prices, I
use a series called "Farm Machinery," but this is defined to
mean farm implements; see ibid., pp. 570-1.
[b]For the price of the tractor, I average figures from two
sources. The Iowa yearbook indicates tractor prices rose 8.8
percent, while national trends show an increase of 5.9
percent between 1929 and 1938. See Iowa Department of
Agriculture, "Prices Paid by Iowa Farmers for Commodities
used in Production," *Fortieth Annual Yearbook* (Des Moines,
1939), p. 553; and the U.S. Department of Agriculture, *Income
Parity for Agriculture* (Washington, D.C.: U.S. Government
Printing Office, 1940), part III, sec. 4, p. 13.
[c]I calculate changes in the average value of horses in the
five Corn Belt states from U.S. Department of Agriculture,
Yearbook of Agriculture, 1931 (Washington, D.C.: U.S.
Government Printing Office, 1931), p. 890; and *Agricultural
Statistics, 1940* (Washington, D.C.: U.S. Government Printing
Office, 1940), p. 418.
[d]Changes in labor wages (and horse care) are calculated for
changes in the average of Iowa and Illinois wages between
1929 and 1939. See *Crops and Markets*, 19 (July 1942), pp.
150-1.
[e]I average two sources to estimate the decline in feed costs.
One source is the Iowa series which reported a 34.4 percent
decline; see Iowa Department of Agriculture, *Fortieth Annual
Yearbook*, p. 553. Although this series is the best
representative of the Midwest, I balanced it with national
trends, for which I calculated changes in three crops (oats,
corn, and hay), as reported in U.S. Department of
Agriculture, *Agricultural Statistics, 1941* (Washington, D.C.:
U.S. Government Printing Office, 1941), pp. 49, 67, 310-1.
[f]I averaged the change in fuel prices from two sources. The

threshold if they experienced a dramatic change in their prices. For example, the price of fuel fell 19 percent, but because this item was small, it had a negligible effect on the threshold. By contrast, major inputs exerted a substantial shift in the threshold. The fall in the price of feed served to bring about large reductions in costs for the two kinds of farms. Furthermore, because farms relying only on horses used proportionately more feed, their costs fell more relative to farms relying on horses and a tractor.

Tables B.2 and B.3 measure the effect of prices and technical improvements on fixed and variable costs for a team of six horses as compared with a smaller team of four horses and a tractor. I use these two tables to calculate a new threshold for 1939 using the same formula I used for 1929 (Appendix A).

All costs are expressed in per-acre terms. The per-acre cost of fixed expenses varies as the number of acres increases, and the acreage is represented by an "x." The cost functions for farms with only horses and farms with horses and tractors are solved simultaneously. X equals the number of acres above which the tractor reduces the cost of production relative to a team of horses.

| | *Team of Four Horses &* |
| *Team of Six Horses* | *a Tractor* |

$$\$519.56/X + \$3.10/\text{acre} = \$556.16/X + \$2.50/\text{acre}$$
$$X = 61.0 \text{ acres}$$

| | *Team of Three Horses &* |
| *Team of Five Horses* | *a Tractor* |

$$\$463.85/X + \$3.18/\text{acre} = \$500.45/X + \$2.53/\text{acre}$$
$$X = 56.3 \text{ acres}$$

Notes to Table B.1 (*cont.*)

Iowa series reported a 17.2 percent decline, while a second series reported a 21.2 percent drop. The second series came from the U.S. Department of Agriculture, *Income Parity for Agriculture*, part II, sec. 4 (October 1940), pp. 39-40. For this series, I calculated the weighted average of changes in the price of gasoline, kerosene, and motor oil.
[g]For changes in the cost of tractor repairs, the one series is found in U.S. Department of Agriculture, *Income Parity for Agriculture*, part II, sec. 4 (October 1940), p. 43.

Table B.2. *The fixed cost for different farms based on changes in technology and prices, 1939*

Item[a]	Six horses	Four horses & a tractor	Five horses	Three horses & a tractor
Equipment	$170.25	$179.70	$170.25	$179.70
Tractor	---	118.98	---	118.98
Wagon	15.05	15.05	15.05	15.05
Horses				
($11.23 each)	67.38	44.92	56.15	33.69
Horse care				
($7.61 each)	45.66	30.44	38.05	22.83
Tractor repairs	---	19.59	---	19.59
Feed				
($36.87 each)	221.22	147.48	184.35	110.61
Total	$519.56	$556.16	$463.85	$500.45

[a]Changes in prices between 1929 and 1939 for the individual items are reported in Table B.1. These rates of change are used to adjust the price of tractors, equipment, wagon, and horses from 1929 (as reported in Table A.1). The interest rate used to calculate the rental rate for all of these items is reduced from 7 to 6 percent. The tractor's cost is adjusted for the increase in its service life from eight to thirteen years.

In 1929, farmers stood to profit from a tractor when the size of their farms crossed a threshold of roughly 65 crop acres. In 1939, the threshold had fallen six acres to roughly 59 crop acres.

There is one other factor to consider, the Agricultural Adjustment Administration's acreage restrictions. The AAA paid farmers to divert land from corn to other crops. In doing so, farmers necessarily altered their cost of production. Of their crops, corn was the most labor-intensive. For every hour a farmer spent raising an acre of oats or wheat or alfalfa, the farmer devoted an hour and a half to two hours tending an acre of corn. The AAA asked farmers to reduce acreage in corn by 15 to 25 percent. On average, corn acreage shrank by 18 percent. In my calculations I consider the consequences of redistributing land from corn to other crops. The amount of land is reduced roughly 18 percent from 52 out of every 100 crop acres to 42.5 acres. Acres freed from corn production are redistributed among other crops (based on the

Table B.3. *Variable costs per acre, adjusted for*
changes in technology and prices, 1939[a]

Variable costs	Six horses	Four horses & a tractor	Five horses	Three horses & a tractor
Feed	$0.665	$0.299	$0.690	$0.302
Labor	2.434	1.816	2.489	1.846
Fuel, oil, grease	---	0.381	---	0.381
Total	$3.099	$2.496	$3.179	$2.529

[a]Variable costs (dollars per acre) are determined by the
estimated number of hours spent by horses, tractors, and
farmers (Tables A.5, A.7, and A.8) times the cost per hour.
1929 costs are adjusted for changes in prices between 1929
and 1939 (Table B.1). Hours spent in the fields are also
adjusted in the case of farms with tractors for the adoption
of pneumatic tires. Tractor hours declined 25 percent from
2.11 to 1.58, and labor hours fell by the same amount of time
from 9.20 to 8.67. Hourly rates for the three inputs in 1939
are as follows: feed, $0.0231; labor, $0.2095; fuel, oil,
grease, $0.2408.

other crops' relative share of total cropland), as shown in Table B.4.
Once land is redistributed, farm costs decline for all farms, but costs
decline relatively more for farms that rely only on horses. If one includes the effects of the AAA, the tractor's threshold increases from
roughly 65 crop acres in 1929 to roughly 68 acres in 1939 (Table B.4).

In reporting the tractor's 1939 threshold, it is important to be
cautious in selecting the values of different inputs. I argue that
changes in technology and prices between 1929 and 1939 caused no
significant fall in the tractor's threshold. One might wonder whether
changes in technology could have brought about larger declines in the
tractor's cost or whether prices might not have reduced the tractor's
advantage by as much as I indicate. To bolster my choice of figures, I
review my selection of figures for changes in technology and prices.

In the case of technological improvements, I use a value of thirteen
years for the tractor's life expectancy. In 1941, a survey found that
midwestern farmers anticipated that tractors would last fourteen
years. It is likely that in 1939 a tractor was expected to last fewer
years: at least one less and perhaps two or three fewer years. Warren

Table B.4. *Effect of AAA acreage restrictions on distribution of crops and variable costs measured in hours per acre, 1939*[a]

Crops	Percent of total	Six horses[b]		Five horses & a tractor[b]		
		Labor	Horses	Labor	Horses	Tractor
Corn	42.5%	6.46	17.17	4.76	7.48	1.19
Oats	27.5	1.65	3.27	1.65	1.32	0.36
Wheat	12.0	1.31	3.12	0.97	0.98	0.29
Hay	10.8	0.69	0.89	0.69	0.89	----
Soybeans	7.2	0.80	2.03	0.73	1.35	0.13
Total	100.0%	10.91	26.48	8.80	12.02	1.97

[a]Hourly rates (hours per acre) are calculated by multiplying the rates given per crop in Table A.4 by the crop's percentage share of the land. Adjustments for the cases of four horses and three horses and a tractor are reported in Tables B.5 and B.6. Adjusting for the effect of pneumatic tires, tractor hours are cut 25 percent from 1.97 to 1.48 hours and labor hours are reduced by the same amount of time from 8.80 to 8.31 hours.

Using 1939 prices to calculate variable costs, results for six horses in a cost of $2.898 per acre, and for four horses and a tractor in a cost of $2.375 per acre. In the case of the two smaller farms, the variable cost of five horses amounts to $2.962, and for three horses and a tractor, $2.405. Substituting these figures into the two equations, the threshold for six horses versus four horses and a tractor rises to 70 acres, and that for five horses versus three horses and a tractor to 66 acres.

[b]Weighted hours per acre for labor, horses, and a tractor.

Whatley, in his study of the Cotton South, investigated the relationship between the tractor's life expectancy and its actual improvements between 1930 and 1950. Using a twelve-year lifetime in 1940, Whatley concluded that twelve years was "equivalent to assuming that over 80 percent of the durability improvements successfully adopted during the period 1930–50 were actually embodie[d] in the marketable tractor of 1940. This leaves only 20 percent of the improvements for the following decade." Any lifetime greater than twelve years seems unlikely by these standards. Whatley himself considered an estimate of a twelve-year lifetime to be very generous, and used twelve

Table B.5. *Adjustments to hours per acre spent by five horses, as compared to six horses, in raising crops, based on distribution of crops with the AAA acreage restrictions, 1939*

A. *Increase in time spent plowing, disking, and harrowing for corn*

Operation	Five horses[a]		Six horses[a]	
	Horse[b]	Labor[b]	Horse	Labor
Plow	11.81	2.15	10.50	1.81
Disk	3.09	0.60	2.29	0.45
Harrow	1.09	0.22	1.08	0.22
Total	15.99	2.97	13.87	2.48

B. *Adjustments to hours and costs per acre for a team of five horses[c]*

	Horses	Labor
Adjusted hours	40.4 + 2.12 = 42.52	15.2 + 0.49 = 15.69
Weighted share	42.5% of 42.52 = 18.07	42.5% of 15.69 = 6.67
Total hours[d]	18.07 + 9.31 = 27.38	6.67 + 4.45 = 11.12
Cost per acre[e]	$0.632	$2.330

[a]Hours per acre for labor, horses, and a tractor.
[b]The increase in horse hours per acre: 2.12 hours; percent change in hours: 15.3%; the increase in labor hours per acre: 0.49 hours; percent change in hours: 19.8%.
[c]The increase in time associated with five horses came in the three jobs: plowing, disking, and harrowing fields. For other jobs, farmers would have used five or fewer horses. Variable costs per acre are calculated using 1939 prices.
[d]Corn and other crops.
[e]The cost per acre for horses amounts to $0.0231 times 27.38 hours, or $0.632; the cost per acre for labor amounts to $0.2095 times 11.12 hours, or $2.330.
Sources: See Tables A.7 and B.1.

years in his calculations for the year 1939.[2] Had I used twelve rather than thirteen years, the tractor's fixed cost would have declined by less from 1929 to 1939.[3] The tractor's threshold, adjusted for other

[2] Warren C. Whatley, "Institutional Change and Mechanization in the Cotton South: The Tractorization of Cotton Farming" (Ph.D. dissertation, Stanford University, 1983), p. 127.
[3] Using a service life of twelve years, 1939 prices, and an interest rate of 6 percent, the tractor's rental fee amounts to $125.55, not $118.98.

Table B.6. *Adjustments to hours spent by three horses and a tractor, as compared to four horses and a tractor, in raising crops, based on the distribution of crops with the AAA acreage restrictions, 1939*

A. *Increase in time spent cultivating corn and cutting wheat*

Operation	Three horses and a tractor[a]		Five horses and a tractor[a]	
	Horse	Labor	Horse	Labor
Cultivating corn[b]	2.34	0.82	2.33	0.59
Cut wheat[c]	4.33	1.10	3.20	0.86

B. *Adjustments to hours and costs per acre for three horses and a tractor*

	Horses	Labor
Adjusted hours		
Corn	0.01 + 17.6 = 17.61	0.23 + 11.2 = 11.43
Wheat	1.13 + 8.2 = 9.33	0.24 + 8.1 = 8.34
Weighted share		
Corn	42.5% of 17.61 = 7.48	42.5% of 11.43 = 4.86
Wheat	12% of 9.33 = 1.12	12% of 8.34 = 1.00
Total hours[d]	12.16	8.93
Adjusted labor hours[e]		8.44
Cost per acre[f]	$0.281	$1.78

[a]Hours per acre for labor, horses, and a tractor.

[b]The increase in hours for horses in cultivating corn: 0.1; percent change: 0%; the increase in hours for labor in cultivating corn: 0.23; percent change: 39%.

[c]The increase in hours for horses in cutting wheat: 1.13; percent change: 35.3%; the increase in hours for labor in cutting wheat: 0.24; percent change: 27.9%.

[d]Corn, wheat, and other crops. Total hours for horses amount to 7.48 + 1.12 + 3.56 = 12.16; total hours for labor amount to 4.86 + 1.00 + 3.07 = 8.93.

[e]Labor hours are reduced for the savings from pneumatic tires, or 25 percent of the tractor's time (0.49 hours), to 8.44.

[f]The cost per acre for horses equals $0.0231 times 12.16 hours, or $0.281; the cost per acre for labor equals $0.2095 times 8.44, or $1.78.

Sources: See Tables A.7 and B.1.

technical improvements and prices (but not for the AAA), would have risen to 69 crop acres, a level above the 1929 threshold of 65 crop acres.

In the case of pneumatic tires, studies showed that these tires reduced time spent plowing and disking by 25 percent. In my calculations, however, I assume reductions took place in all operations for which a farmer used a tractor. Had I restricted the gains to just plowing and disking (or roughly half the time in the fields), then the tractor's hours would have declined by less, from 2.11 to 1.85 hours. Variable costs would have dropped by a smaller amount, and the final threshold would have risen to roughly 72.5 crop acres, again well above the 1929 threshold.

My figures for changes in prices also compare with those reported by Warren Whatley in his study of the tractor's diffusion in the Cotton South. With respect to labor and feed, he reported changes of greater magnitude than I did. For example, I reported a 27 percent decline in labor costs, whereas Whatley found a 39 percent decline; I estimate a 32 percent drop in feed, whereas Whatley reported a 40 percent decline.[4] Since the declines in labor and feed costs are smaller in my case, they exert less pressure to raise the threshold and reduce the tractor's competitiveness than was the case with Whatley's study.

In the case of the tractor my changes are greater than Whatley's: I report a 7.4 percent increase, Whatley a 6 percent increase. Our two figures, however, are not fully comparable because Whatley reports changes for tractors and trucks together. The estimated costs also differ insofar as I use a longer service life of thirteen instead of Whatley's twelve years. I also adjust the fixed costs for a decline in interest rates for short-term loans. On net, then, I report a decline in the tractor's fixed cost of 23 percent.

It is possible that not all costs can be compared directly between the Cotton South and the Corn Belt. In selecting prices for the Corn Belt, I also tried to be conservative. For instance, for measuring the decline in labor costs I use an estimate for Iowa and Illinois that amounts to a 27 percent drop. Had I used an estimate for all five states in the Corn Belt, then wages would have fallen 30 percent, and the tractor's threshold would have averaged roughly 62 crop acres (a

[4] Whatley gives the value of these inputs for 1929 and 1939 in table 4.2. I calculated the changes in prices based on this table. See Whatley, "Institutional Change and Mechanization of the Cotton South," p. 126.

level close to its 1929 threshold). For the cost of horses, I report an increase of 14.4 percent based on the average of the value of horses in the five Corn Belt states. Of these states, Missouri reported an unusually large increase of 31 percent in the price of horses (perhaps because droughts had been severe in that state). Excluding Missouri, the increase would have been 10 percent, and the tractor's threshold would have been 58 to 63 acres. Furthermore, in calculating changes in the costs of the tractor, feed, and fuel, I average figures specific to the Midwest with figures for national trends. Of the two sources, those specific to the Midwest are more appropriate because they represent that region. Had I used only rates of change as reported by midwestern sources, then changes in these three items would have resulted in the tractor's threshold in 1939 amounting to 65 to 70 crop acres, or slightly above those levels reported in 1929.

This review suggests three conclusions. First, the calculations indicate that the tractor's threshold fell roughly six acres between 1929 and 1939 if only changes in technology and changes in prices are considered. Factoring in the effect of regulation, the threshold actually rose slightly. Second, this conclusion is reached using figures that are similar to those used by another economic historian, Warren Whatley, in his analysis of the Cotton South. Finally, had I made a few adjustments – such as relying on midwestern sources to calculate changes in rates, or using a service life of twelve years to estimate the tractor's fixed cost – then the tractor's threshold in 1939 would have exceeded its 1929 level. On net, then, the figures indicate that the tractor's threshold changed little from its 1929 level.

APPENDIX C Sources of preharvest and harvest labor productivity, 1929–1939

In the 1930s, New Deal regulation contributed to a new climate for investment, one that was directly associated with the diffusion of expensive machinery, notably the tractor and the mechanical corn picker. Inasmuch as farmers purchased expensive machinery, did this machinery contribute to significant gains in labor productivity during the 1930s? In this appendix, I estimate changes in preharvest and harvest productivity associated with tractors and mechanical corn pickers. I also assess the role of related equipment, notably pneumatic tires and one new implement, the four-row cultivator. I conclude by comparing my calculations for changes in labor productivity during the 1930s with estimates reported by the Works Progress Administration for the 1920s.

For preharvest labor, I first report official estimates of the number of labor hours spent performing specific tasks (such as plowing, planting, and cultivating) using either tractors or horses. I then report the percentage of farmers who performed specific jobs using each method, based on state and federal data.[1] From these two steps, I calculate a weighted average of the total number of preharvest labor hours per acre in 1929 and again in 1939 (Table C.1). For 1929 the average was 6.63 hours per acre, but in 1939 it had dropped 14 percent to 5.70 hours per acre.

These estimates of the tractor's contribution to preharvest productivity assume no change in the time spent performing specific tasks, but performance times for certain activities fell in the 1930s thanks to

---

[1] The figures for 1939 are weighted according to each state's share of the five states' total corn acreage. The shares were as follows: Ohio, 11.7 percent; Indiana, 14.0 percent; Illinois, 27.1 percent; Iowa, 32.5 percent; and Missouri, 14.7 percent. Calculated from the U.S. Department of Commerce, *Sixteenth Census of the United States: 1940* (Washington, D.C.: U.S. Government Printing Office, 1942), Agriculture, vol. 1, part 1, pp. 428, 538, 652, and part 2, pp. 114, 234.

Table C.1. *Preharvest labor hours in 1929 and 1939*

A. *Performance rates (hours per acre) for the general-purpose tractor and horses*		
Operation	Tractor	4-6 Horses
Plow	1.25	2.00
Disk (two times)	0.33	0.50
Harrow	0.19	0.25
Plant	0.49	0.65
Cultivate (four times)	0.51	0.80

B. *Percentage of operation performed by tractor*		
Operation	1929	1939[a]
Plow	38%	73%
Disk	34	72
Harrow	20	56
Plant	00	9
Cultivate	05	48

C. *Total preharvest labor hours per acre*			
Weighted labor hours	1929	1939	Change (%)
Hours per acre	6.63	5.70	-14.0%

D. *Total preharvest labor hours per acre adjusted for pneumatic tires[b]*			
Weighted labor hours	1929	1939	Change (%)
Hours per acre	6.63	5.58	-15.8%

[a]The percentage of an operation performed by a tractor in 1939 is the average of the five midwestern states weighted according to each state's share of the total corn acreage for the five states.
[b]By reducing a tractor's time by 25 percent, pneumatic tires in turn reduced the hours per acre for plowing from 1.25 to 0.94, for disking from 0.33 to 0.25, and for cultivating from 0.51 to 0.38. I weight these figures under the assumption that by 1939 roughly 25 percent of the land farmed with tractors was worked by operators who employed rubber tires.
Sources: Performance rates for horses are found in H. C. M. Case, R. H. Wilcox, and H. A. Berg, "Organizing the Corn-Belt Farm for Profitable Production," University of Illinois Agricultural Experiment Station No. 329 (revised, June 1934; originally June 1929), p. 289; and for tractors see, L. A. Reynoldson, W. R. Humphries, S. R. Speelman, E. W. McComas, and W. H. Youngman, "Utilization and Cost of Power on Corn Belt Farms," U.S. Department of Agriculture Technical Bulletin No. 384 (October 1933), p. 19.   For usage rates,

a new improvement, pneumatic tires. Rubber tires could save farmers perhaps 25 percent of their time in plowing, disking, and cultivating the crop. It is not clear what percentage of farmers used rubber tires. Warren Whatley notes that by 1937 43 percent of all general-purpose tractors sold came with rubber tires and by 1940 the rate had reached 96 percent.[2] One survey found that while most farmers preferred rubber tires, 80 percent of farmers still used steel wheels in the spring of 1938.[3] Assuming that by 1939 the percentage had shifted to the point where 25 percent of farmers who used tractors had pneumatic tires and that they attained a 25 percent savings in plowing, disking, and cultivating their land, then their productivity would increase in the 1930s. Overall, average labor preharvest productivity amounted to 5.70 hours without pneumatic tires in 1939, and to 5.58 hours with the tires. Labor hours fell 16 percent with the tires, as compared with 14 percent without them.

I perform similar calculations for gains in harvest productivity (Table C.2). I first report the performance rates of picking corn by hand as compared with rates achieved by mechanical harvesting. For 1929, I estimate that no more than 5 percent of the corn was machine-harvested, but farmers machine-harvested roughly 28 percent of the corn by 1938. Given these usage rates, in 1929 harvest productivity amounted to 5.75 hours per acre, but declined 20 percent to 4.60 hours in 1938. This figure for 1939 may be somewhat low. Rates of change are calculated for 1938 because that was the year in which survey results were reported, but actual calculations should be made for 1939. The use of mechanical harvesters no doubt increased between 1938 and 1939, although the exact amount is not

[2] Warren C. Whatley, "Institutional Change and Mechanization in the Cotton South: The Tractorization of Cotton Farming" (Ph.D. dissertation, Stanford University, 1983), p. 128.
[3] The survey "covered 1,300 representative farmers." Of states surveyed, four were from the Midwest (Illinois, Iowa, Missouri, and Ohio). See "Tractor Survey," *Farm Implement News*, 59 (April 21, 1938), p. 31.

Notes to Table C.1 (cont.)

see Works Progress Administration, *Changes in Technology and Labor Requirements in Production: Corn*, National Research Project A-5 (Philadelphia, 1938), p. 53; and U.S. Department of Agriculture, *Agricultural Statistics, 1941* (Washington, D.C.: U.S. Government Printing Office, 1941), p. 568.

Table C.2. *Harvest labor hours in 1929 and 1939*

A. *Performance rates for hand harvesting and mechanical harvesting*

	Hand picker	1-row picker	2-row picker
Hours per acre	5-7	1.2	0.8

B. *Total harvest labor hours per acre*[a]

Weighted labor hours	1929	1939[b]	Change (%)
Hours per acre	5.75	4.60	-20.0%

[a]Few farmers used mechanical corn pickers in 1929. I estimate that the rate was 5 percent of farmers. The machine's usage rate for 1938 was 28 percent. This is calculated as the average of the five midwestern states weighted according to each state's share of the five states' total corn acreage in 1939.
[b]Calculations are actually made for 1938, the year in which farmers were surveyed for their use of mechanical harvesters. In 1939, the usage rate was in all likelihood higher, harvest hours somewhat lower than 4.60 hours, and labor savings somewhat greater than 20 percent.
Sources: Performance rates are reported in P. E. Johnston and K. H. Myers, "Harvesting the Corn Crop in Illinois," University of Illinois Agricultural Experiment Station Bulletin No. 373 (September 1931), pp. 360, 366; for usage rates, see U.S. Department of Agriculture, *Agricultural Statistics, 1940* (Washington, D.C.: U.S. Government Printing Office, 1940), p. 563.

clear. Had the increase been roughly 10 percent, say from 28 to 31 percent of the acreage, then labor would have amounted to 4.45 hours, for a 23 percent reduction.

In Table C.3, I total preharvest and harvest labor hours and calculate the percentage change for each category between 1929 and 1939. Overall, total labor hours fell 18 percent in the 1930s. These figures include the effects of pneumatic tires. Had the tires been excluded, then total labor hours would have declined by 17 percent for the decade.

These calculations require different qualifications. The gains in productivity are based on the contribution of the two mechanical inventions and exclude the effects of improvements in implements, such as increases in the size of disks and cultivators. The introduction

Table C.3. *Total labor savings, 1929-39*[a]

Season	Labor hours per acre		Change (%)
	1929	1939	
Preharvest	6.63	5.58	-15.8%
Harvest	5.75	4.60	-20.0
Total labor hours[b]	12.38	10.18	-17.8

[a]Calculated from Tables C.1 and C.2.
[b]Excluding the effect of pneumatic tires, total labor hours
in 1939 would have amounted to 10.30 hours per acre for a 17
percent decline from 1929.

of better implements obviously reduced labor time, but the question
is how much time.

The one item that received important improvements in this period
was the cultivator. To cultivate corn, a farmer ran the piece of equipment through rows of young corn, grinding out weeds. Farmers cultivated corn four times between May and July. Unlike plowing, which
had to be completed in a short span of time, cultivating did not
require speed. But the job consumed up to 40 percent of the total
time a farmer spent raising corn. An improvement in the cultivator
could bring about significant labor savings.

Manufacturers gave farmers the chance to save time and cost when
they introduced the four-row cultivator in the 1930s. On an individual basis, four-row cultivators replaced two-row cultivators and
could save one out of every two hours spent cultivating. Overall, a
farmer could reduce total preharvest labor requirements by 20 percent. Whether these potential savings translated into actual gains
depended on the four-row cultivator's rate of diffusion. As late as
1936, the WPA reported that most farmers used two-row cultivators,
and unfortunately, no source tells us how many farmers used the
four-row models in the late 1930s or early 1940s.[4] Suppose, however,
that two-thirds of all land cultivated with tractors was worked by
farmers who used the four-row cultivator. Preharvest labor hours

[4]Use of the two-row cultivator is taken from a WPA survey. See Works
Progress Administration, *Changes in Technology and Labor Requirements
in Production: Corn*, National Research Project A-5 (Philadelphia, 1938),
p. 58.

would have declined not by 16 percent but by 21 percent (assuming all farmers also employed rubber tires).[5] Even so, with a 21 percent savings in preharvest labor, three-quarters of the savings would have been due to the tractor's diffusion. One-quarter of the savings would have been attributed to an implement that, while less expensive than a tractor, still entailed a large outlay of roughly $260.[6]

A second qualification concerns the comparison I make in Table 6.1 between changes in productivity in the 1920s and 1930s. I calculate changes in productivity for the 1920s from data collected by the WPA. The WPA reported that for four midwestern states – Illinois, Indiana, Iowa, and Ohio – labor savings amounted, on average, to 11 percent for the decade. The WPA also reported changes in productivity for the corn area, which included these four states plus the southeastern part of South Dakota, eastern Nebraska, and northern Missouri.[7] Overall, the WPA calculated savings for the corn area not as 11 percent, but as 13 percent.[8] The higher figure, though, reflects changes that took place in these other states. In particular, the proportion of corn acreage shifted from Missouri to the two western states.[9] Further, farmers spent less time raising corn in the western states than in Missouri.[10] This shift plus the reductions in labor hours within South Dakota and Nebraska in the 1920s contributed to further reductions in labor hours. In my analysis, I do not include South Dakota or Nebraska. I also find that the share of corn acreage

---

[5] Including the effects of a four-row cultivator, the time devoted to preharvest tasks declined from 6.63 to 5.24 hours per acre. Supposing that those farmers who used four-row cultivators did not have pneumatic tires, then the drop in labor hours would have been 19 percent, from 6.63 to 5.39 hours per acre.

[6] Warren Whatley estimated the cost of a four-row cultivator at $266.88. See Whatley, "Institutional Change and Mechanization in the Cotton South," p. 207.

[7] Works Progress Administration, *Changes in Technology and Labor Requirements in Production: Corn*, p. 47.

[8] Ibid., p. 149.

[9] The WPA reports that from 1909 to 1929, corn acreage in South Dakota increased by more than 100 percent, and in Nebraska, it increased by 11 to 30 percent. In Missouri, by contrast, acreage slipped from 10 to 29 percent. Ibid., p. 8.

[10] South Dakota and Nebraska fit within the western region that reported the lowest number of hours per acre for raising and harvesting corn in 1929 among the five regions. Missouri was represented mostly by the livestock grazing region, which reported that total hours in 1929 were almost 50 percent higher than levels in the western section. Ibid., p. 64.

among the five midwestern states remained fairly stable between 1929 and 1939.[11] Given the effect of South Dakota and Nebraska on the WPA estimates, I compare my figures for the 1930s to the WPA's figures for the average of Illinois, Indiana, Iowa, and Ohio.

This approach, though, tends to reduce the relative increase in labor savings in the 1930s as compared to that recorded in the 1920s. One factor concerns improvements or changes in farm practices, aside from mechanization, that boosted levels of productivity. In the case of harvesting, the WPA found that reductions in labor hours in Indiana and Ohio in the years from 1909 to 1936 were affected, in part, by changes in methods. In some sections of these two eastern states, farmers had harvested corn from the shock, which entailed three times the amount of labor as husking from standing stalks. The WPA reported that the proportion of corn husked from the shock fell from 64 percent in 1909 to 47 percent in 1936. Although it is not possible to determine the exact contribution, the figures suggest that a small part of the labor savings from 1909 to 1936 were attributed to changes in harvesting methods.[12]

Whereas the estimates for the 1920s include both the effects of mechanization and changes in harvesting (or other) practices, my estimates for the 1930s are limited to the effects of mechanization. As a result, it is possible that labor savings were larger in the 1930s than what I have reported. Even so, the diffusion of expensive machinery after the coming of regulation had contributed to significant new gains in productivity. If the figures could be revised so as to compare the 1920s and the 1930s on a similar basis (that is, to exclude factors other than mechanization in the 1920s, or to include factors other than mechanization in the 1930s) the rate of savings in the 1930s

[11] From 1929 to 1939, the share of corn acreage for Ohio increased from 10.6 to 11.7 percent, for Indiana from 12.8 to 14 percent, and for Illinois from 26.1 to 27.1 percent. In Iowa, the share fell from 33.6 to 32.5 percent, and for Missouri from 16.9 to 14.7 percent. Calculated from U.S. Department of Commerce, *Sixteenth Census of the United States: 1940, Agriculture*, vol. 1, part 1, pp. 428, 538, 652, and part 2, pp. 114, 234.

[12] I made a rough estimate of this effect based on figures the WPA reported for time spent husking from standing stalks versus husking from the shock in the eastern section of the Corn Belt. The weighted time fell from 13.68 to 11.64 harvest hours within the eastern region. Since Ohio and Indiana accounted for roughly 25 percent of the corn acreage, the change in hours translated roughly into a 4 percent savings for harvest labor over these years. Ibid., pp. 52, 60, 66.

would have been more than two-thirds larger than the rate of increase reported for the 1920s. Put another way, the calculations indicate the extent to which mechanization within the context of the coming of regulation raised productivity during the Depression relative to over-all gains in productivity during the 1920s.

One last qualification concerns the states used to estimate changes in productivity. I calculate changes in productivity based on the diffu-sion of technology among all five midwestern states, whereas the WPA estimates are based on four states; Missouri is excluded. In my calculations, Missouri tends to reduce changes in productivity because farmers in this state were comparatively slow to adopt technology during the 1930s. To directly compare my figures to the WPA's figures for the 1920s, I recalculate figures on the basis of the four remaining states. Doing so, I find that for 1939 preharvest labor amounted to 5.47 hours per acre, for a 17.5 percent decline; harvest labor amounted to 4.40 hours per acre, for a 23.5 percent decline; and total labor savings were almost twice that of the 1920s – a decline of 20 percent as compared to 11 percent among the four states.

During the Great Depression, regulation created a new climate for investment. The effects of price controls and special sources of credit served to create, in particular, incentives to invest in labor-saving, but expensive, machinery. The two primary examples, tractors and mechanical corn pickers, indicated that these incentives had been important. Overall, savings in productivity in the 1930s increased by roughly 18 percent. Tractors and mechanical corn pickers had accounted for most of these savings. Compared to the estimates re-ported by the WPA for the 1920s, labor savings in the 1930s were at least two-thirds and perhaps twice as large as savings in the 1920s.

Index

Adams Act, 31
Aetna Life and Casualty Insurance Company, 71, 72, 113–14, 116, 190–1, 226–7, 228
Agricultural Adjustment Act, 143
Agricultural Adjustment Act of 1938, 159
Agricultural Adjustment Administration, 136, 143–4, 146–7, 155, 159–60, 171, 248
  farm relief, 181–7
  land productivity and, 165, 166, 170, 199, 249
  relation to Commodity Credit Corporation, 145, 155, 157, 159, 181–2, 186, 187, 196, 250
  soil conservation, 166
  tractor's threshold and, 179–80, 199, 290–1
  also see United States Department of Agriculture
Agricultural Credits Act of 1923, 75–6
agricultural engineering, 22, 43, 46–7
Allis-Chalmers, 35, 41, 42
Alston, Lee J., 66n24, 149n30
American Bankers Association, 227, 240, 242–3
American Farm Bureau Federation, 156–7, 159
Anderson, O. E., 221–2
Ankli, Robert E., 90, 95, 279–86

Bankers Life, 71, 150, 192
Bankhead–Jones Tenant Act, 161
Biermann, Frederick, 185, 188
Broehl, Wayne G., Jr., 39, 197–8
Bureau of Agricultural Economics, 151, 152, 186, 207, 211–12, 218–20

commercial banks, 16, 20, 27, 67, 75–6, 206–7, 248
  Commodity Credit Corporation and, 145, 156
  credit crisis in the Corn Belt, 1920s, 109, 113–15

criticism of loan policies, 67–8
decline of farms and, 242–3
diffusion of tractor in Corn Belt, 125, 131–3
farm loan distress, 240, 257, 259–60
farm mortgage debt held, 73, 74 T 3.2, 228
farm mortgage loans, 67–8, 69 T 3.1, 227, 268
federal lenders and, 17, 193, 221–2, 225, 249–50
Great Depression and, 139–40
life insurance companies and, 70, 71, 72, 107, 113–15, 224–7
non–real estate debt, 67–8, 70, 104, 228
suspensions in Corn Belt during the 1920s, 108 T 4.3, 115, 131
Commodity Credit Corporation, 3n1
  acreage controls and, 215–16
  corn prices during the 1930s, 163, 182, 184 T 6.5
  criticism of, 211, 212, 256–7, 261–2, 269–70
  effect on cash costs and income, 182–6, 184 T 6.5
  effect on farm investment, 165–6, 182–6, 193–4, 196, 249, 252–3
  effect on prices after World War II, 212, 216, 218, 218 T 7.2, 220 T 7.3, 242, 251
  farm crisis of the 1980s, 263–5, 268
  farm income subsidies, 215–16, 252
  farm land values and, 241
  farmers' support of, 155–6, 186, 206, 211, 218, 220
  implement manufacturers and, 196, 250
  politicians and, 136, 154–9, 185, 206, 211, 220, 256–7
  relief efforts in the 1930s, 181–2, 187
  status of during the 1930s, 136, 145–7, 154–9
  surplus crops, 212, 214 T 7.1, 265
  target prices, 265
  World War II and, 205–6, 209, 211

Connecticut Mutual Life Insurance Company, 70, 71–2, 116
Coolidge, Calvin, 74, 139, 147
corn, 87, 238, 265
    acreage restrictions and, 143–4, 155, 180, 241, 249, 268
    open-pollinated, 45n60, 167–8
    prices, 62, 65, 71, 99, 137, 144–6, 182, 206, 213 F 7.3A, 215–16, 220 T 7.3, 249
    yields, 25–6, 53, 124, 163, 164 T 6.1, 166–70, 171, 173n14, 249
    also see Commodity Credit Corporation; hybrid corn
Corn Belt, 17–19, 51, 77–9, 211, 218, 220, 247–50
    farm crisis of the 1920s, 106–11
    farm land values, 107, 108 T 4.3
    farm size, 77–8, 200n64
    farm wages, 94
    geographic regions within, 117, 120–1
    labor productivity, 133–5, 164 T 6.1, 198–9, 250, 297–304
    number of farms, 200n64
Cornell University, 29–30
cotton, 26, 62, 65, 206, 238, 265–6, 268
    during the 1930s, 137, 143, 144, 145, 157–8, 159, 166
    prices after World War II, 212, 217 F 7.3B, 215–16,
Cotton Belt, 18, 144, 279, 292, 295
    sharecropping and, 18, 58–9, 77–8
    tractor and, 58–9, 95, 279, 292–3, 295
cultivators, 178n20, 199, 301–2

David, Paul, 14–15, 53–4, 55n9, 58
debt moratorium during the 1930s, 148–50
Deere & Company, 20, 35, 37, 39, 41, 46, 87, 137, 179, 197, 246
Dickinson, Lester Jesse, 98–9
domestic allotment plan, 143
Dust Bowl, 78–9, 144, 160
Duncan, S. Lysle, 50, 53

Emergency Farm Mortgage Act, 141
Equitable Life Assurance Society, 20, 207, 223–9, 251

Farm Credit Act, 142
Farm Credit Administration, 136, 141–2, 147, 159, 206–7, 209, 211

    farm crisis of the 1980s, 260–1, 263, 267, 269
    private creditors and, 148–54, 189–93, 200, 221–9, 249–50, 251
    also see federal land banks; production credit associations
Farm Credit Banks, 261
farm crisis of the 1920s, 64–6, 74, 206, 240, 247–8
    Corn Belt and, 106–7, 108 T 4.3, 109–11, 112 F 4.4, 113–16, 125, 131–2
    creditors and, 111, 113–16
    effect on indebted farmers, 64–6, 111
    also see farm foreclosures; farm mortgage debt
farm crisis of the 1980s
    commercial banks and, 257, 260, 268, 269
    commodity prices, 262, 266, 270
    export boom, 263–7
    farm debt, 258–9, 266, 267, 268–9
    farm loan distress, 257, 259, 267–8, 269
    federal creditors and, 260–1, 267, 269
    life insurance companies and, 257, 260, 261–2, 267, 269
    price supports, 256–7, 261–3, 265, 268, 269–70
    small farms and, 255, 257–9, 270
farm foreclosures, 65, 148–9, 207, 208 F 7.1, 240
    Corn Belt and, 108 T 4.3, 109–10, 189n38
    during the 1980s, 257, 258 T E.1, 266
    after World War II, 239–42
    also see farm crisis of the 1920s; farm crisis of the 1980s; federal land banks; life insurance companies
farm investment climate, 15–17, 19, 60, 66–7, 77, 79, 211, 244–5, 246–7, 249, 252–4
    during the 1930s, 161, 165, 181, 193–4
farm land values, 65, 66n24, 209
    Corn Belt and, 107, 108 T 4.3
    during the 1980s, 255, 267
    after World War II, 241, 243, 251
farm mortgage debt, 139–40, 228, 229, 259, 261, 263
    amount of, 207, 232, 234 T 7.6, 266, 268–9
    burden of, 64–5, 110–11, 108 T 4.3,

125, 131–3, 187–9, 240–2, 249,
  266–7, 268–9
delinquencies, 111, 137, 138 T 5.1,
  151, 190, 240, 260, 267, 269
interest rates, 67–71, 69 T 3.1, 114,
  141–2, 143n16, 191 T 6.6, 222,
  229, 267, 268–9
maturity of loans, 67–71, 69 T 3.1,
  114, 116, 142–3, 222, 229
private individuals and, 67, 68, 69 T
  3.1, 73, 74 T 3.2, 113, 151–2, 207,
  228–9
relation to assets, 108 T 4.3, 125, 131,
  234 T 7.6, 236, 241, 257, 259
World War II and, 206–9
also see farm crisis of the 1920s; farm
  crisis of the 1980s
farm non–real estate debt, 63–4, 66–8,
  70, 75–6, 104, 142, 193, 224–8,
  232, 235
farm sales, voluntary, 209, 210 F 7.2,
  243
farms, 59–61, 233 F 7.4
commercial and noncommercial, 236,
  237 T 7.7, 259, 262, 267, 270
decline in number of, 4–5, 200n64,
  204–5, 242–4
financial leverage of, 64–6, 234 T 7.6,
  236, 259, 259 E.2, 266, 267
size of, 77–8, 78n47, 200n64, 236,
  237 T 7.7, 238, 243, 255, 258–9
Federal Farm Loan Act, 75
Federal Intermediate Credit Banks, 75–6
federal land banks, 16
credit crisis in the Corn Belt, 1920s,
  111, 113–14, 116
farm crisis of the 1980s, 261, 267, 269
farm loan distress, 111, 137, 138 T
  5.1, 140–1, 269
farm mortgage debt held, 74 T 3.2, 76,
  114, 189, 228
farm mortgage loans, 69 T 3.1, 141–2,
  188, 189–90, 191 T 6.6, 222
Great Depression and, 137, 140–1
organization of, 75
private creditors and, 116, 150–4,
  189–93, 221–5, 229, 249–50
relief activities during the 1930s, 140–
  2, 148, 151, 153 T 5.2, 153–4, 87–
  9
also see Farm Credit Administration
Federal Trade Commission, 37, 102–3,
  179
Ford, Henry, 23, 36–40, 42
Fordson tractor, 36–40, 46

Great Depression, 3, 7, 58, 78, 94, 137–
  40, 162–3, 200, 205
Griliches, Zvi, 53n5, 55n9

Hatch Act, 28
Hoover, Herbert C., 74, 136, 139
horses, 25, 26, 39–40, 47, 48
compared to the tractor, 83, 87, 89–
  90, 98, 100–2, 105–6
expenses of, 61, 96, 98, 100–2, 103,
  105–6
reaper and, 59
threshold calculations, 1929, 91–2,
  94, 271–6, 279, 281–6
threshold calculations, 1939, 179, 289,
  290–1, 296
threshold model and, 53, 91–2, 93–4
hybrid corn, 18–19, 47, 165, 184
development of, 32, 45
diffusion in Corn Belt, 167–8, 170,
  198–9
mechanical technology and, 171

Illinois, 26, 31, 96, 100, 102, 105, 114,
  168, 200n64, 232, 302
cost of production, 182
credit crisis of the 1920s and, 107,
  109, 111, 131–3
diffusion of mechanical corn picker,
  171–3
diffusion of tractor, 93, 117, 118 F
  4.5, 120–21, 122 F 4.7, 123–33,
  175
farm foreclosures, 110, 189n38
implement manufacturers, 15, 17, 20,
  70, 97–8, 104, 137, 179, 194, 196–
  8
dealers, 102–3, 115, 176, 196–7
farm machinery and, 33–44, 46, 247
regulation and, 165, 196–7, 200, 250
also see Allis-Chalmers; Deere & Company; International Harvester Company; tractors
Indiana, 96n19, 107, 110, 111, 172,
  182, 189n38, 200n64, 302
International Harvester Company, 20,
  37, 87, 178–9, 194, 196–8
capital expenditures in the 1930s, 197
credit for machinery, 66–7, 70, 104
efforts to sell tractors, 37–8, 83, 84 F
  4.1, 85 F 4.2, 86, 88 F 4.3, 97–8,
  103, 162, 179
Farmall tractor, 38–40, 43, 83, 87,
  103
Ford and, 37–9, 40, 42–3, 46

International Harvester Company (*cont.*)
  industrial research staff, 40–2, 197
  merger, 34–5
Iowa, 26, 51, 99, 105, 114, 150, 188–9,
    189*n*38, 200*n*64, 232, 302
  cost of production, 99, 182
  credit crisis of the 1920s and, 107,
    109, 111, 131–2
  diffusion of hybrid corn, 167–8, 170
  diffusion of mechanical corn picker,
    172–3
  diffusion of tractor, 93, 117, 118 F
    4.5, 120–1, 122 F 4.7, 123–33, 175,
    176
  farm foreclosures, 110
Iowa Farm Bureau, 232

Johnston, Edward A., 40
joint stock land banks, 75–6, 114
Jones, Jesse, 157–9

Kahn, Alfred, 8–9
Kloppenburg, Jack C., Jr., 24, 27, 45,
    45*n*60
Kohn, Frederick, 203–4, 243–4
Kraschel, Nelson G., 150, 188

Lamoreaux, Naomi R., 7–8
Land Bank Commissioner loans, 142–3,
    150, 151, 153 T 5.2, 189
land grant colleges, 27, 28–9, 30, 32, 33,
    43–4, 45
Legge, Alexander, 37
life insurance companies, 16, 20, 248,
    249–50, 251
  competition with federal lenders, 116,
    136, 148, 189–93, 221–9
  farm crisis of the 1980s, 257, 260,
    261–2, 267, 269
  farm foreclosures after World War II,
    240, 258 T E.1
  farm mortgage debt held, 73, 74 T 3.2,
    114, 227–8
  farm mortgages, terms of, 69 T 3.1,
    70–3, 114, 116, 190, 191 T 6.6,
    192–3, 223, 226–7
  Great Depression and, 137, 138 T 5.1,
    140, 148–54
  loan experience in the Corn Belt, 110,
    111, 112 F 4.4, 113–16
  World War II and, 206–7
  also see Aetna Life and Casualty Insur-
    ance Company; Equitable Life As-
    surance Society; Metropolitan Life
    Insurance Company; Northwestern
    Mutual Life Insurance Company

livestock, 61, 62, 63, 67–8, 78, 100,
    106, 117, 120–1, 230–1
  during the Great Depression, 144, 156,
    181, 185
Lucas, Scott, 185

McCormick, Cyrus, 34–5, 42–3, 46
McCraw, Thomas K., 8
McNary–Haugen bill, 74, 139
mechanical corn picker, 47, 101, 175
  cash outlays, 101, 170, 175
  diffusion in Corn Belt, 171–4
  labor productivity and, 198, 199,
    299–300
  sales of, 194, 198
  threshold calculations for, 171–5
Metropolitan Life Insurance Company,
    New York, 106–7, 113–16, 148,
    150–1, 152
  also see Rogers, Glenn E.
Midwest, *see* Corn Belt
Missouri, 51, 110, 111, 173*n*14,
    189*n*38, 200*n*64, 302, 304
Morrill Land Grant Act, 28
Mortgage Bankers Association, 192
Murray, William G., 16*n*22, 63, 193

National Research Council, 40–2,
    42*n*49, 197
New Deal, 3, 7–8, 59, 154–5, 194, 205,
    253–4, 255
  farm relief and, 141–9, 159–61, 180–
    2, 187–9
  also see Agricultural Adjustment Ad-
    ministration; Commodity Credit
    Corporation; Farm Credit Adminis-
    tration
Northwestern Mutual Life Insurance
    Company, 72, 152, 190
Nowell, R. I., 224, 225*n*38, 226*n*41,
    227, 228–9

Ohio, 51, 96*n*19, 110, 111, 172, 182,
    189*n*38, 200*n*64, 302, 303
Olmstead, Alan, 90, 279
Olsen, Nils, 223

Parker, William N., 19, 24
pneumatic tires, 42, 176, 287, 295, 299,
    300
price supports, *see* Commodity Credit
    Corporation
prices, crop, 228, 252–3
  competition and, 51–2, 56–7, 60, 246
  farm crisis of the 1920s and, 65, 106–
    7, 240, 248

farm crisis of the 1980s and, 253–4,
262–3, 266, 270
Great Depression and, 137
parity and, 141, 154, 159, 162, 182,
206, 212, 249
pattern after World War II, 216, 218,
240–1, 242, 251
political efforts to stabilize, 73–4, 139,
143, 145–6, 154–9, 181–2, 185,
205, 206, 209, 211–12, 215–16
volatility of, 15–16, 61–6, 98–100,
165, 182, 184, 216, 218, 220 T 7.3,
246–7, 249, 263
production credit associations, 16, 142,
193, 197, 221, 222, 225, 228, 235
productivity, 5, 9–11, 211, 230 T 7.4,
236, 238, 262
changes between 1920 and 1940, 4,
50, 59, 133–5, 163, 164 T 6.1,
166–7, 170, 198–200, 250, 297–
304
competition and, 13, 14, 48, 76–7,
246–7, 248, 250–1, 253–4
diffusion of technology and, 3–4, 14,
15, 23–4, 77, 165–6, 198–200,
229–30, 231 T 7.5
farm labor, 4, 6, 229–30
farm sector, 4, 203, 229–30
manufacturing sector, 5–6
safety and, 60–4, 77, 79, 98–102,
124, 182, 184–6, 199–200, 211–
12, 216, 218, 220–1, 241–2, 247–8
sources of knowledge and, 24–6, 27,
45, 48–9
also see Corn Belt; mechanical corn
picker; tractors

Reagan, Ronald, 256–7
reapers, 26, 58, 59, 77, 90
regulation, farm, 3,
competition and, 205, 244–5, 246–7,
251–4
criticism of, 3, 7–8, 9, 20–1, 136, 147,
148, 158–9, 211, 238, 251
dynamic versus static analysis of, 17,
251–3
farm investment climate and, 15, 16–
17, 19, 21, 161, 193–4, 198–200,
205, 211, 229, 238–9, 244–5
Great Depression and, 137, 140–7
productivity and, 4, 6, 13–14, 16–17,
20–1, 161, 165–6, 170, 198–200,
238–9, 240–1, 250, 251, 253–4
relief activities during the Great Depression, 140–7, 159–61, 181–2,
187–9

subsidies of, 215–16, 238
World War II and, 205–7, 209
also see Agricultural Adjustment Administration; Commodity Credit
Corporation; Farm Credit Administration
regulation, nonfarm, 6–7
airlines, 8–9, 251
research
agricultural sector, 17, 23, 28–33, 44–
5
manufacturing sector, 11, 12–13, 17,
22–3, 47–8
also see agricultural engineering; land
grant colleges; tractors
Rogers, Glenn E., 106–7, 113, 115–16,
152
Roosevelt, Franklin D., 3, 136, 139, 143,
154, 156, 206, 248
Rosenberg, Nathan, 12–13

Schumpeter, Joseph, 9–11, 17, 244–5
science-based inputs, 4, 25–6, 30, 44–5,
48–9, 61, 77, 184, 250
cost analysis and, 53, 57
farm investments after World War II,
229–32
also see hybrid corn
sharecropping, 18, 58–9, 77–8, 160
Smith, Earl, 156
Smith–Lever Act, 28, 31

technology, 13
agricultural researchers and, 15, 28,
43–4, 97, 101–2, 105–6
cash expenses and, 61, 62, 63, 77, 78,
95–7, 165, 168, 182, 236
competition and the diffusion of, 14,
17–18, 48–9, 51–2, 76, 199–200,
205, 246, 252–3
cost analysis of, 50, 51–7, 60, 76, 79,
101–2, 135
farmers' finances and, 50–1, 59, 60–1,
77, 79, 101–2, 111, 229–30, 232,
235–6
farmers' investments in during the
1930s, 163, 194, 195 T 6.7, 198–
200
regulation and, 3, 14, 16–17, 161,
165–6, 180, 187, 198–200, 205,
244–5, 252–3
also see agricultural engineering; land
grant colleges; research; science-
based inputs; tractors
threshold calculations for tractor, 91–5,
101, 121, 175–6, 178–80

threshold calculations for tractor (*cont.*)
  acreage restrictions and, 179–80, 199, 290–1
  changes in prices, 178–9, 287, 289, 295–6
  comparative analysis of data, 95, 276–86, 291–3, 295–6
  fixed costs, 92, 271–4, 287
  technological improvements, 176, 178, 287, 291–3, 295
  variable costs, 92, 176, 179, 275–6, 287
  also see Ankli, Robert E.; Whatley, Warren C.
threshold model, 14–15, 18, 53–4, 57–9, 60, 77, 90–1, 93–5, 97, 134–5, 271
  also see David, Paul; threshold calculations for tractor
tractors, 18, 70, 86 T 4.1, 89–90, 104, 250
  advertisements of, 83–6, 87, 97–8, 162
  agricultural researchers and, 43–4, 97, 98, 100–2
  cash expense of, 95–8, 100–2, 106, 247
  changes in prices, 178–9
  development of, 35–44, 46
  diffusion in Corn Belt, 83n1, 92–3, 93 T 4.2, 175, 176 T 6.4, 194, 195 T 6.7
  farm crisis of the 1980s, 268
  labor productivity and, 133–5, 199, 248
  lag in diffusion of in Corn Belt, 93, 121, 123–4, 175, 247–8
  quantitative analysis of lag in diffusion of, 123–5, 126–8 T 4.4, 129 T 4.5, 130 T 4.6, 131–3

sales of, 83–6, 103, 137, 194n52, 198
technological improvements of, 87, 176, 178
  also see Fordson; International Harvester Company; threshold calculations for tractor
Trick, Deane W., 192–3

United States Department of Agriculture, 19–20, 31, 32, 33, 65, 171, 236, 238, 257, 259, 261
  acreage controls, 211, 212, 215–16, 265
  cost of production data, 99, 182
  also see Bureau of Agricultural Economics
University of Illinois at Urbana-Champaign, 29, 79, 90, 139–40

Wall, Norman, 152, 206–7
Wallace, Henry A., 25, 26–7, 45, 143, 144, 156, 159, 166, 185
Whatley, Warren C., 58–9, 91n12, 95, 299, 302n6
  threshold calculations for tractor, 1929, 271, 279, 281–5
  threshold calculations for tractor, 1939, 291–3, 295–6
wheat, 25, 51, 58, 59–60, 62, 63, 65, 120, 206, 238, 265, 268
  during the 1930s, 137, 143, 144, 159, 160, 182
  prices after World War II, 212, 215–16, 219 F 7.3C
Wheat Belt, 51, 72–3, 78
Works Progress Administration, 133–4, 166, 168, 171, 273, 301–4
World War I, 65, 106, 205–6, 240
World War II, 5, 19, 205–8, 209
Wright, Gavin, 62n18, 282n9

Printed in the United States
By Bookmasters